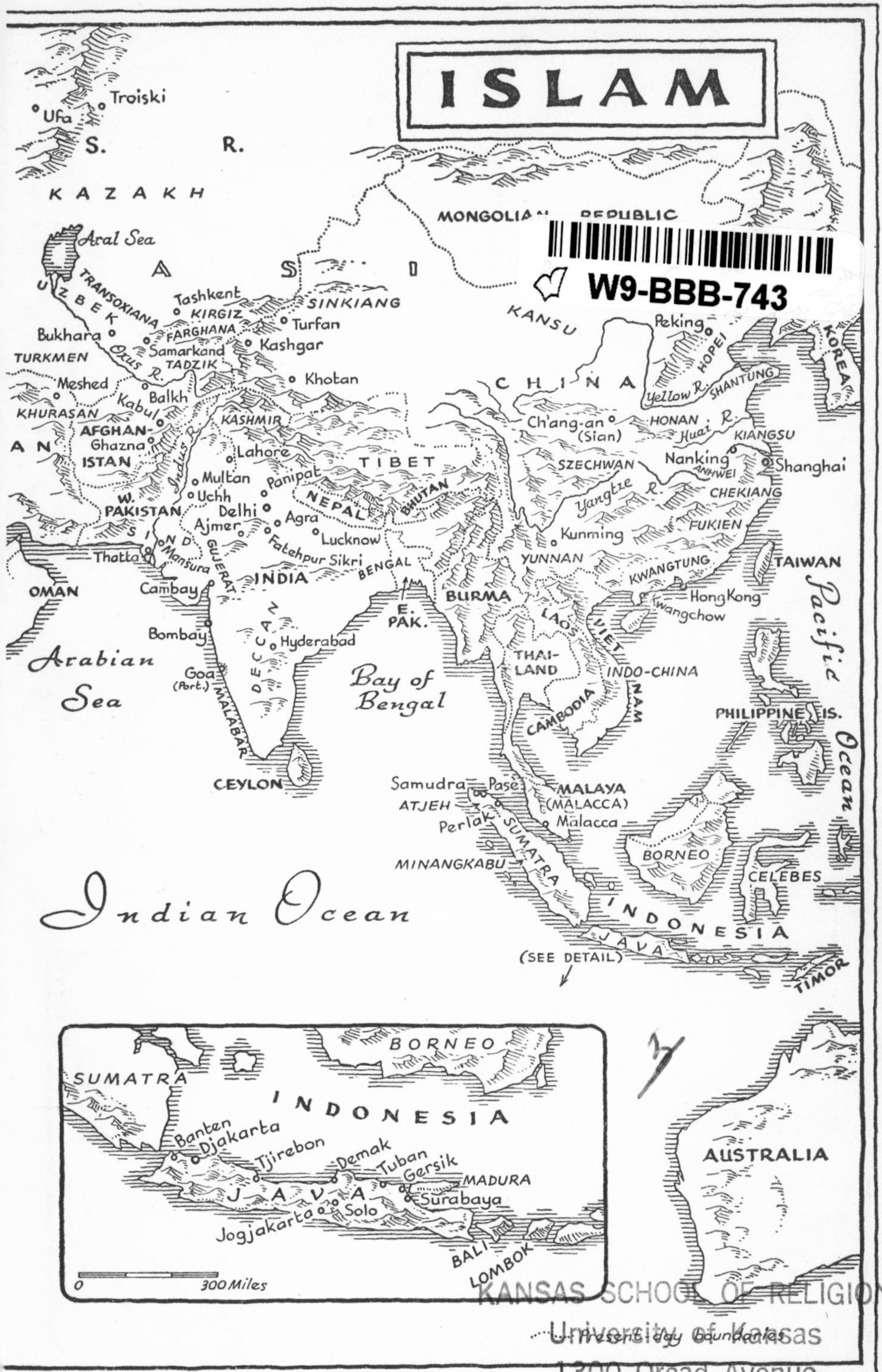

W9-BBB-743

KANSAS SCHOOL OF RELIGION
University of Kansas
1300 Oread Avenue
LAWRENCE, KANSAS

In this book the religion of Islam is described and interpreted by leading Muslim scholars. In the words of devout followers of the religion revealed to Muhammed, the book retells the story of the prophet's life, expounds his teaching, and traces the spread of Islam into Asia, Africa, and Europe. It vividly portrays the attitudes of Muslims toward the Qur'an as the revealed word of God, the Traditions of the Prophet as the guide to righteousness, and the schools of Islamic law as the basis of daily life. Muslim culture and practice in each of the major Islamic areas, from Egypt and Turkey to Indonesia and China, are described by contributors intimately acquainted with the countries concerned. All the main schools of thought are represented, and full justice is done to the rich veins of mysticism and rational philosophy that run through the history of Islam and live in today's practices. Above all, the book gives a warm authentic picture of the religious life of the contemporary Muslim at home, at prayer, and in the mosque.

THE HISTORY OF THIS BOOK

The book is a companion volume to *The Religion of the Hindus* and *The Path of the Buddha*, also edited by Kenneth W. Morgan. The three books form a series initiated by the National Council on Religion in Higher Education and supported by the Edward W. Hazen Foundation, to promote better understanding of the major non-Christian religions. Kenneth Morgan traveled from Egypt and Turkey to Indonesia and Hong Kong talking with Muslim leaders, and on their recommendations selected the scholars best qualified to write a book presenting to Western readers Islam as it is seen by Muslims. Each chapter was written to an outline prepared by the editor in consultation with Western and Muslim scholars. When the manuscripts were completed Professor Morgan discussed them with the writers, edited them to insure continuity and intelligibility to Western readers, and returned them to the writers for approval in their final form. The result is a clear, vivid, and authentic account of Islam for the Western reader.

BP 161
.M63

Islam—The Straight Path

Islam interpreted by Muslims

Edited by

KENNETH W. MORGAN

PROFESSOR OF RELIGION, COLGATE UNIVERSITY

Contributors

Mohammad Abd Allah Draz, Egypt
Shafik Ghorbal, Egypt
Mahmud Shaltout, Egypt
A. E. Affifi, Egypt
Mahmood Shehabi, Iran
Ishak M. Husaini, Egypt
Hasan Basri Çantay, Turkey
Mazheruddin Siddiqi, Pakistan

Dawood C. M. Ting, China
P. A. Hoesein Djajadiningrat, Indonesia
Mohammad Rasjidi, Indonesia

THE RONALD PRESS COMPANY , NEW YORK

Copyright, ©, 1958, by
THE RONALD PRESS COMPANY

All Rights Reserved

The text of this publication or any part thereof may not be reproduced in any manner whatsoever without permission in writing from the publisher

2

Mohammedanism
Mohammedan civilization

Library of Congress Catalog Card Number: 58-9807
PRINTED IN THE UNITED STATES OF AMERICA

Preface

The faith of Islam, and the consequences of that faith, are described in this book by devout Muslim scholars. This is not a comparative study, nor an attempt to defend Islam against what Muslims consider to be Western misunderstandings of their religion; it is simply a concise presentation of the history and spread of Islam and of the beliefs and obligations of Muslims as interpreted by outstanding Muslim scholars of our time.

The method used in the writing of this book is the same as that used in the preparation of the two previous volumes—*The Religion of the Hindus* and *The Path of the Buddha*—which I have edited in an attempt to present to Western readers the major religions of the world from the point of view of the followers of those faiths. First, an outline was prepared for a book designed to present Islam to Western readers. Then that outline was checked with Muslim scholars in Turkey, Egypt, Syria, Lebanon, Iraq, Iran, Pakistan, Indonesia, and with refugee scholars from China, by asking them whether a book written to that outline would give a fair and representative picture of Islam, and who, in their opinion, would be the best writer for each chapter. In the light of their suggestions the outline was extensively modified and the men most highly recommended and most frequently mentioned by their fellow Muslims were asked to write. They recognized that they were not writing independent essays but were creating sections of a carefully planned volume and were aware that their fellow Muslims looked over their shoulders as they wrote.

The eleven able scholars, recommended by their fellow Muslims to speak for the contemporary Muslim world, have given generously of their time and counsel in the creation of this book. Shaikh Mohammad Abd Allah Draz is a Member of the Body of the Grand Ulama, and Professor of Interpretation of the Qur'an at Al Azhar University in Cairo. Shaikh Draz, who received his doctorate at the Sorbonne, is recognized as one of the leading authorities in the Muslim world on the Qur'an and the life of the Prophet.

Dr. Shafik Ghorbal, who has now retired from university teaching and from government service, is the head of the Institute of Higher Arabic Studies of the Arab League, in Cairo. His work as a teacher and writer of history and as an administrator in the Ministry of Education of the Government of Egypt has made him one of the most highly honored scholars of Egypt today.

Shaikh Mahmud Shaltout is a Member of the Body of the Grand Ulama and Professor of Comparative Law at Al Azhar University. He is famous in the Arab world for his radio broadcasts on Islam and for his fearless and outspoken interpretations of Islamic law.

Professor A. E. Affifi, Professor of Islamic Philosophy at the University of Alexandria, is recognized as one of Egypt's leading scholars and a specialist in the Muslim rationalists and mystics.

Professor Mahmood Shehabi, Professor of Jurisprudence in the Faculty of Law and Professor of Eastern Philosophy in the Faculty of Theology at the University of Tehran, is recognized among the Shi'as as qualified to speak for them because of his great learning and his deep devotion to the faith.

Dr. Ishak Musa Husaini is Professor of Arabic Literature both at the Institute of Higher Arabic Studies of the Arab League and at the American University at Cairo. He comes from an old Palestinian family which has long been known for its scholarly leadership in Islam; until recently he was a teacher at the American University at Beirut. Muslims from several Arab countries recommended him as one of the scholars ably qualified to speak for the Arab Muslims.

Hasan Basri Çantay of Istanbul is a retired scholar who has recently translated the Qur'an into Turkish. Even in his retirement many people come to him for instruction and guidance in Islam, for he is highly regarded as a learned and devout Muslim who is representative of the best in Islam in Turkey today.

Mazheruddin Siddiqi, who, like Dr. Husaini, has studied at McGill University in Montreal, is Reader and Head of the Department of Muslim History at the University of Sind, Hyderabad, Pakistan. As editor of the monthly journal *Islamic Literature*, and a contributor to other Islamic publications in Pakistan, he has become widely known as one of the leaders in Muslim thought in his country.

Dawood C. M. Ting, at present a member of the Consulate of the Republic of China at Beirut, was a leader of the Muslim community in China before moving to Taiwan. He has studied at Al Azhar in Cairo, has served on several diplomatic missions for the Republic of China, and is one of the chief spokesmen for the Chinese Muslims.

Dr. P. A. Djajadiningrat is Professor of Islam on the Faculty of Literature at the University of Indonesia. He was formerly Professor of Islamic Law in the High School of Law at Djakarta, a Member of the Council of Netherlands India, Director of the Department of Education of Indonesia, and Secretary of State for Education in Indonesia. He is the senior Muslim scholar of Indonesia, highly respected and honored by his countrymen.

Dr. Mohammad Rasjidi is the Indonesian Ambassador to Pakistan and one of Indonesia's leading Muslim scholars. He has studied at Al Azhar in Cairo and received his doctorate from the Sorbonne. He served on diplomatic missions in Egypt and Iran before going to Pakistan and has traveled widely throughout the Muslim world. Few Muslims can equal Hadji Rasjidi's first-hand knowledge of Muslim culture in both the Far East and the Middle East.

Each of these men has generously undertaken the writing of his chapter in addition to the heavy obligations of his regular work. Not only have they faced the difficulties of language, but they have all been required to cover in a few pages material which could scarcely be covered adequately in a whole book, and to fit that material into a common outline. Their competence, patience, and diligence have amply justified the confidence of their fellow Muslims who recommended them so highly. The unity of Muslims throughout the world is clearly shown in the chapters they have written. Where there are differences on minor points, they should be recognized as inevitable minor variations which have developed through the centuries in a religion which has found its home from Morocco to Indonesia and China.

The eleven chapters of this book were written in seven different languages: *Two*, *Four*, *Eight*, and *Eleven* in English; *One* in French; *Three* and *Six* in Arabic; *Five* in Persian; *Seven* in Turkish; *Nine* in Chinese; and *Ten* in Dutch. After they were all available in English they were carefully checked with each writer to make sure that there were no misunderstandings; then they were extensively edited so the book would read as a unified whole and be clear to Western readers. After the editing, each writer approved his chapter as it appears in the book.

For the sake of simplicity the generally accepted Arabic spelling of names and technical terms has been followed, although in a few cases it seemed to do less violence to follow a form which has gained wide acceptance in a particular Muslim country. When a new word is introduced for the first time it is italicized and defined but after that it is used as if it were a part of the vocabulary of the reader. Definitions may be found either in the glossary or through the first reference in the index. Diacritical marks have been omitted in the text, but are used in the index. The quotations from the Qur'an are either from Pickthall's *The Meaning of the Glorious Koran*, or are translated by the writer of the chapter in which they are found. All quotations from the Qur'an which vary from Pickthall are the writer's unless specific credit is given; verse references follow the numbering in Pickthall, which sometimes varies slightly from other versions. It should also be noted that Islam is not referred to as Muhammadanism since

Muslims do not like to use a word which might imply that they look upon Muhammad as divine or place him above the Qur'an.

The dates are given first according to the Hijrah Era, followed by the date according to the Christian calendar. The Hijrah Era starts with July 15, A.D. 622, as established by Caliph Umar. The Muslim year is a lunar year divided into twelve months with the odd months having thirty days and the even having twenty-nine, with 354 days most years, but 355 days eleven years in each cycle of thirty. Since the lunar year begins roughly eleven days earlier each solar year, any one month may eventually fall at any season of the year.

Among the many people who helped in the preparation of this book, I am especially indebted to Professor Resid Ayda of Istanbul, Mr. Hussain Yurdaydin of the Theological Faculty at Ankara, Dr. Aly Ansari of the Ministry of Education in Cairo, and Miss Christine Laurens of the Faculty of Literature of the University of Indonesia.

In the preparation of the three volumes on Hinduism, Buddhism, and Islam many of the Fellows of The National Council on Religion in Higher Education have given valuable counsel and encouragement. The writing of these books was made possible by grants from The Edward W. Hazen Foundation.

The Oxford University Press has generously given permission to quote from *The Legacy of Islam* by T. W. Arnold and A. Guillaume. The passages from Pickthall's classic translation, *The Meaning of the Glorious Koran*, have been used with the permission of George Allen & Unwin Ltd., publishers of the clothbound edition, and of the New American Library, publishers of the paper-backed edition.

KENNETH W. MORGAN

Hamilton, New York
A.H. 1377, A.D. 1958

Contents

Islam—The Straight Path

CHAPTER ONE

The Origin of Islam

Mohammad Abd Allah Draz

In the Name of God, the Merciful, the Compassionate

Praise belongs to God, the Lord of all Being,
the All-merciful, the All-compassionate,
  the Master of the Day of Doom.
Thee only we serve; to Thee alone we pray for succour.
  Guide us in the straight path,
the path of those whom Thou hast blessed,
not of those against whom Thou art wrathful,
  nor of those who are astray.

(The first Surah of the Qur'an,
Arberry translation)

The straight path of Islam requires submission to the will of God as revealed in the Qur'an, and recognition of Muhammad as the Messenger of God who in his daily life interpreted and exemplified that divine revelation which was given through him. The believer who follows that straight path is a Muslim.

The word *Islam* literally means "peaceful submission to the will of God—without resistance." This complete submission presupposes as an acceptable minimum a firm belief in the truth and justice of all that God has revealed in human history. In the Qur'an it is made clear that from most ancient times the word *Islam* has been used by all divine messengers and their followers as the name for their religion. Islam is thus the generic term applicable to every revealed religion so long as that religion is not altered by men. The Qur'an assures us of the intimate relation of its revelation to the previous revelations: "God has ordained for you that religion which He has already commended to Noah, Abraham, Moses, and Jesus" (Surah XLII, 13).

Thus it is that Noah declared, "I was commanded to be among the Muslims" (Surah X, 73). Abraham and Ishmael, (Isma'il), when they were constructing the Ka'ba as a place of worship at Mecca, addressed God in these words: "Our Lord! Make us Muslims unto Thee and of our seed a nation of Muslims unto Thee" (Surah II, 128). Jacob gave his sons this counsel: " . . . and die only as good Muslims" (Surah II, 132). His sons reassured him with their reply, "We do worship thy Lord, the unique God, the God of thy fathers Abraham, Ishmael, Noah, and Isaac, and we are good Muslims" (Surah II, 133). When Moses was instructing his people, he said, "Trust yourselves to God if you are true Muslims" (Surah X, 85). The disciples of Jesus avowed, "We have believed and you can be witness that we are Muslims" (Surah V, 111).

The Qur'an makes it clear that Islam is the only religion acceptable to God when it says, "Lo! religion with God is Islam" (Surah III, 19). That is, religion is submission to God's will and guidance. Again the Qur'an says, "And who seeketh as religion other than Islam, it will not be accepted from him" (Surah III, 85). Thus there has been but one true religion on earth, the religion of God, to which believing men have belonged at all times and places. Each of the holy messengers of God who has taken part in revealing the nature of the religion of God has been a stone in the building of that edifice. For the Qur'an this unity of believing humanity is not only a fact, it is above all an essential part of religious belief.

The prophets are required to show mutual recognition and acknowledgment of each other. The believers must accept and respect all revealed books and all messengers of God without distinction between them. To show preference among the revelations of God is to be guilty of a mortal sin which destroys the very basis of our belief. "Those who wish to separate God from his envoys, those who say we believe in some and do not believe in others, those are all the true infidels, and we have prepared for the infidels a terrible torture" (Surah IV, 150–51). Showing preference among the revelations of God is infidelity because it makes our own desire, our own passion and fanaticism, a criterion and principle of belief; because it resists the will of God which has been authenticated by the divine signs which appear with each one of His messengers.

The fundamental mission of the messengers of God has been to teach true belief about the one God and to establish justice among men. The unity of this belief springs from the one God and creates a union of the prophets and of their followers, who together form a unique spiritual nation, Islam. Thus, after enumerating the prophets from Noah to Jesus, the Qur'an says, "Here is your nation, one and united, and I am your Lord. Worship me, then" (Surah XXI, 92).

The belief in the divine revelation and in the spiritual peace which comes from submission to God is expressed in daily life by obeying His commandments and avoiding that which is forbidden. A humble obedience to the divine commandments is a second essential part of Islam, completing the act of faith —which is belief in God's revelation—by obeying God's commandments in practical affairs. For example, in our personal life we are commanded in the Qur'an to act with righteousness, to be straightforward in speech, to control our passions, and to purify our souls. In family life, we are commanded to treat women kindly, with full regard for their rights, and to be generous in our dealings with them. In social life, God commands that all cases shall be judged with equity; justice and charity are required; no injustices shall be done to people because of hatred toward them; all life is made sacred by God and may not be ended except through justice. In spiritual life, the Muslims must have always present in their minds the idea of God and must never despair of the forgiveness of the Lord; it is in God that believers must put their trust.

"The Muslim," said Muhammad, "is he who spares others all his bad words and evil deeds." Thus, Islam is external peace and internal peace, peace with God and peace with all creatures, the peace which comes through submission to God.

It is noteworthy, however, that historically speaking the meaning of the term *Islam* has undergone a continuous and gradual evolution in the successive divine revelations. Each new book and each new prophet constitutes a new element to be added to our creed. The most complete revelation has naturally been reserved for the latest revelation which summarizes and confirms all the others. It is thus justified to consider those who accept the last relevation as the Muslims. It is in that spirit that Qur'an calls them not only Muslims, but *the* Muslims.

God's latest revelation is given in the Qur'an; therefore, it is necessary to know the Qur'an in order to follow the straight path of Islam. The message of the Qur'an, however, is better understood by those who know the Prophet Muhammad who was the Messenger of God, the interpreter of the Qur'an and its living example.

Muhammad

Muhammad, the son of an illustrious Arab family known for its religious accomplishments and political activities, was born in Mecca on Monday, the ninth of the month Rabi Awwal (April 20, A.D. 571), in the fifty-third year before the beginning of the Muslim Era. His father died before the child was born. When Muhammad lost his mother in his sixth year he was taken into the house of his grandfather, who foresaw for him a splendid future. The grandfather died two years later, leaving him to be cared for and educated by his uncle Abu Talib who had always shown a fatherly interest in him.

The affectionate bond between the young lad and his uncle was so strong that he often traveled with him on caravan journeys. Tradition says that when he was twelve he accompanied his uncle on a commercial journey to Syria, where they met a Syrian monk called Bahira who recognized in the young man the characteristics of a prophet. He advised the uncle to take good care of Muhammad always, and to mistrust especially the Jews who might wish him ill if ever they learned of the prophetic mission he would be called to fulfill.

Muhammad spent his youth in humble circumstances, much of the time working as a shepherd. As he later pointed out, herding sheep was also the occupation of many other prophets, Moses and David in particular.

As a young man he distinguished himself by his refined manners, his extreme shyness, his absolute chastity, and his avoidance of the easy pleasures pursued by other young men of his community. All those who knew him showed complete confidence in him for he fully deserved the name by which he was called, al-Amin, which means the true and reliable one. When he was only twenty years old he was called to sit with the most venerable shaikhs of the Fudul league, an association which cared for the weak and helpless and sought to assure peace between the tribes.

At the age of twenty-five he married the rich and virtuous Khadijah, and in his married life he revealed to his family and the community his excellent human qualities. The trade which he carried on with his wife's funds kept them in comfortable circumstances, but he used his resources only as a means of spreading happiness. For instance, in order to repay his uncle for having taken care of him in his youth, he took responsibility for the education of Abu Talib's son, Ali.

Muhammad remained a faithful, loving husband during the quarter-century of his marriage to Khadijah, and after her death he was so fond of recalling the sweet memories of their married life that he caused not a little naïve jealousy in his second marriage. He was an excellent father and grandfather, showing an ideal tenderness toward his children and grandchildren. He allowed them to hang on his neck or to mount on his back, even while he was praying; he interrupted his speeches in order to greet them and made them sit with him on his chair. Some Bedouins, seeing him kiss one of his grandchildren, said, "You kiss the children? We never do that." To which the Prophet replied, "What can I do if God has deprived your hearts of all human feeling? God does not grant

His mercy to those who are not merciful." (al-Bukhari, *Al Adab*, Chapter 18).

His most famous action between the time of his marriage and his prophetic calling came when he was thirty-five years old. The sacred shrine in Mecca, the Ka'ba, was being rebuilt, and when the time came to place the Black Stone (the revered angular stone of the traditional monument), there was a furious competition among the Arab tribes for the honor of lifting it into position. The controversy was about to break out into a fight, with swords drawn, when Muhammad was seen to enter. The crowd started shouting, "al-Amin, al-Amin!" and all submitted to the arbitration of the true and reliable one. With his remarkable presence of mind and the impartiality which he always showed, Muhammad spread his coat on the ground, put the Black Stone on it, and asked the chiefs of the principal tribes to grasp the edges of the coat and together lift the stone to the required height. Then he took the stone and placed it with his own hands, thus resolving the dispute and restoring harmony among the tribes.

By this time Muhammad was physically, intellectually, and morally a mature person, endowed with those characteristics which made him a leader throughout the rest of his life. His figure was taller than average, solidly built, with a large chest and shoulders. He had a noble and always serene countenance, a large mouth with white, slightly separated teeth, black eyes set in a somewhat bloodshot background, a white, rosy skin, and black, wavy hair falling just below his ears. His walk was lively yet dignified. He wore simple clothes which were always clean and well-groomed.

He was very sober and normally restrained; he talked little, but always agreeably and with good humor. His sweet temperament and extreme delicacy would never allow him to force the pace of a conversation with anyone, nor would he ever show a desire to finish a discussion. He never withdrew his hand first from a handshake. While he was inflexible and impartial in applying justice to others, he was indulgent and yielding when his personal rights were involved.

When he later became sole master of the state he was not tempted by earthly wealth but remained as simple and frugal as he had always been, deliberately avoiding all luxury and pomp for his family as well as for himself. After his death his few possessions were not inherited by his relatives but were distributed among the poor.

In his fortieth year he approached the decisive event which wrought a complete change in his life and in the history of mankind.

The first sign of his prophetic vocation, according to his own words, was the discovery that everything which he dreamed happened in his waking hours precisely as he had foreseen it. After a time he felt a strong inclination to seek solitude and withdrew to Mount Hira, or the Mount of Light, north of Mecca. This was a spiritual withdrawal, broken only occasionally by visits to the town for food.

Muhammad received his first revelation on the seventeenth day of Ramadan (February, A.D. 610) in the thirteenth year before the beginning of the Muslim Era. This revelation took the form of a discussion between teacher and pupil, between the Archangel Gabriel and Muhammad.

"Read!" commanded Gabriel. "I am not of those who know how to read," replied Muhammad. "Read!" Gabriel repeated. "What shall I read?" asked the astonished pupil. "Read!" insisted Gabriel. "But how shall I read?" asked the solitary hermit. The Archangel then recited the first five verses of Surah XCVI:

> Read: In the name of thy Lord who createth,
> Createth man from a clot.
> Read: And thy Lord is the most Bounteous,
> Who teacheth by the pen,
> Teacheth man that which he knew not.

This is the first fragment of the Qur'an. The Angel then disappeared and Muhammad, completely overcome, was starting to leave the grotto when he heard a voice calling to him. He lifted up his head and saw the Angel filling all the horizon in its immensity, and heard the Angel tell him, "O Muhammad: Really, you are the messenger of God, and I am Gabriel." After that, Muhammad saw nothing else.

When he reached home he told Khadijah of these happenings and expressed his fears. His devoted wife reassured him with wise and consoling words, "No," she said, "do not worry. God would surely not do you any harm, nor heap shame upon you, for you have never done harm. You always speak the truth, you help the feeble, you always assist those who suffer for a just cause." To comfort him further she accompanied him on a visit to her cousin, Waraqa Ibn Nawfal, who said to him, "This is good news which should fill you with rejoicing. I declare that you are the prophet announced by Jesus. Oh, that I could live until your countrymen will chase you, Muhammad, from your country." "How is it," cried Muhammad, "that they will chase me from here?" "Of course," replied Waraqa, "never has a man brought his fellowmen what you brought with you without becoming the object of persecution and hostility."

Muhammad often returned to the grotto where he had received his first message to seek another revelation. He placed himself in the same condition, he walked the mountains, he turned his eyes in all directions. Days passed, weeks went by, month followed month, one year was gone, another began, and according to the account of al-Cha'bi even a third year came without another revelation. His only comfort was that each time when he felt himself on the brink of despair he heard, "O Muhammad, you are the messenger of God, and I am Gabriel," but without hearing the message he so ardently expected.

By this time Muhammad was forty-three years old. He continued to wake up almost every night in the hope of hearing this "heavy and grave" promised word. Each year he withdrew to Mount Hira in the month of Ramadan. Finally one day, when he had finished his retreat and was descending to the town, he heard someone calling him. He looked around, to the right, to the left, and behind him, but saw no one. Then he lifted his eyes toward heaven and recognized the Angel whom he had seen at Mount Hira. The suddenness of the apparition, the majestic immensity of the heavenly being, struck him so strongly that he could not remain standing. The sublime visitor then gave him the decree which invested him with his second responsibility: "Oh you, who cover yourself carefully, get up, and spread your announcement" (Surah LXXIV, 1–2).

Thus Muhammad must not only receive his divine knowledge, he must also transmit it to the people. To his role of Prophet was added that of Apostle.

After this second message, the revelations succeeded each other without the long interruption which came between the first and second.

Muhammad's career as the Messenger of Islam lasted for twenty years, with ten years in Mecca before the Hijrah (the move from Mecca to Medina in A.D. 622, which is the starting date for the Muslim Era) and ten years at Medina before his death.

He began his preaching in Mecca by discreetly speaking only in his most intimate circles. Abu Bakr was the first man to be converted to Islam and Khadijah the first woman; Ali was the first young man. The first foreigners were Zaid Ibn Haritha, the Yemenite; Bilal Ibn Rabah, the Abyssinian; and Sohaib Ibn Sinan, the Roman. Islam spread slowly in Mecca, privately at first, and then, in the tenth year before the Hijrah the calling to Islam became public. At first it was kind and courteous and evoked no animosity among the unbelieving. But when the message became reproachful of paganism the Arabs rose in opposition and showed their hatred.

The opposition of the Arabs was at first directed mainly toward the Prophet. It was relatively mild toward those of his believers who had a distinguished family or tribal position, but tended to be cruel toward the humble and the powerless. Therefore, in the middle of the ninth year before the Hijrah the Prophet allowed eleven men and four women to seek refuge with the King of Abyssinia, who received them well and was himself converted to Islam. By the beginning of the eighth year before the Hijrah there were scarcely forty men and about ten women who were Muslims in Mecca, and they met in secret. The conversion of such important people as Hamzah and Umar in this year gave such strong support and encouragement to the followers that they were able to say their prayers openly near the Ka'ba, and the new religion began to spread more rapidly.

This new growth of Islam aroused the unbelieving to redouble their violence and persecution, and in the seventh year before the Hijrah a second contingent of refugees, eighty-three men and eighteen women, emigrated to Abyssinia. The Prophet himself became the target of a conspiracy but was protected by the two family branches most closely related to him, the Bani Hashim and the Bani al-Muttalib, who rallied around him in the Hashimid quarter. The other branches and tribes thereupon banded together in opposition and took a written oath to boycott the protecting quarters until Muhammad was handed over to them. They maintained their severe boycott for three years, abandoning it in the fourth year before the Hijrah.

The ending of the boycott would have been a great relief to the Prophet if it had not been that just at this time he suffered two cruel losses: the death of his uncle Abu Talib and shortly afterward the death of his wife Khadijah. The Prophet calls this year "the year of suffering." Having become a widower without the consoling intimacy of a wife, he married Sawdah, a courageous believer whose suffering during the persecution and emigration had just been crowned by the loss of her husband after their return from Abyssinia. Accordingly, this marriage must be considered more a compensation for her than for him.

When Muhammad lost the support which his uncle afforded him in Mecca, he left the town to look elsewhere for allies and adherents. He spent ten unsuccessful days with the tribe of Thaqif, at at-Ta'if, but he was received badly and returned disappointed to Mecca to devote his proselytizing efforts to the pilgrims' encampment at the Ka'ba. Toward the end of the third year before the Hijrah he saw a faint hope in six men from Medina. These good men, who had heard the message of the Prophet during a brief encounter at Mina, responded enthusiastically to his appeal and carried the holy message to Medina where they made many converts.

Toward the end of the following year, the second before the Hijrah, five of those men from Medina with seven new converts visited the Prophet and took an oath to abstain from any polytheistic cult, from all vices, and to observe strict discipline. A year later, seventy-five men from Medina came to swear allegiance, confess their faith, and declare their submission. They also promised to defend the Prophet and their Muslim brothers if they should choose Medina as their refuge. This represents the first defense treaty in Islamic history.

Immediately after receiving this promise from the men of Medina the Prophet authorized and even obliged those men among his followers who had sufficient means to settle in Medina with their new brothers. Those who insisted upon remaining in Mecca without valid reason were to be regarded as hypocrites. But the Prophet himself did not hasten to leave his post and join the community of his faithful followers. He awaited an express authorization by revelation, an authorization which came after three months, on the day before the unfaithful had planned to carry out a plot against him.

Before the Hijrah, when Muhammad joined his followers in Medina, the Muslims did not form a nation or even a community; they did not even have a majority in Mecca. In Mecca they occupied no post of authority. They could not make a solemn call to prayer or come together for a public gathering. In Medina, however, Muslims could settle openly and Islam could develop. Communal prayer was observed solemnly even before the arrival of the Prophet. The day after his arrival in Medina the Prophet assumed full authority, started forming the state, and began the building of the great mosque.

Muhammad's authority in Medina was of an entirely new and original kind: it was at the same time absolute and consultative, theocratic and socialist. It was religious and absolute in its framework, based on revealed commandments and general rules, but socialistic and consultative in the details and the application of the rules.

The Muslim state which the Prophet created in Medina remains the model of every Muslim state worthy of the name. It is unique in human history, for although this Muslim state was fundamentally religious, it established two principles which are not found elsewhere except in a nonreligious state or in a religion which has no state government associated with it. The first is the principle of freedom of religion, a freedom which the Muslim state not only admits and authorizes but must even defend and guarantee. The second is the principle which defines the idea of fatherland or nation in the most tolerant and human sense, a principle which guarantees equality of rights and national duties for those of all races, colors, languages, and ideologies existing in the country.

The first year and a half after the Hijrah were entirely devoted to purely pacific and constructive activities, to the development of religious and social institutions such as fasting, almsgiving, fraternization of the immigrants with the original inhabitants, agreements between tribes, and the like. Thus far nothing suggested the use of force. It was only because they wanted to be indemnified for the loss of their houses and worldly goods, which had been left behind in the hands of their enemies in Mecca, and because they wanted to put an end to the persecution and violence which the enemies were inflicting upon their brethren in Mecca that the Muslims tried several times, unsuccessfully, to intercept enemy caravans passing near Medina.

In Ramadan of the second year after the Hijrah the pagans reacted to these fruitless attempts to intercept the caravans by declaring an offensive against Medina. The Muslims thereupon sought to defend themselves, in a rather improvised manner, and although inferior in numbers and weapons they obtained a decisive victory. In the month of Shawwal in the third year the Meccans took their revenge, and for the next few years actions and counteractions followed until in the sixth year a ten-year truce was concluded. This truce was very favorable for the growth of Islam. Not only did it spread among the Arabs of the Hijaz—the western side of the Arabian peninsula—who were in frequent contact with the

Muslims, but during this time the Prophet sent his messages and messengers to the Roman Emperor Heraclios, and to the kings and princes in Persia, Egypt, Bahrein, and Yemen.

In the year A.H. 8 the Meccans broke the truce, and this time the Prophet marched victoriously into the capital. The indulgent and merciful character of the Prophet, which he had always shown, was clear to all the people of Mecca after this conquest when, without repressive action or loss of life, he generously pardoned all his former persecutors. The conversion and submission of the whole Arab peninsula came soon after the conquest of Mecca, but in the northern part of the peninsula the Romans (Byzantines) prepared themselves for a strong attack against the young religion. In A.H. 9 the Prophet himself led an expedition as far as Tabouk (halfway between Medina and Damascus) which made the Romans renounce their enterprise. When the Prophet returned to Medina he had concluded nonaggression treaties with the neighboring countries to the north.

It was also in the ninth year of the Hijrah that the Prophet ordered Abu Bakr, his closest disciple, to lead the pilgrims to Mecca and to proclaim that the approach to the Ka'ba from that time onward was to be forbidden to all pagans and polytheists.

In the tenth year after the Hijrah the pilgrimage to Mecca was led by the Prophet himself. This is known as the "farewell pilgrimage," during which the Prophet received the divine message that his mission was fulfilled and foresaw that the end of his life was near. "This day have I perfected your religion for you and completed My favor unto you, and have approved for you as religion AL-ISLAM" (Surah V, 3).

Those who heard his sermon on Arafa day in the tenth year recognized that they were hearing his last will and testament. With great emphasis he reminded all human beings of their brotherly love, their common origin, their equality without distinction except by means of virtue. With clear authority he commanded respect for the person, the family, and for property. With kindly compassion he recommended gentleness toward women. With great vision he enjoined his listeners to retain and transmit his message to all those who have not heard it, for, he said, "Who knows? Maybe I shall not see you again after this year." Finally, addressing himself to the pilgrims who had come from all the surroundings countries in such numbers that they reached the horizon and spread over all the desert, he said, "God will ask you about me: did I transmit to you His message?" "Yes! Yes!" Thereupon, looking toward heaven and pointing his fingers, Muhammad prayed in a loud voice, "My God, be witness."

Less than three months after this sermon, on the twelfth day of Rabi Awwal, A.H. 11 (June 7, A.D. 632), Muhammad's soul returned to his eternal resting place.

The question of miracles in relation to Muhammad has often been debated. Did he perform miracles other than the Qur'an?

The Qur'an, revealed to the world by the voice of Muhammad, is a miracle—yes, rather THE Miracle. Everything proves it: its style, its contents, the extraordinary events by which it was revealed, taught, and written down; its constant conformity with past, present, and future truth; its transcendent character which never shows a trace of a particular man, of any one society or epoch of history or specific region of the globe. The Qur'an is not a passing event in history which appears one day and disappears the next, to be known only by more or less correct hearsay reports. No, it is a fact, stable and durable, which remains unchanged and eternally present for the admiring contemplation of all men.

The Qur'an is not a temporary wonder which deceives the mind and is alien to the new knowledge which it has come to influence. It is the truth, the truth which proves itself, and while it appeals to reason it transcends reason and thus shows its divine origin.

The recognition of the Qur'an as THE Miracle does not diminish the value of other material and tangible miracles, known through our senses. These miracles, too, can very well bring us conviction; they are often the best means to reinforce our faith. That is why our earlier prophets have performed miracles.

Was it the same with the Prophet of Islam? Has he performed miracles other than the transmission of the Qur'an?

There are current tendencies toward answering in the negative, pretending to find proof in the Qur'an itself. The Qur'an, it is said, tells us that the Prophet Muhammad systematically refused to satisfy those who asked him to produce miracles.

> And they say: We will not put faith in thee till thou
> cause a spring to gush forth from the earth for us;
> Or thou have a garden of date-palms and grapes, and
> cause rivers to gush forth therein abundantly . . .
> Or thou have a house of gold; or thou ascend up into
> heaven, and even then we will put no faith in thine
> ascension till thou bring down for us
> a book that we can read. (Surah XVII, 90–93)

> And they say: Why are not signs sent down upon him
> from his Lord? Say: Signs are with Allah only,
> and I am but a plain warner.
> Is it not enough for them that We have sent down unto
> thee the Scripture which is read unto them?
> Lo! herein verily is mercy, and a reminder for
> folk who believe.
> (Surah XXIX, 50–51)

At the basis of the theory that the Prophet refused to perform miracles we find a grave misinterpretation, not only of the meaning of these quotations, but more so of the Islamic conception of the author of miracles in general. In those quotations the possibility of a miracle is not denied. Rather, they point out that miracles come from the supreme authority which alone is capable of any form of creation, and above all of creating supernatural things. It is a matter of demarking the frontier which separates human and divine power. The man is not yet possessed of the true Islamic faith who confounds those two powers, believing that the prophets themselves created their miracles. For the prophets are only human; they cannot overcome physical laws nor can they overcome the laws of the mind. God alone does so, if and when He wants to, in order to prove the divine origins of the message which the prophets transmit.

Therefore, it was not Moses who transformed the stick into a living snake, for this transmutation took place to his great surprise. It was not Jesus, either, who by his own power revived the dead; he did it only by the authority of the Lord. And when he refused the demands of those who once asked him to produce a sign from heaven, does this mean that he no longer performed miracles? Evidently not!

It is the same with Muhammad in his refusal to comply with certain pagan requests. The answer with which he avowed his own incapability to perform miracles is the same which he gave concerning the Qur'an. It is not Muhammad who is the author of the Qur'an, but it is "the faithful spirit"; it is the Archangel Gabriel who, on God's command, brought the Qur'an down from heaven and deposited it in Muhammad's heart so that it may guide and rejoice those who believe in it. Not only could Muhammad not modify an iota of it, he did not even expect to be its bearer and was not sure that he would continue to receive it.

Thus no miracles, material or spiritual, are of human origin, for all are exclusively within God's domain and competence. All prophets have avowed that they are subject to the same limitations. Neither they nor the people to whom they were sent could demand a certain miracle or substitute one miracle for another according to their preferences. God gives His mandate to whomsoever He wills, in the form which He deems proper to persuade any epoch of history or any age of humanity. To each epoch its book. To each people, its guide.

> And verily We sent messengers (to mankind) before thee,
> and We appointed for them wives and offspring,
> and it was not (given) to any messenger that he should
> bring a sign save by Allah's leave.
> To each epoch, its book.
>
> (Surah XIII, 38)

In Islamic terminology a miracle is most often defined as a fact contrary to general rules, opposed to the normal course of events, with a cause which escapes human comprehension;

and this fact is also a challenge to anyone who doubts it. Now the only fact which most obviously fulfills all these conditions is, of course, the Qur'an, which repeatedly and in many ways cries out its challenge to all beings visible and invisible and predicts their impotence to prove that it is not the miraculous message of God. It invites them first to imitate its text in its entirety, then to create ten Surahs similar to those in the Qur'an or to create but a single similar Surah, and finally asks but for a Surah only slightly resembling one in the Qur'an.

The question as to whether or not the Prophet performed any miracle other than the revelation of the Qur'an thus depends on the definition of a miracle. If it is required that such a challenge must have been explicitly expressed, then it must be said that in Islam there has been no miracle other than the Qur'an. But once we eliminate the arbitrary stipulation that the challenge must have been expressed, we find an uncountable number of miracles performed by the Prophet.

Some of those miracles are mentioned in the Qur'an itself:

The Prophet's journey made by supernatural means from Mecca to Jerusalem in a single moment of the night; a journey during which he saw many divine signs, and distinguished clearly all topographical details of the place, details which he later described, to the surprise of all (Surah XVII, 1).

The prediction of a cleavage on the surface of the moon, a celestial phenomenon which indeed took place immediately in the presence of the crowd of people he was addressing and which was observed and confirmed by travelers (Surah LIV, 1).

The miraculous victory over the army of his enemies which was accomplished by a small number of faithful, poorly armed followers, but men who were assisted by divine power (Surah VIII, 17).

The fact that the society in Medina, which had been divided and eaten by hatred and civil war for dozens of years, became overnight a united group of intimate friends—a sudden change of mind which could not have been accomplished by earthly forces (Surah III, 103; VIII, 63).

The revelation by the Prophet of secret facts which had been carefully hidden from his knowledge (Surah IV, 113; LXVI, 3).

Innumerable predictions fulfilled, such as the announcement of the precise date of a coming victory of the Romans over the Persians (Surah XXX, 2–6).

Also innumerable truthful reports of historic facts which were unknown to him and his people (Surah XI, 49; XII, 102; XXVIII, 44–46).

Among other miracles not mentioned in the Qur'an only a few can be cited here. The knowledge of these miracles, performed publicly by the Prophet, has been transmitted from generation to generation by reporters who have been identified and are known to be trustworthy historians. These examples are taken from the first chapter of al-Bukhari's *Alamate El Noboua:*

The prediction that the Roman and Persian empires would cease to exist immediately after the death of their emperors who were contemporaries of the Prophet.

The announcement of the death of the King of Abyssinia on the date of his death.

The assurance he gave that, after the battle against the pagans of Mecca in the fifth year of the Hijrah, the Meccans would never again march against Medina and that Mecca would be conquered by the Muslims.

The prediction that his grandson al-Hasan would re-establish unity and end the conflict between two great parties of Islam, a prediction which was fulfilled in the days of Mu'awiya, the fifth Caliph.

A miracle which was often repeated during times of drought and general thirst in the army was the production of an abundant yield of water from a little vessel which the Prophet blessed by putting his fingers in it. Fifteen hundred soldiers were able to quench their thirst, perform their ablutions, and water their animals with the water from that little vessel.

During a Friday sermon, when a Bedouin complained about the continuing dry weather and the famine which would ensue, the Prophet prayed for rain, and storm-clouds gathered from all directions, bringing rain which continued until the following Friday.

> The next Friday the same Bedouin complained of the destruction being caused by the rain, and after the Prophet prayed the sky above Medina cleared immediately.
>
> Once when the Prophet had been sitting on a tree stump and then abandoned it for a higher seat in order that the increased number of listeners might hear him better, all the audience heard the wailing complaint of the stump, a wailing which continued until the Prophet took the stump in his arms and consoled it as one would console a baby.

These are only a few of the many authenticated examples of miracles, other than the great miracle of receiving the revelation of the Qur'an, which were performed by the Prophet Muhammad, the Messenger of God.

The Qur'an

The greatest miracle was the revelation of the Qur'an which was transmitted by the Prophet in passages of unequal length at different times over a period of twenty-three years.

As soon as the Prophet received each inspired message he recited it to his audience and they in turn repeated it to the community, which was made up of people who were fond of literature and eagerly awaited each new message, whether they were partisans or adversaries.

As the Prophet dictated each new passage it was written down by the scribes on anything within reach, on thin white stones, pieces of parchment, wood, leather, or whatever was available. Tradition counts up to twenty-nine different persons in Medina who served as secretaries; a lesser number of scribes recorded the revelations received in Mecca. From the very beginning the faithful never failed to record the revealed messages, even during the persecutions. Among these scribes were included the first five Caliphs: Abu Bakr, Umar, Uthman, Ali, and Mu'awiya.

Thus the holy book of Islam became known in both an oral and written form. In its oral form it was called *Qur'an*, that is, Recital. In its written form it was called *Kitab*, or Scripture.

At the beginning the written extracts were not put in order or even gathered together, for other messages were expected.

As time went on several groups of verses began to grow up and tended to become independent unities as new verses were added according to the instructions given by the Prophet, who was following the orders of the Revealer Spirit. Although the text was originally scattered in its written form, it always had a definite order in the Prophet's mind and in the minds of the faithful, with each verse or group of verses fitting into its proper place in the structure of the whole. In the Prophet's lifetime there were hundreds of his Companions, called "Qur'an bearers," who were specialists in reciting the Book and knew by heart every Surah in its proper place in the structure.

At the death of the Prophet the Qur'an was preserved in the memories of the faithful as well as in writing. While in its oral form every Surah was complete and in its proper place in the order known today, in its written form it was nothing but scattered documents written on many different materials. During the year following the death of the Prophet no one worried about the written form because there were innumerable oral witnesses among them as living copies of the Qur'an complete in its final form. But about a year after the Prophet's death seventy of the Qur'an bearers were killed in the battle with Musailima, the false prophet, and it became clear that it would be necessary to guard against the loss of the oral tradition by gathering the written documents into a book easy to handle and use for reference. The idea of preparing the book was suggested by Umar and carried out by Zaid Ibn Thabit, a Qur'an bearer who had attended the last recital of the Qur'an by the Prophet and a man known for his intelligence, integrity, and competence.

Under the guidance of Zaid Ibn Thabit the correct written form of the Qur'an was determined by including only those passages which were verified by two witnesses as having been written down at the dictation of the Prophet and as being in the oral text of the last recital by the Prophet. This official collection is distinguished from the other personal, oral versions by an absolute rigorism which excluded from the text any explanatory notes and even eliminated the Surah titles. When the written form was completed it was given to the first Caliph, Abu Bakr, who entrusted it to Umar when he designated him the second Caliph. Since the third Caliph had not been chosen at the time of Umar's death, he gave it to his daughter Hafsah who was one of the widows of the Prophet.

The universal authority of the written form of the Qur'an dates from its publication by the third Caliph, Uthman, who received it from Hafsah and ordered four secretaries to write as many copies of the document as there were big towns in the Islamic Empire. From that time the Uthman edition has been the only one in use in the Islamic world.

Ever since the earliest days the question has been raised as to whether the Qur'an was of divine or human origin. The explicit and implicit testimony of the Qur'an is that the author is God Himself. It is never the Prophet who speaks in the Qur'an. The Scripture either refers to him in the third person or addresses him directly—O Prophet, O Messenger, We reveal to thee, We send thee, do this, recite this; such is the language of the Qur'an.

The direct proof of the divine origin of the Qur'an is manifest all through the Scripture itself. It is also shown by the peculiar phenomena which accompanied every revelation of the Qur'an, according to the testimony of the true tradition. The Prophet's contemporaries were objective witnesses of the visible, tangible, and audible signs of the mysterious accompanying phenomena which made evident the real source of the Qur'an and opened the eyes of the truth-seekers. In the presence of the Revealer Spirit the Prophet's inspired face was illumined, like a mirror; there was silence; conversation stopped as if in moments of absence of mind; his body relaxed as if in sleep and a mysterious buzz was heard around him—as in a telephone conversation where the one listening is the only one who can hear distinctly enough to understand. There was nothing voluntary about these phenomena, for the Prophet could neither avoid them when they came nor bring them into being when he earnestly desired to receive a message. On many occasions the Prophet sought a revelation but it was not given; then, sometimes after an interval as long as a month, the mysterious phenomena would come, appearing suddenly and vanishing abruptly, after which the people with him would listen to the wonderful text.

The literary style and contents of that text are conclusive evidence of the divine origin of the Qur'an, but before considering that evidence let us turn to the arguments by which attempts have been made to prove that the origins were human. It is to the honor of Islam that the Qur'an records all hypotheses, reasonable or absurd, by which the contemporaries of the Prophet attempted to establish human origins for the Scripture. If the origins were human, they must have come from Muhammad's environment, from other religions in that environment, or from the meditations and reasoning of the human author. Let us examine the activities of the Prophet before and during his apostolate and see what he could have learned from his surroundings or from his own meditations.

It is scarcely necessary to point out that at the beginning of Islam neither the ideas nor the practices of the people of Mecca show any resemblance to the teachings of the Qur'an. There is no relation between the pure unitarian system, the most perfect and refined ethics of the Holy Book of Islam, and the ignorance, paganism, superstitious idolatry, arrogant materialism, infanticide, prostitution, incest, dowry extortion, oppression of orphans, disregard for the poor, and scorn of the weak which were characteristics of Mecca in those times.

An effort has been made to show that the teachings of the Qur'an are similar to those of the Sabians, a sect well-known in Mecca at that time. But the Sabians were idolatrous and polytheistic, worshiping the stars and angels with a mixture of pagan, Christian, and other rites. Their pilgrimage was not to the Ka'ba, but to Harran in Iraq, and their prayers were to the stars at sunrise, at noon, and at sunset—three times when prayer is prohibited in Islam.

It was also suggested that Muhammad might have been influenced by the travelers and immigrants who came to Mecca: the Abyssinians or Romans, the laborers or wine merchants. It is clear that our Personage could not have known the vulgar class of immigrants for he lived either alone, in complete solitude, or as a shepherd, or as a big merchant in a caravan, or in the high society with the leaders of the community. Even if he had any contact with such people, their lack of religious knowledge would have been evident, and as the Qur'an points out, their foreign language would have made communication impossible (Surah XVI, 103).

It has been argued that in Muhammad's travels he became acquainted with Arab tribes which had been converted to Christianity and got his ideas from them. Many scholars, ancient and modern, have pointed out that such contact with Christianity is unlikely but that, even if it did happen, the Christianity practiced in that part of the world was so debased that it was indistinguishable from paganism. The fourth Caliph, Ali, said that the tribe Taghlib had taken from Christianity nothing but the habit of drinking wine. Wherever Muhammad traveled he found beliefs to be rectified, deviations to be brought back to the right way. Nowhere did he find a moral or religious model which could have been copied for his work of reform.

Again, it has been suggested that the Prophet gleaned his teachings from the reading of books recording previous revelations. But the Qur'an categorically denies that he knew how to read or write (Surah XXIX, 48). Furthermore, the Bible was not available in Arabic until many centuries after the Prophet's time, and the Bible in other languages was out of reach of the common people. The few biblical ideas which may have circulated among the common people were so vague and often contradictory that they cannot be the basis for the precision, extensiveness, unity, and vigor of the material in the Qur'an.

Nor can it be argued that Muhammad was influenced by Jewish teachings after he came to Medina, where he was in contact with Jewish scholars. Even before the Hijrah the Holy History had been revealed in all its true details in the Meccan Surahs, and the Qur'an had condemned the believers in the Pentateuch as followers of satanic inspiration, unworthy of being accepted as teachers or examples (Surah XVI, 63). In the revelations in Medina the Qur'an goes even further in its condemnation of the followers of the Pentateuch (Surah II, 79–80; III, 75; IV, 161). The psychological attitudes on both sides made Jewish influence on Islamic thought practically impossible. The majority of the Jewish scholars adopted an antagonistic position which was far from the benevolent attitude of teachers. Those of the Israelite scholars who were impartial enthusiastically welcomed the Prophet in Medina and declared their conversion to Islam, thereafter as disciples recognizing him as their Master. Between the two categories of the hostile or the submissive, there was no place for a third group of friendly tutors.

Thus it is clear that the teachings of the Qur'an cannot be attributed to the influence of the environment on Muhammad. There remains the question as to whether or not he could have created the Qur'an by himself through the use of meditation and reason. To a limited extent, reason could have revealed the falseness of idolatry and the senselessness of superstition, but how could it know how to replace them? It is not by mere thinking that facts can be known, that previous events can be described, yet the Qur'an was always in perfect accord with the essential data of the Bible, even those hidden from Muhammad by scholars. Mere intellect by itself could not have given such details. The Qur'an confirms that before the revelation Muhammad did not know any book nor even the meaning of faith (Surah XLII, 52). He could not possibly have guided others, for he did not even know how to guide himself in religious matters. He was ignorant of all the legislative, moral, social, and ritual details which are included in the revelation of the Qur'an. It was not by reason, or by the study of books, but only by revelation that Muhammad could know the creative God and the divine attributes. Only as it was revealed to him could he define the relation between God and the visible and invisible worlds and specify the future reserved to man after death.

We have seen that the Qur'an could not have human origins traceable either to the experience of Muhammad in the environment of his time or to his ability to construct the Holy

Book by use of his reason. We have seen that the divine origin of the Qur'an is attested by the mysterious phenomena which always preceded a revelation. Now let us look further and consider the internal evidence for the divine origin in the literary form and contents of the Qur'an.

The literary form of the Qur'an is distinguished clearly from all other forms, whether they be poetry, rhythmic or non-rhythmic prose, the style of the common people, or that of the Prophet himself. The exceptional eloquence of Muhammad was always acknowledged and is known to us in countless instructions which he gave after careful thought, or dictated as non-Quranic insights. In all such passages there is not the slightest resemblance between them and the revealed messages.

We feel such ascendant power in the revealed texts that they penetrate the soul. The infidels in the time of the Prophet considered the form of the text such an extraordinary phenomenon that they used to call it magic. Even in modern times those who can understand the Arabic text recognize its sublime character without being able to explain it.

In our lectures on exegesis at Al Azhar University in Cairo—the oldest university in the world—the following analysis is used to point out the ways in which the literary form of the Qur'an transcends the powers of man and defies imitation.

> The form of the Qur'an reflects neither the sedentary softness of the townsman nor the nomadic roughness of the Bedouin. It possesses in right measure the sweetness of the former and the vigor of the latter.
>
> The rhythm of the syllables is more sustained than in prose and less patterned than in poetry. The pauses come neither in prose form nor in the manner of poetry, but with a harmonious and rhythmic symmetry.
>
> The words chosen neither transgress by their banality nor by their extreme rarity, but are recognized as expressing admirable nobility.
>
> The sentences are constructed in a dignified manner which uses the smallest possible number of words to express ideas of utmost richness.

> The brevity of expression, the conciseness, attains such a striking clearness that the least learned man can understand the Qur'an without difficulty.
>
> At the same time there is such a profundity, flexibility, suggestivity, and radiance in the Qur'an that it serves as the basis of the principles and rules for the Islamic sciences and arts, for theology, and for the juridical schools. Thus it is almost impossible in each case to express the ideas of a text by one interpretation only, either in Arabic or in a foreign language, even with the greatest care.
>
> Quranic speech appears to be superhuman in its transcendence of the psychological law that intellect and feeling are always found in inverse proportion to each other. In the Qur'an we find constant cooperation between the two antagonistic powers of reason and emotion, for we find that in the narrations, arguments, doctrines, laws, and moral principles the words have both a persuasive teaching and an emotive force. Throughout the whole Qur'an the speech maintains a surprising solemnity and powerful majesty which nothing can disturb.
>
> Finally, when we pass from the structure of a sentence, or a group of sentences dealing with the same subject, to the structure of the Surah and of the Qur'an as a whole, we find an over-all plan which could not have been created by man.

We know that the Qur'an was revealed in long and short fragments over a period of twenty-three years and that they have been arranged according to neither their chronological order nor their subject matter but in an independent, complicated order which appears to be arbitrary. As each revelation appeared it was placed in its fixed place, given its number among the verses, and its place was never changed. Thus, for every revealed verse there are two different orders, the chronological order based on the date of its revelation and the architectural order which determined its place in the composition of the Book. Throughout the long period of the revelations these two orders were strictly followed for every verse, every Surah, and the whole work.

In the chronological order, every revelation meets the need of the hour and links with the previous and following ones in a gradual progress in teaching and legislation. For instance, consider the main outline of these successive stages: it begins with the simple command, "Read!" (Surah XCVI, 1); then goes on to the apostolic charge, "Preach!" (Surah LXXIV, 2); then the call at first to the near relatives only (Surah XXVI, 214), extended next to the whole town (Surah XXVIII, 59), then to the neighboring towns (Surah VI, 92), and at last to humanity (Surah XXI, 107). Consider also the general outline of the progress in teaching in its two big divisions: first the fundamental bases of the work in the Surahs of Mecca; then the codified application of those general principles in the Surahs of Medina. This long course of events continued from the day of the grotto, when Muhammad was simply warned that he would receive a divine teaching, until the day of the last pilgrimage, when he was told that his mission was accomplished and he had nothing else to do on earth. After receiving the revelations for twenty-three years, he was called back.

Nothing, therefore, has been improvised in the Qur'an. Everything was foreseen and formed as a whole and in every detail, from the beginning to the end, including the death of the Prophet. Who could have formed and carried out such a complete plan? Who other than God from whom came this heavenly mission?

In addition to the chronological order there is the architectural order in the Qur'an. The very texts which follow in the chronological order the most wise educational plan were taken from their historical positions and fixed in the architectural order, every one in a definite frame already built to receive it, taking its place in those units of different length called Surahs. What makes it so wonderful is that once each Surah is completed from those scattered parts it is a unit faultlessly formed, artistically, linguistically, and logically. A special musical rhythm runs equally through all parts of the speech; there is a common, harmonious style, and a logical plan in the development of the ideas expressed.

It is clear that to establish such a scheme in advance the author would have had to foresee not only the problems which would arise from the events of the next twenty-three years, and their solutions, but also the literary form, the musical tone and rhythm in which it would be expressed, the appropriate structure for all the revelations yet to come, and the precise spot in that framework where each revelation would be fixed.

It must be confessed that no man or any other creature is capable of knowing the future in such detail or creating such a Book. Only the Divine Omniscience could be the creator of the Qur'an.

The teachings of the Qur'an are universal, addressed to all people throughout the world regardless of their origins and revealed to mankind to enlighten man's spirit, to purify his morals, to unify his society, and to replace the domination by the powerful with justice and fraternity. As is confirmed in Surah XVI, 89, all human problems can be solved through the Qur'an, either directly or indirectly: "And We reveal the Scripture unto thee as an exposition of all things."

This revelation in the Qur'an deals primarily with the Supreme Truth and with virtue. All the rest of the contents of the text—such as knowledge of the soul, the sciences of the nature of the heavens and the earth, history, prophecy, warnings, and the like—are only means to strengthen the message of the Qur'an, to give it more weight and conviction. The great theologian al-Ghazali, who died A.H. 505 (A.D. 1111), pointed out in his *Pearls of the Qur'an* that 763 verses are concerned with knowledge, and 741 verses with guidance in virtue. For him these 1504 verses represent the most precious substance of the Book, while the remaining 5112 verses are, so to speak, the envelope or shell of the teachings.

According to the Qur'an, the act of faith must include these three elements:

Belief in God
Belief in His messages addressed to humanity
Belief in the Day of Judgment.

The starting point in Islam is belief in God, the Almighty, the Benefactor, the Creator of everything, the only proper object of worship. In the attempts to persuade the polytheists to accept this pure monotheism, the chief point at issue is the question of the proper object of worship. The Qur'an in many passages points out that the pagans confess that there is but one Creator and Administrator of the universe (Surah XLIII, 9), but their mortal mistake is that in their worship they associate secondary gods with God and claim that those secondary gods are capable of interceding with Him on their behalf and winning His favor. The Qur'an uses arguments based on reason and on tradition to bring back those who have strayed from monotheism into polytheism.

In the rational arguments directed at the polytheists, the Qur'an emphasizes their agreement that creation and providence are attributed exclusively to God and seeks to persuade them to the exclusive worship of God. How can one equate the creature to the Creator? Is it conceivable that the being which has created nothing equals the One who has created everything? (Surah XVI, 17). Is it not illogical to invoke that which never answers us, which never even hears our appeal? (Surah XLVI, 5). Is it not ungrateful on our part to forget the Benefactor who grants us our happiness, the Benefactor to whom we address all our supplications in times of disaster? Is it not ungrateful to associate with Him in worship others who are incapable of either good or evil actions? (Surah XVI, 53–54). And finally, those polytheists who pretend that any man or saint or other being has the power of mediation or intercession with the great God must prove that it can be done (Surah II, 255; XIII, 33; XXXIX, 3).

In addition to the rational arguments against polytheistic worship, the Qur'an points to the unanimous testimony of the prophetic traditions. "There has not been one previous prophet to whom We have not revealed this truth that there is no God but Me, therefore worship Me" (Surah XXI, 25). "Ask the divine messengers who preceded you: Have We allowed them to worship other gods than the Merciful?" (Surah XLIII, 45).

While the starting point of faith is belief in God as the Creator, the Benefactor, and the only object of worship, it must be recognized that God is also the Legislator. He commands our actions and our emotions. He requires our trust and obedience. This truth can be known by natural intelligence, by common sense and conscience, and also by the confirmation given in the Qur'an. God has given man the natural power to discern good and evil, justice and injustice (Surah XCI, 7–8), but the experience of all time shows that passions, work, and material and worldly preoccupations sometimes turn our minds away from the highest ideals and lead us to erroneous judgments and practical mistakes. Therefore the Divine Mercy did not abandon us to our natural intelligence alone. To check any tendency in us toward declining our responsibilities, God has reinforced our natural intelligence with revealed Truths (Surah XXIV, 35).

In order that His commandments might be known to men without dependence on reason alone, God chose among men and Angels those worthy of receiving and transmitting the divine light, sending to every nation or large tribe His warning (Surah XVI, 36). Those who refuse to believe in any spokesman of God refuse to believe in God himself, for every divine messenger has been given proof of the divine origin of his revelations (Surah LVII, 25).

The first two elements in the faith of Islam—belief in God and in His messages—are not complete without the third: belief in the Day of Judgment. God is Creator, God is Legislator, and God is also the supreme Judge. He is the beginning and the end; to Him all men must turn to give an account of their deeds and to receive from Him equitable retribution according to their merits (Surah XL, 16; LVII, 3; II, 281). The doctrine of life after death includes belief in the survival of the soul and the resurrection of the body. The belief in the survival of the soul did not give rise to difficulties, but the impious objected with irony to the doctrine of the resurrection of the body: "Give us back our fathers if you speak the truth!" (Surah XLIV, 36).

The Qur'an opposed such superficial reasoning by pointing out the argument from nature, how the earth is at one time dead and dry and then living and fertile. (Surah XXII, 5–7; XXX, 50). The Qur'an establishes that resurrection is not only possible, it is certain. It is certain because God has promised it, and it is certain because it is required by wisdom and justice in order to give to each creature a just retribution for his deeds. Otherwise, the creation of man would have been in vain. "Deemed ye then that We had created you for naught, and that ye would not be returned unto Us?" (Surah XXIII, 115). Nor should it be thought that good and bad men would be treated in the same way, giving them similar life and death (Surah XLV, 21). In the Day of Judgment, justice will be given to all men.

Belief in God the Creator, God the Legislator, and God the Judge is not enough in itself. The Qur'an teaches that a genuine believer must have that faith and must also observe the law; it requires sincere belief and laborious obedience. In giving its commandments it awakens in us a sense of good and evil, of beauty and ugliness. "God could not order indecent things" (Surah VII, 28). "Tell them: My Lord forbids only what is indecent done in public or in private; deeds of the limbs or of the heart, such as any impious action and any unjustified violence" (Surah VII, 33). "The faithful do not defame the reputation of those who are absent. Would any one of you like to eat his dead brother's flesh?" (Surah XLIX, 12). The Qur'an points out that such ideals of universal duty were always taught by wise men and the saints. The names of Abraham, Isaac, Ishmael, Jacob, Moses, and Jesus are often mentioned as having taught such virtues and the necessity for prayer, charity, fasting, and the like.

Thus it is clear that the Qur'an has preciously preserved these previous teachings concerning virtue which were true, but we must notice that the Qur'an does not synthesize the sometimes divergent previous teachings; it marks out its own way by a spontaneous impulse. While it preserves the religious and moral patrimony, it adorns it more, crowning the divine building on which all the prophets have collaborated. By means of a variety of proofs convincing to the mind and attractive to the heart, the teaching concerning the divine attributes, the destiny of the soul, and the moral duties of man is much more developed in the Qur'an than anywhere else.

For instance, instead of only prohibiting drunkenness, the Qur'an stops the evil at its source by strictly forbidding the use of all intoxicants. Again, after reconciling the two apparently opposed principles of the Old and New Testaments, the principles of Justice and Charity, the Qur'an adds quite a new dimension which can be called the Code of Politeness, Discretion, and Propriety (Surah IV, 86; XXIV, 27–28, 31, 58–62). With the Decalogue of Moses, we are still in the fundamental and elementary laws, as if on the ground floor of morality. With the Sermon on the Mount we already find ourselves on a very high level at which charity excels justice and the heavenly kingdom scorns the earthly realm. Finally, through the laws of the Qur'an we reach the summit where charity and justice are combined and there is a total disinterestedness which aims at the absolute Good which is God. It is God Himself who must be borne in mind while carrying out His will by living a virtuous life.

In the revelations of the Qur'an, as in every previous revelation, a new and original contribution is added to the earlier ones. It is the purpose of the Qur'an to "confirm and to safeguard the former books" (Surah V, 48). "Safeguard," in that verse, means to discard the alterations and false interpretations unjustly attributed to the earlier revelations (Surah XVI, 63–64). The text of the Qur'an itself is safeguarded against any additions or changes because God Himself promised to be its protector (Surah XV, 9). As for the other books, they were written by men and left to their protection (Surah V, 44).

In addition to the Qur'an's primary aim of revealing religious and moral truths, there are secondary objectives designed to strengthen faith in the Creator or to support the faithful in their hope. It is striking to discover the extent to which the explanations of the natural world, God's creation, correspond precisely with the latest discoveries of cosmology, anatomy, physiology, and the rest of the positive sciences. For instance, consider these remarkable examples of scientific knowledge: the sphericity of the earth (XXXIX, 5), the formation of rain (XXX, 48), fertilization by the wind (XV, 22), the aquatic origin of all living creatures (XXI, 30), the duality in the sex of plants and other creatures, then unknown (XXXVI, 35), the collective life of animals (VI, 38), the mode of life of the bees (XVI, 69), the successive phases of the child in his mother's womb (XXII, 5; XXIII, 14).

A constant support to the faithful in their hope is the fulfillment of prophecies. In a short passage in Surah XLIV the Qur'an predicted accurately the different stages through which the Islamic preaching would pass and the different attitudes toward it which would be taken by the first adversaries, how they would at first be heedless and careless, then conciliatory and interested, and finally opposed and obviously hostile. At the same time it was predicted that the ungrateful town of Mecca would at first endure an awful misery which would bring some of the people from incredulity to an attraction of their souls toward heaven, then it would have prosperity which would make them forget God, and finally Mecca would suffer a humiliating defeat in the first battle (Surah XLIV, 9–16). Other verses announce the triumph of Islam, the permanence of its doctrine, the growth of the empire of young Islam, and the inability of any earthly power to annihilate Islam (XIII, 18; XIV, 24; XXIV, 55; VIII, 36).

The Qur'an also predicted the eternal schism in Christendom (V, 14), the dispersion of the Israelites (VII, 168), their persecution until the end of the world (VII, 167), their everlasting need of a protecting ally (III, 112), and the dominance of the Christians over the Jews until the day of resurrection (III, 55).

It must be noted that not only have the prophecies of the Qur'an been confirmed, but the Qur'an has thrown out this challenge: nothing can ever contradict the prophecies of the Qur'an, neither in the past, the present, nor the future (XLI, 42).

Who could ever give guarantees against space and time other than the Master of Space and Time Himself?

The divine origin of the Qur'an is evident for all the reasons which have been considered in this discussion. The possibility of human origin has been eliminated. Nowhere in the Qur'an is the personal character of the Prophet reflected, nowhere is there an echo of his daily joys and sorrows or of his earthly surroundings. There are no indications of geographical, atmospherical, racial, tribal, or individual peculiarities in the subjects treated. Only that which is necessary for the education of humanity is found in the Qur'an. The revelations were accompanied by visible signs of their divine origin. The linguistic and stylistic form of the Qur'an give positive signs of its divinity. The religious and moral teachings are clear evidence of its divine origin, free from the possibility of borrowing from other books.

It is for this reason that the Qur'an holds the highest place in Islam. For Muslims, the Qur'an is not only the text of prayers, the instrument of prophecy, the food for the spirit, the favorite canticle of the soul; it is at the same time the fundamental law, the treasure of the sciences, the mirror of the ages. It is the consolation for the present and the hope for the future.

In what it affirms or denies, the Qur'an is the criterion of truth. In what it orders or prohibits, it is the best model for behavior. In what it judges, its judgment is always correct. In what it discusses, it gives the decisive argument. In what it says, it is the purest and most beautiful expression possible in speech. It calms or incites most effectively.

Since the Qur'an is the direct expression of the divine will, it holds supreme authority for all men. The obedience due to our parents, our superiors, our community, or the Prophet himself is given only when it is based on a principle found in the Book of God. Their commands are obligations to us only so long as they transmit the divine commandment or do not contradict it.

It is edifying to know how the Prophet himself regarded the text of the Qur'an. He could not by his own will retouch it in the slightest; he interpreted it exactly as any commentator would a text which was not his own. And when he postponed carrying out any of its commandments even for a short time, in order to treat kindly the souls of the faithful and to forestall the objections of adversaries, we see the Revelation reproaching him most severely. Those reproaches he accepted with resignation and left engraved forever in the text (Surah XXXIII, 37). This constantly humble, submissive, and reverential attitude toward the words of God is sincerely confessed in the Qur'an itself: "Recite: my prayer, my acts of devotion, my life and my death belong exclusively to God, the Ruler of the Universe, lone Ruler and without partner. Of this I received the order and I am the first of the submissives" (Surah VI, 163–64).

Sunnah

The prophetic teachings outside the Qur'an are called the *Sunnah,* the Traditions. The base of Islam, as we have seen, is the Qur'an, and nothing is believed or commanded which is contrary to any revelation in the Holy Book. The Sunnah is the derived law of Islam which every Muslim is obliged to obey.

The Prophet taught in three ways: by oral instructions; by the example of his personal behavior; and by his silence, his tacit approval of other people's actions, by letting others do as they pleased without comment or reproach. These three aspects of the Prophet's teaching—speaking, acting, and approving—are the basis for the Muslim tradition called the Sunnah, and are considered to be the second source of Islamic legislation and instruction.

The Prophet draws this triple authority from the Qur'an itself, for it commands us to obey the Messenger's orders (Surah IV, 59; XXIV, 56), tells us that he who obeys the Prophet obeys the very commandments of God (Surah IV, 80), and recommends that we follow his example (Surah XXXIII, 21). In the Qur'an the Prophet is commanded to behave in such a way that his behavior will be a model for believers (Surah XXXIII, 37). It also describes the Prophet as one who gave to mankind all good instructions and forbade all bad actions; therefore, the action he does not forbid is permitted (Surah VII, 157).

The great majority of Muslim learned men hold, with good reason, that the Prophet's teachings follow either the directive of divine, though nontextual, inspiration or, if it was a personal, purely human effort, he applied the very essence or spirit of the law of the Qur'an. If in his instruction as a human being, without specific revelation, he ever was in error, he was immediately brought back to the truth through a revelation (Surah IV, 106–13; VIII, 67; IX, 43, 113). In the absence of such correcting revelations, all his orders, permissions, judgments, and behavior are rightly considered as implicitly approved and having full legislative and educative authority, subject only to the condition that they have been transmitted through authentic and strictly verified sources. Thus the Muslim tradition in Islam is related to the Qur'an as a nation's laws are related to its constitution.

It is a significant fact that regarding our two most essential practical duties—prayer, which is our obligation to God, and alms, which is a duty to our fellow men—the Qur'an refers us directly to tradition for detailed instruction. Speaking of prayer, the Qur'an says explicitly, "Do that which God has taught you" (Surah II, 239). Again, speaking of alms, it says that it is a "precise and known" right of the needy to receive a share of the possessions of pious men (Surah LXX, 24–25). And similar references are found concerning the season of pilgrimage and the sacred months. Now, in the absence in the Qur'an of any further elaboration on these subjects, any clear details as to how these duties are to be performed, it is obvious that through these references the Qur'an establishes the authority of the Sunnah, and grants to it the right to elaborate and define the general precepts of the Qur'an. Without the Sunnah, these texts would have been incomprehensible, stating as known things which were not known.

The role of the Sunnah is not limited to clarifying the duties implied in general commandments revealed in the Qur'an. Often the Sunnah establishes new obligations and prohibitions for which no clear reference can be found in the Qur'an. This is not, however, an addition to the legislation of the Qur'an, for a careful study will show that each of these traditions expresses the spirit of a more general teaching in the Book, even though the ties connecting each tradition with its appropriate foundation in the Qur'an are not easily discovered.

For example, the Qur'an made compulsory the alms deducted from gold, silver, and the crops, using also the more general terms "possessions," and "things granted by God"; the Prophet added the requirement that alms should be deducted from the herd. The Qur'an instituted the fast during the month of Ramadan as training in piety and patience and an opportunity to express thankfulness for divine blessings; the Prophet added the requirement that alms be given at the end of the fast of Ramadan as an act which is an additional means of accomplishing those purposes. The Qur'an forbids usury; the Sunnah forbids those usurious sales in which the increase in price has the same effect. Since such sales, halfway between a legitimate sale and forbidden usury, fell within a doubtful and suspect area of business activity, tradition rightly forbids them under the legislation of the Qur'an which recommends that we abstain from any action when in doubt. Again, the Qur'an prescribes scourging as the punishment for lewdness, while the Sunnah specifies scourging for unmarried persons and calls for death by stoning for adultery—justified by the passage in the Qur'an which says that the punishment for lewdness in women should be confinement to the house up to death, until the time when another punishment should be revealed.

The Sunnah, based on the verified traditions concerning the teachings, actions, and tacit approval of the Prophet, is justifiably binding on all Muslims. Since the Qur'an gave the Prophet full power to enlighten men concerning the meaning of the revelations, he was the best qualified to legislate in matters requiring clarification. The Prophet knew better than any other possible legislator the essence and spirit of the Law. Therefore, it is not surprising that he took new legislative steps, creating the Sunnah, the Traditions binding on all Muslims, through legislation by analogy, by precise definition, and by extension of the revelations given in the Qur'an.

Conclusion

We now see how Muslims regard the Qur'an and the Prophet.

The Qur'an is a purely divine work, a textual revelation which reached the world through a heavenly Messenger, the Faithful Spirit, the Archangel Gabriel, who deposited it in the heart of Muhammad.

Muhammad's role was limited to receiving the revelation, learning it, writing it down, transmitting, explaining, and applying it. Muhammad could not go beyond or change or modify the Qur'an in any way, nor can any other believer. Any human work can be discussed, controverted, or contradicted by events in the past, present, or future. But the Qur'an, the Word of God, is perfection itself; it is unchallengably true, infallibly just, and inimitably good and beautiful.

The Prophet Muhammad was but a man, of a purely human nature. He was neither a great god, nor a small god, nor a subgod, nor even an auxiliary of God. He could not acquire any good or avoid any evil except through God's will. He knew only so much of the past or the future as God revealed to him. He was infallible in his judgments only when sustained by revelation. But he was set apart from the rest of mankind by an excellent inborn morality, by the divine knowledge granted to him, and by the dignity of his apostleship: he is the head of all believers. As the faithful interpreter and living example of the Qur'an, we owe him obedience, respect, and love. The Qur'an urges us to treat him with particular reverence.

The Prophet led us out of the darkness of ignorance into the light of truth. Lost and vicious as we were, he brought us back to the straight path of Islam. But however great our respect for him may be, and however deeply we may love him, in our eyes he is not raised above the level of man. Muhammad never aspired to the rank of divinity; he was God's apostle and servant. In our confession of faith, the Prophet's role as a servant surpasses his role as apostle. For us, he is not an object of worship; we do not pray to him, but pray to God for him, asking God to heap blessings on him.

Islam's monotheistic system is infinitely pure and unmixed.

> There is no God but Allah.
>
> Muhammad is his servant and apostle.
>
> All men are brothers.

Such are the three elements of the Muslim creed, as they are stated in three successive Surahs of the Qur'an (XLVII, 19; XLVIII, 29; XLIX, 13). Such is the straight path of Islam, the path of those who submit to the will of God as revealed in the Qur'an, God's Word as given by the Archangel Gabriel to Muhammad, the Messenger of God.

CHAPTER TWO

Ideas and Movements in Islamic History

Shafik Ghorbal

Al-Ghazali, the great mystical philosopher, in his book *The Rescuer from Error* gives a vivid account of the spiritual crisis he endured until, by the mercy of God, his way was enlightened and he regained the power to guide himself to the truth. When he studied the lives of those who gave themselves to the search for truth, he saw that they might be classified in four groups: the scholastic theologians, who proclaimed themselves the followers of reason and speculation; the Isma'ilis and other Shi'as who held that to reach truth one must have an infallible living teacher, and that there always is such a teacher; the philosophers, who relied on logical and rational proofs; and the Sufis, who held that they, the chosen of God, could reach knowledge of Him directly in mystical insight and ecstasy. In his perceptive classification of the searchers for truth al-Ghazali has gone right to the heart of the matter. We will be guided by his classification in this discussion of the ideas and movements in Islamic history.

Both the Muslim and the Christian have sought to bring as much as possible of the worldly affairs of their communities under the rule of the divine law and to make effective what their faiths teach about the origin and destiny of human society. It is generally admitted that the realization of this hope has always been imperfect, or even, in the view of some members of their communities, undesirable. But the fact that the realization of this hope has been as imperfect in Islamic society as in Western Christian society is usually not clearly grasped. The real difference between the two societies has been the tendency in the Islamic world to condemn or ignore the secular factors. One of the consequences of this attitude is the absence of terms for many human activities and relationships, such as church, secular, lay, ecclesiastical, state, political, social. Such key terms either do not exist or are rendered as approximately as possible, although people are aware of the existence of what these words stand for. In the course of this discussion we shall meet this difficulty and shall have to use such terms as "the ruling institution" and "the religious institution."

Professor H. A. R. Gibb has called attention to the fact that Islam spread in a series of rapid bounds. In slightly more than a century, between the years 10 and 133 (A.D. 632–750), the armies of the Caliphate carried the rule of Islam from Central Asia in the east to Morocco and Spain in the extreme west. Islam remained confined within these boundaries for some two and one-half centuries, and then between 400 and 500 (*ca.* A.D. 1000–1100) Muslim domination was extended to West Africa, Asia Minor, Central Asia and Northern India. Two centuries later there was another wave of expansion thrusting out into the Balkan Peninsula, the steppes of Russia and Siberia, the rest of India, and into Indonesia. Thus by the beginning of the ninth century (A.D. 1400), the map of Islam was very much the same as it is today, except for the total disappearance of Islam from the Iberian Peninsula and Sicily, and except for minor advances which have been made since that time, chiefly in Africa.

It is significant to note that the faith and practice of Islam were fully matured in the period between 133 and 400 (A.D. 750–1000). Since that is the case, the regions to which Islam spread subsequent to that period cannot claim to have made an original contribution to the development of Islamic culture. That is why Islam in Indonesia and in Africa south of the Sahara have been dealt with separately here.

The Foundation of Islamic Society

The First and Second Centuries of the Hijrah (A.D. 622–750)

The Prophet Muhammad lived most of his life in the city of Mecca in the Hijaz region of the Arabian peninsula. He was forty years old when he began to preach that Allah is the only God, the Almighty, the Creator of everything, the Lord of the Worlds, the Beneficent, the Merciful, the Sovereign of the Day of Judgment.

Mecca in the days of the Prophet was a city-state, a commercial republic, and also a great religious center built around the Ka'ba, which at that time attracted many pilgrims who came to worship the idols housed there. The Meccans made detailed arrangements for the safety of the pilgrimage routes to the city, for the sale of supplies to the visitors, and for the order and propriety of the elaborate rituals at the Ka'ba. Since the care of the pilgrims and the conduct of commercial transactions were the main occupations of the Meccans, the life of the city was dominated by a class of able administrators and negotiators, men who distrusted violence and were suspicious of enthusiasm.

Mecca remained a city-state because Arabia had never been effectively controlled by a central authority. The influence of the geographic environment has always militated against the growth of centralized control in the Arabian peninsula. The chief characteristics of that environment have been the unstable relations between a settled and a nomadic society, the constant interpenetration of those two societies, the extension of those conditions northward into the desert areas between Syria and Iraq, and finally, the international relations of the Arabian fringes of the peninsula with the outside world and the transpeninsular traffic created by those fringe areas.

The distinction between the commercial and agricultural settlements and the nomadic way of life is due mainly to climatic conditions. Nomadic life is tribally organized, with the tribal unit being neither too large nor too small for the conditions of existence in the desert. While a tribe is held together by ties of blood relationship, strangers can be attached to a tribe as "clients" or "allies." Because of the mobility and instability of the nomadic society, the settlements are greatly affected by what happens to their Bedouin neighbors. Usually, the people of the established communities have descended from nomadic tribes which settled down. After they have settled as traders or agriculturists they try to control by force and persuasion the neighboring Bedouin tribes in an effort to maintain some measure of peace and order. While they may succeed for some time, they often are overpowered by a new wave of nomadic unrest and the settled community is engulfed in nomadism. Sometimes the nomadic conquerors settle down and adopt the way of life of the conquered—and the cycle starts again.

It is important to remember that even when the Bedouins have settled down to a new way of life they preserve many of their old ways and much of their old instability of character. There are many illustrations of their nostalgic attachment to the old ways, such as their tendency to escape into the desert for sports and physical and spiritual refreshment, the practice of sending their children to be reared in Bedouin encampments to protect them from the effects of city life, and the legends of the desert which beguile their evening hours.

It is important to note the role of the interpenetration of the settled and the nomadic life because it is not confined to Arabia or to the days before Islam. It runs through the history of Islamic society. The history of Islamic North Africa, or Egypt, Syria, or Iraq cannot be understood without a clear understanding of the role which this interpenetration has played.

Mecca, the birthplace of Muhammad, is a good illustration of the phenomenon of interpenetration. The clans of Mecca belonged to the tribe of *Quraish*, which traced its descent to Ishmael, son of Abraham, both of whom are recognized in the Qur'an as prophets of God. The building of the Ka'ba as a House of the Lord and sanctuary and place of pilgrimage is attributed to Ishmael and Abraham. The clan of the Prophet was descended from Hashim, and a closely related clan was descended from his brother Umayyah. The Umayyads were more wealthy and influential than the Hashimids. It was Abu Talib, the leader of the Hashimids, who cared for Muhammad in his youth; his son, Ali, one of the first converts to Islam, married Muhammad's daughter, Fatimah, and was one of the stalwart champions of Islam. He and his descendants were destined to occupy a unique place in the history of Islam. Another uncle of Muhammad was Abbas, the ancestor of the Abbasids who were Caliphs of Islam for five centuries.

In order to understand the position of Mecca in the days of the Prophet, it is necessary to consider not only the role of the nomads and their clans but also to know something of the external relations of Arabia. Arabia provided the neighboring areas with such desired products as frankincense and livestock, and Arabian ports were links in international trade, with goods moving back and forth between Mediterranean areas and India by transpeninsular trade routes, many of which went through Mecca. The instability of Arabian nomadic society and the rivalry between Persia and the Byzantine Empire caused those two powers to create satellite states on their borders for the security of their frontiers and as a means of intervening in Arabian politics. The Byzantine Empire sought to counteract Persian influence in eastern Arabia, and to advance Christianity by overcoming Judaism in southern Arabia by encouraging Abyssinia to invade the Yemen. As is well known, the Abyssinians used the Yemen as the basis for an attempted attack on Mecca to destroy the Ka'ba. By divine mercy the expedition was an utter failure. Because the Abyssinians used African elephants in the attack, the year of the expedition is known as the "Year of the Elephant." It is the year of the Prophet's birth, according to some sources.

It is clear, therefore, that Mecca was not a cultural backwater at the time of the Prophet. Its leaders were men who had traveled far conducting important commercial transactions, who had dealt with Roman and Persian officials as well as with their sophisticated fellow Arabs, and were skilled in managing Bedouin tribesmen. There were Christian and Jewish communities in many parts of Arabia; Medina, which figured prominently in the life of the Prophet, was particularly influenced by the Jews who settled there.

The tradition of Islam refers to the age in which the Prophet was born as the age of ignorance, *Jahiliya*, but the ignorance here is not to be taken as the antithesis of knowledge. Rather, it is used in the sense of "lawlessness" or "not being aware of something better." Some scholars have thought that the word refers to a relapse into barbarian or nomadic customs some time before the apostleship of Muhammad, but it should be taken to mean the falling away from the pure monotheism of Abraham and Ishmael to the idolatry which, more than anything else, the Prophet denounced with all his power.

This aspect of the situation in Mecca at the time of the Prophet must be clearly understood if one is to see the mission of the Prophet in the right perspective. For while his message was a reaffirmation and renewing of what earlier prophets, named and unnamed, had been instructed to convey to various peoples, in a very special sense it was a restoration of the religion of Abraham. The central theme of his message was above all the creation of a community dedicated to the worship of Allah and to righteousness. It was Muhammad's ardent hope that his own people, the Quraish, could be transformed into a community which would restore the Ka'ba to its pristine purity.

But it was not to be, for the Meccans did not respond to his preaching. In fact, they were temperamentally opposed to religious zeal and, being businessmen, tried to make Muhammad see sense by placing the Hashimids under an economic and social boycott! The weak and lowly among the early converts to Islam were subjected to physical torture, but the Meccans did not dare inflict such punishment on those who had strong connections. It is a measure of the strength of kinship solidarity that men stood by their converted relatives even when they disapproved of their change of religion. Muhammad eventually saw that it was hopeless to expect the conversion of the Quraish, and withdrew to Medina.

Muhammad in Medina went on with the building up of the community under a new set of circumstances. His objective, his cherished ideal, was to make Mecca the spiritual center of the community and to extend the community to include all humanity. To achieve this end he merged two constituent elements, the Meccan emigrants (*Muhajirun*) and the Medinese helpers (*Ansar*), into the brotherhood of Islam, a new relationship which was destined to transcend every other relationship of family, clan, tribe, or nation. The community was to be made secure by an elaborate system of alliances based on a recognition of mutual interests and even by covenants with non-Muslims. Until the brotherhood of Islam should include all humanity, the "striving" to make the Word of Allah supreme over all should never cease. But "striving" never meant compulsion. In the thought of the Founder, and after him in the thought of the community, the main objective is the security and supremacy of the Islamic community. Any particular good must be subjected to the general good. The treatment of non-Muslims within the community or outside it, the relations of peace and war with the rest of the world—all must be governed by the supreme good of the community as a whole.

For ten years the Prophet toiled to turn his followers into a society of the Select, the community described in the Qur'an, "You are the best community that hath been raised up for mankind. You enjoin what is right and forbid what is reproachable, and you believe in Allah." The Qur'an embodied the tenets of the faith, the principles of righteous living and social relations. The Prophet, by word and deed, sought to set before his followers the living model, never sparing himself, never finding anything too trivial for his attention. The system of traditions created by his sayings and deeds, the spirit which permeates all that he did, and the outlook on things sacred and profane which was revealed in his life form the Sunnah of the Prophet, the binding force of Islamic society.

Eight years after the Prophet's withdrawal from Mecca (in A.D. 629) he returned to his native town in triumph. During those eight years he had managed by war and diplomacy to isolate Mecca so that it fell into his power like ripe fruit. He forgave his people for their past bitterness and cleared all the idols from the Ka'ba; then he returned to Medina, his adopted home. He died in Medina in the tenth year of the Hijrah (A.D. 632), after a short illness. Muhammad was a great-hearted man of supreme vision, the greatness of his vision equalled only by the extent of his delicacy of feeling and genuine humility.

The responsibility for guiding the fortunes of the community in the difficult times following the death of the Prophet fell to two men, Abu Bakr and Umar, who, although different from each other in almost everything, were singularly united in outlook and aim. Abu Bakr "succeeded" the Prophet as guide and leader and was known as "successor (or Caliph) to the Apostle of God." It was abundantly clear that general opinion in the community would accept only Abu Bakr as the first successor to the Prophet. Two years after he became the leader he designated Umar as his successor and the two men carried the evolution of the community a stage further.

Abu Bakr declared war to the bitter end against the assertion of some of the tribes that their covenants with the Prophet were not valid after his death and that therefore they were free to shape their attitude toward the community as they saw fit. He denounced such claims and crushed by force those who made them. In addition, he began the policy of expansion outside Arabia which was carried on so vigorously under Umar, and under the third Caliph, Uthman, that within ten years the Arabs became masters of Syria, Iraq, Upper Mesopotamia, Armenia, Persia, Egypt, and Cyrenaica. These conquests served later as bases for further expansion in the east into Central Asia and the Indus Valley, and in the west to North Africa, Spain, and some of the islands of the Mediterranean.

Abu Bakr and Umar continued the work of the Prophet in founding the Islamic community, looking upon their responsibilities as a trust, a calling to guidance and leadership, with the supreme authority residing in the community. They were undoubtedly chosen by the general agreement of the community. They belonged to two of the less powerful clans of Mecca. There was general reluctance to have as Caliph a man belonging to the Umayyads or the Hashimids, for it was feared that a Caliph enjoying the support of the Umayyads or the prestige of the Hashimids would have too much power. Abu Bakr and Umar showed a combination of just dealing and severity in their relations with the others who had been close associates of the Prophet. Umar, particularly, did not hesitate to break any man who fell short of the required standards of integrity and devotion to duty. The two men had their way because it was obvious that in not sparing others they spared themselves least in serving the community.

Abu Bakr and Umar were faced with many problems of which the most pressing were the question of the position of the community after Mecca had become the spiritual center, the decisions as to the kind of governmental organization to be adopted, and the necessity for striking a balance between conservatism and change in the conduct of practical affairs. They met the first problem by deciding on a policy of expansion which resulted in the creation of an Islamic world reaching from Spain to the Indus. In evaluating their motives it is impossible to ignore the view that the desirability of employing the newly converted tribesmen in military expeditions outside Arabia influenced the decision of the Caliphs. It is also necessary to consider the view that Meccan statesmanship counseled expansion. But the chief motive that led to the dispatch of the expeditions was the fact that the security and prosperity of a community confined to the Hijaz would have been precarious indeed unless their domain was extended to the bordering Arab territories which were under Byzantine and Persian control. It was the surprising ease of the earliest conquests which encouraged Umar and the Meccan generals to extend the operations much further afield.

It is important to note the great care with which the Caliphs and generals prevented the economic ruin of the conquered territories. They refused to partition the agricultural lands among the Arabian tribesmen, for those Bedouins would have ruined the land and impoverished the treasury. Care was taken to isolate the Arabian conquerors in garrison towns and to provide them with regular pensions and their share of the spoils of war. Some of the new garrison towns were founded on direct desert routes communicating with Medina, such as Basra and Kufa in southern Iraq, or Fustat just south of modern Cairo; others were old Syrian cities like Homs.

Although Islam theoretically denounced the loyalties of the pagan society of the age of ignorance, the tribal structure with its internal strength and its method of adopting strangers was too useful to be done away with. Thus the fighting forces were organized on tribal lines and the quarters in the garrison towns were allotted according to tribal divisions. The newly converted provincials were brought into Islam not merely as members of the community, but were affiliated with the tribes as clients, or *mawali*, who did not find themselves treated as equals by their Arabian brethren of the faith. This problem of the mawali, the provincial converts who were affiliated with the Arab tribal structure, continued to plague Islamic society until the advent of the Abbasid Caliphs, when the tribal structure inherited from the days of Umar broke down.

Those of the provincials who preferred to keep their Christian or Jewish or Zoroastrian faith were included in the social organization as *zimmi*, or protected persons, subject to special taxes and various restrictions. They were second-class citizens—a category which is regarded by historians as having been injurious to the first-class citizens as well. Although the problem of the provincial converts, the mawali, was solved by the disappearance of the tribal structure, the problem of the protected persons, the zimmi, has been solved in the Muslim states of modern times simply by deviating from the practice of old Islamic society.

In spite of the expansion of the Islamic domain, the two Caliphs tried to get along with a very simple form of government. They would ask this or that Companion to do whatever was needed. Very early they found it necessary to establish a central treasury and a recorder of the pensions granted, and other offices were created as required. As the new issues arose the two Caliphs faced every new situation with a tremendous searching of heart. They sought to avoid being innovators as they would a mortal sin, but once they were satisfied that a new step must be taken, they would not shirk their responsibility.

Abu Bakr and Umar had worked closely together for two years when Abu Bakr died, leaving Umar the responsibility of carrying on as second Caliph. Umar himself was stabbed to death by a Persian slave who thought that the Caliph did not give him a fair deal against his exacting taskmaster and who seems to have felt deeply the defeat and enslavement of Persia. Before he died, in 23 (A.D. 644), Umar appointed a panel of six senior Companions of the Prophet to select the next Caliph from among themselves.

The Companions chose Uthman for the third Caliph because he belonged to the powerful Umayyad clan but was a mild old man. The combination of mildness and membership in a powerful clan caused his undoing, however, since there was jealousy of the power of the Umayyads and he was too gentle to protect that power. His reign witnessed the Sedition (*Fitna*) when the firm leadership established by Umar failed to function. The charges brought against Uthman, such as nepotism, were not so heinous as to justify the march of malcontents from the garrison towns against him at Medina or their penetration of his house and their brutal murder of the aged man in his room. It is an indication of the spirit of the early Caliphate that the head of the Islamic community which ruled a domain extending from the Indus almost to the Atlantic had no bodyguard to protect his person.

Uthman met his end gently and resignedly. He was perplexed, for he could not understand why his people should not be friendly and happy. He had good reason to count on the gratitude of the community because he was an early convert to Islam who had contributed of his fortune to the needs of the community, he had married successively two of the daughters of the Prophet, under his rule the domain of Islam had been further extended, and he had established the authorized, written version of the Qur'an. But he was murdered, and in his grave was buried the ideal of a leadership that tried to rule without the sanctions of force.

The Sedition was possible only because the kind of leadership established by Umar was based on a climate of opinion, a standard of morality, and a degree of discipline which were rapidly vanishing. Uthman did not receive from his fellow Companions the same collaboration and obedience that Umar knew how to get, for they were torn by private animosities and jealousies and did not rally to his support. He was faced with the undisciplined men from the provinces, some of whom were Bedouin tribesmen who turned the faith of Islam into a weapon of Bedouin instability, while others were men who were moved by anti-Umayyad prejudice. Even his kinsman Mu'awiya, the Umayyad governor of Syria, did not bring his forces to Medina to defend him.

For a time it looked as if opinion would support Ali, another of the senior Companions, an early convert, a cousin and son-in-law of the Prophet, the father of the Prophet's only grandchildren, and a respected warrior-ascetic. But, alas, the forces let loose by the Sedition could not be brought under control. Ali now paid in full for his attitude of reserve during the attack on his predecessor, when he did not come out openly as a defender of law and order. Some of the people held him responsible for the murder of Uthman and demanded that he should prove his noncomplicity by punishing the perpetrators of the outrage. He could not do so, not because he was an accomplice, but simply because the responsibility for what happened was so diffuse. Others were sincerely aggrieved by the resort to the horrors of civil war and pressed for arbitration between Ali and Mu'awiya, the Umayyad governor of Syria. When Ali agreed, a section of his followers seceded in protest against what they took to be his admission of the invalidity of his title to the Caliphate. Thus began the party of *Kharijism.*

In essence, Kharijism represents the literal adherence to ideas with utter disregard for reality. The Kharijites' doctrine, which led the community to treat them as outlaws, was that people who disagreed with them concerning the consequence of committing a mortal sin should no longer be accepted as Muslims and should be killed on sight. Some Kharijites went even further and held that the children of such renegade Muslims were to be killed with their parents. The Kharijites held that the Caliph was to be elected by the whole Muslim community and could be deposed by the will of the people. He need not belong to any special family or tribe; he might even be a slave, so long as he was a good Muslim ruler. Some of them even denied the need for a Caliph at all, and held that the Muslim community could rule itself. Kharijism thus represents the reaction of the slender stock of ideas and experience of the tribesmen of Arabia to the impact of Islam. But so great was the force of Kharijism that it led to two important reactions. It led the community, out of fear of anarchy, to acquiesce in the doctrine that the actual possession of power suffices to make it legitimate. It also led to the doctrine of *irja*, that is, to the postponement of judgment on the actions of believers, a doctrine of acquiescence and convenient latitudinarianism.

The Caliph Ali tried to crush the Kharijites by force and actually slaughtered thousands of them in battle, but at too great cost, for in the year 40 (A.D. 660) he was assassinated by a Kharijite.

It should be noted that it was only after the death of Ali that the development of Shi'ism began. We say "after his death" purposely, for Shi'ism is not merely the desire to proclaim Ali as Caliph and to claim that only the descendants of the family of the Prophet should be Caliph. Shi'ism grew up after the death of Ali because it involved a view of Ali's claim to the Caliphate which the early community did not hold and it involved the endorsement of the person of Ali with a timeless significance which was not held by his generation. Shi'ism also inculcated a conception of the function of the Caliphate which was developed later; it is based on a reconstruction of historical events and personal tragedies, and thus has to be later than these events. It should also be noted that there have been descendants of Ali on Muslim thrones, as in Iraq and Morocco today, who were not followers of Shi'a doctrines. The story of the rise of Shi'a and its role in Islamic history is told more fully in another chapter of this book.

After the death of Ali, Mu'awiya stepped into the void. He was already in possession of considerable power as the governor of Syria and the community accepted him as Caliph, even if some hated the necessity of doing so. Mu'awiya—skillful, liberal, moderate, and sagacious—represented the Meccan aristocracy at its best. He healed for a time the ills of Islamic society, but he healed them by political methods which took man at his worst, and he did not hesitate to suppress by force or to win support by an appeal to cupidity. He saw that there was no alternative to the establishment of the dynastic principle if civil war was to be avoided in the selection of successors to the Caliphate. Beginning with Mu'awiya, the Umayyads ruled from Damascus for nearly one hundred years, until 133 (A.D. 750).

The Umayyads have been represented as a reproduction on a larger scale of the old Arabian dynasties of Petra and Palmyra which in pre-Islamic days combined Arabian traditions with a Hellenistic, Byzantine, or Persian veneer. Superficially it seems so, but there was enough of Arabism and of Islam in the Umayyad state to enable the rulers to adapt to the needs of the Islamic society of their day what they copied from their neighbors and the conquered provincials. The machinery of government was organized with the help of the provincials and, at the opportune moment, was Arabicized. A coinage was introduced, the foundations of intellectual pursuits were laid down, and adaptations of art and architecture were made to serve Arabian taste and Islamic needs. Spain was added to the domain of Islam.

The Maturing of Islamic Society

The Second to the Fifth Centuries of the Hijrah (A.D. 750–1055)

The period covered by this section begins with the assumption of the Caliphate by descendants of Abbas, an uncle of the Prophet, and ends with the Seljug Turkish Sultan Tughrul, who assumed effective management of the affairs of the capital of the Abbasid Caliphs. It is a period in which the Congregation founded by the Prophet and expanded by the skillfully conducted warfare of Arabian tribesmen became an Islamic Society with a formulated creed, a system of law derived from the source of its beliefs and ideals, a ruling institution, and a brotherhood which transcends accidents of race and station in life. The maturing of the Islamic Society in these three centuries was not complete, for some issues continued in all their urgency, but much of the pattern for later times was determined in this fascinating period of Islamic history.

The most important development of the early centuries of Islam is beyond doubt the Sunnah. It is not merely a doctrine, it is also a way, an outlook, a temperament; it is the way a Muslim should view law, or dogmatics, or ethics, or ritual. The chief characteristic of the Sunnah is that it must be as universal as possible. It attained its universality from the generations of men who lived in the Hijaz, in the new cities of the Islamic world, and in the old cities of Iraq, Syria, Egypt, and elsewhere; it was developed there by the will of the Congregation and not imposed by force, nor was it associated with any earthly authority. The Sunnah was the most important force which bound together in a spiritual unity the communities in Asia, Africa, and Europe—communities without a common geographical environment or a common racial inheritance, but with common social forms and institutions.

Another characteristic of the Sunnah is its traditionalism, based on a desire to protect the Prophetic Revelation from modifications by establishing the authority of social tradition, institutional forms, and orthodox theology and law.

A third characteristic of the Sunnah is that it has been orally transmitted by men who have voluntarily devoted themselves to gaining religious knowledge and to teaching it.

Such, in brief, are the chief characteristics of the Sunnah. By the end of the Umayyad rule the Sunnah was substantial enough to stand up to Kharijism and the heresies which arose from pre-Islamic sects, and to provide the ruling powers with principles of law to guide them. Although the upholders of the Sunnah did not have a program of dynastic or political change, they supported the parties which actively worked for an end of the Umayyad rule.

The Umayyads deserved well of the community. After the murder of the Caliph Uthman, the civil war, and the murder of the Caliph Ali, it is difficult to see any alternative to the assumption of the Caliphate by Mu'awiya and the establishment of the principle of hereditary succession. The dynasty which he established lived up to the tradition of the Meccan aristocracy with some notable feats of constructive statesmanship. But there were fatal weaknesses in their position which led to their downfall. The Umayyads were too deeply involved in the tribal feuds of the first century; they could not offer a better justification for their rule than the fact that the founder had stepped in to fill a void; and they could not find a satisfactory settlement for the strained relations between the Arab and non-Arab Muslims. As a consequence, they were assailed from many quarters and could not defend their position by better means than ruthless suppression and naked force.

The fall of the Umayyads was due to a successful conspiracy led by a Persian aristocrat, Abu Muslim al-Khurasani, whose motives are still a mystery. He organized a fighting force made up of Arab colonists of Khurasan and converted Persian landowners. Ostensibly he worked to establish a Caliph who was a "member of the house of the Prophet," without specifying a particular person, so as to have the support of the Alids, the descendants of Ali. Secretly, his candidate was a descendant of Abbas, an uncle of the Prophet. Abu Muslim's revolt was successful. The last Umayyad was defeated, pursued, and murdered. Abu Ali-Abbas al-Saffah assumed the title of Caliph, beginning a new dynasty which held the Caliphate for five hundred years.

Before anything else, the new rulers were state-builders. Without meaning to reflect on the sincerity of their beliefs, we must note that religion for the Abbasids was no more than an element in a well-organized, well-administered society. They saw the absolute necessity of the Islamization of society and did all they could to help it. They encouraged religious leaders, lawyers, scholars; they organized heretic hunts; they carried out periodic campaigns against the bordering territories of the Eastern Roman Empire; they helped to destroy the distinction between the Arabs and the non-Arab Muslim converts; they destroyed the tribal structure of the armies. One of the Abbasid Caliphs, al-Ma'mun, tried to give state support to the doctrines of the *Mu'tazilites*—rationalist theologians (to be discussed later)—but he failed. One of the Persian converts to Islam, the famous man of letters Ibn al-Muqaffa, advised the Caliph al-Mansur, who founded the new capital at Baghdad, to promulgate a code of Islamic law, but the lawyers, theologians and scholars, inspired by the general sense of the community, resisted all such attempts at control of belief by the ruling powers.

In another direction, the policy of the Abbasids went in direct opposition to the spirit of Islam. They built up an elaborate machinery of state despotism modeled on the old Persian monarchy with all its paraphernalia of an elaborate bureaucracy, court etiquette and ceremonial, fulsome flattery, and seclusion of the monarch. With this went an utter disregard of the Muslim's rights of life, honor, and property.

The despotic ruling power established by the Abbasids had important consequences for the development of Islam. In the eyes of the devout the "secular affairs" became so tainted that they were condemned out of hand or ignored, and the creative spiritual and intellectual movements became entirely otherworldly and divorced from reality or went into open revolt against the community, aiming at destroying rather than reforming it. It is true that the patronage of the rulers contributed to a considerable flourishing of the arts and sciences, but this does not qualify the judgment that the vital creative forces of the community were divorced from or in open revolt against society.

The core of the Sunnah is the Qur'an as explained and interpreted by the acts and sayings of the Prophet. Two sciences grew up in connection with the Qur'an and the Sunnah: *Tafsir*, exegesis, or explanation, or commentary; and *Hadith*, Tradition. The schools of Tafsir have been classified in many ways; one of the most useful is by Goldziher. There is the Tafsir based on materials ascribed to the Prophet and his Companions and handed down from generation to generation, such as the great work done by al-Tabari (224–311; A.D. 838–923); the Tafsir, or commentary, made by men primarily interested in dogmatics, such as al-Zamakhshari (467–538; A.D. 1074–1143); the Tafsir as written by the mystics, illustrated by the wide range of attitudes toward the Qur'an of men like Ibn Arabi on the one hand and al-Ghazali on the other; the Tafsir as written by the sectarians, such as the commentaries on the Qur'an by the Shi'as of the Imami and Isma'ili persuasions; and the Tafsir as written by the modernists such as two twentieth-century Shaikhs, Muhammad Abduh and Muhammad Rashid Rida. The choice among these various schools of commentary on the Qur'an and Sunnah depends on one's attitude with respect to three basic issues: the credence to be attached to historical tradition; the weight to be given to the claim for a hidden meaning in the Qur'an; the amount of subjectivity to be allowed in interpretation.

As for the Hadith, the Tradition, it is remarkable to note the facility with which even men of undoubted piety did not hesitate to attribute to the Prophet sayings made up by themselves to promote sectarian interests. It is difficult to explain the popularity of that practice when it was obvious that it had been so abused as to expose even genuine sayings to suspicion. At any rate, in obedience to the firm resolution of the community to uphold the Hadith as a foundation for faith and practice, the learned men did their best to establish principles of criticism and grades of authenticity to serve as a guide in accepting true traditions. Two collections of "genuine" sayings have become particularly celebrated: those of al-Bukhari (195–257; A.D. 810–70) and Muslim (206?–62; A.D. 821?–75).

The two disciplines of Tafsir and Hadith—learned commentary and study of traditions—served the development of theology and law, but before turning to them a few words must be said about the auxiliary disciplines needed by Tafsir and Hadith. These auxiliary disciplines were chiefly linguistic and historical. The language of the Qur'an and the Hadith is Arabic, which was not the mother tongue of the early generations of converts. Grammar, script, and lexicography were developed to preserve Arabic and to make it teachable. It was necessary for the purpose of lexicography to accumulate as much as possible of the legendary and poetic lore of pre-Islamic Arabia, thus bringing this heritage to a certain extent into the cultural patrimony of every lettered Muslim, whether of Arab or non-Arab descent. It is not quite true to say that this Arabian past became the past of all Muslims, that Islam, for example, obliterated for the Muslim Egyptian his Pharaonic past. As a matter of fact, the Egyptian was a Christian before he became a Muslim, and Pharaoh was damned in the Christian writings before he was damned in the Qur'an. The lore in which the cultured Muslim was brought up was presented to him in an Arabic garb, but it was an amalgam of the wisdom literature drawn from divers sources, of historical narratives of prophets and kings, of the wonders of every clime, and of the pre-Islamic Arabian legends. To the unlettered Muslim, the folk literature was a composite of many strands, of which the pre-Islamic Arabian was the least.

More remarkable than the fashioning of linguistic tools was the creation of an Arabic prose style beautifully adapted to serve the needs of the Islamic society whose maturing we have been trying to describe. It was perfected by men of non-Arab as well as of Arab origin and proved its adequacy as a medium of expression in theology and philosophy and for describing the mystic's experience and aspirations, as well as in the precise statement of the lawyer's formulae and the observations of scientists.

In the field of law we note the same impulse toward Islamization. Going back to the beginning, we note that the Qur'an contains varied prescriptions concerning religious, ritual, military, political, family, and other practical matters. The Prophet, in his lifetime, interpreted and carried into effect by his acts and sayings the legislation of the Qur'an. After his death, his immediate successors endeavored, in agreement with the most eminent of the Companions of the Prophet, to direct the community in the path which they believed to be the "straight path" by adhering to the letter and the spirit of the Prophet's practice. At the same time, a body of customary law, derived from the usage of the communities before they became amalgamated with the Islamic Society, was administered by the officials of the Caliphate.

As time went on, however, the religious impulse led certain of the learned men living in the Hijaz, Iraq, Syria, and Egypt to construct an ideal picture of what the law in an Islamic Society should be. Four founders of systems of jurisprudence (*fiqh*), who created the four systems of law which have persisted to the present day, are Abu Hanifah of Iraq (80–150; A.D. 699–767), Malik of Hijaz (died 179; A.D. 795), al-Shafi'i of Egypt (died 205; A.D. 820), and Ibn Hanbal of Iraq (died 241; A.D. 855). Space does not permit elucidation of the specific principles on which they worked, but it may suffice for our purpose to note that the law, the *shari'a*, as built up by the founders and generations of commentators, embraces all the rules of God's prescription for the conduct of men—domestic life, political and social activities, religious and ritual duties. It is restricted, of course, to the external relations of the Muslim to his fellow men and to God, as distinct from matters of conscience.

The place of the shari'a in the history of Islamic Society is not easy to define. If one considers only the forms in which it was transmitted, the methods used by the legalists, the material of its content, and the restricted field of its application as the whole field of positive law, then its role is quite limited. But looked at as a common ideal to be realized by the Muslim communities everywhere, or as a standard by which state policy and acts are judged, its role has been great. But it is not enough to use it, as it is used in our day, as a rallying cry in battles which, strictly speaking, have nothing much to do with religion, or to put it on a pedestal to be admired, or in a spirit of haphazard eclecticism to pick and choose from the shari'a only the material which pleases us most. What is required is to relate the shari'a to the great world-currents of legislation which predominate in our day. It is clear that this is a task of immense difficulty. It is perhaps the greatness of the difficulty which caused the Turkish Republic in our time to exclude the shari'a altogether from its society!

Before turning to a brief consideration of some of the forms taken by the community to express its spiritual and intellectual yearnings—those adopted by the Mu'tazilites, Shi'ites, and Sufis—we should stop to remind ourselves of the background against which these developments took place. It is necessary to remember, in the first place, that two distinct worlds were brought together for the first time within the Islamic Society:

the ancient and diversified Mediterranean tradition of Rome, Greece, Israel, and the Near East; and the original civilization of Persia with its distinctive pattern of life and thought and its fruitful contacts with the great civilizations of the Far East.

It should be borne in mind, in the second place, that there continued to exist within the Islamic Society churches, monasteries, synagogues, and temples serving Christians, Jews, Zoroastrians, and others; that all these survived, not as ghost communities or depressed classes, but as communities of living men and women who pursued their callings, professed their faith openly, and entered into polemics in defense of it; who continued to develop their religious, philosophical, and scientific legacies; and who were at all times in communication with their Muslim neighbors. One aspect of this Islamic phase of their history, if we may so describe it, was their adoption of Arabic for their daily life and for theological, devotional, historical, and other writings.

A third point to be remembered is that there is no trustworthy evidence to justify the tendency of some scholars to impugn the sincerity of the converts to Islam, or to attribute to some of the mystics or philosophers or founders of sects a deliberate intention to corrupt or destroy Islam. A good example of this is the current representation of Isma'ilism (Shi'a) as a conspiracy initiated with devilish cunning by one individual. It is much more probable to imagine generations of Muslims agitated by the same mysteries, moved by the same yearnings, troubled by the same questionings and doubts, and aspiring to the same peace as had generations of their ancestors who lived in the same environment. It is a proof of their sincere adherence to Islam that they sought to find within Islam the solutions of their problems. It should also be pointed out that, in the areas to which Islam spread, the termination of one chapter of existence and the beginning of the new Islamic culture, with all that this change entailed in the forming of new relationships and acceptance of basic ideas, restored the vigor and revived the energies of nations which had been weighed down by age and tradition.

The Hellenic material which was transmitted to Islam was used for the advancement of philosophical and scientific speculations and for many practical applications. But that material was, as Duncan B. Macdonald has ably noted, "a tangled system," "a welter of translations and pseudographs." Men like al-Farabi (died 339; A.D. 950) and Ibn Sina (died 429; A.D. 1037), who is known in the West as Avicenna, wholeheartedly devoted themselves to the study of those materials, and generations of men toiled and managed, sometimes by sheer brainpower, to reject nonsense and falsehood. It is a matter of supreme regret that the transmission of the classical legacy was not accompanied by the development of even a rudimentary method of textual and historical criticism. Even so, the Greek patrimony contributed to the development of the mystical outlook and had a great deal to do with the elaboration of the Muslim system of belief.

Against that background of a variety of intellectual, religious, and racial traditions the Islamic community created several distinctive ways of expressing its spiritual and intellectual yearnings. The followers of the orthodox Sunnah became known as Sunnis; a brief introduction to the Sunnah has already been given. To complete this picture of the maturing of Islamic society a few words must be said about three strands woven into the fabric of the community of Muslims: the Mu'tazilites, with their emphasis on reason; the Sufis, who are the mystics and ecstatics of Islam; and the Shi'ites, who have placed special emphasis on Ali and his descendants as spiritual guides.

The early attempts at elaborating the Muslim system of belief grew out of the issues raised by Kharijism—due to the impact of Islam on the Arab Bedouin society—and the perplexities of the non-Arab communities which were gathered under the banner of Islam. The individuals who, impelled by a genuine piety, attempted to meet the difficulties of the times are known as Mu'tazilites. Their thought is not a unified body of doctrine but a collection of distinct interpretations. Their central doctrine was an insistence on the unity and justice of God. They taught that the qualities attributed to

God are in danger of being hypostatized, of being regarded as distinct persons like those in the Christian Trinity; they taught that the Qur'an was created; and they insisted on man's free will.

It is their teaching about the Qur'an which is the core of their system, for, if accepted, all kinds of very grave conclusions could be drawn. A Book which has existed from all eternity is a Logos, unalterable. But a book which has been created could have a human and a divine side, and things which it seemed desirable to omit or change in it could be ascribed to the human side. It was in order to modify some of the teachings of the Qur'an that the Abbasid Caliph al-Ma'mun, seeking to impose by force what he conceived to be an "enlightened" religion, issued a decree in 212 (A.D. 827) proclaiming the doctrine of the creation of the Qur'an as the only truth, binding on all Muslims. This was a truly revolutionary decree because by it a Caliph attempted to usurp for himself a function which Islam reserved for the whole community. Al-Ma'mun insisted that those who held that the Qur'an was uncreated sinned against the unity of God, and he established a test of views on the Qur'an which had to be passed by all judges and by all witnesses in court before their testimony would be accepted. Those who refused the test were punished as idolaters and polytheists. This policy was continued under al-Ma'mun's successor but was given up in 234 (A.D. 848). It was never repeated.

The glory of standing against this test through imprisonment and scourging belongs to Ibn Hanbal, the founder of one of the four schools of law. For him, the tradition handed down from the forefathers was the only basis on which the Qur'an could be explained. This Hanbalite position represents a main strand in Sunni Islam. Another strand is represented by the position taken by al-Ash'ari (died 324; A.D. 935), a prominent Mu'tazilite who used the same dialectical methods as his teachers did but came to the conclusion that their position was wrong, and on the basis of his teaching the Ash'arite theology of Sunni Islam was formulated.

Mu'tazilite trends continued in Shi'a Islam. Shi'a is based on the belief that to reach truth one must have an infallible teacher in the person of the Imam, the carrier of the divine light-spark transmitted from Adam through Muhammad and his cousin and son-in-law, Ali, and the descendants of Ali. Mu'tazilism, with its insistence on the use of reason to reach truth, finds a place in Shi'ism because the occult relation with the Imam allows a great deal of latitude for the exercise of individual reasoning.

The three main divisions of Shi'ism today are the Zaidis, now living chiefly in Yemen; the Imamis, or Twelvers, now living chiefly in Iran, Iraq, India, Pakistan, Lebanon, Syria; and the Isma'ilis, or Seveners, now living in India, Arabia, and East Africa. The numbers refer to a difference in belief about the order of succession among Ali's descendants.

Historically, the Isma'ilis have played a dazzling and substantial role. Out of Isma'ilism was born the widespread Qarmatian movement of revolt against Sunni authority which was at one time in control of the Holy City of Mecca (316–17; A.D. 928–29). We have suspiciously tendentious reports of the way the Qarmatian community organized itself spiritually and socially. A more solid outcome of Isma'ilism is the Fatimid Caliphate which began in Tunisia in 298 (A.D. 910), extended its sway into Egypt, founded there the city of Cairo and the mosque of Al Azhar in 363 (A.D. 973), and continued to rule Egypt and parts of Syria and the Hijaz until 567 (A.D. 1171). Whatever may have been the social implications of Isma'ilism—and scholars claim a good deal—the doctrines of the Fatimid Caliphate did not appreciably affect the procedures of the Egyptian administrative system, and Egypt emerged from two hundred years of Isma'ili rule and intensive indoctrination as solidly Sunni as before the coming of the Fatimids. Perhaps this indicates the possibility that we are apt to look at the differences between Sunnism and Shi'ism from an overly intellectual point of view, emphasizing the differences with a degree of subtlety that may well never have been imagined by their common adherents.

There can be no doubt of the supreme importance of Sufism in molding the attitude toward life of the individual Muslim. Sufism as an organized system with teachers, pupils, and rules of discipline appeared in the latter part of the third century of the Hijrah (after A.D. 865). Since that time, the mystics and ecstatics of Sufism have, as we shall see, done much to shape the beliefs and practices of the Islamic world. It may be that the supremacy of Sufism represents the victory of the common man over the earthly mighty and the learned professors and scholars. For under Sufism the common man finally managed to live in a world of ideas and emotions of his own construction, and to have the satisfaction of seeing the powerful and the learned bow before the uncouth "saintly" vagabond and beggar.

To conclude this section on the maturing of the Islamic Society, some account must be given of the rise of autonomous dynasties in the provinces of the Caliphate. The movement is indicative of the maturing process in the sense that it is a passing from the earlier phase in which the Islamic world was made up of Arab settlers and Arab garrison towns set apart from the native peoples of the provinces. In the new phase, the distinction between Arab and provincial fades away, and provinces and regions regain their individuality and autonomy within the consciously recognized Islamic unity.

Spain was the earliest region to be separated from the Caliphate. When the Umayyads fell, one of the princes of that house escaped to Spain and after many adventures established the Amirate of Cordova in 139 (A.D. 756). The Amirate was turned into a Caliphate in 316 (A.D. 928) which produced some brilliant achievements before it fell in 423 (A.D. 1031) and was split into petty principalities. In the meantime a great Berber power, the Almoravids, had arisen in North Africa. The Almoravids added Spain to their North African Empire and later lost it to another Berber dynasty, the Almohads. Both dynasties were the outcome of movements of religious revival in Berber tribes.

In Tunisia the Aghlabids, who became autonomous in 184 (A.D. 800), were interested in maritime expansion and conquered Sicily in 216 (A.D. 831). Sicily was a center of Islamic civilization under Islamic rule until it was conquered by the Normans, beginning in 452 (A.D. 1060).

In Egypt, Ahmad Ibn Tulun founded an autonomous dynasty in 256 (A.D. 869). His rule, though brief, was brilliant. The rise and fall of the Fatimids has been noted. Moving eastward from Egypt, we note the Hamdanids, an Arab dynasty whose capital was Aleppo. The Hamdanids gained fame for their warfare against Byzantium and for the brilliant circle which was gathered at Aleppo, including the famous philosopher al-Farabi.

In the eastern provinces of the Caliphate a brilliant dynasty arose in Transoxiana in the third century of the Hijrah (ninth century A.D.) under the Samanids, whose rule was adorned by the life and work of Ibn Sina (Avicenna). A century later they were succeeded by the Ghaznavids who are famous for their conquests in India under Sultan Mahmud. His court is remembered as the residence of that great master of many sciences, al-Biruni (died 440; A.D. 1048), and Firdawsi, the famous author of the Persian epic *The Book of Kings.*

The Caliphs themselves came under the control of a Shi'ite dynasty which ruled Iraq and western Persia from their Baghdad court from 338 to 447 (A.D. 949–1055) when they were dislodged by the Seljuq Turks. With the coming to power of the Turks we enter a new phase of the development of Islamic society.

The power of the various dynasties in this period was based on the command of a war band, the support of a tribal or national sense of solidarity, or religious sectarianism. It was a characteristic of the dynasties of Egypt and eastward that they tried to copy as much as possible the Abbasid court and organization in Baghdad. The rulers were generous patrons of the poets, scientists, philosophers, and theologians of their areas, for these men shed lustre on their courts and enhanced their prestige. The fact that the intellectual pursuits of the times were not concentrated in one center made it difficult and at times impossible for political or religious authority to control the intellectual movements.

The Contributions of the Berbers and Turks and the Invasions of the Crusaders and Mongols

The Fifth to the Tenth Century of the Hijrah (Eleventh to Sixteenth Century A.D.)

The fifth century of the Hijrah (eleventh century A.D.) was of critical importance in the Islamic community which was at that time organized around the three Caliphates—the Umayyad of Cordova, the Fatimid of Cairo, and the Abbasid of Baghdad—together with the various provincial dynasties which had grown up. But the decline of the Caliphates, the apparent disruption of the society through revolutionary activities and unrestrained speculation, and in the case of Spain, the advance of Christian power to reconquer the peninsula, led to the resurgence of nomadic power in western Asia and North Africa. This resurgence of nomadism took place among the Arabs, Berbers, and Turks.

The new wave of nomadism which occurred on the borderlands of Egypt, Syria, Iraq, and Persia was of the unobtrusive, cumulative kind which continued until well into the fourteenth century (nineteenth century A.D.) with such strength that the established authority in those countries could just manage to keep it partially under control. Far more sensational and fateful was the wild, destructive activity of the Bedouin tribesmen of North Africa and the constructively planned action of the Turks in western Asia and the Berbers in Morocco and Spain. Of the activities of the Bedouins in Tunisia it need be noted only that they and their descendants gave active support to their co-religionists in the expanding arena of conflict between Christendom and Islam.

The Berber movement grew from a religious revival which began in the Sahara and crystallized in the establishment of a dynasty of religious warriors, the Almoravids. The dynasty extended its power to Spain, where it defeated the Christians and stopped their advance for a time. As happens regularly in Islamic history, the dynasty lost its vigor and gave way to a new one, this time the Almohads (Unitarians), another revivalist movement. The Almohads also built up a Morocco-

Spanish Empire. While they maintained a literalist system of law and dogmatics, they were quite willing to allow individuals liberty for philosophical pursuits so long as they maintained proper outward discretion. Ibn Rushd, the great Arabic philosopher known in the West as Averroes, flourished under the Almohads.

The Turks, like the Berbers, had nomadic origins, but they differed from them in that the nucleus of Turkish power was a folk, or a nation, rather than a tribe or confederation of tribes. The Turks were known as Seljuqs after their leader who settled his people near Bukhara and went over with them to Islam. While the Turks had a religious policy which played an important part in their activities, they did not owe their rise to power to a religious founder as did the two Berber dynasties. The cultural tradition of the Turks, going back to the pre-Islamic Persia of the Sasanids, was far richer than that of their Berber contemporaries. Also, the social and political organization of the Turks was more advanced than that brought to North Africa and Spain by the Berbers.

The Seljuqs stepped into the center of the picture when their Sultan Tughrul entered Baghdad in 447 (A.D. 1055) and liberated the Caliph from the tutelage of the Shi'ites, thus asserting the central point in the Seljuq policy—the championship of Sunni Islam. In their dedication to the service of Islam, the Seljuqs expanded the domain for the first time in Anatolia. In 464 (A.D. 1071) they defeated the Byzantine Emperor. It was this defeat and the expansion of Turkish power into Syria and Palestine, the control of Jerusalem, and the reports of their harsh treatment of the Christian pilgrims that inflamed feeling in Christendom and favored the extension of the holy war from Spain and Sicily to the Holy Land.

Seljuq institutions were essentially military in character, not only because of the kind of life the Turks had lived in their original steppe environment, but also because the Turks adopted a role in the Islamic Society which necessitated such an organization. They made themselves the champions of Sunni Islam; they sought to expand and defend the domain of Islam and to extirpate the forces of material, moral, and intellectual anarchy. This led to two important results. In the first place, the sultanate claimed the right to rule and control the affairs of men. Naturally, it sought a formal sanction from the Caliphate, for what it was worth, but the sultans were confident of the legitimacy of their claim. This is important, for it provided the historical basis and model for the Islamic states of the last century. It is interesting to note that Ibn Khaldun (died 809; A.D. 1406), the great Tunisian historian, dealt in the *Prolegomena* of his universal history with these non-Caliphate sultanates and institutions as existing in their own right.

A second important result of the Seljuq rule was that the sultans paid great attention to the creation and elaboration of social institutions. They created a ruling institution for purposes of war and government which was based on the division of the empire into military fiefs; a chancery for the preparation of state documents and communication throughout the empire; and a religious institution which, in addition to maintaining the legal and cult services, was expected through the control of education to be an instrument of social cohesion.

Under the Seljuqs, colleges, or *madrasas*, were founded and endowed to carry out a carefully graded program of instruction in the religious sciences and humanities. Subjects were classified as being taught for their intrinsic worth or as tools for the study of the main subjects. In these colleges the professors received regular stipends and students were given board and lodging. No effort was spared to attract outstanding scholars to teach in these colleges. Al-Ghazali was a professor for a while and later, when he wanted to withdraw and lead a life of contemplation, he was almost compelled to go back for a time to his chair. Outside the madrasas there were independent teachers and a free cultivation of studies was allowed, but their influence was limited. The official organization of higher education, although it achieved the immediate end of the restoration of order, unfortunately led to those characteristics of Islamic education which have come down almost to our time—the addiction to memorization of prescribed texts and study of the same materials in generation after generation. The result was that any hope for a creative intellectual movement had to be looked for outside the regular institutions of learning.

The major trends in the intellectual life of Islam from the sixth century of the Hijrah (twelfth century A.D.) to modern times begin with the influence of al-Ghazali (died 505; A.D. 1111). He brought Islam back to its fundamental and historical facts as found in the Word of God and the tradition of the Prophet; he aroused new interest in philosophy; and he gave a place in his system to the emotional religious life. But it is rare to find the same balanced and harmonious combination in contemporary and later thinkers. After al-Ghazali what do we find? We find some men—the Sufis—putting their faith in the "unveiling" of the mystic, others placing theirs in the transmitted tradition, and the philosophers continuing their old neglect of the objective study of the outside world. It is no wonder that the Sufis were accused of heresy by the traditionalists and the traditionalists were charged by the Sufis with formalism, hypocrisy, and the inability to reason logically.

Sufism had its speculative philosophers, such as Ibn Arabi (died 638; A.D. 1240), and its poets, such as Ibn Farid (died 633; A.D. 1235), but its greatest influence was not in its speculations or poetry or emotional outpourings. By the sixth century after the Hijrah (twelfth century A.D.) Sufism had become an all-embracing social institution which gave ample scope for the exercise of talents and satisfied all levels of individual aspirations. This was the Sufism of the orders such as the darwishes and faqirs. There are many distinctions noted between the various Sufi orders—as to whether they observed seemliness or extravagance in their exercises, whether they were urban or rural, whether they tried to propagate the faith among non-Muslims or wandered about with no particular mission, whether they set up new dynasties dedicated to holy war or the extirpation of heresy, and the like. Important as these distinctions are, there is a great deal of uniformity in the Sufi attitude toward life, and this attitude has permeated the Muslim's character and outlook throughout the world of Islam. Most of the superficial labels attached to Islam by Europeans derive from the more obvious Sufi characteristics.

Although no one individual could really be typical of a movement of such wide ramifications and subtle shades as the Sufi brotherhoods, it is possible to recognize in the Egyptian al-Sha'rani (died 973; A.D. 1565) characteristics which can be found in different proportions in all Sufi brothers, except that he is no representative of the extremely discreditable orders—and these are not representative of Sufis in general. Al-Sha'rani has gathered in his attitude and writings all the elements which constitute the Sufi legacy. He was superstitious and at the same time a man of high ethical principles, humble in social life and arrogant in intellectual affairs. To al-Sha'rani the Jinn and Angels were most intense realities with whom he held familiar converse. He believed in a hierarchy of saints who held dominion over the divisions of the world of Islam, saints who had their jealousies, conflicts, and divided loyalties and were kept in check by a balance of power. The reality of this way of looking at the world can be gathered by anyone who studies the historical material of this age, and remnants of it can be found in memories which linger to the present day.

But the mystics were not the only influence in the intellectual development of this period. Ibn Taymiyya (died, Damascus, 729; A.D. 1328) fought against what he considered to be the idolatry of saint worship, pilgrimage to holy shrines, vows, offerings, and invocations with all his might, and paid for his courage with imprisonment. Mystics, philosophers, and scholastic theologians all fell under the lash of his denunciations. He bowed to no earthly authority and drew his arguments from the traditions and practices of early Islam. Curiously enough, Ibn Taymiyya, who fought the worship of saints so vehemently has become a saint in spite of himself.

Ibn Taymiyya's doctrine based on traditionalism was carried on by Muhammad Ibn Abd al-Wahhab (1115–1207; A.D. 1703–92) and serves as the doctrinal basis of the movement known as Wahhabism, which has been influential in the last two centuries.

The ruling authorities, while personally more sympathetic to the Sufis, tried to prevent the antipathies between the Sufis and the Traditionalists *(Salafiya)* from breaking out into open clashes. In their attempts to prevent extremism they were true to the Seljuq program of stability and discipline.

The Seljuqs were the prototype of later Muslim dynasties. Their immediate successors were the Ayyubids in Syria, Egypt, and western Arabia, a dynasty founded by the famous Saladin (died 589; A.D. 1193). The Ayyubid Sultanate was seized by warriors of slave origin, setting up the dynasty of the Mamluks.

The Ottoman dynasty began in Seljuq territory in Asia Minor and conquered Asia Minor, the Balkan Peninsula, Hungary, Arabia, Egypt, Syria, Iraq, and North Africa as far as Morocco to become the chief Islamic power in the modern age.

The story of the dynasties which derive from the Seljuqs is inextricably involved in the resurgence of active hostilities with Christendom. These new hostilities are fundamentally a western European movement, quite distinct from the wars between Islam and the Byzantine Empire. This European drive against the Islamic world had several objectives. It sought to expand the papal power against the "infidels," the Muslims, and against the schismatics, the Greek Orthodox and eastern churches. It also sought the establishment of the commercial domination of the Italian republics and the carving out of principalities for the feudal lords of western Europe (as it has been expressively put, it attempted the solution of the problem of the landless younger sons); and the Crusades also provided scope for all who desired to strike a blow for the faith or do penance by enduring the hardships of a holy war.

Historically, the roots of the crusading movement lie in the fight to restore Spain to Christendom. The movement was given a great impetus by the success of the Normans in destroying Muslim power in Sicily. The appeals of Byzantium for help and the alarm aroused by Seljuq victories in Anatolia provided the occasion for the call made by the papacy for a crusade. The so-called "First Crusade" achieved the entry of the Crusaders into Jerusalem in 493 (A.D. 1099) and the foundation of the Latin principalities on the Lebanese coast. It is not part of our purpose to trace the fortunes of these

European foundations in the Levant, but we should note that the theatre of operations was by no means restricted to the Levant. It involved Egypt, Tunisia, the islands of the eastern Mediterranean, the Balkan Peninsula, and Constantinople. Islam was not the sole enemy, for the Fourth Crusade was directed against the Byzantine Empire and led to the foundation of a Latin Empire in Constantinople and Italian and other West European principalities in the Balkans.

Although Saladin regained Jerusalem for Islam in 583 (A.D. 1187) and a century later the Crusaders were expelled from their last stronghold in the Levant, the memories of the Crusades continued to cloud the relations between Islam and Christendom. Christians and Muslims may have learned some things from each other during that time, but fundamentally they continued for centuries to look upon each other as mortal enemies.

The Crusades also helped to stiffen the principle of holy war as the main justification for the existence of dynasties and states with large military forces. The advent of Saladin, his destruction of the Fatimids in Egypt, and his building up of an Egyptian-Syrian state were aimed solely at the deliverance of Islam. The Mamluk, or Slave, Sultans could claim no other justification for their power than the necessity to protect Islam. In this we have the main reason for the depression of the nonmilitary classes of Islamic society. Since much of the military was recruited from certain races outside the domain of Islam and the main body of the Muslim people made up the nonmilitary class—especially in the Arab countries—we can easily see how the Islamic society came to be made up of a minority of war-lords and a majority of mere subjects. There can also be no doubt that the course of the holy war against the European forces speeded up the process of separating the Islamic Society into an Arabic western portion and Persian and Turkish eastern portions. The eruption of the Mongols into the domain of Islam completed that process.

The first big wave of Mongol advance into western Asia was that led by Genghis Khan early in the seventh century (thirteenth century A.D.), but the wave which left the deepest mark was that of Hulagu whose forces captured Baghdad and executed the last Abbasid Caliph in 656 (A.D. 1258). The Mongols were stopped by the Mamluk Sultans of Egypt before they could establish themselves in Syria, but some of those Sultans were certainly influenced by Mongol ideas and practices. The Mongol Timur (Tamerlane, died 808; A.D. 1405) tried again after his conversion to Islam to conquer Anatolia and Syria, but, although he had military successes against the Ottoman and Mamluk Sultans, he turned back eastward to India and even planned to go on to China. It was left to his descendant Babar to have the honor of founding in the next century the celebrated Mughal dynasty of India.

Although the Mongols did cause a good deal of destruction, it was not as extensive or irreparable as is usually represented. Iraq suffered most, not only because of the destruction by Hulagu, but also because no dynasty arose to establish a settled order again. The country became a prey to nomadic Arab, Kurdish, and Turkoman groups, and to the rivalries of the Ottoman and Persian Empires.

The Mongol eruption and its aftermath created a new phase of Asiatic and world history, extending beyond the area of Islamic Society. Out of those disturbed times grew up the Ottoman Turkish Sultanate, beginning in northwestern Anatolia as a Seljuq dependency and expanding into the Balkans, capturing Constantinople in 857 (A.D. 1453), extinguishing the Byzantine Empire, and finally conquering Egypt and Syria in 922–23 (A.D. 1516–17). At about the same time Persia emerged as a Shi'a state under the Safavid dynasty and the Great Mughals established their rule in India. With these three dynasties Islamic society entered a new phase of its history.

The Islamic Society in the Modern Age

The Tenth to the Fourteenth Century of the Hijrah (Sixteenth to Twentieth Century A.D.)

By the tenth century of the Hijrah (sixteenth century A.D.) there were three major Muslim powers: the Ottoman Empire, the Persian Monarchy, and the Mughal Empire of India. The Ottoman Empire extended into central Europe, from Iraq to the frontiers of Morocco, and southward to the Persian Gulf and the Red Sea and Aden. With the exception of Morocco and most of the Arabian Peninsula, it included among its subjects all of the Arabs. The great cities of Arab culture—Baghdad, Damascus, Aleppo, and Cairo—were under its rule, and the great sanctuaries of Mecca, Medina, and Jerusalem were under the special care of its sultans. They were conscious of their great Islamic prestige during all these centuries and developed gradually an Islamic policy which came to an end only with the dissolution of the empire at the end of the first World War.

One element of the policy of the Ottoman Sultans was their championship of Sunnism, which brought them into conflict with the monarchs of Persia who had adopted the creed of Imami Shi'ism as the religion of their government. Persian history from the tenth century of the Hijrah onward, in spite of transient imperial episodes on the Afghan and Central Asian borders, became more and more the history of a national state, thus anticipating a development which has become the dominant feature of present-day Islam.

The Mughal Empire in India shared many religious and cultural features with the other two powers, but it was destined to lose its sovereignty much earlier than they did, leaving the great body of Indian Muslims in a situation very different from that of their co-religionists in the Ottoman Empire and Persia.

In the tenth century (sixteenth century A.D.) the great geographical discoveries, the navigation of the ocean routes, and the building up of the European colonial empires brought a turning-point in modern history. The European powers which had hitherto been encircled by the world of Islam broke through in this century and encircled Islam. As a result of these changes, some of the Islamic areas passed under direct European rule, notably in Southeast Asia and in East and West Africa. But until the last century such Christian rule in Muslim lands did not penetrate very deeply and therefore did not call forth the reactions of later times.

In the territories of the Ottoman, Persian, and Indian Empires, the European powers generally followed the policy of building up enclaves based on extraterritorial rights and of establishing connections with the non-Muslim communities. In some cases they encouraged Christian proselytizing and in others they sought to bring the schismatics into the Roman Catholic fold, but their aim was always to create a "clientele" of the European power. Until the beginning of the last century, these enclaves did not strike a deep root, except in the case of the Mughal Empire where the East India Company was supplanting the Emperors as the paramount power.

Because of the decline of the central authority in the three empires during this early period (to the beginning of the last century), the local tribal leaders, adventurers, and leaders of war bands tried to build up autonomous rule in the provinces and sometimes sought aid from European powers. Conscious of the dangers from Europe and from their own ambitious subordinates, the central authorities began to take measures to reaffirm their authority and increase their power, but their political activities did not greatly concern the common people. The movements of revival and reconstruction which were born out of the experience of the common people were more significant than the actions of their rulers.

There was renewed activity of the Sufi orders in the twelfth century (eighteenth century A.D.), but the most notable movement was that of Muhammad Ibn Abd al-Wahhab. We have already seen how al-Wahhab adopted the ideas and spirit of Ibn Taymiyya—the return to the Qur'an and the traditions of early Islam, and the revolt against the strict application of the shari'a. Ibn Abd al-Wahhab converted to his views certain Arab leaders, the Saudi barons of Dar'uya, who dedicated themselves to the realization of his doctrines. Toward the end of the twelfth and for the first two decades of the thirteenth century (eighteenth and nineteenth centuries A.D.), they were in control of the Holy City of Mecca and Medina and of the territories extending to the Persian Gulf and the southern borders of Iraq and Syria.

The activities of these early Wahhabis, however, shocked the sense of the community and exposed them to punitive action on the part of the Ottoman Empire and the viceroy of Egypt, Muhammad Ali. By 1236 (A.D. 1820) the power of the Wahhabis had been destroyed, but not their doctrines. Wahhabism influenced Islam in the Arab countries and India in the last century in fruitful ways.

Since the beginning of the last century, the Islamic Society has found itself in a critical stage of its development. The period of a hundred and fifty years which began with the French invasion of Egypt in 1213 (A.D. 1798) witnessed the merging of our Islamic Society into the world society of the present era. We, the members of the Islamic Society, have not been fully aware of all the implications of the events of this period. To become aware of these implications is, in my view, the greatest single problem of the Islamic Society of our day.

This merging into a world society was a process which occupied only a relatively short span of time, a mere century and a half. During this time, until the conclusion of the second World War, practically all of the Islamic people were under some degree of effective control by a European power. Also during this time the life of all the Islamic people has been influenced materially and morally by contacts with Western civilization. The influence has been so great that even when the Islamic people have regained their political independence they have found that a return to the traditional way of life was not possible—even if it were desirable. It needs to be emphasized that such a return is not deemed desirable even when lip-service is paid to the glorious traditions of the past.

If we look around in modern times for representatives of al-Ghazali's four categories of the searchers for truth, we cannot say that they can be found anywhere in the Muslim world. There are, of course, scholars who deal with theology, philosophy, and mysticism, but they deal with them only as historical expositions. Modern authors write to prove that Islam is this or Islam is that, that it does not hinder progress, or is socialism, but the search for truth in al-Ghazali's sense is not found. In the field of action, the religion of Islam has been used to promote causes such as nationalism, or fascism; religious associations do not exist to promote spiritual fellowship —they seek to realize the aims we associate with political clubs or parties.

These developments can be understood in the light of the circumstances in which the Islamic Society has lived for the past century and a half. But it must be realized that although the long history of Islam has bequeathed to modern times a rich legacy, no society can meet the needs of our times by drawing on its inner resources alone. The Islamic Society—as well as all other societies—must recognize the inadequacy of its own resources and its duties to humanity at large. The possession of a world religion is not only a privilege, it is also a responsibility.

ISLAM IN THE SUDAN AND EAST AFRICA. Although Islam in the Sudan and East Africa lay somewhat outside the main stream of events, it has grown to include many millions of Muslims. Most of the area of Africa below the countries of North Africa is controlled by European colonial powers, but for our purposes it is more convenient to refer to the traditional divisions of the Sudan—Eastern, Central, and Western. Western Sudan contains the basin of the Senegal, the Gambia, and the Middle Niger; Central Sudan includes the basin of Lake Chad; Eastern Sudan lies in the Nile basin and covers what is now the newly-constituted independent Sudanese Republic.

Islam reached Western Sudan through the Berbers of the Sahara. The vast movement of religious revival which took place in the fifth century of the Hijrah (eleventh century A.D.) and led to the establishment of the Almoravid dynasty in Morocco and Spain gave a strong impetus to the spread of Islam among the subjects of the great pagan African Ghana Empire, whose sway extended at one time over the gold mines of the Upper Senegal and over the majority of the Berber tribes of the Sahara. In the seventh century (thirteenth century A.D.) Timbuktu was the center of Islamic culture. Five centuries later Muslim expansion received a new impetus with the founding of Sokoto State and the subjugation of the major portion of Western Sudan with the help of the Moroccan Sufi brotherhood, the Tijani order.

In Central Sudan, along Lake Chad, Islam was introduced as early as the fifth century (eleventh century A.D.) but did not gain a firm foothold until some five centuries later.

Eastern Sudan, bordering on southern Egypt, retained its independence and Christianity long after Egypt became a province of the Islamic Empire in the first century after the Hijrah. While there were no intimate relations between Eastern Sudan and the Muslim world of Egypt, North Africa, and Arabia, there was enough communication to prevent complete isolation. There was active intervention in the affairs of the Sudan by the Mamluk Sultans of Egypt in the seventh century (thirteenth century A.D.), but the conversion of the Sudanese Christians and pagans to Islam was the direct result of the settlement in the Sudan of Arab tribesmen who had left their homes in Egypt. It is surmised that they were seeking a more congenial place to live after the government of Egypt passed into the hands of Turkish rulers.

The ruling house in Eastern Sudan from the tenth through the twelfth century (sixteenth-eighteenth century A.D.), called the Funj, claimed descent from the famous Umayyads, but they are believed to have been of African stock and relatively recent converts to Islam. Their power rested on slave armies recruited from African tribes. When the Sudan was united with Egypt in the last century, the process of Europeanization and innovation that was going on in Egypt was extended to the Sudan area. There was a brief period of revolt in the last century; then the Sudan came under British colonial power until recently. Islamic society in Eastern Sudan was characterized by the survival of pre-Islamic African ideas and practices, by the permeation of their religious life by the ritual of the Sufi brotherhoods, by a zeal to acquire religious learning and by efforts to secure the settlement there of holy and learned men.

The East African coastal areas, extending from Cape Guardafui in the north to Delagoa Bay in the south, have from pre-Islamic times been for Arabian, Persian, and Indian seafarers a field for cooperative action which resulted in the creation of prosperous communities and the blending of their diverse cultural traditions. Those early seafarers explored the west Indian Ocean and colonized the East African coast. They usually built their towns on islands adjoining the mainland for purposes of defense against the tribes of the hinterland, settled down and married African women, and traded in gold, slaves, ivory, and other African products.

The intimate relations with Arabia, Persia, and India resulted in the propagation of Islam in East Africa. The area became a land of refuge and settlement for certain sects which in other lands could not resist absorption in the conformist mass around them. Thus we find in East Africa today Isma'ili, Imamite Shi'a, and Ibadi groups enjoying mutual toleration and leading prosperous lives. There is also a tendency toward blending the cultural elements of their diverse origins in one whole, as is evidenced in the building up of the Swahili language and culture out of Arabic and African elements. Swahili is now one of the cultural languages of the Muslim world and bids fair to become the common language of East Africa.

The early prosperity of the East African settlements was soon ended by the coming of the Portuguese. Following the new route to India around the Cape of Good Hope, the Portuguese pioneers set about subjugating the Islamic settlements in East Africa, seeking to acquire strategic bases, further their commercial interests, and carry out their commitment to an anti-Islam crusade. Portuguese domination was replaced by British, and the partition of Africa in the last century brought into the area French, German, and Italian colonial powers as well. In modern times, the position of Islam in East Africa is similar to that in Western Sudan. Here, too, the people are subject to European domination, and divided into many areas of varying size, with differing cultural traditions.

Islam in Malaya and Indonesia. Long before the preaching of Islam, Arab seafarers had made settlements along the trade routes between the Arabian Peninsula and China. These trade activities were given an added impetus when the Arabians were converted to Islam—and when they were joined in the propagation of the faith by Indian converts. We hear of Arabian merchants and mariners who were sufficiently strong to sack Canton in South China as early as 141 (A.D. 758). We hear also of Muslims from India settling in several ports on the routes to China, winning the favor of the local chieftains by suitable gifts and the confidence of the common people by the distribution of amulets. Thus they acquired a reputation for affluence and magical knowledge and, on the strength of their claim to "noble birth," obtained the daughters of the local chieftains in marriage.

It is due to the Islamization and rise to power of Malacca on the Malayan Peninsula that Islam was firmly established in both Malaya and Indonesia. Malacca, which began as a center for piracy, managed to force all vessels passing through the straits to put into its harbor for passes and became the center for the spice trade of the East. The rulers of Malacca became Muslim in the ninth century (fifteenth century A.D.) and encouraged the intimate relations with the Javanese which led to their conversion to Islam. The army and the trade were in the hands of the large Javanese colony in Malacca. The Muslims of Malacca also propagated Islam in the Malay Peninsula and along the coasts of the island of Sumatra.

The Portuguese conquered Malacca in 917 (A.D. 1511), but Islam continued to spread throughout Malaya and the islands of Indonesia. Portuguese domination gave way to the British and Dutch colonial empires, and thus Malayan and Indonesian Muslims were subjected to European control earlier than in other parts of the Islamic world. However, in evaluating the effect of the colonial control a distinction should be made between the early centuries and the gradual transformation during the last century into an intensive system of planned penetration. In the earlier phase the European colonial powers were not in a position to establish complete control over immense regions so remote from their shores. They sought to monopolize commerce, to exercise control indirectly through native rulers, and to secure their position by naval power and fortresses. The Portuguese were pledged to a crusade against both Islam and Theravada Buddhism, but their missionaries had little success. The Dutch and British made no attempt before the last century to interfere with established religion. France, on the other hand, launched at one time a grandiose scheme of missionary enterprise. But it did not accomplish much.

The last century brought a new era in the relations of Europeans with the people of Malaya and Indonesia, characterized by a policy of capital investment and economic development, and by introduction of elementary education and social services on Western lines. Provinces became dependent upon external markets, agricultural indebtedness increased; and there were large-scale migrations of Chinese and Indians to Malaya and Indonesia. The effects of these changes upon Islamic Society were great. One positive reaction was a tendency of the Muslims of Southeast Asia to turn to the mother society for revivification. The chief method adopted was to send out students for intensive study in the Holy Cities of the Hijaz and in Al Azhar University in Cairo. On their return home, these men were active in the Islamic educational program in its broadest sense. This attachment to the older Islamic centers accounts for the marked enthusiasm of the Indonesians for the pilgrimage to Mecca.

The Muslim World Today

In this chapter we have traced the spread of Islam from Mecca and Medina west to the Atlantic Ocean and east to the Pacific. Only on the fringes of Europe has Islam been expelled from areas where the people had accepted the teachings of the Prophet. Although there has been no exact census of the Muslim population of the world, conservative estimates indicate that today there are more than four hundred million Muslims. The following table shows the distribution of the Muslim population by countries.

Far East		42,005,000
China & Korea	42,000,000	
Japan	5,000	
Southeast Asia		79,180,000
Indonesia	74,200,000	
Philippines	790,000	
Indo-China	250,000	
Malaya	3,300,000	
Thailand	640,000	
Pakistan-India		107,450,000
Pakistan	66,000,000	
India	40,200,000	
Burma	750,000	
Ceylon	500,000	
Turkish areas		64,250,000
Sinkiang	3,000,000	
Afghanistan	12,000,000	
Turkey	23,600,000	
Soviet Union	22,000,000	
Albania	700,000	
Yugoslavia	1,900,000	
Bulgaria	800,000	
Greece	200,000	
Romania	50,000	
Iran		20,700,000
Arabic areas		64,200,000
Iraq	5,000,000	
Arabian Peninsula	12,500,000	
Syria, Lebanon, Jordan, Israel	5,000,000	
Egypt	20,000,000	
Libya	1,100,000	
Tunisia	3,200,000	
Algeria	8,000,000	
Morocco	9,400,000	
Africa		35,000,000
Somaliland	1,800,000	
Ethiopia	3,200,000	
Tanganyika	1,500,000	
Sudan	7,000,000	
French Equatorial Africa	1,500,000	
French West Africa	6,300,000	
Other African countries	13,700,000	
Western countries		800,000
	Total	413,585,000

These figures are only estimates based on the available census figures and informed guesses as to the percentage of Muslims in the population. Chief reliance has been placed on census figures of the United Nations and the figures given in

Atlas of Islamic History, compiled by Harry W. Hazard; *Unity and Variety of Muslim Civilization*, edited by Gustave E. von Grunebaum; and *Annuaire du Monde Musulman, 1954*, edited by Louis Massignon.

There is little agreement as to the number of Muslims in China. The official figure given by the present government is 10,000,000 but that seems to include only the recognized racial minorities of Huis, Uighurs, Kazakhs, Khalkhas, Tadziks, Tartars, Uzbeks, Tunghsiangs, Salas, and Paoans, and takes no account of the Chinese who call themselves Muslims. The figure of 42,000,000 for China and Korea is based on the estimates as to the size of the Muslim community before the present government came into power, with a conservative allowance for population increase. Chinese Muslims estimate the total as at least 50,000,000.

The Turkish area includes those Muslims whose ties are closer to Turkey than to the Arab or Iranian world. Not all the Muslims in the Soviet Union fall properly in that classification since more than 2,000,000 of them look to Iran as their cultural center. The figure for the Soviet Union is open to question because it has not been possible in recent years to get accurate information concerning the fate of Islam under Communism and it is known that efforts have been made to curtail Islam, partly for ideological reasons and partly to break the ties of the Muslims with the Turkish and Iranian areas.

Because of the recent shifts of population in the Near East, the figures for Syria, Lebanon, Jordan, and Israel have been grouped together. The estimates for Africa vary widely, with the figure chosen representing a conservative judgment. The figure for the Western countries includes 350,000 Algerian Muslims who have settled in France.

These figures indicate that the Muslim population of the world may be conservatively estimated at around 400,000,000. Approximately half of the Muslims of the world live in eastern Asia, from China and Indonesia to Pakistan. The largest Muslim country is Indonesia, followed closely by Pakistan.

There are five major cultural areas in the Islamic world. The Indonesia–Malaya area can claim more than 75,000,000

Muslims; their chief relations with the Muslims of other areas have been with the Arab world, although recently they have shown a new interest in China. The Pakistan–India area, including Burma and Ceylon, is the largest with more than 105,000,000 Muslims using Urdu as a language fairly widely known; their ties have been more with the Arab and Iranian areas than with others. The Iranian area includes some 3,000,000 Shi'as in Iraq, 1,100,000 in Afghanistan, and 1,400,000 in Tadzhik, in the Soviet Union. If the Shi'as in Pakistan, India, Arabia, and Africa are included, the total area of Iranian influence would include more than 30,000,000 Muslims. The Turkish area extends from Sinkiang to the Balkans and includes most of the Muslims in the Soviet Union, some 60,000,000 Muslims. The Arab world, where the Arabic language and culture is dominant, includes more than 60,000,000 Muslims. In addition, the African Muslims, some 35,000,000 of them, tend to look to the Arab world for leadership. The Chinese Muslims have had little contact with their brothers in the rest of the Islamic world, but have had some ties with Arabia, Egypt, and the Turkish area.

It is interesting to note that almost half of the Turkish Muslims, a tenth of the Iranian, and all the Chinese Muslims—a total of 71,000,000—are in Communist-dominated areas.

CHAPTER THREE

Islamic Beliefs and Code of Laws

Mahmud Shaltout

In the Name of Allah, the Beneficent, the Merciful

Islam is the religion of Allah revealed to the Prophet Muhammad (Allah bless him and give him peace) in order that he might proclaim it to all mankind and men might be able to believe in it and put its teachings and regulations into practice. The Apostle transmitted the Scripture precisely as it was revealed to him, explained its fundamental teachings, and in his own life followed the principles and regulations of the Holy Revelation. Since the time of the Prophet, Muslims have for generation after generation received the Qur'an as it was given to the Apostle himself from Allah, passing it on precisely as it was taught at the beginning—whereof there is no doubt whatsoever.

It has been definitely proved that the Qur'an could not possibly be the work of Muhammad or of any other human being, as is clearly seen when one considers its style, the treasures of teachings contained in it, and the environment in which Muhammad lived. In the Scripture itself Allah defiantly stressed the impossibility of imitating the Qur'an when He said to the unbelievers, "And if ye are in doubt concerning that which We reveal unto Our slave (Muhammad), then produce a surah of the like thereof, and call your witnesses beside Allah if ye are truthful. And if ye do it not—and ye can never do it—then guard yourselves against the fire prepared for disbelievers, whose fuel is of men and stones" (Surah II, 23–24). Such a final demonstration that the Scripture was revealed by Allah to Muhammad is the Muslim's authority for recognizing the Qur'an as the principle source of Islamic beliefs and the Islamic code governing practices.

After the Apostle had been called by Allah, the *ulama*—those leaders who were well-versed in Islam—recognized that there were two types of texts in the Qur'an: those which are clear and definite and those which could have more than one meaning. The Quranic texts which are clear and definite are concerned with the basic beliefs like belief in Allah and the Last Day. These texts also cover the origin of law, whether religious laws governing prayer, religious tax, and fasting, or prohibitions against such acts as manslaughter or attacks on the chastity of a woman, and laws governing the use of property. For them no freedom of interpretation is allowed. The texts which could have more than one meaning are concerned with subsidiary aspects of Islam, but not its fundamentals, and have given rise to a plurality of Muslim theories and attitudes which are more or less personal points of view and are far from being obligatory.

Islam, except in matters concerning its basic beliefs and the principles of its code of practices, is not limited to one type of thinking or one specific legislative method. It is a tolerant religion which authorizes and permits wise liberality. As it has demonstrated throughout the Muslim world, Islam fits into all major cultures and constructive civilizations—and will continue to do so forever.

The Qur'an, the principal basis of Islam, shows us that Islam cannot find its way into any heart or mind without the acceptance of its two basic branches: the beliefs and the code of laws. Islam requires, first of all, a deep belief in it without any doubt or suspicion, as is made clear in many texts of the Qur'an and in the general agreement of the ulama of Islam. This emphasis on the primacy of belief was the first message of Muhammad to the Arabs, just as it was the message of all apostles and prophets; as the Qur'an says, "Say (O Muslims): We believe in Allah and that which is revealed unto us and that which was revealed unto Abraham, and Ishmael, and Isaac, and Jacob, and the tribes, and that which Moses and Jesus received, and that which the Prophets received from their Lord. We make no distinction between any of them, and unto Him we have surrendered" (Surah II, 136).

The code of laws provides the regulations which create the proper relations between man and God, such as saying prayers, fasting, and other religious duties; they guide man in his relations with his brother in Islam or the non-Muslim community, in organizing the structure of the family and encouraging reciprocal affection; they lead man to an understanding of his place in the universe, encouraging research into the nature of man and animals and guiding man in the use of the benefits of the natural world.

The Qur'an makes clear that the result of belief is faith, and the result of the code of laws is good behavior, as is shown in many texts: "Lo! Those who believe and do good works, theirs are the Gardens of the Paradise for welcome, Wherein they will abide, with no desire to be removed from thence" (Surah XVIII, 108–9). "Lo! Those who say: Our Lord is Allah, and thereafter walk aright, there shall no fear come upon them neither shall they grieve" (Surah XLVI, 13).

Islam is both belief and legislation which organizes all the relationships of man. Belief is the basis of the code of laws and the code of laws is the result of belief, for legislation without belief is a building without a foundation—and belief without a code of laws to put it into effect would be merely theoretical and ineffective. Thus, in Islam there is an intimate interrelation between belief and the code of laws governing all conduct, and those who deny this can by no means be considered to be Muslims.

Islam calls upon all people to accept its beliefs and code of laws regardless of race, sex, color, rank, or any other difference. All people are equal before Allah and must bear their own responsibility to accept the revelations of the Qur'an: "O mankind! Lo! We have created you male and female, and have made you nations and tribes that ye may know one another. Lo! the noblest of you in the sight of Allah, is the best in conduct" (Surah XLIX, 13). "It will not be in accordance with your desires, nor the desires of the People of the Scripture [i.e., Jews and Christians]. He who doeth wrong will have the recompense thereof, and will not find against Allah any protecting friend or helper. And whoso doeth good works, whether of male or female, and he (or she) is a believer, such will enter paradise and they will not be wronged the dint in a date-stone" (Surah IV, 123–24).

Those two verses make clear that the descendants or relatives of any of the apostles have no more rights in His sight than any common believer. They also emphasize that men and women bear equal religious responsibility, regardless of their sexual differences. The woman's responsibility is quite independent of that of her mate; his good behavior will not benefit her and his bad actions will not harm her. Each will receive in the eternal abode the reward or punishment which his—or her—actions merit. "Allah citeth an example for those who disbelieve: the wife of Noah and the wife of Lot, who were under two of our righteous slaves yet betrayed them so that they (the husbands) availed them naught against Allah and it was said (unto them): Enter the Fire along with those who enter" (Surah LXVI, 10).

The son is also responsible for himself once he attains majority. The belief and behavior of his parents neither benefit nor harm him, nor does his belief and behavior benefit or harm his parents. Thus says the Qur'an, "O mankind! Keep your duty to your Lord and fear a Day when the parent will not be able to avail the child aught, nor the child to avail the parent" (Surah XXXI, 33).

Thus it is clear that it is the individual responsibility of each person to accept the revelation of Allah—the Islamic beliefs and code of laws governing conduct—regardless of sex, rank, race, or any other difference.

The Fundamental Beliefs of Islam

A man announces his acceptance of the beliefs of Islam and his commitment to its code of regulations, he manifests the existence of Muslim beliefs in his heart, when he repeats the Word of Witness: *I witness that there is no God but Allah and that Muhammad is His Prophet.* To witness that Allah is One includes a perfect belief in Him as the source of creation and knowledge and the object of worship. To witness that Muhammad is His messenger includes a perfect belief in the Angels, the Scriptures, the messengers, the Day of Resurrection, and the principles on which the code of laws is based. This witness is the key to Islam, subjecting one to its beliefs and regulations. "The messenger believeth in that which hath been revealed unto him from his Lord and (so do) the believers. Each one believeth in Allah and His angels and His scriptures and His messengers—We make no distinction between any of His messengers—and they say: We hear, and we obey" (Surah II, 285). "It is not righteousness that ye turn your faces to the East and the West; but righteous is he who believeth in Allah and the Last Day and the angels and the Scripture and the Prophets" (Surah II, 177).

We must believe in the existence and oneness of Allah, that He is the only creator and disposer of the universe, that He has no partner, that there is no comparable being, and that none but Allah is worthy of worship. "Say: He is Allah, the One! Allah, the eternally Besought of all! He begotteth not nor was begotten. And there is none comparable unto Him" (Surah CXII). "Say: Shall I seek another than Allah for Lord, when He is Lord of all things?" (Surah VI, 165). "Say: Shall I choose for a protecting friend other than Allah, the Originator of the heavens and the earth, who feedeth and is never fed?" (Surah VI, 14).

We must believe in all the messengers of Allah of whom we are informed by the Qur'an from Noah to Muhammad (Allah bless them and give them peace). Allah selects some of his slaves and prepares them through ideal education to be His messengers to mankind. Some of these apostles are mentioned in the Qur'an and other are not mentioned; we must believe in all of them.

We must believe in Angels, the ambassadors of the revelation from Allah to His apostles, and, of necessity, in the Scriptures, His messages to humanity. The principles of legislation of Allah are His laws that we must follow; we must not sanction that which Allah has forbidden, nor forbid that which He allows us to do. We must believe in the contents of all the messages concerning the code of laws which aims at the organization of human life in a way which meets the needs of mankind and promotes human welfare in accordance with His justice and mercy.

We must believe in the Day of Judgment and the Other World, which is the only eternal life and is the life of reward and punishment.

We have to believe in all of these facts.

Anyone who denies one of these Muslim facts cannot be treated as a Muslim nor subjected to the Muslim rules. Yet it does not follow that he who does not believe in any of these facts would be considered a nonbeliever by Allah and would therefore suffer eternal damnation. It simply means that he would not be treated as a Muslim; he would not be under any obligation to worship Allah according to Muslim rules. He would not be prevented from doing things prohibited by Islam—such as drinking wine or eating pork—and on death he would not be washed and prayed for by Muslims.

Man will, however, be considered to be an unbeliever if, after having been freely convinced of the truth of these beliefs, he rejects them, or any part of them, through obstinacy, pride, love of mammon or the pomp of power, or the fear of being criticized. But if these beliefs had not been presented to him at all, or were presented in a hateful way, or were presented in a true and right way but he was incapable of fully understanding them, or even if he were capable but died before being fully convinced—in such cases a man is not an unbeliever according to Almighty Judgment and will not suffer everlasting punishment. The only disbelief mentioned in the Qur'an for which man will suffer judgment is a disbelief arising from obstinacy and pride. Hence the distant peoples to whom Islam has not been introduced, or those to whom it has been introduced in a hateful way, or those who have not understood the evidence even though they tried, will not suffer judgment. But they will by no means be treated as Muslims for they have not adopted the Word of Witness; they have not said with conviction, "I witness that there is no God but Allah and that Muhammad is His Prophet."

Islam, when it invites one to adopt its beliefs, does not use any compulsion, for it detests compulsion. Faith cannot be attained by force; there can never be true faith through obligation. The Scripture says, "There is no compulsion in religion" (Surah II, 256). "And if thy Lord willed, all who are in the earth would have believed together. Wouldst thou (Muhammad) compel men until they are believers?" (Surah X, 100). Not only is there no compulsion to adopt Islam, but Islam does not lead people to faith through spellbinding miracles which seek to convince without thought or the exercise of free choice. "If We will, We can send down on them from the sky a portent so that their necks would remain bowed before it" (Surah XXVI, 4).

Islam, in its invitation to accept its beliefs and to submit to its rules, rejects any methods which are not based on liberality and freedom of choice. Everyone has full liberty to embrace Islam voluntarily and through conviction. Thus Islam supports its beliefs through sound evidence and completely logical proofs. The Quranic evidence for the revelation of Allah—concerning belief in the One God, in Angels, the Scripture, the prophets, and the Last Day—is the Qur'an itself, the Word of Allah, whereof there is no doubt, as we have already seen. The logic of this belief is that all that is mentioned in the Qur'an is a matter of fact because it is supported by a standing miracle which will never cease, the Qur'an itself. "And thou (O Muhammad) wast not a reader of any scripture before it, nor didst thou write it with thy right hand, for then might those have doubted, who follow falsehood. But it is clear revelations in the hearts of those who have been given knowledge, and none deny our revelations save wrong-doers. And they say: Why are not portents sent down upon him from his Lord? Say: Portents are with Allah only, and I am but a plain warner. Is it not enough for them that We have sent down unto thee the Scripture which is read unto them? Lo! herein verily is mercy and a reminder for folk who believe" (Surah XXIX, 48–51).

Belief in Allah. The basic belief in Islam is belief in Allah—His existence, His unity, and His perfection. The evidence by which the Qur'an draws people's attention to the belief in Allah is based on reason and inner consciousness or intuition.

The rational evidence for belief in Allah is based on Islam's call to ponder on the nature of the universe—the earth, the heavens, the mysteries, the natural laws, the harmony and unity of the universe. Thus one comes to see that it is impossible that the universe could be self-created, or created by opposed or contradictory forces, or purposeless. This universe was created by an ultimate creative force; it was created by a supernatural force which guides and manages it through ultimate knowledge and wisdom. This universe is attaining its purposes through the will of the Almighty Creator. One of those purposes is its ultimate dissolution, after which comes the eternal abode, as we are told in many places in the Qur'an.

When the heaven is split asunder
And attentive to her Lord in fear,
And when the earth is spread out
And hath cast out all that was in her, and is empty
And attentive to her Lord in fear!

(Surah LXXXIV, 1–5)

When the heaven is cleft asunder,
When the planets are dispersed,
When the seas are poured forth,
And the sepulchres are overturned,
A soul will know what it hath sent before (it) and
what left behind.

(Surah LXXXII, 1–5)

When the sun is overthrown,
And when the stars fall,
And when the hills are moved,
And when the camels big with young are abandoned,
And when the wild beasts are herded together,
And when the seas rise,
And when souls are reunited,
And when the girl-child that was buried alive is asked
For what sin she was slain,

And when the pages are laid open,
And when the sky is torn away,
And when hell is lighted,
And when the garden is brought nigh,
(Then) every soul will know what it hath made ready.
(Surah LXXXI, 1–14)

By such rational evidence we are instructed in the Qur'an as to the ultimate end toward which the universe is moving, the final destruction which awaits all created things. In almost every Surah we find rational evidence proving that the universe was created and is sustained by Allah. "Lo! in the creation of the heavens and the earth, and the difference of night and day, and the ships which run upon the sea with that which is of use to men, and the water which Allah sendeth down from the sky, thereby reviving the earth after its death, and dispersing all kinds of beasts therein, and (in) the ordinance of the winds, and the clouds obedient between heaven and earth: are signs (of Allah's sovereignty) for people who have sense" (Surah II, 164). "And in the Earth are neighboring tracts, vineyards and ploughed lands, and date-palms, like and unlike, which are watered with one water. And We have made some of them to excel others in fruit. Lo! herein verily are portents for people who have sense" (Surah XIII, 4). "We have built the heavens with might, and We it is who made the vast extent (thereof)! And the earth have We laid out, how gracious was the Spreader (thereof)! And all things We have created by pairs, that haply ye may reflect" (Surah LI, 47–49). These are only a few examples illustrating the many texts which give rational evidence of the creative power of Allah.

The intuitional evidence for belief in Allah, the belief based upon the recognition of Allah by our inner consciousness, is brought to our attention in the Qur'an by pointing out the important psychological fact that there is an instinctive feeling of faith in Almighty Allah, the Creator of the universe, which comes to men when they are free from inclinations, or the distractions of dull routines, or when surprised by the question of the origin of the universe, or when faced with hardships or misfortunes which they cannot overcome by themselves. These facts are illustrated by many texts of the Qur'an. "And if thou (Muhammad) ask them: Who created the heavens and the earth, they will surely answer: The Mighty, the Knower created them" (Surah XLIII, 9). "When We show favor unto man, he withdraweth and turneth aside, but when ill toucheth him then he aboundeth in prayer" (Surah XLI, 51). "And if a wave enshroudeth them like awnings, they cry unto Allah, making their faith pure for Him only. But when He bringeth them safe to land, some of them compromise. None denieth Our signs save every traitor ingrate." (Surah XXXI, 32).

The Qur'an illustrates this sudden, instinctive faith in Allah by describing in detail Pharaoh's feeling when he was faced with death by drowning and realized the impossibility of escape, "And We brought the Children of Israel across the sea, Pharaoh with his hosts pursued them in rebellion and transgression, till, when the (fate of) drowning overtook him, he exclaimed: I believe that there is no God save Him in whom the Children of Israel believe, and I am of those who surrender (unto Him). What! Now! When hitherto thou has rebelled and been of the wrong-doers? But this day We save thee in thy body that thou mayest be a portent for those after thee. Lo! most of mankind are heedless of Our portents" (Surah X, 91–93). Thus we see that the belief in Allah is based on both rational evidence and intuitive insight, evidence which is available to all men who are not heedless of the Divine portents.

The Scripture also guides us to the Names and Qualities of Allah, all of which refer to His power, His wisdom, and all His perfections. Many of the Names are difficult to translate from the Arabic, for example, Allah is the One, the Eternally Besought of All, the First, the Last, the Beneficent, the Powerful, the Almighty, the Wise, the Knower, the Creator, the Shaper out of Naught, the Fashioner, the Guardian, the Majestic, the Superb, the Glorified. The Creator names Himself in this manner, "He is Allah, than whom there is no other God, the Knower of the invisible and the visible, He is the Beneficent, the Merciful. He is Allah, than whom there is no other God, the Sovereign Lord, the Holy One, Peace, the

Keeper of Faith, the Guardian, the Majestic, the Compeller, the Superb. Glorified be Allah from all that they ascribe as partner (unto Him). He is Allah, the Creator, the Shaper out of naught, the Fashioner. His are the most beautiful names. All that is in the heavens and the earth glorifieth Him, and He is the Mighty, the Wise" (Surah LIX, 22–24).

These names which show His superiority, mercy, and perfection are recognized by wise men to be true and justly applicable, because a true understanding of the nature of the universe indicates that these are the qualities of Allah. The wise man recognizes also that no other being in the universe is worthy of such names, for all these beings are creations—changeable, needy, and deficient. In the Qur'an the proper and comprehensive name which emphasizes His individuality is the *Ultimate Being*, known to Muslims as Allah, or the name of the Almighty and the Sublime.

Muslims call Him and worship Him by such names. For thus He saith: "Allah's are the fairest names. Invoke Him by them. And leave the company of those who blaspheme His names. They will be requited what they do" (Surah VII, 180). It is forbidden for a Muslim to invoke Him by a name or an adjective that is not mentioned in His Scripture or by His Apostle.

The Ultimate Being can be described, but not conceived by man. When the Qur'an guides men to belief in Allah, it aims at turning man's thought from the fruitless attempt to know the essence and reality of His Ultimate Being and instead to guide men to know His creative ability and the activities which reveal His qualities, His might and perfection. The Qur'an shows that He is above all qualities possessed by His creation, that His qualities are divine and superior and that attempts to know His essence, to describe Him by such concepts as monism or pantheism, will fail. For He saith, "Such is Allah, your Lord. There is no God save Him, the Creator of all things, so worship Him. And He taketh care of all things. Vision comprehendeth Him not, but he comprehendeth (all) vision. He is the Subtile, the Aware" (Surah, VI, 103–4).

The story of Moses (the Blessing of Allah be upon him) when he asked his Creator to show him Himself, is a good illustration of the impossibility of knowing the essence of the Ultimate Being. "And when We did appoint for Moses thirty nights (of solitude), and added to them ten, and he completed the whole time appointed by his Lord of forty nights; and Moses said unto his brother: Take my place among the people. Do right, and follow not the way of mischief-makers. And when Moses came to Our appointed tryst and his Lord had spoken unto him, he said: My Lord! Show me (Thy self), that I may gaze upon Thee. He said: Thou wilt not see Me, but gaze upon the mountain! If it stand still in its place, then thou wilt see Me. And when his Lord revealed (His) glory to the mountain He sent it crashing down. And Moses fell down senseless. And when he woke he said: Glory unto Thee! I turn unto Thee repentant, and I am the first of (true) believers" (Surah VII, 142–43). It is by such texts that the Qur'an makes clear that Allah can be described, His qualities can be partially known, but His essence cannot be conceived of by man.

One final point should be stressed in relation to the Islamic belief in Allah. Islam rejects all forms of polytheism. Allah is One. The Qur'an often reprimands those who believe in the existence of two gods, or in Trinitarianism, and those who worship any part of His creation such as the sun, the moon, or idols. The Qur'an calls upon such polytheists to consider the numerous evidences of His ultimate Unity. "If there were therein Gods beside Allah, then verily both (the heavens and the earth) had been disordered" (Surah XXI, 22). "Allah hath not chosen any son, nor is there any God along with Him; else would each God have assuredly championed that which he created, and some of them would assuredly have overcome others. Glorified be Allah above all that they allege" (Surah XXIII, 91). "Say: O People of the Scripture: Come to an agreement between us and you: that we shall worship none but Allah, and that we shall ascribe no partner unto Him, and that none of us shall take others for lords beside Allah"

(Surah III, 64). "Lo! I have turned my face toward Him Who created the heavens and the earth, as one by nature upright, and I am not of the idolaters" (Surah VI, 80). Thus it is seen that Islam clearly rejects all polytheism, Trinitarianism, and idolatry and worships only the One.

Belief in Angels, Jinn, and the soul. The first of the basic beliefs of Islam is the belief in Allah, as we have said. The second basic belief is the belief in Angels. The Scripture describes Angels as supernatural and says that such is their real nature that they do not appear in the material world generally, but only by divine command. The Qur'an says, "And they say: The Beneficent hath taken unto Himself a son. Be He glorified! Nay, but (those whom they call sons) are honoured slaves; They speak not until He hath spoken, and they act by His command" (Surah XXI, 26–27). The Angels' functions are concerned with spirits and souls. Some of these functions, through which they carry out His orders and His will, are recorded in the Quranic texts. Some of the Angels carry His revelations, His orders, His messages to His prophets and apostles: "And lo! it is a revelation of the Lord of the Worlds, Which the True Spirit hath brought down Upon thy heart, that thou mayest be (one) of the warners" (Surah XXVI, 192–94). Other Angels support the prophets and make the believers stand firm. "And we gave Jesus, son of Mary, clear proofs (of Allah's sovereignty) and We supported him with the holy Spirit [i.e., the angel Gabriel]" (Surah II, 253). "When thy Lord inspired the angels, (saying:) I am with you. So make those who believe stand firm. I will throw fear into the hearts of those who disbelieve" (Surah VIII, 12).

Other Angels are preachers who preach the true and the good and encourage believers by His good tidings of His eternal Paradise. "Lo! those who say: Our Lord is Allah, and afterward are upright, the angels descend upon them, saying: Fear not nor grieve, but hear good tidings of the paradise which ye are promised. We are your protecting friends in the life of the world and in the Hereafter. There ye will have (all) that your souls desire, and there ye will have (all) for which ye pray" (Surah XLI, 30–31).

Others are Angels of Death, such as Azrad. "Say: the Angel of death, who hath charge concerning you, will gather you, and afterward unto your Lord ye will be returned" (Surah XXXII, 11). "Those whom the angels cause to die (when they are) good. They say: Peace be unto you! Enter the Garden because of what ye used to do" (Surah XVI, 32). "Lo! as for those whom the angels take (in death) while they wrong themselves, (the angels) will ask: In what were ye engaged? They will say: We were oppressed in the land. (The angels) will say: Was not Allah's earth spacious that ye could have migrated therein? As for such, their habitation will be hell, an evil journey's end" (Surah IV, 97).

Other Angels are registers of the deeds of human beings, preserving the records until the Day of Judgment when they are shown to man. "Lo! there are above you guardians, Generous and recording, Who know (all) that ye do" (Surah LXXXII, 10–12).

Such exemplary functions, like all other functions of the Angels, are supernatural. The Qur'an describes Angels as "Messengers with wings and force." "Allah chooseth from the angels messengers, and (also) from mankind" (Surah XXII, 75). "Praise be to Allah, the Creator of the heavens and the earth, who appointeth the angels messengers having wings two, three, and four. He multiplieth in creation what He will. Lo! Allah is Able to do all things" (Surah XXXV, 1). As has been demonstrated previously, the Qur'an is the basic resource of Islam and therefore the Muslim's belief in Angels must be fully limited by definite Quranic texts, which are the only source of such supernatural facts.

Another kind of supernatural creature is the Jinn. The Qur'an differentiates between Jinn and Angels in several ways. Concerning the substance of the Jinn, the Qur'an states several times that He created them from fire. "And the Jinn did We create aforetime of essential fire" (Surah XV, 27).

Some of the Jinn are virtuous, others are wicked. According to the Qur'an, speaking of the Jinn, "And there are among us some who have surrendered (to Allah) and there are among us some who are unjust. And whoso hath surrendered to Allah, such have taken the right path purposefully. And as for those who are unjust, they are firewood for hell" (Surah LXXII, 14–15). In contrast, we have seen above that the Angels are "honoured slaves."

Angels, as we mentioned previously, are the messengers of Allah to His prophets and apostles, but Jinn, like mankind, receive the revelations through His apostles. This is shown in the Quranic text, addressed to Muhammad, "And when We inclined toward thee (Muhammad) certain of the Jinn, who wished to hear the Qur'an, when they were in its presence, said: Give ear! and, when it was finished, turned back to their people, warning. They said: O our people! Lo! we have heard a Scripture which hath been revealed after Moses, confirming that which was before it, guiding unto the truth and a right road. O our people! respond to Allah's summoner and believe Him. He will forgive you some of your sins and guard you from a painful doom" (Surah XLVI, 29–31).

Jinn share with mankind the responsibility of hearing and believing Muslim teachings. On the Judgment Day, both mankind and Jinn will be called by Allah in the same way and will be responsible in the same degree. "In the day when He will gather them together (He will say): O ye assembly of the jinn! Many of humankind did ye seduce. And their adherents among humankind will say: Our Lord! We enjoyed one another, but now we have arrived at the appointed term which Thou appointedst for us. He will say: Fire is your home. Abide therein for ever, save him whom Allah willeth (to deliver). Lo! thy Lord is Wise, Aware" (Surah VI, 129). But the Angels do not share with mankind the same responsibilities.

The Qur'an makes it clear in many passages that Angels possess all the spiritual virtues and none of the shortcomings of human beings, while the Jinn are described as sometimes being whisperers and provocators—evils which are sometimes found in men.

Concerning the soul, or spirit, the Qur'an says very little. "And (remember) when thy Lord said unto the angels: Lo! I am creating a mortal out of potter's clay of black mud altered, So, when I have made him and have breathed into him of My spirit, do ye fall down, prostrating yourselves unto him" (Surah XV, 28–29). There is another text in which He says, "Why, then, when (the soul) cometh up to the throat (of the dying) And ye are at that moment looking" (Surah LVI, 83–84). All that we can deduce from such texts is that the soul is the source of life, and that it is the vital force of existence without which beings become lifeless. As to the precise nature of the soul, the Qur'an says nothing. However, there is no Quranic text which prohibits searching for such a supernatural spirit, whether or not such researches might be fruitful. His saying, "They will ask thee concerning the Spirit. Say: The Spirit is by command of my Lord, and of knowledge ye have been vouchsafed but little" (Surah XVII, 85), indicates that the identification of the soul is His own concern and that the human mind is too limited to understand such a supernatural reality. This has been a subject of scientific research, but up to now those who have studied the problem have not reached a clear understanding about the soul.

Concerning the soul after death, the texts of the Scripture and the sayings of the Prophet say nothing except that the soul remains after death, either living in ease and comfort or in torment. Thus He saith, "Think not of those, who are slain in the way of Allah, as dead. Nay, they are living. With their Lord they have provision. Jubilant (are they) because of that which Allah hath bestowed upon them of His bounty" (Surah III, 169–70).

Belief in the Apostles. Belief in Angels is the highest stage of belief which leads to the right way, the belief in Allah. Belief in apostles is not a belief in the supernatural, for they are men with the same human nature that other men have. They differ from other men in that they have been selected by Allah and authorized to receive His revelations through His Angels in order that they may proclaim them to mankind and lead men in practicing their teachings. Such a divine selection preserves them from error in all that they proclaim of His divine messages. At the same time, their very human nature and qualities make it easy for believers to accept what they say and imitate what they do. He saith, "And We sent not (as Our messengers) before thee other than men whom We inspired. Ask the followers of the Reminder [i.e., the Jewish Scripture] if ye know not? We gave them not bodies that would not eat food, nor were they immortals" (Surah XXI, 7–8).

It is a divine fact that in all ages Allah has sent His messages to men through His apostles to direct and strengthen human beings toward good. Since the dawn of creation it has been the aim of the divine will to further the spiritual progress of man by providing the guidance which enables man to arrange his daily affairs so that he lives wisely and correctly, "and there is not a nation but a warner hath passed among them" (Surah XXXV, 24). Thus messages have been revealed again and again with the one purpose of guiding man to perfection. Each age had its message and each generation had the chance to hear His words. In all these messages, the principles taught were the same. "He hath ordained for you that religion which He commended unto Noah, and that which We inspire in thee (Muhammad), and that which We commended unto Abraham and Moses and Jesus, saying: Establish the religion, and be not divided therein" (Surah XLII, 13).

The Messenger Muhammad illustrated the unity of divine messages by saying that all the apostles are builders of one house, the earlier apostles laying the foundation for the later ones who build upon their foundation. The Qur'an calls upon mankind to believe in all His messengers as well as in the scriptures revealed to them. To believe in some apostles and reject others is a fallacy from the Islamic point of view. The Qur'an says, "Say (O Muslims): We believe in Allah and that which is revealed unto us and that which was revealed unto Abraham, and Ishmael, and Isaac, and Jacob, and the tribes, and that which Moses and Jesus received, and that which the Prophets received from their Lord. We make no distinction between any of them, and unto Him we have surrendered" (Surah II, 136). "And who believe in that which is revealed unto thee (Muhammad) and that which was revealed before thee, and are certain of the Hereafter" (Surah II, 4).

Those who believe in some apostles and reject others will be punished, for the Qur'an says, "Lo! those who disbelieve in Allah and His messengers, and seek to make distinction between Allah and His messengers, and say: We believe in some and disbelieve in others, and seek to choose a way in between; Such are disbelievers in truth; and for disbelievers We prepare a shameful doom" (Surah IV, 150–51). On the other hand, those who believe in all of His apostles will receive their reward. "But those who believe in Allah and His messengers and make no distinction between any of them, unto them Allah will give their wages; and Allah was ever Forgiving, Merciful" (Surah IV, 152).

The message of the Apostle Muhammad includes the foundations of all the previous messages which guide humanity to perfection and open the way to human progress, both materially and spiritually. Islam calls mankind to believe that Muhammad is the last of all prophets and apostles, as is made clear in the Qur'an, "Muhammad is not the father of any man among you, but he is the messenger of Allah and the Seal of the Prophets; and Allah is Aware of all things" (Surah XXXIII, 40). "This day have I perfected your religion for you and completed My favour unto you, and have chosen for you as religion AL-ISLAM" (Surah V, 3).

Muhammad's message, or Islam, is addressed to every human being in all ages and all over the world, regardless of color, race, nationality, or any other difference. "Say (O Muhammad): O mankind! Lo! I am the messenger of Allah to you all" (Surah VII, 158). The messages of the apostles before Muhammad differed from his in that they were limited to the apostle's people or tribe, as the Qur'an shows. "We sent Noah (of old) unto his people, and he said: O my people: Serve Allah. Ye have no other God save him" (Surah VII, 59).

"And unto (the tribe of) A'ad (We sent) their brother, Hud" (Surah VII, 65). "And to (the tribe of) Thamuḍ (We sent) their brother Salih" (Surah VII, 73). And the Qur'an reveals concerning Jesus (the Blessings of Allah be upon him): "Allah createth what He will. If He decreeth a thing, He saith unto it only: Be! and it is. And He will teach him [Jesus] the Scripture and wisdom, and the Torah and the Gospel. And will make him a messenger unto the children of Israel" (Surah III, 47–49). Thus we see that Muhammad, the last of the prophets, brought a message which was unique in that it was addressed to all men everywhere.

It should be clearly understood that, according to the Quranic texts, the function of the apostles is limited to guiding and educating people through revelation. They are worthy of the highest degree of honor and respect, for they are fully authorized to assume spiritual and educational leadership for all men, but they have no authority over people's beliefs, minds, or hearts. They are in no way responsible for the unbeliever. They have no power to confer any benefit or to inflict any punishment on themselves or other human beings. He saith, "We have not sent thee (O Muhammad) as a warden over them" (Surah XVII, 54). "Thy people (O Muhammad) have denied it, though it is the Truth. Say: I am not put in charge of you" (Surah VI, 66). "Say: For myself I have no power to benefit, nor power to hurt, save that which Allah willeth" (Surah VII, 188).

The apostles are human beings. The Qur'an asserts that the fact that their messages were divine revelations did not change their human nature or make them into supernatural beings. They were highly honored to be selected as messengers, but they remain human; their only infallibility is that given them by Allah concerning the religious facts revealed through them. The Qur'an says, "Say: I am only a mortal like you. My Lord inspireth in me that your God is only One God. And whoever hopeth for the meeting with his Lord, let him do righteous work, and make none sharer of the worship due unto his Lord" (Surah XVIII, 111). As human beings, in all matters other than the messages of Allah, apostles can be right or wrong like any other human beings. It is recorded in the Qur'an that Allah admonished His Apostle Muhammad for some of his actions, as for instance when the Apostle was distracted from his responsibilities to the Muslims by his honorable aim to preach to the idolators (Surah LXXX, 1–10).

We have seen that worship may be offered only to Allah. Islam states that no Angel or human being is entitled to any kind of worship. No human being can be of any assistance in the Day of Judgment, nor can a human being remit any sins, for himself or for others. Only Allah has the power to pardon or punish, only Allah is entitled to worship. And just as no Angel or prophet is entitled to worship, so also no worship may be offered to any of the educated believers, the leaders in Islam, no matter how distinguished. Islam has no saints in the sense of beings with intercessory powers who may be worshiped. Rather than saints in that sense, Islam has Allah's *Aoulia*, that is, His constant obeyers, His favorites. According to the Qur'an they have no special distinction which gives them any sort of saintliness or supernatural ability such as the authority to intercede or remit sins. The constant obeyers, or favorites of Allah, are true believers who follow the apostles in all that is revealed to them by Allah, obeying the divine commands and avoiding that which He prohibits.

Some people, influenced by non-Muslim sources, say that Allah has, in addition to the apostles, His distinctive slaves who are authorized by Him to rule the universe and to respond and fulfill the people's demands. It is even said that when such "saints" die they should have distinctive tombs, high domed, and lighted at night; that one should seek their blessings, offer them pledges, and bow before them. Such errors have become popular among some Muslims and in other religious congregations, but all such errors are entirely rejected by His religion in all His messages.

Belief in the scriptures. To accept and believe in the messages of Allah is a mere logical consequence of belief in Angels and apostles. The messages are the contents of all His scriptures, which include instruction concerning true beliefs and the fundamental principles for codes of law which guide men in distinguishing the approved from the forbidden in human actions. Islam calls mankind to believe in all His scriptures which have been revealed through the apostles—such as Abraham's Books, Moses' Bible, Jesus' Gospel, and Muhammad's Qur'an. From the Muslim point of view, no one who denies any of these scriptures is considered to be a believer.

It also follows that if Muhammad is the final Apostle, the Qur'an is the final Scripture. The Qur'an, as is known to anyone who is thoroughly acquainted with its contents, states the basic beliefs, the basic principles of worship and of human dealings, and the ideals of morality. The Quranic texts do not give in detail the code of laws regulating dealings—human actions—but they give the general principles which guide people to perfection, to a life of harmony—to an inner harmony between man's appetites and his spiritual desires, to harmony between man and the natural world, and to a harmony between individuals as well as a harmony with the society in which men live. The means of establishing harmony which are revealed in the Qur'an are based on faith and justice, and a wise understanding of human nature.

It is not the function of the Qur'an to explain in detail the facts of the universe, its secrets and the useful ways in which it can serve mankind. It does, however, urge men to use their minds and skills to gain understanding of the universe, its secrets and its wonderful phenomena. It opens the way for man to use his mind and powers in whatever vocation falls to his lot, to increase his knowledge, and to strengthen his faith in the Almighty. It guides mankind to individual and social welfare and establishes justice among men. The Qur'an limits the human mind only in basic beliefs and principles of legislation, a wise limitation which is necessary to guide the people's faith and bring them to submission to Allah.

Belief in the Last Day. The fifth principle of faith in Islam—after faith in Allah, Angels, apostles, and the scriptures

—is belief in the Day of Resurrection, the Judgment Day. It is the end of man and His goal in the creation of man. "And that man hath only that for which he maketh effort, And that his effort will be seen, And afterward he will be repaid for it with fullest payments (Surah LIII, 39–41). What happens to a man on the Last Day—his reward or punishment, his pleasure or pain,—is determined by what he has chosen to do in this world. The Other World is the world of judgment for what man has done. "On the day when We shall summon all men with their record, whoso is given his book in his right hand—such will read their book and they will not be wronged a shred. Whoso is blind here will be blind in the Hereafter, and yet further from the road" (Surah XVII, 71–72). Thus the belief in the judgment of the Last Day is the strongest motive for man to seek perfection and progress in this world in order that he may be accepted and favored by Allah in the Other World.

The Qur'an mentions in various places the rewards and sufferings which will come to men in the Other World. Although it uses phrases that are commonly used by man in his daily life, Islamic sources emphasize that life in the Other World is a new life that differs from life in this world in everything except the names.

> But for him who feareth the standing before his Lord
> there are two gardens.
> Which is it, of the favors of your Lord, that ye deny?
> Of spreading branches.
> Which is it, of the favors of your Lord, that ye deny?
> Wherein are two fountains flowing.
> Which is it, of the favors of your Lord, that ye deny?
> Wherein is every kind of fruit in pairs.
> Which is it, of the favors of your Lord, that ye deny?
> Reclining upon couches lined with silk brocade,
> the fruit of both gardens near to hand.
>
> (Surah LV, 46–54)

Concerning the sufferings in the Other World, He saith, "The guilty will be known by their marks, and will be taken by the forelocks and the feet" (Surah LV, 41). "While the reward of disbelievers is the Fire" (Surah XIII, 35). "And lo! for all such, hell will be the promised place" (Surah XV, 43). Thus in many passages does the Qur'an describe the blessings and sufferings of the Other World in a way which urges men to believe according to the teachings of Allah's messages and to act in accordance with the principles of dealings laid down in the Quranic texts.

A Muslim never doubts, nor hesitates to hold a firm belief in, the eternity of the blessings of the Other World. He knows that those who obstinately continue to be disbelievers will be punished for that disbelief which contradicts the natural disposition of man. That punishment, according to the Qur'an, will continue eternally. It is not definitely stated in the Qur'an whether Hell is everlasting or not, but it is clearly stated that Paradise and its blessings are eternal. In all matters of belief concerning the Last Day and the Other World, the human mind is subject to the definite Quranic texts and the sayings of the Apostle.

These, then, are the beliefs of Islam: belief in Allah the One God, in Angels, in the apostles, in the scriptures, and in the Day of Judgment. These beliefs are, according to Islam, the basis of every divine religion; therefore, the religions which are not founded on them are false religions. Allah rejects the disbelievers, those who are polytheists, who do not believe in Angels, or in the apostles, or in the scriptures, or in the Last Day—and He invites them all to believe in Islam through logical thought and acceptance of the evidence revealed to men.

Man was called by Allah to adopt these beliefs. As an expression of His mercy and His goodness to His slaves, He has made man master of the earth, God's deputy on earth to make use of its blessings by using and developing its natural resources. Allah has called upon man to study the universe in order that he may see and understand the wonders of His creation which confirm man's faith and lead him to spiritual and material progress. The Qur'an says, "He it is Who created for you all that is in the earth" (Surah II, 29). "See ye not how Allah hath made serviceable unto you whatsoever is in the skies and whatsoever is in the earth and hath loaded you with His favors both without and within?" (Surah XXXI, 20). "Allah it is Who hath made the sea of service unto you that the ships may run thereon by His command, and that ye may seek His bounty, and that haply ye may be thankful; And hath made of service unto you whatsoever is in the heavens and whatsoever is in the earth; it is all from Him. Lo! herein verily are portents for people who reflect" (Surah XLV, 12–13).

Islam states that Allah created man with a disposition which leads him sometimes to choose the good and sometimes to choose the evil way of life. His good deeds lead him to his own happiness, to social welfare, and to his being acceptable to Allah, while his evil deeds lead him to unhappiness and to destruction in this life and damnation in the next. For thus saith Allah,

> Did We not assign unto him two eyes
> And a tongue and two lips,
> And guide him to the parting of the mountain ways?
> But he hath not attempted the Ascent—
> Ah, what will convey unto thee what the Ascent is!—
> (It is) to free a slave,
> And to feed in the day of hunger
> An orphan near of kin,
> Or some poor wretch in misery,
> And to be of those who believe and exhort one another
> to perseverence and exhort one another to pity.
>
> (Surah XC, 8–17)

The purpose of Allah's messages and revelations is to strengthen the good tendencies of men and guide them to perfection in this life, thus laying the foundations for the next life. Islam points out that each man must choose for himself the way to happiness through good deeds or the way to unhappiness and punishment through wickedness. Islam, in placing the responsibility on each individual, makes no distinction between human beings; each is given the same rights and responsibilities regardless of his sex, race, color, or other differences. Blessed are faithful and true believers. The Qur'an says, "Whosoever doeth right, whether male or female, and is a believer, him verily We shall quicken with good life, and We shall pay them a recompense in proportion to the best of what they used to do" (Surah XVI, 97).

In the eyes of Islam a man chooses either good or evil by his own free will and is rewarded or punished according to his deeds. He is only guided and advised by the messages of Allah and by the apostles but is still completely free to choose as he wishes. It is quite clear that if Allah wanted to He would have created man wholly good and completely ignorant of all evil. Since man has been created free to choose between good and evil, he will be rewarded or punished on Doomsday according to what he has chosen. There is no supernatural force which limits a man or compels him to adopt any mode of behavior. What is called fate, or testing, is nothing but the operation of natural laws, such as the principles of cause and effect and of the freedom of man.

In former times, disbelievers excused themselves by saying that they had been predestined to certain actions by His will. But the Almighty rejected such an excuse and made it clear that full responsibility is thrown on each man because of his free mind and the guidance given by the apostles. "They who are idolaters will say: Had Allah willed, we had not ascribed (unto Him) partners neither had our fathers, nor had we forbidden aught. Thus did those who were before them give the lie (to Allah's messengers) till they tasted of the fear of Us. Say: Have ye any knowledge that ye can adduce for us? Lo! ye follow naught but an opinion. Lo! ye do not guess. Say—For Allah's is the final judgment—Had He willed He could indeed have guided all of you" (Surah VI, 149–50). It is true enough that the Almighty foresees how man will act; but this foresight is nothing other than divine knowledge of the freedom of choice, which is a natural law.

Therefore, Islam does not allow a man to wander from the rightful faith and then offer the workings of fate as his excuse. For if that were so, His commandments, the missions of the apostles, the scriptures, and the promise of reward and punishment would all be null and void, impossible to reconcile with the Almighty's Wisdom and Justice.

The Islamic Code

In the name of God, the Merciful, the Most Compassionate

In the introduction to this chapter it was stated that the Qur'an, the all-embracing source of the true concept of Islam, says that Islam is both a faith and a code. Up to this point we have discussed the beliefs that must be held with the head and the heart if one is to be a Muslim. The acceptance or rejection of these beliefs determines the dividing line between loyalty to Islam and infidelity.

The Islamic code is the name given to the principles and laws which God revealed and which He requires all Muslims to adhere to strictly in all their actions, whether in their relations with Him or in their dealings with mankind. The actions through which Muslims draw near to their Lord, recall His greatness, and show their trust in Him by their observance of His divine rules are known in Islam as *worship of God*. The actions through which Muslims uphold their interests and repel evils in themselves, between themselves and their neighbors, and between Muslims and non-Muslims, the actions through which they prevent maltreatment, preserve rights, fulfill the general good, and establish peace and security, are known in Islam as *dealings*. The great number of laws which make up the Islamic code are classified under these two headings: worship and dealings.

Worship of God. The worship of God is made up of prayers, fasting, payment of religious tax, and pilgrimage. Basic to the worship of God is the acknowledgment of God's oneness and Muhammad's heavenly purpose in life, the cleansing of the heart and soul, the strict observance of obedience to God in all actions. This is the foundation, these are the pillars on which Islam is built. Therefore the Prophet (may God bless him) has said, "Islam is put upon five principles: belief in the single God and in Muhammad as His Messenger, performance of prayers, payment of religious tax, keeping of the month of Ramadan, and pilgrimage to the Holy Mosque by whoever finds the way clear to do it."

Prayer. Prayer is a form of physical worship assigned to the Muslim five times a day at specified times. In prayer he stands wherever he happens to be at the appointed time and turns his face toward the Divine Mosque in Mecca. He begins his prayer by saying in a fairly loud voice, "God is the Most Great," praying reverently with profound intent to worship God. He then recites the Good Book's first Surah, along with a passage of the Qur'an which he has learned by heart, trying to understand its inner meaning. He then bows by bending until his back makes a straight horizontal line, holding his knees with his hands, and saying to himself as he bows, "Great God." Then he lifts his head, saying, "God the Most Great," and kneels down, touching his forehead to the floor, saying as he goes down, "God the Highest." He then lifts his head, saying "God the Most Great," and sits comfortably on his heels. Then he touches the floor with his forehead a second time. This process is called one kneeling.

There are five daily prayers. First is the morning prayer which the Muslim performs at the beginning of his day between the small hours of the morning and sunrise. It is made up of two kneelings, at the end of which the worshiper sits to salute his Lord, admitting His oneness and the mission of His Prophet in a manner which has been universally copied from Muhammad (may God bless him). He then salutes the right side and the left side with the words, "Peace be upon you together with God's blessings." The second prayer is the midday prayer which is performed from noon until halfway between noon and sundown. The afternoon prayer comes between midafternoon and sunset. Each of those prayers is made up of four kneelings. The early evening prayer is three kneelings and is offered between sunset and the vanishing from the horizon of the twilight. The late evening prayer is performed after the twilight disappears; it is the last prayer of the day when the Muslim welcomes the night, and is made up of four kneelings.

With these prayers the Muslim thinks of his Lord five times during each day and night, appearing before his Lord repeatedly and saluting His name within his heart and soul, submitting himself to God, looking forward to His favor. Therefore he perseveres in obeying His commands.

The Muslim can perform these prayers anywhere—at the mosque, at home, in the field, at the factory, in the office—wherever he happens to be when the time falls due for prayer. He can pray alone, or he can pray with others standing in a line or lines arrayed closely in straight formation, like a highly-disciplined military parade, behind a leader who is followed by the congregation in all that he does. Congregational prayer in Islam is the best form of prayer because it encourages acquaintanceship, intimacy, cooperation, joint entreaty, remembrance, and cheerful submission to God, the Lord of all peoples.

Muslims are reminded of the time for prayer by the call to prayer which is given from the minaret of the mosque in the form taught by the Prophet, "God is Most Great. God is Most Great. I avow that there is no God other than Allah. I avow that there is no God other than Allah. I declare openly that Muhammad is the Messenger of God. I declare openly that Muhammad is the Messenger of God. Welcome prayer. Welcome prayer. Welcome good fortune. Welcome good fortune. God is Most Great. God is Most Great. There is no God but Allah."

Islam also has a weekly prayer, known as the Friday prayer because it is performed at noon on Friday. It is a congregational service with preaching before the prayer, which is made up of two kneelings. There are also two other prayers like the Friday prayer which are performed twice a year on the mornings of the two Islamic feasts, the first day following the month of Ramadan and the tenth day of the month of Dhu'l Hijja. These two prayers are known in Islam as the prayers of the two feasts, Ramadan and al-Qurban.

In addition to the daily prayers, the Friday prayer, and the prayers of the two feasts, there is in Islam the funeral prayer, a religious ceremony expressing the Muslims' loyalty toward their dead. Muslims are required to prepare their dead for burial by cleaning the body and wrapping it from head to foot in unstitched cloth; the body is then placed on a bed and the mourners stand in line and, led by one of them, join in the prayer for the dead person. They repeat four times the phrase "God is Most Great" and recite together the preface to the Qur'an; then they ask God's blessing on the deceased. The body is later buried. According to Islam the grave may be in the ground or on the surface level, but should not be elevated either for a member of the masses or for a prophet who has completed a heavenly mission.

In this connection it should be pointed out that Islam has no other funeral ceremonies than those mentioned above. The elaborate rituals, the special places for ceremonies, the special funeral processions which are sometimes seen, the domes built over graves, all these have nothing whatever to do with Islam. Nor is there any basis in Islam for the great respect paid to certain mausoleums with the object of securing blessings. Islam has nothing to say about visiting graveyards for inspiration or blessing. These customs have been copied by Muslims from others.

Islam is also opposed to the practice of withdrawing into monasteries or caves to repeat prayers. It looks upon the daily work to support one's family and to improve the life of the community as an obligation as important as prayer. Indeed, the daily prayers are assigned merely to fulfill the debt owed to God, and as a means of securing His aid in the daily struggle in the world. The Islamic code states clearly the everyday obligations of the Muslim which provide him with food for the soul through worship and further his material standing as an individual and promote the welfare of his community. Islamic law provides the best way for a man to maintain the right relationship with his Lord and a proper participation in the life of the world. This is not possible except for the Muslim.

Except for the five daily prayers which distinguish the Muslim from the non-Muslim, the daily routine of the Muslim is like that of other men. He carries on the business for which his talents qualify him, earning his livelihood, guarding his family and his interests, and abstaining from sin in matters of food and drink and evil amusements. Then he retires at night to relax from work and fatigue. Islam does not prevent the Muslim from enjoying the beautiful things of life and the favors of God. "Say: Who hath forbidden the adornment of Allah which He hath brought forth for His bondmen, and the good things of His providing?" (Surah VII, 32).

Fasting. Prayer is the first form of physical worship. The second is fasting—refraining from eating, drinking, and sexual intercourse all day from dawn to sunset during the whole month of Ramadan each year with the intention of showing submission to God's command. The act of fasting during Ramadan is the means by which the Muslim recognizes the favor God did to His subjects in the month of Ramadan when He began the revelation of the Qur'an to the Prophet Muhammad (may God bless him).

Fasting is the means by which the Muslim voluntarily abandons certain legitimate frivolous enjoyments as a means of putting his soul to a test and promoting its capacity for perseverence, thus strengthening his will to keep away from sins, both obvious and obscure. The Muslim thereby samples enough of starvation to make him a warm-hearted, hospitable person, sympathetic with the poor who are in constant want. This is precisely the spirit Islam endeavors to create in the Muslim's heart and mind by requiring fasting as a mode of worship. Therefore, Islam attaches no significance to the kind of fasting that does not inspire this great humanitarian spirit, and a person fasting for any other purpose has nothing to gain except hunger and thirst.

Religious tax. The third form of worship is the religious tax, *zakat*. This is a fiscal worship by which Islam requires the well-to-do to care for the needs of the poor and to pay a subsidy to maintain public benefits like hospitals, educational institutions, and a defense force. It is a sacred duty incumbent upon the rich to pay out of their possessions in excess of their requirements, and those of their dependents, portions which are universally recognized by Muslims as fair, and which in the aggregate meet the needs of the poor and the general interests of the community without adversely afflicting the owners. It is customary to give one-tenth of the product of the land if it is watered by rain and one-twentieth if it is irrigated by human effort; two and one-half per cent of savings is suggested, with equal proportions of the increase in cattle or in trade in goods. The motive for giving the religious tax is internal; there is no external pressure.

Worship through the giving of the religious tax is the best means of promoting the welfare of society, linking the classes of the community with reciprocal sympathy and compassion, and spreading throughout the people a sentiment of love and cooperation. Through the religious tax the nation protects itself from creating financial tyranny through the concentration of the bulk of the national income in the hands of a few individuals, or of the ruler who might claim it in the name of the state. The divine legislation which requires the religious tax preserves for the ordinary man freedom of choice as to his means of livelihood and at the same time provides the community with the aid and cooperation owed it by the individual. The Muslim who fails to pay the religious tax is failing in his religious duty and undermining one of the main pillars of Islam.

Pilgrimage. Pilgrimage is also a form of physical, or external, worship in Islam. The pilgrimage is an annual form of congregational worship in which those Muslims who are able to make the trip assemble from all over the world at Mecca, the home of the revelation to Muhammad (may God bless him). There they visit the Holy Mosque and pray to God in Arafat, a narrow defile some thirteen miles from Mecca. It is a public worship expressing the full equality among Muslims gathered together from all over the world with a common objective—all performing the same actions, all seeking to gain God's favor. At Mecca all pilgrims stand on equal footing whether rich or poor, rulers or ordinary people, scholars or laborers. There all of them, wearing similar white, seamless robes and shorn of class distinctions, assemble around a single center which inspires them with a strong sense of unity. There their views and aims are unified and their resolution is strengthened to work cooperatively for the fulfillment of the general good.

This, then, is worship in Islam—based on the beliefs required of all Muslims, worship is performed through prayer, fasting, payment of the religious tax, and pilgrimages. These forms of worship are required by Islam as owed to God in order that Muslims may please Him, observe His commands, and show their gratitude to Him. As Muslims perform their worship they always think of God and of His gifts related to the body, wealth, and society. At the same time the Muslim realizes that these ceremonies performed in honor of God are of benefit to himself. Prayer and fasting give the Muslim discipline which he needs and further the development of his spiritual life; the religious tax encourages communal cooperation to meet the requirements of the poor and of society; and the pilgrimage widens the circle of acquaintances and increases mutual understanding and cooperation under the shadow of revelation and divine guidance.

The mosque. Although the prayers may be performed at the appropriate times wherever a Muslim happens to be, the mosque has since the dawn of Islam been the best environment for Islamic learning and the performance of religious ceremonies. It has been the center for preaching and guidance, it has served as a court of law where disputes are reconciled, and has been like a social club where Muslims assemble to discuss topics of common interest. The mosque was not invented by Islam but is copied from ancient divine establishments. The Qur'an states that the first building set aside for worship for the people was the Holy Mosque erected by Abraham and his son Ishmael. The Good Book says of mosques in general, "He only shall tend Allah's sanctuaries who believeth in Allah and the Last Day and observeth proper worship and payeth the poor-due and feareth none save Allah. For such (only) is it possible that they can be of the rightly guided" (Surah IX, 18).

The Qur'an mentions two mosques by name, the Divine Mosque in Mecca and the Aqsa Mosque in Jerusalem. "Glorified be He who carried His servant by night from the inviolable Place of Worship [Mecca] to the Far Distant Place of Worship [Jerusalem], the neighborhood whereof We have blessed" (Surah XVII, 1).

Among the first things the Prophet did on his return to Medina was to establish his own mosque as a means of bringing the Muslims closer together and forming the Muslim community, and as a place for performing the magnificent communal prayer.

Following the example of the Prophet, the Caliphs set up mosques where Muslims worshiped their Lord on an equal footing without any distinctions whatsoever. Today mosques are found throughout the Islamic world as the symbol of Islam, the center for Islamic worship, teachings, and service.

Dealings. Within the Islamic code, which provides guidance for all human activities, the distinction between worship and dealings is made for convenience in the exposition of Islam. We have seen the nature of the true worship of Islam; in considering the dealings we shall be concerned with the dealings within the Muslim community—the family, monetary affairs, relations with fellow Muslims, and government—and dealings with non-Muslims both as individuals and nations. Islamic law has clearly stated the obligations of the Muslims in all areas of life and the penalties to be inflicted for offenses and irregularities.

Under the guidance of its code of laws Islam preaches the one God and, by acknowledging the principle of equality, asserts the unity of the human race and denounces discrimination based on color, racial, or regional differences. It aims at justice through the eradication of oppression and tyranny. It mistreats no stranger merely because he is a stranger in a strange land, nor the infidel because of his infidelity, nor the enemy because of his enmity; nor is a near relative given special treatment in Islamic law because of his relationship, nor is a friend shown partiality for his friendship, nor is a

Muslim treated leniently because of his adherence to Islam. "Be steadfast witnesses for Allah in equity, and let not hatred of any people seduce you that ye deal not justly. Deal justly, that is nearer to your duty" (Surah V, 8).

The family. Marriage in Islam requires the full agreement of both parties without compulsion being brought to bear on either person. A marriage which takes place forcibly is considered null and void. When an agreement is reached between the two, the man pays to the woman the bride money, which is a token of admiration, not a purchase price or a form of remuneration. The actual amount of the bride money is determined by agreement and is the exclusive property of the prospective wife; the husband is not entitled to use it in any way without her consent.

The marriage contract is repeated in the presence of two or more witnesses. The bride says, "I marry you to myself," and the groom replies, "I accept your marriage to me." It is quite in order for the two accredited agents for the bride and groom to repeat the phrases of the marriage contract also. If the contract is not authenticated by two witnesses it is unlawful, and no marriage exists between the two. Properly witnessed, this verbal contract completes the marriage and the man and woman may establish their home.

In Islam, the husband, by virtue of his physical strength and ability to secure means of livelihood, is given the responsibility of guardianship of the wife and of the home, within the framework of their reciprocal legal rights and obligations. Such guardianship is not an autocratic authority which excludes the wife from expressing her views or from the right of consultation; it is merely a rank of honor and control which must respect the wife's point of view.

Thus it is seen that the marriage in Islam is a simple agreement between two parties without any participation by religious or civil authorities. Nor does it curtail the wife's freedom of action or her control of property, so long as she lives up to the responsibilities of married life and cares for the home and children.

Islam authorizes a man to marry a second wife in special circumstances in which the objectives of the initial marriage, such as the begetting of children, cannot be fulfilled. There can be no doubt that marriage to a second wife is the best solution to the problem in cases in which the first wife, if divorced, might not be able to remarry or might have no one to look after her. Islam permits a man to have not more than four wives and stipulates that he may have not more than one wife unless he is able to discharge the rights of each wife and maintain absolute equity between them. Islam authorizes the woman to bring her case before justice if she believes that by marrying another wife her husband sought to injure her.

Islam permits marriage with Christians and Jews. In the Qur'an He saith, "This day are (all) good things made lawful for you. The food of those who have received the Scripture is lawful for you, and your food is lawful for them. And so are the virtuous women of the believers and the virtuous women of those who received the Scripture before you" (Surah V, 5). But Islam forbids Muslims to marry disbelievers or polytheists, for He saith, "Wed not idolatresses till they believe; for lo! a believing bondwoman is better than an idolatress though she please you; and give not your daughters in marriage to idolaters till they believe, for lo! a believing slave is better than an idolater though he please you" (Surah II, 221).

Islam seeks to stabilize married life and reconcile differences between the husband and wife. It orders, for instance, that when there is a disagreement between husband and wife they should turn to their family or near relatives for arbitration. But if ill feelings gain such a hold on the married couple that their union is endangered, and no arbitration can succeed, and married life develops from a state of tranquillity, love, and compassion into one of anxiety, hardship, and boycott, and indeed is almost hell, then in such a situation, and only in such a situation, the husband is allowed by Islam, against its better judgment, to seek the remedy of divorce. Strictly speaking, divorce is a right bestowed on the husband in view of his ability to shoulder the marriage obligations and because of his aptitude for better self-restraint than the wife can display.

If the shock of divorce fulfills the purpose for which it is intended and both the husband and wife return to their senses, then they are permitted by Islam to resume their marriage within the terms of the Islamic code. Islam permits the husband to resort to the remedy of divorce twice, and to remarry each time if a satisfactory reconciliation is attained, but a third divorce is decisive and a woman so divorced cannot be made a legitimate wife a fourth time unless she first marries a different man and is then divorced by that man of his own free will, and there have been no consequences of that marriage. If that marriage had been arranged with the intention of divorcing him so that she might go back to her original husband, the contract for the second marriage was unlawful.

It is thus seen that Islam has not allowed divorce in order that a man may use the threat of divorce as a sword which he waves in the woman's face. On the contrary, Islam allows divorce as a bitter medicine to be used by a man to cure a situation or get rid of an association that defies remedy. Islam holds that if a man trespasses on a woman's rights by divorcing her without cause he is abusing his power and is therefore liable to be held responsible for committing a breach of duty. Islamic courts are allowed to censure the man for misusing the right of divorce.

The law of Islam permits the woman to ask the courts of law to look into her case if her husband maintains an unpleasant association with her, or causes real hardship to her unjustifiably, or if she finds that he suffers from a disease of the body or mind which prevents him from preserving her chastity. The court is authorized to order her to be divorced if she is justified in her contentions and her husband refuses to divorce her.

Just as Islam maintains equality between husband and wife in married life it insists on equality in the termination of the marriage. It does not allow the man in any circumstances to take undue advantage of the woman's innate weakness to deny her any of her rights or to abuse the rights which she owes to him. At the same time, it does not require a woman to go beyond her obligations to keep intact her purity and to preserve her husband's property and the home.

The family bears a special responsibility for the education of the children in Islam. The training begins with teaching the child to repeat lessons concerning Islamic beliefs and to perform correctly the worship rites. The family is also responsible for seeing that the child receives further training in the school and the mosque where legitimate and illegitimate actions and beliefs are expounded so that when the child attains maturity he will have been guided along the way to a true understanding of Islam.

Monetary affairs. Inheritance in Islam is based on the blood relationship of parents, brothers and sisters, and children, and on the marriage relationship of husband and wife, without regard for sex or age in the right of inheritance. The parents, the children, and the consorts do not in any circumstances lose this right, though the amount of their share may be affected by the number of heirs. However, brothers and sisters are not entitled to inheritance in case the parents are living. If men and women are both heirs, the man receives twice as much as a woman except in the case of maternal half-brothers and half-sisters, who each get an equal share.

Islamic law has ruled that, since the man bears the support of the woman and the expenses of her children as well as the cost of her marriage, his share of the inheritance should be double that of the woman. Her share is allowed to stand her in good stead in case she loses the source of her livelihood. Islam has taken into consideration the fact that to allocate the inheritance among blood relatives and consorts strengthens bonds of affection and promotes among relatives a reciprocal interest in their common good. Jealousy would prevail and the family structure would be exposed to disintegration if favoritism were allowed among heirs of equal standing. Thanks to this system, Islamic society has been guarded against the threat of financial tyranny which may result when the entire inheritance goes to a single person. It is also guarded against the danger which would come from paying the inheritance into the state treasury, for that would deprive members of the family of the results of the efforts made by parents, children, relatives, husbands, and wives, and would be damaging to society.

Islamic law also sets the standards for financial dealings through its regulations governing such things as the terms of sale and lease, things liable to sale and lease and those liable to neither, ways to employ capital, conditions regulating deposits, authentication of debts, and like matters which could become sources of controversy. All these financial dealings must be based on truthfulness, fidelity, and a willingness to discharge obligations.

Government. The necessity for some sort of government in the Muslim community is indicated by many texts in the Qur'an, such as, "Retaliation is prescribed for you in the matter of the murdered" (Surah II, 178). "Lo! Allah commandeth you that ye restore deposits to their owners, and, if ye judge between mankind, that ye judge justly" (Surah IV, 58). The obligations imposed upon the community by the Qur'an can only be discharged by the community deputizing a spokesman from its midst, a man possessing the mental qualifications, will power, and skills which enable him to secure unity of thought and cooperation in carrying out the tasks required for the common welfare. Such a man is known in Islam as the Caliph or Imam.

It is the duty of the Caliph or Imam, the leader in Islam, to consolidate public opinion, execute judgments, administer state machinery, encourage the faithful in the practice of their faith, such as prayers and the religious tax, and look after affairs of public interest with the guidance of a parliamentary democracy, the basis of government in Islam. The Caliph, in Islamic practice, is subject to control by the nation; he has no authority other than that given to him as a representative of the people and that which is required of him as the enforcer of supernatural laws. If he violates the terms of national representation or breaks God's orders, it is up to the nation to depose him and replace him. The Caliphate or Imamate in

Islam is not based on a heavenly sanction which gives the Caliph power from God to rule the nation; he has no divine authority which makes it the duty of the people to obey him at any cost. The Caliph or Imam is only a member of the society whose actions are determined by divine laws and orders. The Caliph and the nation form an inseparable whole linked together by the strong tie of religious faith, worship of God, fair dealing, and interest in the public welfare. The Prophet (may God bless him) says, "The Muslims are equal before God." The first Caliph in Islam said, "Obey me so long as I obey God and the Prophet in dealing with you. Once I cease obeying them you are no longer obliged to obey me."

Thus in Islam we find no distinction in community life between that which is called religious and that which is outside religion. In Islam religion is concerned with faith and worship, and also with the upbringing, education, and guidance of the people, and with all economic and social dealings as to those which are legitimate and illegitimate, sound or corrupt; and religion is concerned with the government of the people and the administration of state machinery, with the operation of all the functions of the community or nation. Religion provides the guiding principles for the individual and for the state. There can be no state which has a separate framework for the government and for religion. Those Islamic regions which separate the state from religion are following a mere private school of thought, contrary to the teachings of Islam.

Islam recognizes equally the rights and responsibilities of the individual and the community. It has built its legislation on the recognition that a man has a personality independent of his compatriots and his community, a personality which forms an element in the social structure. He has rights and obligations as an independent individual and rights and responsibilities as a part of the nation to which he belongs. As an independent person, man is required by Islam to believe in God, worship Him, and to live in a manner which assures him a clear conscience; it is incumbent upon him to work for a living, to control himself and his children, and to realize his interests and maintain his existence without encroaching upon the life and welfare of other people. It is his right to own property and to enjoy the legitimate pleasures of life. As a member of the community it is the divine duty of man to contribute to the general good, to guide and aid his fellow men, to do his full share in furthering the social amenities of the community, and to take part in fighting the common enemy.

In return for the individual's fulfillment of his obligations, the community is required by Islam to protect the individual's life and property, and to safeguard the chastity of his womenfolk. Islam has legislated for this purpose, clearly defining the functions of the legitimate ruler who is representative of the community, and outlining the penalties which the ruler must enforce.

Within the Islamic framework the individual and the community have defined for them the rights and obligations which ensure life and happiness through cooperation and equity in assigning privileges and tasks without encroaching upon the rights of the individual or the community. Should the individual deny to the community any of the rights due to it, he deserves God's denunciation, and it is the duty of the ruler to censure him on behalf of the nation. And if the society, as represented in the ruler, fails to ensure the rights of the individual, then the individual is entitled to insist upon his rights, and the ruler deserves God's condemnation and anger. When the ruler does not protect the rights of the individual, the community is empowered to depose him and to replace him with a man who is able to live up to the functions of his high office.

Dealings with non-Muslims. Islam does not hold any enmity or hatred toward non-Muslims. It stands for peaceful coexistence and cooperation in daily life with them. For thus the Qur'an says, "Say: O disbelievers! I worship not that which ye worship; Nor worship ye that which I worship. And I shall not worship that which ye worship. Nor will ye worship that which I worship. Unto you your religion, and unto me my religion" (Surah CIX). "Unto this, then, summon (O Muhammad). And be thou upright as thou art commanded, and follow not their lusts, but say: I believe in whatever Scripture Allah hath sent down, and I am commanded to be just among you. Allah is our Lord and your Lord. Unto us our works and unto you your works; no argument between us and you. Allah will bring us together, and unto Him is the journeying" (Surah XLII, 15). When non-Muslims are resident in the same country with Muslims, the most important thing is to ensure freedom of belief and the opportunity for non-Muslims to worship God in their own sanctuaries and hold their religious ceremonies, and to maintain full equality between them and their Muslim compatriots in public rights and obligations.

As we have seen, Muslims are permitted to marry Christian or Jewish women, and such wives enjoy the same rights and duties as Muslim wives with full liberty to cherish their own religion and perform their religious duties.

Even if parents are polytheists and even if they strive to mislead their Muslim son to follow them, he is commanded by the Qur'an to be good to them and to treat them gently, for Allah saith, "And We have enjoined upon man concerning his parents . . . But if they strive with thee to make thee ascribe unto Me as partner that of which thou hast no knowledge, then obey them not. Consort with them in the world kindly, and follow the path of him who repenteth unto Me" (Surah XXXI, 14–15). It is said in history that Abu Talib, the Prophet's uncle, who was a polytheist until his death, was a good helper and protector of Muhammad.

Islam is strongly averse to resorting to force to expound its cause or to compel people to embrace its faith. Islam's invitation to non-Muslims to embrace Islam is made by an explanation of its advantages—its easily understandable faith, its simple obligations in religious ceremonies and dealings, its tolerant ethical principles, freedom of research, deep understanding of the universe, and the fact that it makes no distinction between men except by virtue of piety and good achievements. It points out that in Islam no man has authority over another person's beliefs, and that only God has authority to introduce beliefs and to require or receive worship.

Islam bases its policy for relations between Muslims and other people of varying beliefs on acquaintanceship, cooperation, and working for the common good. Non-Muslims who live in the community in cooperation and peace are looked upon by Islam as equal to Muslims, each of them holding to his faith and preaching its aims with wisdom and friendly argument without bringing pressure to bear on anyone or encroaching on each other's rights. Islam requires of non-Muslims only abstention from hostility to Muslims and from sedition or opposition to the Islamic way of life.

In the relations between Muslim and non-Muslim states, Islam stands for "inviting the world to do good." Islam permits treaties and cooperation with non-Muslim powers in time of peace so long as the treaties do not contradict the basic principles of Islam. "Allah forbiddeth you not those who warred not against you on account of religion and drove you not out from your homes, that ye should show them kindness and deal justly with them. Lo! Allah loveth the just dealers. Allah forbiddeth you only those who warred against you on account of religion and have driven you out from your homes and helped to drive you out, that ye make friends of them. Whosoever maketh friends of them—(All) such are wrong-doers" (Surah LX, 8–9).

Islam does not turn from friendly relations with non-Muslim countries unless it is the victim of an aggressive attack, or obstacles are placed in the path of Islam, or attempts are made to seduce the people. When Islam is exposed to such hardships, its believers are permitted, and indeed it is made incumbent upon them, to repel aggression, to restore peace, and to establish a just situation in which people can think and act freely. Islam forbids Muslims to launch aggressive war motivated by a spirit of cruelty, or a desire to drain the resources of a people, or to cause suffering, or to eject people from their homes. After an approved war breaks out, Islam rejects devastation or extermination as methods of war. It does not permit the killing of members of the civilian population who are not actively engaged in hostilities, such as women, children, the old, and the disabled. The Prophet said, "Do not exterminate the young ones." When he was asked, "Aren't they the children of the infidel?" he replied, "Are not the best among you children of infidels?"

Islam does not permit participation in war until after the causes are clearly known and the enemy has received a warning. Islam condemns maltreatment of prisoners of war, their persecution, or their murder. It is made clear in the Qur'an that the prisoners must be fed in order to win God's satisfaction. "And feed with food the needy wretch, the orphan and the prisoner, for love of Him" (Surah LXXVI, 8). The termination of an approved war does not require that the enemy forces embrace Islam. It is considered sufficient if the enemy stops his evil aggression and signs a treaty which preserves the rights of the people, and protects them from tyranny or sedition.

Such are the principles which govern the relations of Muslim and non-Muslim nations and the code of *jihad*—the Holy Struggle. The basis for the Islamic code of war was laid in the Qur'an and it was carried out in practice by the Prophet and his foremost successors.

Penalties and rewards. Up to this point we have been discussing the Islamic code—worship and dealings. The code also states the rewards and penalties which are in store in this world and in the Second World. Islam has specified the death penalty for murder, the cutting off of the hand for theft, and flogging for adultery and slander. The punishment is definitely stated for these three categories of offences only; the penalties for other offences and irregularities are left to the ruler who is representative of the nation and who acts after consultation with the people.

Concerning the rewards and penalties in the next world, Allah has said, "Whoso obeyeth Allah and His messenger, He will make him enter Gardens underneath which rivers flow, where such will dwell for ever. That will be the great success. And whoso disobeyeth Allah and His messenger and transgresseth His limits, He will make him enter Fire, where such will dwell for ever; his will be a shameful doom" (Surah IV, 13–14). The penalty for the aggressor and the corrupt is stated in God's saying, "The only reward for those who make war upon Allah and His messenger and strive after corruption in the land will be that they will be killed or crucified, or have their hands and feet on alternate sides cut off, or will be expelled out of the land. Such will be their degradation in the world, and in the Hereafter theirs will be an awful doom" (Surah V, 33).

Thus we see that in both worship and dealings man stands before his Lord and receives rewards or punishment in the afterlife according to his merits. In Islam, both worship and dealings are religious ceremonies and the Muslim must answer for all his actions before God in the Second World just as he must answer before a court of law in this world.

If a Muslim commits a breach of divine law through intent and premeditation, it constitutes a dangerous sin for which he alone is responsible. Even an accomplice who seduces him to commit the sin cannot relieve him of responsibility; he must, as an accomplice, bear his own sin. According to the Qur'an it is a law of God of long standing that it is only the sinner who bears responsibility, "That no laden one shall bear another's load" (Surah LIII, 38). One of the clearly established principles of Islam is that only God forgives sins, and that God has given no authorization to anyone whatsoever to pardon sins, "Who forgiveth sins save Allah only?" (Surah III, 135). Another principle is that all sins are pardoned by God as he pleases except the sin of infidelity. This is expressly stated in the Qur'an, "Lo! Allah pardoneth not that partners should be ascribed unto Him. He pardoneth all save that to whom He will" (Surah IV, 116). Infidelity includes doubt in God's oneness and divinity. Therefore those who denounce the Creator, and those who worship other than God, and those who disagree with God's legislation as to that which is legitimate or illegitimate are all infidels.

It is also a principle of Islam that if a sinner repents and abstains from committing further sins because of fear of God and a determination to uphold His orders, God has pledged to forgive the sin. "And He it is Who accepteth repentance from his bondmen, and pardoneth the evil deeds, and knoweth what ye do" (Surah XLII, 25). And Islam holds to the principle that man is born free from sins and remains free of sin until he is mature and has heard God's teachings. If, then, he closes his eyes to God's teachings and refuses to observe them, only then is he regarded as a sinner, with exclusive responsibility for his sins.

THE MORAL FRAMEWORK. Thus far in this chapter we have dealt with Islamic beliefs, Islamic worship, and Islamic dealings. The moral framework of Islam is a fourth element of equal significance in the life of a Muslim, entailing reward or punishment in the afterlife according to its observances or neglect. The moral principles of Islam strengthen the Muslim's resolve to adhere strictly to Islamic teachings and rules of conduct for polite society. They consolidate the bonds of understanding and unify sentiment and common feeling among Muslims. Allah urges Muslims to speak the truth, forget and forgive, and display compassion, mercy, valor, and love in all their relations with others.

The moral framework of Islam states the principles of etiquette for polite society for the common people as well as for the most advanced. The Qur'an says concerning the etiquette of walking and modesty in one's bearing, "Turn not thy cheek in scorn toward folk, nor walk with pertness in the land. Lo! Allah loveth not each braggard boaster. Be modest in thy bearing and subdue thy voice" (Surah XXXI, 18–19). Concerning the etiquette of calling on one's neighbors, "Lo! those who call thee from behind the private apartments, most of them have no sense" (Surah XLIX, 4). And also, "Enter not houses other than your own without first announcing your presence and invoking peace upon the folk thereof" (Surah XXIV, 27). And in closing the door to sexual irregularities, the Qur'an says, "Tell the believing men to lower their gaze and be modest. That is purer for them. Lo! Allah is Aware of what they do. And tell the believing women to lower their gaze and be modest" (Surah XXIV, 30–31). And concerning unkind conversations, "Let not a folk deride a folk who may be better than they (are), nor let women (deride) women who may be better than they are; neither defame one another, nor insult one another by nicknames" (Surah XLIX, 11).

By these and similar rules of social etiquette Islam guided the steps of people in backward stages of development, urging them to rise to an appropriate standard and attain the level of the more advanced social classes. At the same time Islam invites men of all levels to live up to the highest point of ethical and spiritual progress. "Keep to forgiveness (O Muhammad), and enjoin kindness, and turn away from the ignorant" (Surah VII, 199). "The good deed and the evil deed are not alike. Repel the evil deed with one which is better" (Surah XLI, 34). "Those who spend (of that which Allah hath given them) in ease and adversity, those who control their wrath and are forgiving toward mankind; Allah loveth the good" (Surah III, 134). "If ye publish your almsgiving, it is well, but if ye hide it and give it to the poor, it will be better for you" (Surah II, 271).

In calling upon the people to guide their lives by these ethical principles, Islam insists, in the main, that they should be moderate in all things, sparing themselves misery and not lowering their status in life. Islam requires courage of Muslims and warns them against cowardice and extravagance. It demands forgiveness and renounces both submissive humbleness and revenge. It upholds hospitality and condemns spendthrift and miserly economy. It preaches perseverence and rejects panic and defeatism. It constantly urges, "Give the kinsman his due, and the needy, and the wayfarer, and squander not (thy wealth) in wantonness" (Surah XVII, 26). It praises moderation in all things, "And those who, when they spend, are neither prodigal nor grudging; and there is ever a firm station between the two" (Surah XXV, 67).

These illustrate, briefly, the ethical principles which guide the actions of the Muslim.

SOURCES OF ISLAMIC LEGISLATION. The fundamental source of Islamic legislation is the Qur'an, which has been proved beyond all doubt as God's own book brought down by His Prophet to guide the people to obey its commands and to refrain from actions which it prohibits. The legislation of the Qur'an is of two kinds: that which has a crystal clear and decisive meaning not open to debate, and legislation liable to have two or more meanings.

The secondary sources of Islamic legislation are the Sunnah and the schools of thought, dealing with those areas not decisively covered in the Qur'an, the areas of probable meaning. After the Qur'an, the chief interpretative authority for Islamic legislation is the Sunnah—Muhammad's own sayings, deeds, and legislative decisions which have been correctly and authoritatively transmitted. If a problem arises which is not dealt with clearly in the Qur'an or in the Sunnah, the answer is sought in the schools of thought, the theories worked out by "leaders of thought" who have been careful students of the Qur'an and the Sunnah, have thought profoundly about their inner meanings and understand their general principles, and who have special knowledge of virtue and the general welfare.

The order of merit of the three sources of Islamic legislation has been recognized by Muslims from the days of the Prophet. They will continue to be the basis of Islamic legislation to the end of time.

The Qur'an. In the previous discussions of the Qur'an we have seen that it contains many specific passages calling upon the people to follow its teachings and be guided by its legislation. "Lo! We reveal unto thee the Scripture with the truth, that thou mayest judge between mankind by that which Allah showeth thee" (Surah IV, 105). "These are the limits (imposed by) Allah. Transgress them not. For whoso transgresseth Allah's limits: such are wrongdoers" (Surah II, 229).

The Qur'an legislates concerning worship, enjoining fixed hours for prayer; it prescribes fasting, the giving of alms, and pilgrimage. It lays down the regulations for family life—

marriage and divorce. It gives clear directions concerning financial dealings, contracts and pledges, relations with the people of the scriptures and with infidels, holy war and fighters and non-fighters, the administration of community life, sources of legislation, and the penalties for disobedience.

Thus the Qur'an is established as the foundation of the faith and of the code of legislation. Although the legislation in the Qur'an which may have two or more meanings is the subject of theory and study, the legislation which is explicit and open to only one meaning is binding on all Muslims. Should the Muslim fail to follow such legislation in his practical affairs, he is looked upon as rejecting Islam. Whoever alleges that the Qur'an is the product of a particular people, or a special age, or a limited aspect of human life is a disbeliever in Islam and in God's Book.

The Sunnah. There are two aspects to the Sunnah: legislation given by the Prophet on matters not specifically detailed in the Qur'an, and traditions based on the actions and utterances of Muhammad as a human being.

The legislation given by the Prophet is illustrated by the rules stating the form of prayer, the pilgrimage rites, and giving in detail the limits of legitimacy in marriage. For instance, marriage is illegitimate between two people who in their infancy fed from the same breasts, and a man may not be married at the same time to a woman and to her aunt. This type of teaching is based on the tradition of Muhammad's instructions on matters not specified in the Qur'an.

The second aspect of the Sunnah is not associated with legislation. It deals with the traditions based on the actions and teachings of Muhammad concerning the affairs left to man's discretion, affairs for which God has given no definite command as to their legitimacy or illegitimacy, such as when to stand up and when to sit, the etiquette pertaining to eating and drinking and sleeping, and matters to be dealt with on the basis of experience or expert knowledge like agriculture, industry, medicine, military discipline, and tactics. It is authentically related that the Prophet, in the course of one of his battles, ordered an army contingent to be dispatched to a particular point, but a group of his disciples objected, "Is it a position God commanded you to choose, or have you chosen it as a strategist?" He replied, "No, it is one of my own choosing." His disciples pointed out that it was not an ideal position and gave their reasons for preferring an alternate location. The Prophet was convinced and dropped his plan. At another time he expressed his views as to the proper way to fertilize palm trees, but the trees failed to produce fruit. When he was informed of the result, he said, "You are better acquainted with your own worldly affairs."

Knowledge which depends on human experience and traditions related to the Prophet concerning such matters are not the basis for Islamic legislation. Traditions attributed to the Prophet can only be a source of legislation that must be obeyed if they are based on revelations given to him to guide the people according to God's laws.

The Sunnah as a source of legislation is always subordinate to the principles and fundamental laws of the Qur'an; its importance lies in the fact that it expounds specific aspects of the general principles of the Qur'an. Sometimes the expounding may be done by the example of an action; in the case of prayer, the Prophet showed how it is performed, the number of kneelings required for each prayer, and the proper time limits for its performance. The expounding may also be done by adding certain ceremonies not expressly described in the Qur'an. Expounding is also done by the Prophet in expressing opinions concerning general rules, such as the opinion that the simpler of two possibilities should be chosen in following a general principle stated in the Qur'an.

Hence we may assert that the legislative Sunnah is an attempt on the part of the Prophet to teach the real meaning of the Qur'an, its inner implications and aims. Thus, the legislation based on the Sunnah really springs from the Qur'an.

God's policy in relation to the Prophet's endeavor to interpret the Qur'an was to endorse his endeavor if it was right and proper, and to direct his attention to the correct interpretation and even to censure him if he was in error. Once when the Prophet out of dutiful regard for his faith was willfully denying himself certain good things allowable by God, He said, "O Prophet! Why bannest thou that which Allah hath made lawful for thee, seeking to please thy wives?" (Surah LXVI, 1). This and similar instances in which the Prophet tried to get at the correct answer but failed provide the best proof that the Prophet used his discretion to determine things about which no revelation was forthcoming, and that whenever he made a mistake God directed him along the correct path.

Thus the Prophet used his discretion and received God's endorsement when he was right, and the result became law, binding on the people. So, also, his disciples copied his example and used their discretion when necessary, and on being informed of the outcome of their efforts the Prophet endorsed them if they were in order and God agreed with his approval. If they were in error, the Prophet directed his disciples' attention to the correct answer to which God guided him. In this way the results of his disciples' endeavors in his time were associated with his own efforts to interpret the Qur'an and became legislative Sunnah which it is incumbent on the people to respect. Thus we see that during the Prophet's lifetime there was no source of legislation other than the Qur'an and the Prophet's interpretation of it either through revelation or discretion.

The authenticity of the Sunnah is proved by the Qur'an, for it orders that the Prophet should be obeyed and it made obedience to him a form of obedience to God and a recognition of His love, "But nay, by thy Lord, they will not believe (in truth) until they make thee judge of what is in dispute between them and find within themselves no dislike of that which thou decidest, and submit with full submission" (Surah IV, 65).

If the purpose of the legislation of the Sunnah is to expound the legislation of the Qur'an, and if God's policy with His Prophet was to endorse Muhammad's interpretation when it was correct and to guide him to what was right when he made a mistake, then the Sunnah legislation is the same as the legislation of the Qur'an, and equally binding on all Muslims.

Schools of thought. In the time of the Prophet there were two sources of Islamic legislation: the fundamental source in the Qur'an, and the interpretative source in the Sunnah. After Muhammed's death his disciples found themselves in an expanding Islamic world, facing new issues for which they needed the guidance of explicit legislation. They would refer to the Qur'an and if they failed to find a satisfactory answer there they would turn to the Sunnah, which was preserved for them by reliable men who were fully acquainted with the Prophet's interpretations. If they did not find the answer to their question in either the Qur'an or the Sunnah, they pondered the points at issue—guided by their knowledge of the aims and guiding principles of Islamic legislation—and came to conclusions which are consistent with the Qur'an and the Sunnah, and have the authority of legislation. In this way the schools of thought, under carefully controlled conditions, became a third source of Islamic legislation.

The schools of thought, in their interpretations of the probable meanings of passages in the Qur'an and the Sunnah and in their rulings concerning issues not definitely dealt with in those sources, adopted certain general principles found in Quranic legislation as a guide. These are some of the principles on which the schools of thought based their decisions: all things are fundamentally allowable, unless specifically prohibited; toleration and the lifting of restrictions should be the aim of legislation; eradication of mischief is the aim of administration; necessity permits benefiting by things not otherwise allowable; necessity is given due appreciation; preventing mischief has priority over bringing about welfare; commit the lesser of two evils; mischief is not removed by mischief; one should suffer private damage to avert general disaster. Such general principles are the guides for the creation and interpretation of Islamic law.

Under the first two Caliphs, Abu Bakr and Umar, it was the policy when deciding public issues to consult with the leading disciples who were recognized for their accurate thinking, appreciation of the interests of the people, and grasp of the spirit of the legislation of the Qur'an and the Sunnah. When unity of view was achieved among those responsible leaders of the Muslim community, it was put into practice. In this way, the adoption of a law through consultation and a consensus *(ijma)* of the opinions of the leaders of Islam became a new source of Islamic legislation after the Prophet's death, covering all matters which were not expressly mentioned or clearly implied in either the Qur'an or the Sunnah.

The authenticity of the legislation of the schools of thought is assured by the Qur'an, for it says that the affairs of the people are matters of counsel and it orders that the people should obey the authority of those who are responsible for the common good and are known for sound interpretation. Such legislation is also authorized by the Sunnah, for the Prophet dispatched his lieutenants to remote regions with authority to use their discretion when guided by the consensus of opinion on all issues not defined in the Qur'an and Sunnah.

During the regimes of the first two Caliphs the differences of opinion were quite limited because of the trouble they took to ascertain the authenticity of the Sunnah and the importance they gave to consultations among the students of the law from among the Prophet's disciples, most of whom were resident at the Caliph's headquarters. It is important to note that the regimes of the two Shaikhs Abu Bakr and Umar are the only ones which define the correct use of discretion as a source of legislation. They show that discretion as a source of legislation must reach its conclusions through consultation which arrives at unity of view among Muslims of authority who are qualified to decide issues. Thus unity of view, considered by Islam to be a source of legislation in cases where neither the Qur'an nor the Sunnah is applicable, is the agreement reached by investigation and study by men of thought who understand the spirit of Islamic legislation and are responsible for guiding the interests of the people in the community.

Unity of view as a source of Islamic legislation is not the same as complete agreement among all members of the nation, whether men of thought or mere laymen, scholars or ordinary people. Such general agreement about Islamic principles definitely known to have been enacted is not the subject of thought and discretion and should be held equally by all Muslims. It is simply the general acceptance of the beliefs and code of legislation required of all members of the Islamic community.

For the unity of thought which is considered to be a source of binding legislation, the agreement or disagreement on the part of those not qualified to state views has no weight. Unity of view which can be the source of legislation must be attained through the use of methods of thinking and investigation which have been approved as valid; it must be reached by a limited number of men from among all classes of the nation, whose qualifications for the use of the approved methods are recognized; the views of all the qualified men must be ascertained; and unanimous agreement on a specific ruling must be sought. The unanimous agreement is difficult to attain because of the varying abilities of the men participating and the diversity of interests and regional circumstances influencing each investigator. Therefore it is recognized that unanimity can be achieved only on the basis of the principles that "there is no knowledge of any dissidents," or of "agreement by the preponderant majority." This is all that can be done to attain unity of view which can be a basis for legislation. "Allah tasketh not a soul beyond its scope" (Surah II, 286). However, in seeking unity of thought as a basis for legislation, freedom of thought must be ensured for all those participating and no authority should bring to bear any pressure which would restrict the liberty of thought.

Islamic legislation based upon the consensus of opinion of the leaders qualified to decide is subject to review and alteration. The interests on which the leaders were called to rule vary in different areas, places, and conditions, making it allowable for the successors of the original leaders to review the position in the light of new circumstances and to make a new decision if the changed situation requires it. The new unanimity replaces the former legislation and becomes the new law which ought to be followed.

Individual private discretion. In addition to the discretion employed in communal consultations concerning issues not specifically covered in the Qur'an or the Sunnah, there is the private discretion of the individual man in which decisions are reached by independent thinking. Private discretion *(ijtihad)* is not binding on anyone except the individual who uses it. Islam recognizes that the right of private discretion belongs to any individual who possesses the capacity for clear thinking and study, whether man or woman, ruler or subject, leading government civil servant or private citizen. Just as they have an equal right to engage in individual discretion, so do they have equal responsibility for making mistakes. Islam knows of no one who is immune from committing errors except the Prophet insofar as revelation was concerned. If the Prophet was liable to make mistakes in trying to find the correct answer —and indeed he did try and did make mistakes—then other Muslims, even those of great accomplishment or near relationship to Muhammad, are more liable to commit error.

The exercise of individual discretion was widespread after the time of the first two Caliphs, particularly after the great sedition arising out of the assassination of the third Caliph, Uthman. In its extreme form it transmuted Muslims into contending sects following their own private tendencies in determining schools of thinking and in conveying prophetic sayings.

It should be clearly understood that Islam does not set aside a specific person with the right to interpret the Qur'an or the Sunnah, nor does it make it a duty of the people to adhere to any person's individual views on questions which are open to private opinion. Every Muslim qualified to investigate questions has the right to do so. Muslims who are not qualified ought to enquire concerning the qualifications of those who speak concerning the obligations of Islamic law. Islam does not bind any Muslim to follow a particular person, for no duty is owed other than those duties which were assigned by

God and the Prophet. Nor did God or the Prophet order anyone to follow a given religious school of thought—with the result that since the dawn of Islam Muslims have been asking for right answers from any well-known students of religion they meet, without binding themselves to any specific teacher. Therefore Islam does not recognize as legitimate any tendency to imitate a given school of thought. All those who have legitimately used their discretion have warned others against copying their example unless they have been convinced by proof of the validity of their findings. They have said, "If this talk proves untrue, then it is just my own theory, and it is up to you to disregard all that I have said."

Thus it is understood that the men who hold religious positions in Islam, such as the Caliph or Imam, have no monopoly on thinking and understanding, nor are they immune from making errors, nor do they receive revelation or special inspiration. Such leaders can only advise, and guide, and administer justice within the limits of Islamic laws. The Caliph or Imam is elected to his office by the nation, and he represents the nation while in office. So long as he discharges his functions within the framework of God's orders, the nation aids and obeys him—and it deposes him if he deviates from the right course.

The position of the Judge (*Qadi*), or the *Mufti*, the *Shaikh of Islam*, and the *Mullah* is similar to that of the Caliph in matters of understanding and legislation. The Judge's responsibility is limited to passing judgment on disputes between parties in accordance with the laws of Islam. The Mufti's function is to explain questions put to him. If he happens to be a man of discretion, the Mufti expresses his own views; otherwise he copies someone else's opinions. However, his answers to questions are not binding on those who resort to him; they have the right to insist on proof that the answers are correct and his tradition is authentic, and they are entitled to ask the same or other questions of someone else in whose knowledge they have confidence.

Shaikh of Islam and *Mullah* are titles which gained popularity among Muslims in certain regions and eras, conferred on men who distinguished themselves in religious and legislative knowledge. Neither of them is depended upon for decisions in legislative matters, and they are not immune from committing mistakes. Islam does not recognize one Shaikh or one Mullah who has authority in Islamic knowledge, and certain religious sects which claim such leadership are deviations from Islamic teachings far from being in order.

Within the area in which private discretion is appropriate, whoever believed himself competent to think clearly did his best to understand the correct implications of Islamic teachings, each thinker following his own style of study and inference. Some thinkers confined themselves to a limited number of prophetic sayings, because of the spread of invented sayings which cast doubt on many widely accepted sayings. They preferred to rely upon general rules and the spirit of Islamic legislation. Such thinkers are known in the history of Islamic jurisprudence as rationalists, or men of thought. Others, known as students of the prophetic sayings, convinced themselves of the authenticity of the transmission of many more of the prophetic sayings and preferred to rely upon them for their decisions. Other thinkers based their judgments on the traditions prevailing in Medina because it was the environment where legislation was made at the time of the Prophet and during the first two Caliphates before the outbreak of the sedition.

Out of such varying uses of the right of private discretion there grew up schools of religious thought which in time gained popularity in Islam and were allowed to spread. In modern times there are four of these schools of interpretation, or schools of Islamic law, which are found living amicably together in the Islamic world. The Hanafi school was founded by Imam al-Nu'man Ibn Thabit, who died in Baghdad in the year 150 (A.D. 767), based on the teachings of Abu Hanifah; the Maliki school was founded by Malik Ibn Anas, who died in Medina in 179 (A.D. 795); the Shafi'i school was founded by Muhammad Ibn Idris al-Shafi'i, a native of Gaza who died in Cairo in 205 (A.D. 820); and the Hanbali school was founded by Imam Ahmad Ibn Hanbal, a Persian who died in Baghdad in 241 (A.D. 855).

These four schools of thought are still taught in most institutions of learning in Islamic countries. The Hanafi school is found chiefly in India, the countries which were under the Ottoman Turks, and China; the Maliki school is found today in North Africa and Upper Egypt; the Shafi'is are found in Indonesia, southern Arabia, lower Egypt, and parts of Syria; the Hanbali school is influential in Saudi Arabia.

The fact that Islam has permitted individual as well as communal discretion—limited only by the original definite legislation of the Qur'an and the Sunnah, which define the roads to justice—enabled students of the Islamic code to choose freely the laws regulating the affairs of Islamic society. Such toleration has been the basis for the everlasting usefulness of the Islamic code and for its fitness to regulate the affairs of life everywhere and at all times.

CHAPTER FOUR

The Rational and Mystical Interpretations of Islam

A. E. Affifi

No account of Islam is complete if it does not take into consideration the extraordinary efforts which the various Muslim sects have made to understand Islam, and the results which they have achieved. Islam is not merely a body of doctrines expressed in the Qur'an and the prophetic Traditions; neither is it best represented by the orthodox school at any particular time. It is a living religion which has received and is still receiving its vitality from the people who confess it; it is a great movement which has passed through various stages of development over its long and complicated history, influencing and being influenced by the religious and cultural forces in its environment. Through the interaction between Islam in its original form and those external forces some of the fundamental concepts of Muslim dogmas and practices were reinterpreted and reshaped. Some of these interpretations are not orthodox, it is true, but they are nevertheless Islamic, at least insofar as they are based on Islamic texts, even though the texts are examined under a different light.

It is the purpose of this chapter to discuss the interpretations gleaned from the writings of the old schools of Muslims—mystics and rationalists, including both the theologians and the philosophers—who are not usually regarded by the orthodox school as strict Muslims, but whose influence on Muslim thought and practical religious life is felt even today. The earliest rationalists were known as Mu'tazilites, and the mystics of Islam are the Sufis. The discussion in this chapter will be limited to the theological, philosophical, and mystical attitudes toward certain of the fundamental problems of dogmatic beliefs and religious practices in Islam.

The Theological Attitude

Islam, like all other great religions, has a theology of its own which aims at the establishment of its fundamental articles of faith and the refutation of heresy and innovation. The Prophet Muhammad was no theologian—nor was any prophet before him. In fact, the revelations that prophets have brought into the world defy any serious attempt at a systematic theology. The systematization of religious dogmas in Islam was a task undertaken by the followers of Muhammad when the need for the establishment of a Muslim theology was felt. The criterion for the early theology was taken by writers such as Ibn Khaldun and Adud al-Din al-Iji to be the teachings of the early Muslims and the orthodox party. In the opinion of these writers the Mu'tazilites (rationalists) and the Shi'as and many other theological schools are heretical. This is too narrow a view to be adopted, and in dealing with Muslim theology here the term "theology" is used in a wider sense to include the speculative thinking of orthodox and non-orthodox theological schools.

The fundamental principle which Muslim theology has always endeavored to establish is the principle of the unity of God. On this principle Muslim theologians know no compromise. It is the keynote of Muslim faith and the root from which all other dogmas of Islam are derived. Hence Muslim theology is also called the science of unification (of God), because its object is to determine the nature of God and His attributes, and to explain the relation between Him and His creation, all of which follow as corollaries from a definite concept of Allah as the Absolute One.

The Qur'an, though not itself a book on theology, contains the rudiments of almost all theological problems. It speaks of God as the only one to be served, the Supreme Master and Ruler of the world. It asserts His absolute transcendence in these words, "Say: He is God alone. God the eternal: He begetteth not, nor is begotten; and there is nothing like unto Him" (Surah CXII). The Qur'an contains a long list of the attributes of God over which there has been much discussion and disputation among the Muslim theologians. It condemns polytheism, atheism, and deism; and it emphatically denies the eternity of the world. Although on the whole it is sympathetic to Christianity, it rejects the Christian Trinity and all its implications.

In discussing these theological problems the style of the Qur'an varies considerably. Sometimes it takes the form of a logical argument—a syllogistic proof or an argument based on analogy—but more often it adopts the rhetorical style, calling on man to reflect upon himself and the wonderful world around him so that by means of such reflection he might know his Lord. When dealing with moral precepts the Qur'an appeals to man's own conscience and bids him reflect upon his actions and the actions of his fellow men.

Such were the seeds from which, under favorable conditions, an elaborate theology developed in the Muslim world. There was no science of theology during the lifetime of the Prophet and the first four Caliphs. The early Muslims accepted the word of the Qur'an literally. They raised no metaphysical or theological questions. When they were in doubt about a Quranic verse dealing with God or any of His attributes they were told to accept it as it was stated in the Qur'an with no further explanation or interpretation. The idea was to have faith in Islam, to propagate it, and to defend it, rather than to inquire into its nature. The orthodox party represented by Ahmad Ibn Hanbal (died 241; A.D. 855) adhered strictly to tradition and opposed any form of independent thinking.

Later on they even rejected the theological investigations made on strict Quranic lines, and looked with suspicion upon the teaching of the ascetics of their time. They would only allow discussion of questions related to the law (shari'a) and the practical affairs of everyday life. But soon after the death of Muhammad political questions relating to his rightful successor were raised, and with them arose certain theological questions concerning the nature of the true Imam (Muslim head of state), the meaning of faith, sin, infidelity, punishment in the Future World, and so on. The interest was primarily political, but the contending parties gave their views a religious coloring, and there was much persecution and bloodshed in the name of religion. Political, or rather political-theological, parties appeared on the scene—the Kharijites, the Qadarites, the Shi'ites, the Murjites, and the Umayyads, who were the state party and the bitterest opponents of Ali and his followers. This was a period of strife and dissension within the Muslim community during which the whole future of Islam was at stake.

What interests us here is their discussion of faith, sin, and retribution. The Murjites—literally those who postpone; here, those who postpone judgment until it is pronounced by God on the Day of Judgment—were more tolerant than the others in their political views and more liberal-minded on theological questions. They believed that faith alone is sufficient for man's salvation. The sinful believer who professes the unity of God and acknowledges His Prophet thus will not suffer everlasting punishment in Hell, a view which was diametrically opposite to that of the Kharijites. They even went so far as to say that a believer need not be a professed Muslim, for faith is a confession of the heart while Islam is an outward or public confession of the tongue.

The question was taken up more seriously later when it lost its political significance and became a theological problem of academic interest. What is the real nature of faith, and what is its relation to religious practice? Does faith admit any degrees? That is, can one man be more faithful than another, or can one and the same person ascend higher and higher in the scale of faith? The Murjites denied the quantitative evaluation of faith, while the rest of the theologians held the view that faith admits increase and decrease. Faith is more nearly perfect when it is accompanied by actions, or better still, when it is so deeply rooted in the heart that it becomes the principle from which righteous actions necessarily follow. Faith which is not accompanied by good works is like a tree which bears no fruit, but true faith becomes a "faculty of the heart"—as Ibn Khaldun calls it—which urges the faithful to perform their religious obligations and to abstain from sin. "A true believer," the Prophet says, "commits no adultery and no theft." In other words, to have real faith and to sin is a contradiction in terms. The theory that faith increases and decreases has its roots in the Qur'an in such passages as this, "The believers are they whose hearts thrill with fear when God's name is mentioned, and whose faith increases at each recital of His words, and who put trust in their Lord" (Surah VIII, 2).

Such were the beginnings of the era in which Muslim theology was being formed. But these rudimentary and altogether primitive speculations on certain religious problems soon assumed larger proportions when Muslim scholars who were skilled in the art of dialectic and tolerably conversant with Greek philosophy appeared on the scene. There were now two important factors which helped the development of the new theology, one internal and the other external.

The internal factor is the nature of the Qur'an itself. As has been pointed out in previous chapters, the Qur'an contains two different types of verses, those which form the main substance of the Book and are clear and definite in their meaning, and the comparatively few verses which are dubious or less definite. This is admitted in one of the Medina revelations which runs as follows, "He (God) it is who hath sent down to thee the Book. Some of its verses are of themselves perspicuous; they are the basis of the Book; and others are dubious. Those whose hearts are inclined to error follow the dubious verses, thereby seeking discord and seeking interpretation. But none knoweth its interpretation save God. Those who are firm in knowledge say: We believe therein; it is all from our Lord. But none will bear this in mind save men endued with understanding" (Surah III, 7).

The reason for the presence of these dubious verses in the Qur'an has been discussed by theologians. The majority incline to believe that they are purposely given as a trial in order to test the strength and validity of man's faith. Those whose faith is firm accept them unquestionably, while others whose hearts are inclined to error—as the Qur'an says—reject them or interpret them in such a way as to cause discord in the Muslim community. Whatever the real reason may be, the fact remains that these dubious verses played an important role in stirring up dispute among Muhammad's followers of the second generation. Out of these disputes emerged different parties, each supporting a different point of view. It is worth while quoting Ibn Khaldun on the subject. He says, in his *Prolegomena:*

> In the Qur'an there are passages which describe God as an absolutely transcendent Being. Their meaning is clear and admits of no interpretation. They are all negative statements; and, on account of their clarity, are accepted by all believers. . . . The other passages which are comparatively few are suggestive of anthropomorphism [these are the dubious passages]. They were accepted [by the early Muslims] without any enquiry into their meaning. But the innovators of their time resorted to a different method, by subjecting the dubious passages to critical examination. Some exaggerated their anthropomorphic side and attributed to God hands, face, feet, and so on, thus falling into gross corporealism and violating the absolute transcendence of God which is explicitly mentioned in numerous other passages and with such undoubted clarity. . . . Others admitted anthropomorphism with regard to the attributes of God such as occupying a place, sitting on the Throne, coming and going and speaking in words, and so on. They, like the others, also drifted into corporealism.

The disputes centering around such passages had a far-reaching effect on the course of the development of many theological doctrines which occupied the minds of Muslims for generations. We can even find some traces of these theological disputes in modern times.

The second, or external, factor in the development of Muslim theology is the cultural influences which were brought to bear upon Islam from without. Up to the second half of the second century we meet only the individual men who expressed their opinions on some religious problems. There was no general or recognized system of religious thought; there were no real theological schools, although there were what we might call semi-theological parties.

The course of development changed when foreign influence came into play. Some ethical problems were raised, particularly the problem of determinism and free will. Such metaphysical problems as were inspired by the Qur'an also came to the fore—the problem of the attributes of God, the divine attribute of speech and the Qur'an as the eternal word of God, the problem of beholding the vision of God in the next world, and so on. It is significant that most of the major issues in religion were discussed in Syria, which was an important center of Christian theology. We know that John of Damascus the great doctor of the Greek Church, was a Vizier (Minister) under the Umayyads, and that he and his pupil Theodorus Abucara wrote polemic treatises on Islam summarizing discussions between Christians and Muslims. Some of these treatises were written in a catechetical form: If a Muslim asks you such and such a question, answer so and so. This is taken as an evidence that direct contact between Muslim and Christian scholars must have taken place at an early stage. But while the possibility of such contact is admitted, there is no justification for the exaggerated view put forward by such scholars as De Boer, Von Kremer, and D. B. Macdonald that the development of Muslim theology was largely influenced by Christian thought.

The other foreign factor which influenced Muslim theology, particularly in its mature form, is Greek philosophy. We can see traces of it in almost all the leading theological theories—either in the bearing of some Greek concepts on such theories, or in the way they were presented and discussed. Yet, here again, Greek ideas never remained unaltered; they were given such a turn as to harmonize with the fundamental concepts of Islam.

A consideration of the two major issues in Muslim theology —God and the problem of divine attributes, and man and the problem of free will—will illustrate the significant trends in the development of Islamic theological thought.

THE THEOLOGICAL CONCEPTION OF GOD. A variety of concepts of God, ranging from crude anthropomorphism to absolute transcendentalism, have their roots in the Qur'an. When the Muslim theologians began to reflect on the nature of God, they found themselves faced with two types of Quranic verses: those which describe God in relation to His creation, and those which describe Him in Himself. According to the former, God sees, hears, speaks to His people, creates with His hands, sits on His Throne, comes with His Angels, and will be seen on the Day of Judgment. They also ascribe to God typically human qualities such as pleasure and displeasure, love and hatred, and the like. These attributes are some of the ingredients, so to speak, of the personality of the one God who speaks to His servants and hears their call, loves the righteous, and hates the wicked. The Prophet says, "Pray to God as if thou seest Him, for if thou seest Him not, He seeth thee." That is, picture God as a person, for you cannot address yourself in prayer to the Absolute.

The second set of Quranic verses, those which describe God in Himself, refer to the divine attributes of transcendence by which God is distinguished from created beings. The question is: Can we predicate attributes of God at all? The Qur'an certainly does. God is described as omnipotent, as omniscient, as knowing and willing, as eternal, infinite, everlasting, and unlike all created beings. Some of these attributes are positive, others are negative. Can they all be predicated of God in the same way? The orthodox party maintain that they can, but they do not go into what such predication logically implies. The Mu'tazilites examine the implications of such predication. The negative attributes present no difficulty and are therefore admitted by them. The positive ones are either reduced to negations or denied as separate entities distinct from or added to the divine Essence. They do not deny that God knows, wills, and does things, but deny that His knowledge or will or action is different from and coeternal with His Essence. They are all identical with the Essence. To assert the separate existence of the divine attributes which are eternal because they belong to God is to assert a plurality of eternal beings, which is contrary to the oneness of God. Some Mu'tazilites went so far as to deny all positive attributes. To say that God knows such and such a thing, they say, means that He is not ignorant thereof, and the same with the rest of the attributes.

It is interesting to notice that the first Muslim thinker to deny the divine attributes in the above sense was Wasil Ibn Ata (died 131; A.D. 748) in his refutation of the Christian doctrine of the Trinity, which he considered a plurality of eternal attributes in one Essence. His view received more elaboration in the later circles of the Mu'tazilites who gave it a more philosophical turn. God was reduced by them to a simple monad stripped of all attributes and qualities. Hence they were called by their opponents *Mu'attila*, that is, those who render the divine attributes useless or functionless.

The opposite view was held by the orthodox party and later by the Ash'arite school. Their argument on the whole is not very convincing, and most of it is quibbling with words. God, they say, has attributes, but they are neither identical with His Essence nor different from it. They are "states" which though distinguishable from the Essence are yet inherent in it. The whole trouble, it seems, rested on one fundamental misconception: they personified the attributes but went on thinking they were dealing with the ordinary simple attributes of God. To talk about an eternal attribute which is different from the divine Essence but coexistent with it is to personify it and give it the status of a substance—a position very similar to that of the Christian Trinity. Had these theologians said that the attributes were mere intelligible relations qualifying the Essence, or mere names with which God has described Himself, the question as to their identity or nonidentity with the divine Essence and the other question as to their eternity or temporality would not have arisen.

The failure to realize the significance of describing the attributes of God from two different aspects is responsible for most of the disputes and futile arguments with which Muslim books on theology abound. The two contending parties—the traditionalists and rationalists—concentrated on one set of attributes to the comparative neglect of the other. The result was two extreme views, with corporealism or moderate anthropomorphism on the one side and absolute transcendentalism on the other. The Mu'tazilites, who were the champions of transcendentalism, resorted to a method of interpretation which explained away all the anthropomorphic passages in the Qur'an, and they discarded the anthropomorphic Prophetic Traditions as invalid or not authentic. This was necessary to preserve their conception of the absolute unity and transcendence of God. The traditionalists wavered between immanence and transcendence but were more inclined toward immanence.

The rational interpretation of the Mu'tazilites had its advantages as well as its disadvantages. In one respect it helped to liberate Islam from the materialistic and mythological concepts of God by insisting on the more spiritual and abstract attributes. But it was carried to an extreme by some of the rationalists who reduced the Godhead to an abstraction void of all content.

The enquiry into the nature of the divine attributes naturally led to a discussion on the nature of the Qur'an as the revealed word of God or the external manifestation of the attribute of divine speech. The orthodox, who held the doctrine of the eternity of the attributes, said the Qur'an was eternal. The rationalists said it was created, or there would be something eternal other than God, and this would be a violation of His oneness. The Prophet to whom the Qur'an was revealed did not hear the words of God, but heard a voice which God created in a material medium and which conveyed to him the content of the divine mind. The Qur'an as we know it is therefore created. This was the doctrine of the Mu'tazilites which was championed by the Abbasid Caliph al-Ma'mun.

When the triumphant days of the Mu'tazilites were ended, the orthodox party saw their opportunity once again and declared that all was uncreated, even the very Word written in the Book and recited in man's prayer. The Ash'arite school took up the problem later and discussed it on a higher level. They were influenced by older speculations on a similar subject, particularly the Christian and Jewish theories of the Logos, which in their turn were influenced by ancient Greek theories.

The Ash'arites held that God's speech was eternal. The Qur'an, the divine command, and the creative Word *Be*, were all forms of the eternal attribute of speech. "The command of God," says the Qur'an, "is such that when God wills a thing, He says to it: Be; and it is" (Surah XXXVI, 81). The creative command and the creative Word *Be* are therefore prior to all phenomenal existence. The Qur'an also says, "One of His signs is that the heavens and the earth are sustained by His command" (Surah XXX, 25). Thus the divine command is not only the instrument of creation, it is also the sustaining principle of the created world. Such verses were originally meant to emphasize the absolute sovereignty of God as the supreme Creator and Maintainer of the universe, but a new meaning was read into them by the Ash'arites in support of a Logos theory comparable in many respects to the Christian and Stoic theories. The divine command and creative Word were personified and given power to create and sustain that which they create. Moreover, the Word, or Logos, is in one respect identical with God, in another different from Him and coeternal with Him. Thus the Word of God gradually took a place similar to that of the Memra in Jewish theology, and the Second Person in the Christian doctrine of the Trinity.

The Ash'arites went a step further. They distinguished between two kinds of speech, the external and the internal. The external, which consists of words and sounds and can be put down in writing, is created. The internal, which is expressed by such words and sounds, is identical with the divine consciousness and is therefore eternal. This distinction is certainly borrowed from the philosophy of the Stoics who spoke of potential and actual, or internal and external Logoi. It is also in line with the Christian theory of the Logos which distinguishes the Word which was from eternity with God and was God from the Word which appeared in a temporal manifestation in the form of Christ. Perhaps the earlier Ash'arites did not express themselves in such plain words. They did not work out the metaphysical implications of their theory. They were more concerned with the problems of the eternity of the Qur'an which they thought they had proved. What they actually proved is the eternity of the divine mind or the divine knowledge, and the temporal manifestation of this knowledge when revealed to the Prophet. This position was taken up by al-Ghazali and later Ash'arites.

DETERMINISM AND FREE WILL. The ethical problem of determinism and free will has its roots in the much wider metaphysical problem of the conception of God in His relation to the world in general and mankind in particular. The pessimistic attitude of the Semitic mind toward the world as a fleeting shadow, the notion that it has value only as a place in which man prepares himself for a more permanent life, led to the conception that God is the absolute sovereign power which rules all things, including man and his actions. We have a definite trace of this conception in the Qur'an. God is the supreme King of Heaven and earth whose authority is not to be challenged. The following examples are typical of a large number of similar texts in the Qur'an. "He should not be asked concerning what He does" (Surah XXI, 23). "He createth what He will" (Surah XXX, 54). "He it is Who created you from dust" (Surah XL, 67). "He alone misguides whomever He pleases and guides whomever He pleases" (Surah XXXV, 8). And in talking to his people, Noah says, "Nor shall my counsel profit you if God wills to misguide you, though I fain would counsel you aright. God is your Lord, and unto Him shall ye return" (Surah XI, 34). This is one side of the picture; in its theological aspect it emphasizes the absolute authority of God over His creation, and in its ethical aspect suggests a deterministic theory of man's actions.

The other side of the picture shows the same two aspects closely related to one another. God, who is described as supreme power and will, is also described as just. The following typical passage from the Qur'an illustrates the justice of God. "We will not burden a soul beyond its power; with Us is a Book which speaks the truth, and they shall not be unjustly treated" (Surah XXIII, 62). "These are the signs of God: we recite them to thee in truth and God wills not injustice to mankind" (Surah III, 108). "God does them no injustice; it is they who are unjust to themselves" (Surah III, 117). "In truth has God created the heavens and the earth that each soul shall be rewarded for what he has earned, and that they shall not be wronged" (Surah XLV, 22). Thus, according to the Qur'an, justice is an essential attribute of God, and it is inconceivable that God can be the absolute despot who wills and acts as He pleases even if His actions are contrary to justice.

It is obvious that the two opposite theories, determinism and free will, can be traced back to a conflict between two conceptions of the nature of God—God as absolute power and God as just.

The early Muslims who were the true sons of the desert preferred to think of God after the pattern of a tribal God with unlimited authority, a conception from which they derived their ethical theory of determinism. Their God can do everything, even that which is unjust or unreasonable. On the ethical side they taught that man was nothing but an instrument in the hands of his Lord, subjected to the strictest laws of determinism. This theory, known as oriental fatalism, has caused Islam to be stigmatized as a fatalistic religion, but nothing could be farther from the truth, for Islam attaches the greatest importance to the role which man plays in the sphere of his actions.

The Mu'tazilites, on the other hand, emphasized man's responsibility for his own actions. They argued against the despotism of God as well as against determinism and fatalism and put their whole trust in human reason, which to them was sacred. They taught that appeal should be made to reason first, rather than to the religious law. Reason tells us that we are the authors of our own actions and that some of them are right and others are wrong. Perception of right and wrong is an innate power of the human mind not due to knowledge taught by religion. Man therefore is a free agent and the maker of his own destiny. He is also the maker of his own moral law which must coincide with the religious law because the religious law is rational. There can be no religious injunction which is contrary to reason.

Man, however, is not purely rational, according to the Mu'tazilites. There is an irrational element in man to which he sometimes yields. This is why he sometimes goes astray and falls into error and sin, and this is why religion is needed as a reminder to the forgetful and to those whose rational will is thwarted by carnal desires. The Muslim rationalists were certainly on the road to Kant. The good will is the only thing that has intrinsic value in moral life, and it is man's own. Without freedom of the will and personal responsibility, retribution, punishment and reward, and the Future Life with its Heaven and Hell are all empty words void of meaning.

Rationality is not only the guiding principle in man's actions and beliefs, according to the Muslim rationalists; it is also the ruling principle in the cosmos. This world is the best of all possible worlds because it is the work of a supreme Mind. The so-called evil in the world is an integral part of the goodness of the whole.

The root of the doctrine of free will is to be found in the Qur'an itself and there is no justification for seeking an external source for it. In fact, the Quranic passages in favor of free will by far outnumber those which are suggestive of determinism. "And say: The truth is from your Lord: let him then who will, believe, and let him who will be an infidel" (Surah XVIII, 30). "This truly is a reminder: and whoso wills, takes the road to his Lord" (Surah LXXVI, 29). "Say: Everyone acts after his manner; but your Lord knows who is best guided in his path" (Surah XVII, 84). "He who does evil or acts unjustly against himself, then asks pardon of God, will find God forgiving, merciful. And he who commits a crime, commits it to his own hurt" (Surah IV, 111–12).

According to the Qur'an man is free to choose his actions and beliefs, and he merits punishment or reward according to whether his choice is right or wrong. It is for God to show the right path, and for man to follow it or not follow it. Everything is predestined in the sense that it is predetermined by man's nature and known as such to God from eternity. The eternal knowledge of God does not interfere one iota with man's choice. Only in this sense can any meaning be attached to moral and religious obligations. Man alone works out his salvation, and this by faith and good deeds. Faith is rarely mentioned alone in the Qur'an; it is usually coupled with good deeds as the necessary prerequisites for entering paradise. "Bring good tidings to those who believe and do the good things that are right, that for them are gardens 'neath which rivers flow" (Surah II, 25). "Those who have believed and done the good things that are right, they shall be the inmates of Paradise" (Surah II, 82).

The Philosophical Attitude

The attitude of the Muslim philosophers toward Islam is somewhat different from that of the theologians. The main object of the theologians was to defend, in their own way, Islamic dogmas. The philosophers sought to reconcile Islamic dogmas with philosophic ideas, to arrive at a conception of God which would satisfy the requirements of free thought as well as those of religious beliefs. The conception of God as the ultimate ground of all phenomenal existence had, somehow or other, to be brought into harmony with the conception of the personal God of Islam. To what extent the attempt was successful we shall see later.

The first Muslims to philosophize about the simple ideas of Islam were the Mu'tazilites. They were followed by the philosophers al-Kindi, al-Farabi, and Ibn Sina (Avicenna). The philosophers were on the whole contemptuous of their predecessors. Even al-Ghazali could not conceal his disappointment with the method of the theologians. "Their method," he says, "is right only insofar as it accomplishes their own objective; but it is of no avail to anyone who admits nothing but self-evident truths."

Generally speaking one can say that the theological method had no philosophic basis, though this applies more to the school of the Ash'arites than the Mu'tazilites. The Ash'arites were skeptical in their attitude toward sense data. They denied causality and causal necessity and even refused to call God the First Cause. They taught that natural phenomena appear to be uniform not because they are subject to necessary laws but because the human mind reads sequence into them. At any moment God may interrupt such uniformities and cause miraculous things to happen. Nothing takes place as a result of interrelations between natural phenomena. Everything is fresh creation. Their whole conception of God and the natural world was different from, and directed against, the Aristotelian philosophy which forms the basis of the thinking of the Muslim philosophers.

It is impossible to give an account of the individual systems of all the philosophers of Islam here. In this general treatment of the subject the aim will be to set forth the attitude of the school of al-Farabi and Ibn Sina, who represent Muslim philosophy in its strict and more limited sense. Ibn Sina in particular represents this philosophy in its mature and final form in a clear and well-reasoned manner. His object, like that of all Muslim philosophers before and after him, was to find a formula by which religious dogmas and philosophic principles can be reconciled. In this he was the faithful follower of al-Farabi. For both of them Greek philosophy was almost infallible, yet they acknowledged, in their own way, the basic theological principles of Islam. Their philosophy therefore is a mixture of ideas often irreconcilable except with the help of the drastic method of explaining away the opposite concepts. It is also highly eclectic in character, but eclecticism was not entirely the work of the Muslim mind as some scholars maintain. Two of the most important sources from which the Muslim thinkers drew considerable material reached them in an already eclectic form—Neoplatonism and Hermetic philosophy. Plato and Aristotle had already been brought into some harmony and their ideas interpreted in the light of the ancient wisdom of the Orient with its characteristic religious sentiment. This made them all the more appealing to the Muslim philosophers whose aim was to philosophize Islam.

When Greek thought found its way into the Muslim world, the philosophers found themselves faced with a problem which they attempted to solve. On the one hand Islam called them to a simple faith in God who is the sole creator and sustainer of the world. It offered them no philosophy or even a basis for one. On the other hand, Greek philosophy in the form in which it came to them represented the final achievements reached by the Greek mind in its search for a solution of the problem of existence. It was impossible for Muslims to accept without alteration any religious teaching which, outwardly at least, contradicted their philosophic ideas. But it was equally impossible to go the full length with Greek philosophical theories and accept their necessary consequences. Therefore, the only way left open to them was to reconcile the two. The question was—which of the Greek philosophical theories should they accept? Aristotle's theory of a Prime Mover who set the whole world in motion, then left it to its own fate? Or Plato's theory of God as the supreme Idea of Good—whose relation to the existing world he left unexplained? Or the Stoic's theory of pantheism? Or the Neoplatonic theory of emanation?

Those were the chief Greek theories of the nature of God known to the Muslims, and none of them could possibly be accepted by them without serious modification. The pantheistic view of reality never appeared in the Muslim philosophy of the type we are discussing here, but a full-fledged theory of pantheism was put forward later by the greatest of all Muslim mystics, Muhy al-Din Ibn Arabi. We shall say more about him later. The Muslim philosophers made use of Platonic, Aristotelian, and Neoplatonic ideas in constructing their own metaphysics, in which Islamic ideas also play an important part. But even the Islamic concepts were interpreted in such a way as to make them more philosophical, thus narrowing the gulf between Islamic and pagan thought.

The problem with which Muslim philosophers were faced was that of the relation between the external world, with its multiplicity of spatio-temporal and changeable phenomena, and an ultimate, immutable, and unchangeable First Principle. In philosophical language, the problem was that of the relation between the one and the many, or the noumenon and the phenomena; in theological language it was the problem of

God and the universe. The Greek thinkers were far from the idea of the Godhead as explained in revealed religions. Aristotle's philosophy is one of strict determinism in which both the material world and God are subject to a supreme law of self-necessity. The metaphysical-poetical conception of Plato reduces God to a mere abstraction. It was the Neoplatonists who, though in the main adhering to their pagan tradition, put forward some sort of a philosophy of religion. It is no wonder therefore that they paved the way for establishing Christian and Muslim philosophy of religion, and that their influence in Muslim religious thought in particular was predominant.

The attempt to reconcile Islam with Greek philosophy in general and Neoplatonism in particular was an honest but a very daring one. Whether the Muslim philosophers succeeded or failed is another matter, but the fact remains that through making the effort they made their genuine contribution to the history of human thought. They also exposed themselves to the severest criticism of their adversaries. Ghazali's vehement attacks on their views will be referred to later.

Ibn Sina is generally regarded as a true representative of the philosophy which sought to reconcile Islamic and Neoplatonic thought. His metaphysical views are regarded by no less an authority than Ghazali as being the most typical of his school, and when Ghazali launches his attacks against the philosophers he has Ibn Sina in mind all the time. Al-Farabi is also an excellent type, but he lacks the clarity and comprehensiveness of his successor. Al-Kindi is more of a logician, natural philosopher, and theologian. Ibn Rushd's (Averroes) greatness is to be found more in his commentaries on Aristotle than in independent philosophical thought. The rest of the Muslim philosophers of the West are mere satellites moving around al-Farabi and Ibn Sina.

God and the world. Ibn Sina prefers to call God the Necessary Being, or the Self-Subsistent Being, rather than Allah. His intention is to bridge the gulf between the religious and philosophical concepts of the Deity, and thus to be able to follow up his analysis of being and necessity, or self-subsistence, to their logical conclusions. The name Allah has some Muslim associations which make it unphilosophical.

Ibn Sina starts his analysis of the relation between God and the world with a consideration of the notion of being—a purely ontological procedure—which he divides into necessary and contingent being. The necessary being is that being whose existence is self-necessitated; it exists *per se;* its essence and existence are identical; the supposition of its nonexistence involves contradiction. The contingent being is that which has no essential or necessary reason for its existence; its being or nonbeing are equally possible; its essence is different from its existence. This is the phenomenal world; it is all that is "other than God." Ibn Sina says that the mere fact that we have a notion of the Necessary Being proves that He exists. Existence is a positive quality of perfection, and if we have an idea of the Perfect Being, that Perfect Being must exist, or our idea would be self-contradictory. This is the ontological argument used in modern philosophy by Descartes and Leibnitz, though the consequences which Ibn Sina draws are different.

Ibn Sina also makes use of the Aristotelian distinction between necessity and contingency, but goes far beyond what Aristotle has said in the subject, both in his proof of the existence of God and in his explanation of the relation between God and the universe. He criticizes the cosmological argument of the theologians by which they infer the existence of an eternal Creator from the existence of the phenomenal world. Contingency, he says, not origination in time, is the cause of the dependence of the world upon God. To say that it is origination in time—that is, creation—leads to these absurdities: that God's will and creative power were idle for an infinite time before the creation of the world; that to choose the creation of the world at a certain time, and not before or after that time, must have been due to circumstances outside God's nature, which means that some sort of change must have taken place in Him; and that the world after it has been created could very well be independent of its Creator, since its need of Him is only for creation and not for preservation after creation.

A contingent universe, on the other hand, has no temporal beginning and is dependent for its existence and the continuity of its existence on God. It is an eternal being which derives its existence every moment from God. There is only logical—not temporal—priority between them, the priority of cause to effect. The cause has never existed in time before its effect in this case. We can also call it priority of rank since the cause is usually regarded as superior to the effect. Here Ibn Sina is in complete agreement with Aristotle and in complete disagreement with the theologians who insist on the idea of creation, which is one of the principle dogmas of Islam. The world, they hold, was created out of nothing by the will of God and at the time He appointed. No question should be asked as to why it was not created before or after, because such relations as before and after have no application within the domain of the eternal Will. This is the argument adduced by Ghazali in his refutation of the philosophers' doctrine of the eternity of the world.

In spite of his theory of the eternity of the world, Ibn Sina describes God as the Maker, the Fashioner, and sometimes the Creator of the world. These epithets occur in the Qur'an and have one definite sense in common—bringing the world into existence from nothing. Ibn Sina, who believed in the impossibility of creation out of nothing, explains these terms in such a way as to deprive them of their temporal significance. That which comes into being need not always have a temporal beginning, nor need it be the result of an act of will. It can be the result of a spontaneous and necessary overflowing of being from an original source, like the overflowing of the rays from the sun. This is the case with regard to the world in its relation to God. If eternity and necessity are essential attributes of God as the Primary Cause, so must they be attributes of His actions, which are His effects.

Thus we see how far Ibn Sina went in his deterministic philosophy. Necessity is the fundamental law to which both the phenomenal world and God Himself are subjected.

THE ATTRIBUTES OF GOD. The conception of God in Muslim philosophy, in spite of all that has been said, is not quite the same as the Aristotelian conception. God, according to al-Farabi and Ibn Sina, is not a mere principle of action within the material world but is an independent and transcendent Being over and above the material world, forever producing it and preserving it.

Their conception of the Godhead is both theological and philosophical. God has two different kinds of attributes: metaphysical attributes, which can be inferred directly or indirectly from the definition of God as the Necessary Being; and theological attributes with which God describes Himself in the Qur'an. Even the metaphysical attributes are often tinged with a religious color and explained in a way which makes them partly ethical and partly theological. This is because these philosophers are forever oscillating between philosophy and religion, although their loyalty on the whole is to philosophy.

According to Ibn Sina the divine attributes are simplicity, oneness, absolute perfection, pure goodness; God is the contemplator and the contemplated; God has no equal nor opposite.

Simplicity logically follows from the definition of God as the Necessary Being; for complexity, whether material, quantitative, or even intelligible, is contrary to necessity and self-subsistence. The complex, whatever it is, is dependent on its constituent parts and on something else to make it a whole. It follows, therefore, that God is not a material substance, is not divisible, is not a compound of two or more substances, and is not definable.

Oneness is an attribute of God, for God is one in every respect. He has no partner who participates either in His essence or in His attributes. This is the first article of the Muslim faith. Plurality of gods contradicts the notion of self-necessity.

Absolute perfection is an attribute of God. God is perfect and complete. In Aristotle's language, God is pure actuality; there is nothing that is possible in Him which is not actually realized—His will, His knowledge, and His action, the whole of His nature. Everything else is in the process of becoming. The perfection of everything other than God is a potentiality which God brings into an actuality.

Pure goodness is an attribute inferred from God's being free from matter and potentiality. Goodness here is equivalent to positive being, the opposite of evil or not-being. All other things possess the two aspects of being and not-being, because in one respect they are actual and in another they are potential. God is not only the pure good, He is also the fountainhead from which good—positive being—is forever flowing into everything in the world. The whole realm of existence turns toward Him in love-like fashion for the good it receives from Him, for the qualities of being through which the world advances along the road to perfection. The world in fact does love God, because it loves the good, and good is the only thing that is loved for its own sake. Through love, therefore, God sets the whole world in motion, and whatever takes place in existence is the fruit of this love.

Ibn Sina, who is not so successful in his theory about God as the Active Cause, admirably succeeds in portraying Him as the Final Cause. His argument here is potent, clear, and free from verbal quibbling. In fact, it is the most beautiful part of his metaphysics; it is here that his philosophy and mysticism meet. The relation between God and the external world is here expressed in terms of love and revelation—love on the part of the world, and revelation on the part of the Beloved. The divine act of bestowing being on things is the very act of self-revelation. God reveals Himself to His creatures in a manner suitable to the requirements of their inner nature, which is fixed and immutable, or in proportion to the degree of perfection which they aspire to achieve. The divine Providence is the work of a mind which comprehends an orderly system gradually unfolding itself. The self-unfolding of the phenomenal world is paralleled in the eternal self-revelation of God, and the two processes are inseparable. Ibn Sina's theodicy, aesthetics, and optimistic theory of the nature of the world branch off from this mystical philosophy. It is here that he seems to be more under the influence of Plato and Plotinus than Aristotle.

For Ibn Sina, God is essentially an intellect whose sole activity is to contemplate Himself. He is the contemplator and the contemplated, the subject and the object in one. There is no duality in Him as there is in other minds. Duality of any kind is contrary to His absolute unity and simplicity.

There is a great deal of discussion about the knowledge of the Divine Mind. The theologians, following the Qur'an, hold that God knows everything past, present, and future, seen and unseen. They say that He is omniscient, that nothing takes place in the world which is not in accordance with His prior knowledge. The philosophers, on the other hand, maintain that God's knowledge is primarily of Himself and that, knowing Himself, He knows the world in a general way. He is the Ultimate Cause of things, as we have explained, and knowledge of the cause entails knowledge of the effect. They argue that knowledge of individual happenings in the world depends on a temporal relation between the knower and the known and therefore involves change in the knower, but God's knowledge is above time and change.

Ibn Sina also maintains that God has neither an equal nor an opposite. He has no equal because it is impossible for two necessary beings (gods) to be. He has no opposite because two opposites must be similar in one respect and dissimilar in another respect, in which they are said to be opposites—and God has no similar in any respect whatsoever. Therefore He has no opposite.

The Muslim philosophers do not omit the Quranic attributes of God such as omnipotence, omniscience, justice, generosity, and the like, but they interpret them philosophically or explain them away. We have already given the attributes of knowledge and will as examples. So it is quite evident that their concept of God is neither the pagan conception of the Greek philosophers nor the strictly orthodox Islamic conception. The denial of creation in its ordinary sense and the doctrine of the eternity of the world are definitely non-Islamic. In their view, however, they have shifted the problem to a higher plane by maintaining that the world is the outcome of God's inner necessity and the eternal urge within Him to give an outward manifestation of His bounty and generosity.

Although on the theoretical side the Muslim philosophers certainly seemed to be anti-Islamic, at least in some of their views, on the practical side they were true Muslims, insofar as we can gather from their biographies. Al-Farabi is said to have led a saintly life of religious devotion and contemplation. Ibn Sina, though allowing himself some bodily indulgences, is not reported to have neglected his religious duties. It is true that his conceptions of Heaven and Hell and the Resurrection are somewhat unorthodox, but he does not completely deny the orthodox concepts. We will conclude this section with his own words, taken from his *Nine Epistles:*

> The ultimate object of man wherein lies his greatest happiness in future life is to gain knowledge of the realities of things so far as his nature allows, and do what is incumbent upon him. Only in this way does man's soul become more honorable and perfect, an intelligible microcosm comparable to the existing Macrocosm, and become ready to enjoy the greatest happiness in the world to come.

The Mystical Attitude

The mysticism of Islam is known as Sufism, a name said to be derived from the Arabic word *suf* which means wool, referring to the woolen mantles worn by the Sufis. With Muslim mysticism we see the climax of the development of religious life and teaching in Islam. Neither the philosophers nor the theologians nor the canon lawyers have contributed so much as the mystics toward deepening the meaning of their religion and enriching its teachings. It is due to them that Islam, in the way they understand it, can be compared with other great religions of the world, for mysticism is the only ground on which the great religions meet.

Muslim mysticism has, from the time of its inception, been a spiritual revolution against a variety of forms and systems, both social and religious. After a long period of hard struggle, Sufism established itself in two quite different ways: as a religious philosophy and as the popular religion of Islam.

During some of its flourishing periods, the Sufis were counted by the millions all over the Muslim Empire and in some countries their influence was so great that the heads of their orders were the practical rulers, with supreme authority in every major problem concerning the religious or seculiar institutions. Such influence can be found even now in some Muslim communities.

As an ideal mode of spiritual life, Sufism has passed through various stages. At some times it was thoroughly orthodox, at others so far removed from orthodoxy as to become a mere system of religious philosophy. It has also undergone some periods of stagnation and corruption during which its followers completely lost sight of the noble and lofty ideals of the original founders, preserving an outward appearance of ritual with nothing to correspond to it in the heart. But these remarks belong more to the history of Sufism. Our immediate object here is to try to set forth the mystical attitude toward Islam so far as it can be gleaned from the lives and teachings of the great Sufi masters, leaving everything else out of our account.

The special attitude of the Muslim mystics toward Islam was quite clear from the time their movement started. Until the end of the second century (eighth century A.D.) religious laws were based on the literal texts of the Qur'an and Prophetic Traditions, and scrupulously carried out. They were thoroughly studied and strictly adhered to in practice. Knowledge of the canon law—jurisprudence—was the most venerated of all knowledge, and adherence to its rules was the ultimate aim as well as the true mark of every pious Muslim. When the Sufis appeared on the scene, they came with another religious ideal. To them the examination of the esoteric meaning of the law was a more worthy objective than the study of the law in its exoteric sense. Hence arose the distinction between the outward expression of the law and its inward significance, and with it the distinction between the study of jurisprudence on the one hand and Sufism on the other. The jurists became known as the externalists and the Sufis as the internalists. Gradually the opposition between the two camps grew more and more intense as they realized that they stood for two different conceptions of Islam and its teachings.

The differences between the legalists and the Sufis were apparent in their interpretations of the meaning of religious law and the ways in which it should be derived and justified. They differed as to the nature of worship and the way it should be performed. They did not agree as to which actions are lawful or unlawful or what parts of the law are basic to Islam. Nor did they agree as to the object and value of obligatory and supererogatory religious devotions. Is God the object of formal worship or of love? They differed on many points of Islamic dogma, especially concerning the conception of God in His relation to man, and the meaning of the unity of God.

It is obvious that such disputes touch the very core of Islam, and it is no wonder that the Muslim theologians and jurists became the bitterest enemies of the Sufis and fought them on all fronts for centuries. The first opposition to their movement came from the traditionalist Ahmad Ibn Hanbal (died 241; A.D. 855). He could not conceal his admiration for a Sufi like al-Harith al-Muhasibi (died 243; A.D. 857), but admitted that al-Muhasibi spoke in his sermons a language unknown to him, the language of the Sufis. He did not doubt his sincerity but was full of suspicion and apprehension. Relentless persecution of the Sufis was carried on by Ibn Hanbal's party and other theological sects in order to put an end to their growing influence.

Gradually the new mysticism of Sufism—or rather, the new religious spirit—gained ground. It was realized that Islam as understood by the jurists was ultimately reduced to formal ritual which consisted in the performance of certain bodily movements. Prayer, fasting, and pilgrimage were well-defined and measured physical movements, almost void of genuine feeling. Such an attitude toward Islam was sure to satisfy the externalists whose main concern was to give precise definitions to religious terms, lay down general laws, and see that they were strictly observed. It did not satisfy the religious sentiment of the Sufis, who looked for a deeper meaning behind the outward forms. Qushayri tells us that Ruwaym of Baghdad (died 303; A.D. 915) said, "All people hold fast to external appearances [of religion], but this community [the Sufis] holds fast to realities. All people consider it their duty to observe the external aspect of the religious law; the Sufis consider it their duty to strive after piety and unremitting sincerity." In these few words Ruwaym sums up the whole situation by pointing out the real difference between the Sufis and the rest of the Muslims in their respective attitudes toward Islam. For the Sufis, Islam is *haqiqa*, a reality hidden behind words and forms, while for the rest of the Muslims it is principally words and forms.

Such a distinction was practically unknown to the early Muslims. The idea started with the Shi'a who taught that the Qur'an, like everything else, had two aspects, one external and the other internal. The latter is what the Sufis call the esoteric meaning of the Qur'an, which is only revealed to the chosen people of God. They extended the idea to everything in Islam. A real contrast was made between the shari'a (religious law) aspect of a religious principle or usage and its haqiqa aspect, that is, between the religious law as such and its real meaning.

It is true that the great teachers of Sufism agree that shari'a should be strictly observed, and that the abandonment of shari'a on the pretext that haqiqa, the reality or spirit of the law, has been obtained is not only impiety but infidelity. Haqiqa without shari'a, they say, is baseless, and shari'a without haqiqa is meaningless. A reasonable balance between the two is essential for a truly religious life. Such a balance is described by Ghazali in these words,

> He who says that haqiqa is contrary to shari'a, and the internal [side of religion] is contrary to the external is nearer to infidelity. Every haqiqa that has no root in shari'a should be rejected. Shari'a is the law enjoined upon people; haqiqa is seeing the work of Divine Providence. Shari'a is worship of God; haqiqa is to behold Him. Shari'a is to obey the Divine Command; haqiqa is to know by mystic vision what God has predestined, what He has revealed and what He has concealed.

So, according to Ghazali, haqiqa is the spiritual justification and proof of religion. The true meaning of religious teachings is seen by the mystic in his heart. Its real nature is revealed to him. When, for instance, the mystic is called upon to worship God, the meaning of the Godhead and of worship is freshly perceived by the inner light. This is the general attitude adopted by the majority of orthodox Sufis and ardently defended by such men as Tustari (died 273; A.D. 886), Kharraz (died 277; A.D. 890), Junayd (died 297; A.D. 909), and Ghazali (died 505; A.D. 1111). But some Sufis went too far in emphasizing haqiqa and minimizing the importance of shari'a and were eventually led into various degrees of the erroneous belief that the awareness of inner reality frees one from the moral obligations of the law. They represent the other extreme of Sufism which is condemned by the genuinely pious Muslims. Others among the Sufis held fast to shari'a, but understood it in ways which were much wider and more liberal than the interpretation of the orthodox, looking upon the law as either a system of self-discipline or as a set of symbols representing hidden religious meanings.

Those Sufis who regarded the law as essentially a system of self-discipline rejected the claim that the shari'a is a collection of norms and codes divided and subdivided into more norms and codes. For them it must not be understood within the narrow limits and strict definitions of the lawyers and theologians. The value of any religious work should not be judged on the basis of its compliance with the law; its value should be determined by the degree to which it fulfills the ideal of the lawgiver. Voluntary acts of devotion are considered superior to obligatory acts because they fulfill a higher ideal—the love of God—while obligatory acts of devotion only show submissive obedience to God's commands. The Sufis quote the following Tradition in which God says, "In no way does My servant so draw nigh unto Me as when he performs those duties which I have imposed on him; and My servant continues to draw near to Me through works of supererogation, until I love him. And when I love him, I am his eye, so that he sees by Me, and his ear, so that he hears by

Me, and his tongue, so that he speaks by Me, and his hand, so that he takes by Me."

This means that in the act of devotion he becomes completely absorbed in God and loses every vestige of his individual being and feels himself to be one with his Beloved. Such a state is not attained by the ordinary performance of religious duties. The Sufi seeks the attainment of the spiritual benefits which he gains through his acts of devotion, not the mere performance of outward acts as such. Thus the real essence of religion is that which resides in the heart, not that which is performed by the body. The religious command should be addressed to the heart, not to the bodily organs.

This attitude, noble as it is, seems to have paved the way to antinomianism in some Sufi circles. Religious duties, they argued, are a means to an end, and if the end is reached we can very well dispense with the means. Haqiqa, religious truth, is for them the end and shari'a, religious law, is the means. That there were such men even in the golden age of Sufism who allowed themselves all sorts of license and indulgences under the pretext that they had reached their goal is evident from the scathing remarks which we read in the opening chapters of the treatise on Sufism by Qushayri (died 465; A.D. 1072). He attacks most mercilessly the men of his time who believed that haqiqa frees one from the moral obligations of the law, and appeals for a revision of Sufism in the light of the teachings of the old masters, calling upon the Sufis to lead a true religious life in accordance with the Qur'an and the example of the founders of the Sufi path.

Qushayri's warning was not in vain, for fifty years later it found a remarkable response in the writings of Ghazali who took upon himself the task of reconciling Sufism with Islam. He interpreted the principles of Sufism in the light of Islam and showed their interdependence. It is true that Ghazali was primarily concerned with the solution of his own spiritual problem when he was in search of the truth, but in solving his own problem he solved the problem for thousands of others who were and still are searching for the same truth. This truth he found in the Sufi way of life lived according to strict

Muslim law. Religious truth is the inner meaning of the law revealed in the heart of the Sufi by the Divine Light.

In addition to the Sufis who looked upon the law as a means of self-discipline there were those who looked upon the shari'a as a set of symbols standing for hidden religious meanings. Those symbols are of value only as a reminder or an occasion in which the hidden meanings are realized. The pious Muslim should perform the acts of worship prescribed by the shari'a with his heart set on their spiritual meanings, otherwise his worship is merely an empty mechanical action.

This attitude takes into account the external, physical acts of worship as well as the internal acts of the heart. The danger is that it might lead to discarding the external acts altogether on the ground that they are superfluous. The Sufis who insisted on the observation of both the external and internal acts of worship read into the external teachings of Islam meanings undreamed of by canon lawyers. Prayer, for instance, is not regarded as a set of words to be uttered and movements to be performed but is looked upon as essentially a spiritual discourse between man and his Creator. All movements and words are symbols whose meanings form a part of that inner discourse. Similarly, pilgrimage is not a mere trip to the Holy Shrine of Mecca; it is the spiritual journey of the human soul to God. Each step of the journey, each of the rites of the pilgrimage—such as circumambulation of the Ka'ba, the kissing of the Black Stone, the standing on Mount Arafat—is a symbol of great spiritual significance. Each bodily movement of the pilgrimage has a corresponding movement of the heart.

The mention of God, known as *dhikr*, is another example of the symbolic interpretation of Islamic worship. It is not a mere repetition of the name Allah, but is the silent recollection and contemplation of God, done in such a way that the heart of the contemplator becomes occupied with nothing but Him and the lover becomes completely absorbed in his Beloved.

The Sufis go through the rest of the forms of worship in the same way. The man who performs religious rites without observing their hidden meanings is, according to them, like a child who reads the words of a book without understanding them. His religious life is void because his heart is void. In the case of prayer and dhikr, such a man's heart is occupied merely with the name of God, not with God Himself.

THE SUFI CONCEPTION OF GOD. Just as the attitude of the Sufis toward the religious teachings of Islam was a revolt against the jurists who stifled the true spirit of religion in order to preserve its form, their attitude toward God was also a revolt directed against the theologians and the philosophers. The barren speculations of the Muslim rationalists deprived the Godhead of its positive content, and God was reduced to a logical abstraction. The orthodox theologians made of Him a despot whose absolute power could do everything, even the impossible and the irrational. The philosophers, in their attempt to reconcile Islamic dogmas with Greek philosophy, were obliged to abandon many of the theological attributes of God, or explain them away, and put an active or final cause in place of a creator of the world. To the majority of the Sufis, God is essentially a personal being endowed with attributes which determine His relations with the world in general and man in particular. The outline of their picture of God is taken from the Qur'an, but the details which bring out the main features of the pictures are supplied by them, each in his own way.

God, they say, is the Creator of the world, the Maintainer, the sole Doer of everything, the Light of heaven and earth, the Merciful, the Compassionate, but above all He is the God who abides in the hearts of men. "Neither My heaven nor My earth contains Me," He says in a Tradition often quoted by the Sufis, "but I am contained in the heart of My servant who is a believer." So the Sufi does not look afar for his God, for the kingdom of God is in his heart if he can only see it.

The ultimate goal of the Muslim mystics is to bring this state into full realization, to feel the presence of God in the heart in such a way that nothing else is allowed to occupy it. Their aim is the complete absorption of the individual self in the contemplation of God.

If we pass in review over the long and complicated history

of Sufism, we find that three different conceptions of God—ethical, aesthetic, and pantheistic—appear in successive stages of its development. They all had their roots directly or indirectly in the Qur'an and Prophetic Traditions, or were brought into relation with such texts by means of interpretation.

The ethical conception of God was predominant in the earliest period of Muslim asceticism. The essence of God was regarded as absolute power and will. God was the supreme author of all things, including men's actions. The present life was essentially evil and therefore should be abandoned if the everlasting happiness of the Future World was to be attained. The early Sufis had an exaggerated sense of guilt and of the terrible torments that awaited the sinners in Hell. Consequently an overwhelming fear of God and His wrath seized their hearts, and their pious devotions were regarded as a means of escape from the judgment to come. They had almost forgotten the words of God in which He says, "My mercy embraces all things," and, "God pardons everything except associating other gods with Him." This fear colored the moral and religious life of the early ascetics, and determined their attitude toward God, the world, and their fellowmen.

The aesthetic conception of God in Sufi metaphysics was based on the idea of reciprocal love between God and man. The root of this doctrine is to be found in the Qur'an, but further elaborations of it were due to foreign influences coming from Manichaeanism and Neoplatonism. The first note in this direction was struck by the woman saint of Basra, Rabi'a (died 185; A.D. 801). From the third century onward, the doctrine of divine love became the dominant feature of Sufism. God was the Beloved of the Sufis, and loving Him for His own sake was the end of all their endeavor. It was no longer the fear of Hell or the hope of Paradise, but the hope of obtaining a glimpse of the everlasting beauty of God which motivated the Sufis. Rabi'a says in one of her prayers, "O God! if I worship Thee in fear of Hell, burn me in Hell, and if I worship Thee in hope of Paradise, exclude me from Paradise. But if I worship Thee for Thine own sake, withhold not Thine everlasting beauty." Also attributed to her is the following verse:

Two ways I love Thee: selfishly,
And next, as worthy is of Thee.
'Tis selfish love that I do naught
Save think on Thee with every thought.
'Tis purest love when Thou dost raise
The veil to my adoring gaze.
Not mine the praise in that or this
Thine is the praise in both I wis.

(Translated by R. A. Nicholson in *Legacy of Islam*, pp. 213–14)

As time went on, the idea of divine love went deeper and deeper into the life and thought of the Muslim mystics. On the practical side it became the sole motive of their actions. Moral ideas centered around it, just as they centered around the fear of God in the earlier period. Altruism or selflessness became the highest virtue. This meant the abandonment of worldly pleasures and the absolute denial of selfishness for the sake of God. "The essence of love is self-denial," says Ghazali. "It is the ultimate end of all mystic stations. Every state that comes after it is a fruit thereof; and every station that precedes it is a step toward it." Jalal al-Din Rumi, the great Sufi mystic, says, "Love is the remedy of our pride and self-conceit, the physician of all our infirmities."

The Sufis devoted their lives to the worship of God because they loved Him and were anxious to win His love. On the theoretical side, divine love was regarded as the sole reason for the creation of the world. Creation is an expression of God's love, it is His eternal Beauty reflected in an external form. The Sufis quote the following Tradition in which God says, "I was a hidden treasure and I loved to be known, so I created the creation that they might know Me." Moreover they maintain that love is the key to all Heavenly mysteries, and the essence of all true religion. It brings with it, not reasoned convictions, but convictions based on the infallible proof of immediate intuition. It is the celestial light that guides the traveler on his way to God.

Pantheism did not appear in Muslim mysticism—or at least not in a systematic form—before Muhy al-Din Ibn Arabi (died 638; A.D. 1240), the greatest of all Arabic-speaking mystics of Islam. Pantheistic tendencies were seen as early as the third century, for instance in some of the utterances of Bayazid of Bistam (died 261; A.D. 875), but they were not worked out into a consistent pantheistic doctrine. Ibn Arabi, on the other hand, was the first to produce a full-fledged pantheistic philosophy which left its indelible marks on the whole of Sufism ever since his time. The fundamental principle of this philosophy is the principle of the unity of all Being. His understanding of this principle is best summed up in his own words: "Glory to God who created all things, being Himself their very essence." In his *Fusus* he says,

> O Thou who created all things in Thyself,
> Thou unitest that which Thou createst.
> Thou createst what existeth infinitely
> In Thee, for Thou art the narrow and the All-embracing.

In Islamic pantheism the phenomenal world is reduced to a mere shadow of reality, and God is regarded as the only real Being who is the ultimate ground of all that was, is, and will be. There is no actual duality of God and the phenomenal world, but there is an apparent duality asserted by the unaided intellect, which is incapable of comprehending the essential unity of the whole. It is at most a duality of aspects of One Being—not of two independent beings. Looking at the two aspects within one whole, reality is both God and the universe, the One and the many, the transcendent and the immanent, the internal and the external. If we think—as we usually do—in terms of duality, we predicate of Reality all pairs of opposite attributes. But mystic intuition asserts that God is the only Real Being who is above all description and qualifying attributes, and the world is a mere illusion.

There is therefore a definite place for God in this philosophy, although in some respects He is far removed from the God of Islam. Ibn Arabi makes a distinction which is the dividing line between his metaphysical theory and his theology; it is a distinction between God as the unknowable and incommunicable Reality, and God as the object of belief, worship, and love. His conception of God as the object of belief comes very close to that of the ordinary monotheist, but the gap between pantheism and strict Muslim monotheism was too great for him to bridge. God is the object of worship not in the sense that He is exclusively the God of the Muslims, the Christians, or the adherents of any other religion, but in the sense that He is the Essence of everything that is worshiped. He is not to be confined to any particular form of belief or creed. Everything that is worshiped is one of the infinite number of forms in which He reveals Himself. To confine Him to one particular form to the exclusion of all other forms is infidelity, and to acknowledge Him in all forms of worship is the true spirit of religion.

This is the universal religion which the pantheistic Ibn Arabi preaches, a religion which comprises all religions and unites all beliefs. In his *Tarjumanu al-Ashwaq* he expresses this conviction,

> My heart has become a receptacle of every form;
> It is a pasture for gazelles and a convent for Christian monks,
> And a temple for idols, and pilgrims' Ka'ba,
> And the Tablets of the Torah and the Book of the Qur'an.
> I follow the religion of love whichever way its camels take;
> For this is my religion and my faith.

The religion of love, according to Ibn Arabi, is religion in its widest and most universal sense. All worshipers do in fact worship God, although they appear to worship their particular gods. And since love is the essence of worship—for to worship is to love to the extreme—and since the objects of worship are nothing but the external manifestations of God, it follows that God is both the supremely beloved and the supremely worshiped One.

This brief discussion shows some of the ways in which the interpretations of Muslim theologians, philosophers, and mystics have contributed to the vitality of Islam throughout its long history, making their varied contributions to the development of Muslim thought and influencing Islamic practices. Although they have often been considered as unorthodox by the leaders of Islam, their attempts to provide a rational basis for Islamic beliefs and a mystical basis for Islamic worship have for centuries enriched and stimulated the Muslim community.

CHAPTER FIVE

Shi'a

Mahmood Shehabi

The word *Shi'a,* meaning following, has come to be accepted as the designation for those Muslims who are followers of Ali—who was second only to Muhammad. They are followers of God's revelation in the Qur'an, of Muhammad who was the last of the prophets, and of Ali who was the Prophet's choice for his successor.

Interest in religion is created naturally in every man by God whose divine revelation has been given so that man may know what to do in order to achieve the perfection which is ordained for him, and may be happy and at ease when he goes to the Other World. Thus religion is a set of rules, regulations, and plans which God has set up to guide man's life in such a way that he will become happy in both worlds. The religious man is one who submits himself to God's rules and obeys them.

Among mankind there have been those who have had a purity of spirit, a joyous heart, a strong soul, a powerful mind, and a close tie to the supernatural world which have enabled them to maintain a continuous relationship with the Almighty Power. These souls have been blessedly received by God and have reached the most sublime height that man can attain; inspired by Angels and guided by revelation, they have been linked to the source of creation, elevated by God and appointed to give guidance to men. These men who have been chosen by God are the prophets. They receive revelation and inspiration which enables them to recognize righteousness and wickedness and to guide men along the right path which brings them to happiness and perfection.

The believer eventually comes to the conclusion that there is a need for prophets who have been appointed by Almighty God, the Omniscient. After the believers have seen evidence of the right of the prophet to prophesy they heartily accept the religion which is revealed to them and follow it in order to achieve happiness and perfection. Miracles furnish evidence of the right to prophesy. All true prophets have been the instruments for miracles, and all people are convinced by miracles. A miracle is the performance of a supernatural deed which is related to the claim of the right to prophesy, a deed which ordinary people cannot perform.

The Qur'an

It has been stated in Islamic classics that there were many prophets in many different religions—as many as 124,000 prophets have been mentioned, but the number of true prophets and the number of religions is not a matter of discussion here. It should be noted, however, that the Qur'an mentions all the previous prophets with great respect, especially Moses and Jesus. It also tells of the miracles they performed, for example Moses' stick which could be turned into a snake and Jesus' miracles when he cured the blind and gave life to the dead, and many others. The Qur'an has not only told of these miracles; it has accepted them. But those ugly and unacceptable deeds which are attributed to some of the prophets in the Old Testament are not to be found in the Qur'an, for it portrays the prophets as those whose deeds were holy, whose actions never involved them in anything unpleasant. In several places in the Qur'an it has been clearly stated that previous prophets, especially Moses and Jesus, had predicted the coming of the Prophet Muhammad.

The Qur'an is not particularly directed to special persons but is addressed to all people of every time or place or race. All are invited to accept the Qur'an as a guidebook of life and to behave according to its commands.

The most important of all the Qur'an's characteristics is that the Qur'an is a miracle in itself, an everlasting miracle. It should be so. For, as is stated in the Qur'an and by Muhammad, Islam is the most complete religion, Muhammad is the last prophet, and the Qur'an is the most thorough of all holy books. In truth, the Qur'an is peerless among all holy books in its answer to the most important questions facing mankind —where did man come from, where is he going, and what should he do?

In proving the existence of God and explaining the genesis of all things, the Qur'an has furnished the most reasonable and most mystical proofs. It offers the clearest explanations in such a way that it can be understood by both the learned and the layman. It has been acknowledged as one of the wonders of the world by all mankind.

In explaining the Day of Resurrection and the World to Come, and in describing the stages of the Second World, the Qur'an has made the point clear to us in a simple, straightforward, and intelligent way, and has unveiled the secret. Happiness and unhappiness in this life, and death and the everlasting life, have been explained in such a way that there is no other explanation that is equal to it.

Concerning the duties and responsibilities related to living in this world, one must say that Islam and its rules of conduct are the most comprehensive guides for all aspects of the daily life of the individual and his social relations. The Qur'an is so thorough and complete that it is a miracle in this respect. Islam, with its comprehensive point of view, has no equal when compared with other heavenly inspired rules or man-made regulations. All of the affairs of society are regulated in such a way that they protect the piety of the body and spirit and promote the progress and happiness of the individual in both lives—here and hereafter. The rules are stated so clearly that they are adaptable to every life situation and to any place. Insofar as the world is able to follow the pattern of Islam, man can achieve his ordained perfection and happiness by obeying the rules revealed through the Prophet. The following verse from the Qur'an is good evidence of the comprehensive nature of the Islamic rules of conduct, "It is not righteousness that ye turn your faces to the East and the West; but righteous is he who believeth in Allah and the Last

Day and the angels and the Scripture and the Prophets; and giveth his wealth, in spite of his love for it, to kinsfolk and to orphans and the needy and the wayfarer and to those who ask, and to set slaves free; and observeth proper worship and payeth the poor-due. And those who keep their treaty when they make one, and the patient in tribulation and adversity and time of stress. Such are they who are sincere. Such are the God-fearing" (Surah II, 177).

The Prophet of Islam

More details are known about the life of Muhammad than about any other prophet. Friends and foes alike agree that the Prophet of Islam was superior to all others, even before his call at the age of forty. He was the most pious of his people and all virtues were to be found in him. In truth, although differing good qualities might be found in other individuals, Muhammad alone possessed all good qualities. Because from the very beginning his life was outstanding, the details have been preserved and narrated by others.

In the time of the Prophet the people of Mecca and of Arabia were known as the meanest of all in behavior. One need only recall their gods. They made statues of stone and wood, and then worshiped them by asking for material things. Robbery, murder, plunder, burying their newborn daughters alive, fighting over tribal affairs, doing cruel deeds to weak and harmless people—these were among their daily practices. Women were used for making money in an immoral way, and they had no rights at all. Immoral deeds were so much a part of their life that they boasted of their behavior.

In such a situation the Prophet of Islam arose to guide the people. Before accepting his call and inviting people to his faith, Muhammad delayed in order to assist his uncle Abu Talib, who had several children. He took responsibility for the upbringing of Ali, one of his cousins. After Muhammad received his call from God to invite people to his faith, the first woman who was converted was his wife Khadijah, and the first man who believed in him was his cousin Ali.

When Muhammad gathered all his relatives in one place to tell them of his call, he said to them, "God has appointed me to teach you the right path of living so that you may reach the ordained objectives of perfection and happiness. I was chosen to teach you so that you will gain your happiness in this world and become fortunate in the World to Come where eventually everyone will go." Then he continued, "The one from among you who precedes the others in thoroughly believing in God and puts into action God's Will will be my successor." In that meeting only Ali accepted the call to follow; the others were silent. Some of them even joked about Ali's conversion. Three times Muhammad repeated his call, but only Ali accepted it. The rest stood by quietly.

After issuing his private invitation which only Ali accepted, Muhammad made his call public to all the people of Mecca. For thirteen years there he used regularly to recite some of the verses of the Qur'an, patiently, kindly, and with great tolerance, and he invited the people to do good to one another and to worship God if they wished to realize happiness. But the people of Mecca had been brought up in fighting; pride, selfishness, prejudice, boasting, and ignorance were characteristic of them. Whenever the elder members of Muhammad's clan were tired of ridiculing him they asked the younger ones to stand in his way, to call him bad names, to throw stones at him and even to hurt him physically. Muhammad patiently bore all these troubles and continued to give kindly advice to all of them. His only assistant was Ali, who never left Muhammad alone, who went shoulder to shoulder with him everywhere, and it was he who kept the children from hurting the Prophet.

In the first thirteen years only a few people of Mecca had been converted, but Muhammad's fame had begun to spread beyond the city of Mecca and he was invited to join his followers in Medina. The leaders of the Meccan tribes, when they saw that the number of Muhammad's followers was increasing both in Mecca and in other cities, decided to murder him. They devised a plan whereby fifty men selected from different tribes would gather on a certain night and attack

Muhammad's house. Through revelation Muhammad learned of their plan. He discussed the situation with Ali and they finally decided that someone else should sleep in Muhammad's bed that night while Muhammad himself set out for Medina under cover of darkness. Ali—honest, faithful, trustworthy, and a devoted disciple of Muhammad—offered to be the victim of the assassins' attack. He volunteered to sleep in Muhammad's bed so the assassins would think that Muhammad was there and when they attacked Ali would be killed and Muhammad would have time to reach Medina.

According to their plan, Ali slept in Muhammad's house and the Prophet left Mecca with Abu Bakr, whom he met on the way. The plotters entered the house and at the suggestion of one of them decided to wait around the bed until dawn and then assassinate the Prophet. Ali, who was listening to their words, kept silent so they would not become suspicious and pursue Muhammad. At dawn, when they drew their swords, Ali arose and the plotters were taken aback. What could they do? Ali's courage and self-sacrifice had robbed them of their opportunity.

At Medina a new period in the rise of Islam began. One after another Ali and Muhammad's other followers left Mecca and joined the Prophet in Medina. During the short period of ten years from the day Muhammad entered Medina until his death, tribe after tribe became aware of the truth of Islam and put their faith in it. During this time there were several battles in which the Muslims were attacked by the unbelievers, who were superior in numbers and arms, but the forces of Muhammad were victorious. Ali's bravery, self-sacrifice, resourcefulness, experience, and faith were the determining factors in these battles. It was Ali who led the men to victory and who deserves above all other followers the credit for their success.

In the short time that Muhammad was at Medina he achieved miraculous results in converting the people to Islam. Deep-rooted evil customs disappeared and virtue and good morals took their place. Brotherhood, equality, and justice replaced murder, selfishness, anarchy, and cruelty. The people believed in God, desired to follow Muhammad, and conformed to the regulations of religion to such an extent that inwardly and outwardly the basis of every action was righteousness. Thousands of people in Arabia heard the words of the Prophet and observed his behavior, put their trust in him, received the revelation, and obeyed his commands. They were completely made over; as they changed from disbelievers to followers their character changed inwardly and their actions showed outwardly that they had submitted, they had become Muslims. This is one of the most extraordinary happenings in history.

What other leader ever built up such an organization, established such order, was so successful in such a short time, or converted as many people as the Prophet did? He had no money, no arms, no military experience; he had no formal schooling, and he lived in an environment of anarchy and cruelty under an aggressive and hostile government. Even his own tribe was bitter in its enmity. Yet under such circumstances, without using force, he changed the behavior of a people who were prejudiced, cruel, and aggressive. Those people were changed so that they cultivated good morals and became sincere individuals who offered their lives gladly to further the glory of Islam. His only tools for change were good morals, eloquent words, honorable and natural rules of conduct, good and truthful behavior, kindness, and helpfulness.

In the month of Dhu'l Hijja in the tenth year of the Hijrah —just three months before his death—Muhammad, returning to Medina from his last pilgrimage to Mecca, stopped at a place called Ghadir-Khumm and asked all the people who were in his company—it is reported that the number of his companions was as high as 120,000—to gather around him. He even ordered those who had gone on ahead to return, and he waited for those at the end of the caravan to catch up. Muhammad had something very important to say that day as they stood in the hot midday sun. He went up to a pulpit which had been made of camel saddles and, as usual, spoke to them eloquently. He reminded them of their religious obligations and heaven-sent regulations and spoke to them about the

Qur'an and his own family. Finally he raised Ali until the audience could see him and recognize him. Then Muhammad asked, "Who is the master of all believers?" The people replied, "God and his Prophet know." Muhammad continued, "God is my Master, and I am the master of all believers. Therefore, whosoever I am the master of, Ali is his master." He repeated this sentence three or four times and went on, "Oh God, the one who is a friend of Ali, be his friend, and the one who is Ali's enemy, be his enemy."

That day in those words the Prophet explained the greatness of Ali and indicated who his successor would be. There was no doubt as to what Muhammad intended for he gathered the people in the bright sun and gave them news of his impending death and then made Ali the main topic of his speech. He made Ali the new master of the people, and in relation to God he raised Ali's status to the level of his own. Without doubt the Prophet had Ali in mind as his successor.

When the Prophet died he left a people who had learned to worship God, who had spiritual knowledge, cleanness of heart, a desire to seek justice, a wish to serve the people, the spirit of self-sacrifice; they were doers of good. The Prophet left as a legacy to his people the Qur'an, the Tradition (Sunnah), and his family (*Itrat*). The Qur'an is God's revealed book which includes facts about creation, the Day of Resurrection, and regulations governing man's life. The Tradition is made up of the sayings and deeds of the Prophet and his family.

The family of the Prophet included the children by his first wife Khadijah, and also by some of his other wives. His son Abraham, who died young, died by chance during an eclipse and ignorant people believed that this natural event was caused by Abraham's death. If he had not been a truthful man, the Prophet might have used this happening to his own advantage, but instead he became angry and said openly that such thoughts were not right, for the sun and the moon are also creatures of God and it is by His order that they move as they do. No one's death can have any effect on them nor change them from their course.

The Prophet had a daughter, Fatimah, by his wife Khadijah. Because he loved and honored her very much he married her to Ali, his most trusted disciple. Muhammad was also very fond of their two children, his grandchildren Hasan and Husain. He used to honor them on every occasion, at the mosque and at home, and called them his children and the best youth of Heaven. To hurt Hasan or Husain, or Fatimah their mother, or Ali their father, was considered a defiance of God and of Muhammad.

The Prophet recommended his family to people in private and in public. For instance, at the Ghadir-Khumm meeting he said as guidance to the people, "Oh people, I will die, but I leave two things for you so that if you follow them you will never be misled—they are the Holy Book, the Qur'an, and my family [Itrat]." On the day of Ghadir, as we mentioned previously—and it is mentioned by both Shi'a and Sunni—he indicated that Ali should be his successor and he named him as the master of the people. This was an indication that Ali should be the next Caliph, that is, Successor to Muhammad.

Ali and the Rise of Shi'a

Ali, Muhammad's cousin, had been brought up by the Prophet, was the husband of the Prophet's beloved daughter, and was the closest person to Muhammad. From his early childhood until the day the Prophet died, day and night, on journeys and in the cities, in mountains and on the plains, in battle and in peace, on strenuous days and on calm ones, in public appearances and in hiding—Ali was with the Prophet. He wholeheartedly adopted Muhammad's way of life; he learned about his aims and his methods of instruction so that he understood Muhammad's teachings better than anyone else.

On many occasions Ali made personal sacrifices for the sake of the Prophet and for the sake of Islam. His bravery, which was motivated by his great faith, accounts for the early progress of Islam. In every good quality—in virtues, in knowledge, in bravery, in faithfulness, in generosity and reliability—

Ali was superior to others; he was second only to Muhammad.

The Prophet both explicitly and implicitly affirmed Ali's eminent position, mentioning Ali's superiority over the others a number of times. We have seen that Ghadir-Khumm was a significant event in Ali's honor, for there Muhammad explicitly named himself as the master of the people and Ali next to him, in relation to God. On the day that he invited the Christian leaders for *Mubaheleh* (to pray to God to damn a person and his family if he knowingly misrepresents religious facts and lies willfully), he had his daughter Fatimah, his grandchildren Hasan and Husain, and Ali sit with him; it was on this occasion that he referred to Ali as his soul. In this way he paid tribute to the greatness of Ali. These events, and other similar ones, made Muhammad's choice of his successor quite evident. All the evidence pointed to the fact that Muhammad wished Ali to succeed him with complete authority to guide the people. Ali was justly fitted to lead the Muslims and to head the affairs of Islam.

Consequently, after the death of Muhammad, Ali, who felt assured of his position and was greatly saddened by Muhammad's death, went on to fulfill Muhammad's wishes for his funeral. Meanwhile a few followers, who apparently were driven by selfishness, ambition, and a great desire for power, gathered their followers to decide for themselves the question of the succession. Abu Bakr, Umar, and Abu Ubaydah, with glib tongues and skillful speeches, weakened the position of their rivals. Some of the delegates followed them through hope, some through fear, and some made no commitment at all. With the support of Umar and Abu Ubaydah, Abu Bakr was named Caliph. This choice led to conflict between the supporters of Abu Bakr and the other Muslims, but they recognized that if the conflict continued Islam would be so weakened that it might even lead to its destruction. Furthermore, the followers of Abu Bakr would make trouble for those who did not express an opinion in his favor. Therefore, for the sake of Islam, the people gradually took the oath of allegiance to Abu Bakr as Caliph and showed no opposition when he assumed office.

At the same time, there were people who knew that the position of Caliph should have been given to Ali, and they recognized him as the leader of Islam. It was these people who were to follow Ali and to believe in him, and they eventually became the sect known as Shi'a. They believed that Muhammad's successor should have been appointed by God and the Prophet himself, and that the Caliph should not have been chosen on the basis of men's capricious will and temptation. Many of them took the oath of allegiance reluctantly, and Ali himself did not give his approval until six months later.

Abu Bakr, who was Caliph for about two years, nominated Umar as his successor. Umar was a man of will, a ruthless administrator, and a man who abstained from worldly pleasures. As Caliph he decided to extend the borders of Islam and conquered Iran and some of the Roman territories, organizing a widespread empire.

While Umar was Caliph, Ali's position was supreme; for Umar had to recognize his high position in Islam and ascertain his views on important matters. At times Umar acted on his suggestions and at other times Ali pointed out the Caliph's mistakes. Umar admitted his errors, and once said, "If it were not for Ali I should have perished."

When Umar's warriors vanquished Iran they captured the daughters of Yazdigird, the king of Iran, and brought them to Umar. He was going to sell them like any other slaves but Ali advised him that this would be an unjust treatment for princesses and the religion forbade it. As a result the women were allowed to choose their own husbands, and one of them was married to Ali's son Husain and the other to Abu Bakr's son Muhammad. On another occasion Umar was going to execute Hurmuzan, a captured Iranian prince, but Ali persuaded the prince to become a Muslim and his life was spared. During his life he honored Ali.

For ten years Umar served as Caliph and made great conquests for the glory of Islam. Before he died he made plans for the choice of his successor. Although he knew that Ali was well qualified to replace him, he would not consider Ali as his successor. Instead of making Ali the next Caliph, Umar appointed six persons, including Ali and Uthman, to select one person from among themselves as the next Caliph and spiritual leader of the believers. When the six men were assembled to reach a decision, they were surrounded by fifty brave armed men who were ordered to watch the election committee. If after three days they could not select a successor to the Caliph, they were all to be killed on the spot; if they selected someone but could not agree unanimously, the minority should be killed. If three persons selected one Caliph and three selected another, then the group in which Abd-ar-Rahman Ibn Awf was a member would have the deciding vote and the other three must agree or be killed. This was Umar's plan, which was to be carried out after his death. This plan was set up so that Uthman would become Caliph, because Abd-ar-Rahman Ibn Awf was his relative and supporter.

At the meeting of the committee, Abd-ar-Rahman Ibn Awf asked Ali, "If you are selected will you act according to the Qur'an, the Sunnah, and the policies of the two previous Caliphs?" Ali replied that he would act according to the Qur'an and the Sunnah, but he would not follow the opinions of others. After that, the original plan was followed and Uthman was chosen.

As Caliph, Uthman acted against the principles of the previous Caliphs. He made his own corrupt relatives governors; he used the treasury to further his own interests by giving gold and silver to relatives and friends. Democracy, freedom, justice, and equality, which had more or less prevailed under Umar, were silenced by Uthman's rule. Therefore the people became disappointed in him and rose up against him. Some of the great men and sincere believers in Islam knew that Uthman had been selected falsely and they considered his conduct contrary to the tradition of the Prophet and the previous Caliphs. They warned him by speeches and pointed out his faults with audacity, and even with rudeness. Some of them came from distant Islamic cities to make their objections. Muhammad, the son of Abu Bakr, protested, and even the Prophet's wife A'isha publicly and privately criticized Uthman. Several times Uthman promised to make reforms, but he did not fulfill his promise. He was attacked and killed in his own home in the thirty-fifth year of the Hijrah, twelve years after he became Caliph.

After Uthman's death the representatives of Islamic cities who were in Medina asked Ali to become their Caliph. From that day, Ali's friends and followers freely and openly expressed their devotion to Ali, and they were proud of it. They all vowed their belief in Shi'a and honored it.

When, before his death, Uthman saw that he was surrounded by Muslims who disapproved of his policies, he asked help from Mu'awiya, who was a relative in the Umayyad family, the governor of Syria (Sham), and a man who would be called a politician today. Mu'awiya acted slowly because he was clever and had designs for setting up an Islamic empire; therefore his help did not arrive until after Uthman had been killed and Ali confirmed as Caliph by all the people of Islam except those of Syria, who were ruled by Mu'awiya. Mu'awiya was certain that Ali did not favor him and felt sure that Ali would dismiss him as governor of Syria; so he started a plot against Ali by accusing him of Uthman's murder. He wrote letters and sent messengers to Mecca and Medina to arouse the people against Ali, and in Damascus he proclaimed in the mosques that Uthman's death was an injustice against Islam perpetrated by Ali. By telling lies, distributing gold, and making promises to the ambitious and greedy, Mu'awiya turned some of the people against Ali.

Mu'awiya knew that Ali had a strong faith and that the majority of his followers were sincere believers. Therefore, after he had done all he could to deceive the followers whose religious beliefs were weak, he started a war against Ali with a large army made up of people from Syria. The fighting continued for some time and several thousand people were killed on both sides. Just when victory was close at hand for Ali's side, Mu'awiya turned the battle by means of a devilish trick. He asked Ali to stop fighting so they could arrange a truce, and Ali unwillingly accepted the offer for negotiations. Mu'awiya appointed Amr Ibn al-As, a tricky, clever man, while Ali's group selected Abu Musa Ash'ari, a weak, ambitious man, to represent them. Amr Ibn al-As took advantage of Abu Musa Ash'ari's selfishness and stupidity to deceive him, just as Mu'awiya had planned.

When they saw how the negotiations were going, the same people who had urged Ali to accept the truce started to criticize him for starting the negotiations and for sending as a delegate the man whom they had chosen to represent them. They said that Ali had committed an error and he should either repent or be killed. Ali defended himself by giving them evidence from the Qur'an and citing the reasons for the action, but they were not convinced. Over ten thousand of Ali's men, all Shi'ites, left his army.

It is one of the puzzles of history that a group of people who believed in Ali and had made great sacrifices for his sake, who knew him to be right and his enemy wrong, and who had even risked their lives by going into battle for him should desert him and even take up their swords against him. A group of soldiers who were good Shi'as and who had believed in Ali just a few days previously now suddenly left Ali's camp and became his enemies. It was truly a strange happening.

The men who deserted Ali and abandoned their faith became famous in history as unbelievers and were known as Kharijites—the people who have forsaken their faith. Twelve thousand of these Kharijites formed an army which tried to kill Ali. Therefore it was necessary for Ali to deal with them before he could turn to Mu'awiya. With only four thousand men Ali approached the Kharijites; he heard their protests and answered them, and as a result of his preaching eight thousand changed their minds; but four thousand remained as bitter enemies. When the eight thousand had left the battlefield, Ali spoke to his men in the name of Allah, saying, "Our loss will not be more than their survivors, and in neither case will the number be more than ten." After the battle, just as Ali had miraculously predicted, nine of the enemy remained and nine of Ali's men were dead. Although Ali was victorious, that battle did not eliminate the Kharijites.

During the five years that Ali ruled as Caliph he was busy with emergencies at home which prevented him from returning to the conflict with Mu'awiya. On the nineteenth of Ramadan in the year 40 of the Hijrah, while Ali was praying in the mosque at Kufa he was struck down with a poisoned sword by Ibn Muljam, a Kharijite.

In the last hours while he lay on his death bed, Ali besought the people to act with self-sacrifice, rectitude, and gentleness, to serve the poor, the orphans, and the weak, and to follow religion. He said to them, "O people, we are from God and we will go back to Him. Therefore try to know Him, worship Him, be virtuous and do good. In this short time that you are in the world prepare yourself for the life to come." As a man who revered and worshiped God, Ali wished death to come. He said repeatedly, "By God, Ali is more acquainted with death than a child with his mother's breast!" When he was attacked in the mosque he had said, "I have my wish and I join my God." Before he died he showed again his magnanimous spirit by saying concerning his murderer, "As long as I am alive, do not hurt him, but tolerate him. If I do not die and I remain, I will know what to do. If I die never attack him with more than a stroke for he hit only one." Thus just before he died he protected his murderer from torture.

In writing about Ali's sublime qualities and counting his virtues, one can agree with what was said by one of his followers, "To describe your qualities, it would not suffice to wet the finger with all the water of the seas in order to leaf through your book of virtues." Once when the Sunni authority Muhammad Ibn Idris al-Shafi'i was asked to talk about Ali he said, "What should be said about him when his virtues are concealed by his friends because they are afraid, and by his foes because of jealousy? Yet in spite of this his virtuous character was revealed and has been made known to us."

In praying, in bravery, in eloquence, in modesty, in patience, and in helping the poor and weak Ali was above all others; after the Prophet he has had no equal. Once he fasted for three days and nights and when he was to break the fast he gave his food to a beggar and remained hungry himself. When he became Caliph he used to eat bread made of barley and wear rough woolen clothes. When they asked him to change his behavior he said, "Is it just if I call myself Amir of believers but refuse to participate in the difficulties of the people? Rather I should live in such a way that the poorest will be satisfied with his life, and if he eats barley bread he will be glad and will say that his leader eats the same thing."

It has been said that Ali's words are beneath God's words—the Qur'an—but they are far superior to the words of the people. There can be no conflict between Ali's words and Muhammad's, for Ali speaks on the basis of the Qur'an and of his intimate knowledge of Muhammad's teachings. Ali's speeches, letters, and aphorisms have been preserved in many books and are compiled in *Nahdj al-Balagha.*

Ali gave numerous lectures on many topics, such as how to pray and how to thank God, on Muhammad, on prophecy, on the virtues and morals of Muhammad, on the Qur'an, on the stages of life to come, on ways to live in this world, on holy wars, and the like. These speeches so impressed the people that they used to recite them and gathered them in the book called *Nahdj al-Balagha* which is highly respected among the Shi'a and next to the Qur'an is important for every Muslim. As an example of the variety of speeches recorded in that book one of the shorter sermons is summarized here:

> In truth, God has sent the Qur'an to you for guidance. Righteousness, sinfulness and misbehavior are revealed in it. Follow the path of righteousness so that you may be guided truthfully; keep away from sins until you become moderate and acquire justice. Follow God's given orders until you go to heaven. Verily God has forbidden for you things which are known to be corrupt. God has also provided you with things which lack imperfection and defect. To respect an individual is the greatest tribute one can give to a Muslim. Through monotheism and the worship of God, God has protected the individual's right, for believers in God should not be aggressive toward others, but should respect others' rights. O people! Be virtuous toward God with regard for people and places and always remember Him; for you are responsible for everything and every deed. You will be asked to explain—even if you have destroyed a shelter or even if you have hurt an animal. Obey your God! Do not disobey His commands. When you see good, go toward it, and if you see evil keep away from it.

Not only are Ali's speeches masterpieces which, next to the Qur'an, are without equal, but his letters are also most eloquent and superior to all others. These letters try to guide people to paths of good conduct by discussing such topics as knowing God and knowing one's self, understanding one's situation in this world and in the life to come, seeking knowledge devoutly, and behaving devoutly. The letters were sent to men who were appointed to public office, such as the governors at Basra and Kufa, and also to people like Mu'awiya. One of the most important letters is one to Malik Ashtar who became governor of Egypt, a letter which awakened Malik's heart and taught him how to behave in Egypt, and is a model for statesmen of all times and places. Another letter of equal importance is his last letter of advice to his son Hasan. After talking about life, death, the day of creation, and the Day of Resurrection, Ali says:

> My dear son, take your soul as the criterion when you want to judge deeds which take place between you and others—then desire for others what you desire for yourself, and help others to avoid what you avoid yourself. Do not be cruel, as you do not want to receive cruelty. Do good to others as you would like others to do good to you. What you consider ugly in others, consider it the same in yourself. What you do not know, do not talk about it even though you know a little. Do not say to others what you would not like to be said about yourself. And know that selfishness is the squander of reason. Give away what you have gained and do not save it for others or yourself. And when you have reached such a stage of life, thank God for these things.

Ali is also noted for his aphorisms, some of which were in his speeches and letters and some of which have been recorded independently. These are typical of his aphorisms:

> Behave yourself with others in such a way that if you die, people will cry for you, and if you stay alive they seek your presence.

> Opportunity is just like a passing cloud. Therefore take advantage of the right opportunities while they are within sight.

> Victory depends upon thinking ahead, and thinking ahead upon mental resourcefulness; and decision on keeping secrecy.

> The one who is a dictator will be killed soon and the one who consults with the people will share their wisdom.

The one who observes his own deficiencies will overlook another's inadequacy.

These few examples of the teachings of Ali give only a hint of the greatness of the man who was Muhammad's closest companion and chosen successor, second only to the Prophet in relation to God.

Shi'a Leaders After Ali

After Ali was murdered, Mu'awiya increased his deception and bribery in order to gain power and to establish a strong kingdom under his rule. He swiftly banished all the people who were trained by Ali, who were lovers of freedom, who were Shi'a and as friends of Ali knew the truth. Not only did he kill sincere Shi'ites, but he made every effort to turn others from the support of the family of the Prophet and to turn the spiritual system of Islam into a political kingdom which he would rule. To accomplish his ends Mu'awiya played on the hopes and fears of the people by bribery and threats and issued false statements which he attributed to Ali. Stranger than that was that he asked the people of Damascus to curse and hate Ali as a part of their daily prayers. In spite of all these murders and evil deeds and false propaganda there were still God-worshipers who knew the greatness of the family of the Prophet and remained Shi'as.

Imam Hasan. After Ali's assassination the Shi'as affirmed that his eldest son, Hasan, the grandson of the Prophet, was the next Imam. However, the evil influence of Mu'awiya was so strong that after several months Imam Hasan had to enter into a peace agreement with him. In this way the rule of the Caliph lost its spiritual and religious color and, under pressure from Mu'awiya, took on a worldly, material form. Even though Mu'awiya called himself Caliph and forced the people to recognize him as ruler, there were still Shi'as who knew that Hasan was their Imam and that they should ask him about religious doctrines and heavenly duties.

Even after Imam Hasan made peace Mu'awiya was not sure of his support, for he knew that Imam Hasan would not approve his plan to make the Caliphate hereditary in the Umayyad family by appointing his son Yazid as his successor. Therefore Mu'awiya decided to poison Imam Hasan. Although the Imam recovered from several unsuccessful attempts to poison him, the poison was finally effective and Imam Hasan died in the year 40 (A.D. 660) and was buried at Medina.

IMAM HUSAIN. After Imam Hasan's death the true followers of Shi'a affirmed that the right to be the next Imam belonged to Husain, Ali's second son and the most meritorious of the grandsons of the Prophet. Mu'awiya knew that Muhammad had predicted that Husain would become Imam and that he was honored by all his people. Therefore, although Mu'awiya had taken over the government and called himself Caliph and kept the people silent through fear of punishment, he still had to consider Imam Husain. Imam Husain knew that Mu'awiya held his power over the people through fear and greed, but he could do nothing more than to point out Mu'awiya's evil deeds and to remind the people that he was Caliph only through deceit.

After twenty years of dictatorship and deviations from the rules of Islam, Mu'awiya got the confirmation of the people for Yazid, his son, as successor. Some gave their confirmation as a result of bribery and some through fear, but Mu'awiya did not get even silent assent from Husain and some of the others until he brought them together in the presence of a heavily armed force and said to them, "When I ask you not to oppose my son as my successor, you must be silent; otherwise all of you will be killed." In this way he forced silence.

Mu'awiya died in the year 60 of the Hijrah, and Yazid replaced him. Yazid was a sinful man, quite ignorant of the laws and practices of Islam. The people knew how corrupt he was and that he did not have enough ability even to occupy the lowest office in Islam, and many of them would not accept him as Caliph. Yazid decided to get an open confirmation from Imam Husain and sent orders to the governor of Medina to force Imam Husain to submit. In the meantime Husain had gone to Mecca; so Yazid sent an armed force there with secret orders either to capture or kill Husain; he also sent thirty men disguised as pilgrims to try to kill Husain secretly.

When Imam Husain learned of Yazid's plans he decided to accept the invitation of the people of Kufa and set out on the journey from Mecca to Kufa. Before he could reach his supporters in Kufa he was stopped at Karbala by Yazid's army, which was led by Ibn Ziyad. There at Karbala, in the month of Muharram of the sixty-first year of the Hijrah, Imam Husain and his son, his friends, his brothers, and his relatives were all killed in one of the most tragic historical events ever known.

THE TWELVE IMAMS. Ali was the first Imam, Hasan was the second, and Husain was the third. Husain had a son Ali, whose mother was the princess of Iran and the daughter of Yazdigird, the last Sasanian king. During the battle at Karbala, Ali was sick at home and thus his life was spared. According to the will of his father he was accepted by the Shi'as as their religious leader and became known as Imam Zain al-Abidin, the Ornament of the Pious. He died in the month of Muharram in the year 95 (A.D. 713).

The fifth Imam was Muhammad al-Baqir who lived until the year 114 of the Hijrah. He was succeeded by his son, known as Ja'far as-Sadiq. During the lifetime of Imam Ja'far as-Sadiq the cruelty of the Umayyad rule came to an end, and their kingdom was dissolved. The new Caliph, the first of the Abbasid Caliphs, was a descendant of the uncle of the Prophet. On Friday, the thirteenth day of Rabi Awwal, in the year 132 (A.D. 749), the people gathered to make their affirmation for Abu'l-Abbas as Caliph. He ascended the pulpit in the mosque but could not continue to speak because of an attack of malaria; so his uncle stood on the step below him and said, "By God, after the Prophet and Ali, no one has been as worthy as Abu'l-Abbas to be Caliph."

After the Abbasids became the head of the government the situation was so modified that the family of Muhammad could have a voice in leading the people. This made it possible for Imam Ja'far as-Sadiq to teach the people and to encourage interest in religious laws. Well-educated scholars recorded his teachings, which led some people to refer to the religion of Shi'a as the sect of Ja'fari.

When Imam Ja'far as-Sadiq died in the year 148 (A.D. 765), according to his will his son Musa became the seventh Imam. During Musa's time the Abbasids became more powerful, and Harun al-Rashid decided to make the office of Caliph hereditary. When he found that the friends of Ali's family opposed that plan, he asked Musa to come to Baghdad and held him in prison there for years until he was murdered in the year 183. He was buried at Kazimain near Baghdad.

According to Musa's will, his son Ali al-Rida became the eighth Imam. He was recognized by the people as an authority on Shi'a beliefs and practices. In his time the Caliph was Ma'mun, the son of Harun al-Rashid, a learned man and a good statesman who in many discussions proved the sublime position of Ali and his right to be the immediate successor of Muhammad. Because of his interest in Muhammad's family he decided to make Imam Ali al-Rida his successor so the family could attain its just rights. He brought Imam Rida from Medina and persuaded him to accept the appointment as his successor in the Caliphate. Imam Rida accepted on condition that he should not be required to interfere with state affairs and should be free to devote his time to religion and study. The common people recognized the Imam's good attributes, his scholarship, his character, and his noble virtues, and held him in high respect. But the Abbasid family was jealous of him. Later, when Ma'mun regretted his decision to make Imam Rida his successor, he poisoned him secretly. The Imam died in the year 203 (A.D. 818) and was buried in Meshed, a place of holy pilgrimage to this day.

The ninth Imam was Muhammad Taghi, who became Imam according to his father's will. He was murdered in the year 220 and was buried in Kazimain.

The tenth Imam was Ali Naghi, the son of Imam Muhammad Taghi, and became Imam according to the will of his father. He was eight years old when he became Imam and served until he was murdered in Iraq in the year 254 (A.D. 868).

The eleventh Imam was Hasan al-Askari, taking his title from the locality where he was born. He was murdered in the year 260 (A.D. 873) and was buried at Samarra, near Baghdad, where his father had been killed before him.

After the death of the eleventh Imam his son succeeded him. The twelfth Imam is known by several titles, of which one of the best known is the Arabic title Imam Zaman, the Imam of all time. According to Shiʿa, the twelfth Imam, who was born in the year 255 (A.D. 869), is still living; but he is invisible. As the Prophet and others prophesied, when the earth is full of cruelty he will appear and bring justice.

After he became Imam he learned that the Caliph planned to kill him, so he disappeared. The disappearance is known as the absence, and the Imam Zaman had two absences—the short absence and the long absence. For sixty-nine years the twelfth Imam spent his time in hiding, communicating through four great Shiʿites, and through them guiding the people and answering their questions. As this was a short time and communication was carried on during this time, it is known as the short absence. The men through whom he communicated were known as the ambassadors, or specifically appointed deputies. During this time there were four ambassadors who guided the Shiʿites, and it was the fourth ambassador who was assigned the duty of giving the people the news of the Imam's bodily death through a letter from the Imam. The Imam said that after his bodily death no one was to be the Imam's ambassador and that there would be a long absence. And this took place.

Both Shiʿas and Sunnis have mentioned in their writings the good qualities and sublime conduct of the twelve Imams. According to the Shiʿas, they have had virtues and attributes which have been superior to those of anyone in their time; they were endowed with greatness and the ability to perform miracles; they were infallible and innocent; each one was introduced by the previous Imam as his immediate successor; the

Prophet referred to them by name and designated them by number; they gave the best and clearest statements concerning the origin of man and the Day of Resurrection; and after the Prophet they were the best authority to speak about religious affairs and conduct in the affairs of this world.

THE LONG ABSENCE. Since the year 329 (A.D. 940), when the fourth ambassador died, no one has been appointed as a special ambassador, and according to the testimony of religious authorities, if anyone should claim to be an ambassador he is claiming an untruth. During the short absence the four men who were appointed as ambassadors were known by name. These special ambassadors, whether they were aware of religious doctrine or not, whether they were learned or not, had to follow the Imam's instructions and were not free to act according to their own wishes in regard to religious regulations and actions. The same was true for everyone during the presence of the Imam—everyone had to follow his orders.

It is important for Shi'as to recognize what their duty is during the long absence, how they should carry out the laws and regulations. Since there are no ambassadors during the long absence, Shi'as are responsible to their religious leaders who have a thorough knowledge of jurisprudence and understand religion comprehensively. The order was received that during the long absence the ignorant are to be guided by the orders and the religious ideas of leaders—called public deputies, or deputies not specifically appointed—who know jurisprudence, can protect their religion, and are thus able to save the people from sins, corruption, and earthly desires. Such public deputies who have a thorough knowledge from the proper sources are, during the long absence, like an Imam, and following them is comparable to following an Imam. Since Shi'a depends upon the one who is the most learned and accepts him as the public deputy, in every epoch the person who is the most learned and most pious is regarded as the public deputy, and the people follow his ideas and his decisions concerning religious affairs.

Shi'a Sects

Those believers are called Shi'a who believe that Ali was the immediate successor of Muhammad and who have faith in the eleven descendants of Ali who were the Imams of Islam. Those who accept the twelve Imams are known as the believers in the twelve Imams, *Ithna Ashariya*, and have always been a large majority of the Shi'as. There are several other sects which are also called Shi'a because they believe that Ali was the immediate successor of Muhammad, but most of them are not well known or have disappeared. Three of them, however, should be mentioned—Kaisanis, Zaidis, and Isma'ilis. Of these, the Kaisanis exist only in name today, the Zaidis are mostly in Yemen, and the majority of the Isma'ilis are in India, with a few in Iran and in Africa.

The Kaisanis believed that Muhammad Ibn Hanafiyya was an Imam. He was Ali's son by a Hanafite girl, while Hasan and Husain were sons of Fatimah. Some believed that Muhammad Ibn Hanafiyya was to have been the Imam immediately after Ali, and others believed that he became Imam after Husain was killed. It is said that the first man who believed in this Imam was Kaisan, one of Ali's servants, and thus the sect became known by his name. Others say that the name comes from the name of the man who took revenge for the murder of Husain, saying that he did it on behalf of Muhammad Ibn Hanafiyya. It is not, however, an influential sect in modern times.

The Zaidis have existed as a Shi'a sect since the time of the fourth Imam, chiefly in Yemen, but also to some extent in Iraq and Africa. Zaid was the brother of Imam Muhammad al-Baqir. He believed that the Imam ought to be the ruler of the state and must fight for his rights, so he rose in rebellion against the Umayyad Caliph and was killed near Kufa. Zaidis accept the first four Imams but have maintained their own succession of Imams since that time.

The Isma'ilis are followers of Isma'il, one of the sons of the sixth Imam, Ja'far as-Sadiq. He was greatly loved by his father and might have been the seventh Imam if he had not died before his father. Therefore some of the people said that his descendants should be the Imams and they became followers of his descendants, one after the other. Therefore the followers of this sect are known as Isma'ilis. They founded the Fatimid dynasty in Egypt but today are an influential sect chiefly in India.

While Sufism is not a sect in the sense of a separately organized group within Shi'a, it should be mentioned here because it has had a significant influence on Shi'a thought. Some believe that the name Sufi is derived from the woolen clothes worn by the Sufis; others say that it refers to the purity of insight they possess; but it is most likely that the word is derived from the Greek word *sophos* which was taken into the Arabic language to refer to the special wisdom which they possess.

The Sufi mystics claim that mankind can discover truth through internal purity and mental discipline, which produce insight without the use of logical reasoning. They say that whatever philosophers can discover by means of reason the mystics can perceive by intuition. Such mysticism is not exclusively found in Islam; it has been known in many different cultures. In Islam there were people who, from the first century onward, led others on the basis of Sufism—men like Hasan Basri, for instance. Through the years Sufism developed special rules and regulations, customs, and modes of conduct, and different sects grew up, both Shi'a and Sunni.

Although not all the sects of Sufism relate themselves to Ali, there are quite a number which do. Those who honor Ali say that Islam has a hidden meaning, and they believe that Muhammad revealed the secrets of Islam to Ali—who in turn shared this secret information with those people who showed a readiness to receive it.

There is need for more study and writing on the subject of the Sufi sects and their similarities and dissimilarities and the important role they have played in Islam.

An important Sufi in Iran was Shaikh Safiyyu'd-Din whose ancestors had been Sunnis but who, when they found the opportunity, mentioned their objections and accepted Shi'a.

His son, Shah Isma'il, was the founder of the Safavid dynasty in Iran which made Shi'a the official religion of the country.

Shi'a in Iran

Backed by an old culture, endowed with a rich civilization, and acquainted with logic, philosophy, and other intellectual pursuits, the people of Iran became familiar with the teachings of Islam. Gradually, as they understood the aims of the religion and judged them by intellectual standards, they found that they could aspire to perfection and real happiness. Consequently, they began to accept the religion. They investigated the founder of Islam, his virtues and deeds as well as the rules and regulations he set forth. They sought information on the Prophet's relatives, friends, and successors in order to determine who had most truly inherited his character and his concept of justice.

As a result of these studies they learned about Ali's position and they recognized his great leadership. Therefore they all agreed that Ali was best entitled and best endowed to become Muhammad's successor. They sought his leadership and they followed him wholeheartedly and devoutly. As well-informed Iranians and others who were interested in Islam sought to learn more about Islam, they came to appreciate Ali more and more. They found that Ali was far above all others in telling the truth and in searching for the truth. As they learned about his teachings concerning religion, science, morals, and faith, as well as his close relationship to Muhammad and his personal kindness, it was natural that they should become interested in Ali. Thus they followed him, and believed in him, and appreciated him.

The non-Arab nations, especially those which possessed civilization, culture, and a mature philosophy were undoubtedly more ready than the Arabs to perceive the truth. This was because they were not prejudiced against other people and tribes; they were not motivated by jealousy, anger, or ambition which could mislead their feelings and attitudes. They sought truth, and their emotions could not keep them from the truth.

The Arabs knew Ali very well. They knew how close he was to the Prophet and were aware of his deep faith. They had been informed about his constant association with the Prophet and the careful training he had received from Muhammad. They had heard Muhammad talk about Ali's service, his self-sacrifice, his virtues, generosity, bravery, and other noble qualities. These facts were all known to the Arabs, but their minds were clouded by a thick veil of jealousy, prejudice, selfishness, rivalry, and hostility, and thus their sense of justice was unbalanced. Their hostility to Ali was increased by the fact that there was scarcely an Arab family which had not lost some of its members to Ali's sword in fighting against Islam; for instance, three relatives of Mu'awiya were killed by Ali himself in the battle of Badr. Not only was that a factor, but it is also important to note that the Arabs were prejudiced and considered themselves superior to other peoples, while Ali, like Muhammad, favored unequivocal equality—non-Arabs, the Arab tribes, and Ethiopians all received equal justice from him.

According to these reasons one should have expected that the people of Egypt and Syria, since they were far from Mecca, should have followed the pattern of the Iranians, but it was not so. This is because both Mu'awiya and Amr Ibn al-As were bitter enemies of Ali and would not let the people learn about the greatness of Ali, for they sought to establish themselves as rulers of those countries. Mu'awiya in particular prevented the people from getting the truth about Ali and even spread untruths about him.

In Iran, on the other hand, Ali and his sons were respected and had friends and followers. Learned Iranians, from the first Islamic century on, wrote books and spread the ideas of the religion of the family of the Prophet. In the middle of the fourth century the family of the Buyids, who were ruling in a part of Iran, formally supported Shi'a. During the reign of Muhammad Khudabanda one of the Mongols who wanted to select an official religion investigated the four schools of law of Islam and interviewed their leaders, but he was dissatisfied because each one revealed the weaknesses of the others. He then ordered a Shi'a scholar to discuss Shi'a teachings with him and was convinced of its merits; and Shi'a was made the official religion.

Ever since Shah Isma'il established the rule of the Safavid family at the beginning of the tenth century of the Hijrah (sixteenth century A.D.), Shi'a has been the official religion of Iran. Today, the constitution of Iran continues that tradition by recognizing Shi'a as the official religion.

Shi'a Beliefs

Islam demands two kinds of responsibilities of Shi'ites—belief in the major principles of religion and performance of the particular requirements of religion. The major principles are those which are necessary and desirable for religion. The particular requirements are the rules and regulations, the code of practices, which are accepted with faith as guides for all actions.

MAJOR PRINCIPLES OF RELIGION. Every Shi'a should know and believe in these five major principles or tenets: the unity of God; the justice of God; the Prophet and his prophecies; the twelve Imams; the Day of Resurrection.

According to Shi'a, the Creator has given life to all beings and they will all return to Him. He has all the qualities of perfection and has no defects. God is omniscient and omnipotent, and self-sufficient. Nothing has been before His existence—He is the first. Everything has come into existence through Him. He is eternal; He will be when the rest is not. One of the characteristics of God is His unity, which means that God is One and has no partners. Within His being, His entity is single. There is no dualism between His entity and His attributes—His attributes are His entity, for He is One.

Briefly speaking, God has two kinds of attributes: affirmative attributes which are acknowledged by proofs, and negative attributes acknowledged by denial. The affirmative attributes are: God is omniscient, omnipotent, His being is all will, all perceiving, all hearing, all seeing, all speaking, and all truth. The negative attributes are: God is not composed of anything, He is no thing, He is not seen, He has no place, nor does He have any partner.

By belief in the justice of God, Shi'a means that God is just and directs the beings in this world toward their perfection in such a way that everything is good in its own place. There is no defect in the things in this world in the light of the order of the universe. In the creation of the world, which is moving toward perfection, there is no deviation, and also in the life to come there is neither injustice nor cruelty. Whatever an individual does in this world will be recognized in the Hereafter; the amount of good he does in this world will be correspondingly rewarded in the Other World. If he commits bad deeds in this life, he will, without doubt, suffer his punishment and taste the bitter fruit of his deeds in the hereafter, as is clearly stated in many passages of the Qur'an. Therefore, according to this principle of justice, God will judge everyone according to his deeds. He will give good rewards in the life to come to those who have lived according to the code of religion—spiritual benefits, pleasures, and eternal joys; but whoever has followed only his own desires and passions will receive punishment—spiritual and mental pains and eternal punishment.

Prophets and the role of prophecy have been explained above in this chapter. A prophet is one who through natural aptitude, worship, serving God, and being pious attains the highest point of perfection and is blessed by God and finally appointed to educate others. Such a man is different from others in all the sublime qualities, with attributes that others do not have. One of the qualities which a prophet should have is innocence, or purity. A person who never commits bad deeds, acts only according to truth and righteousness, always seeks God and tries to act according to His will is endowed with purity of soul and is known as innocent. According to Shi'a belief, Abraham, Moses, Jesus, and other prophets were all innocent. The Prophet of Islam was innocent and his ancestors, although they were not innocent, were worshipers of God, gentle, and virtuous. According to Shi'a, whatever the Prophet of Islam said or did was done by the order of God, and perceived through revelation and intuition. Muhammad never did anything on the basis of his own wishes.

The fourth major principle of Shi'a faith is belief in the twelve Imams. The word *Imam* means *leader*, and is used in other sects to refer to anyone who becomes an authority in religion and knowledge and is recognized as a leader. They refer to such a leader as Ghazali as an Imam. The Shi'ites, however, attach a special meaning to the title and use it only for the twelve Imams, never using it for others no matter how learned and great they may be.

According to Shi'a, an Imam is a man who is most learned in all fields of knowledge, and especially in religion; he has the most sublime qualities and must be innocent just as the Prophet was, and he must have been appointed by God and the Prophet to guide the people. The difference between the Prophet and an Imam is that the Prophet received messages and religious regulations through revelation, while the Imam receives regulations through the Prophet and it is his duty to lead the people toward God's will and the Prophet's Tradition.

As we have seen, the Shi'ites put their faith, after Muhammad, in Ali, Muhammad's cousin and son-in-law who was brought up by Muhammad himself. He was the most pious man of his time and the most learned in religious doctrines. From early childhood he was a worshiper of God; he did not commit any sins; he was innocent. Because he had these virtues, Ali was several times cited by Muhammad as his successor and was called Imam by the Prophet. Ali's eleven descendants who succeeded him one after another are called Imams because they had all the same virtues, committed no sins, and were spiritually pure. Their interpretations were according to God's will just as Muhammad's and Ali's were, and each Imam indicated his successor so there could be no possibility of error.

The fifth major principle is belief in the Day of Resurrection, belief that everyone will be alive in the next world after his death here. There everyone's deeds will be weighed and he will be rewarded according to his merit. In this world each man must work and in the world to come he will receive his rewards or punishments; here one cultivates, and there one reaps the harvest. If a human being has followed the rules and acted according to celestial orders, the doors of Paradise are opened to him; but if he has disregarded his duties and disobeyed the religious rules, he will go to Hell to receive perpetual torture and punishment.

Paradise is described in a number of verses in the Qur'an. It is the place to which the doer of good goes in the Hereafter to receive infinite blessings, pleasures, and kindnesses. The Qur'an also clearly tells of the differences in Paradise between the doers of good who have attained a high degree of perfection and those who have committed some degree of misbehavior.

Hell is described as the place set aside for the doers of bad deeds, the place where sinners will receive their eternal torture and punishment. The difficulties, the pains, the tortures, and the eternal sufferings of Hell are mentioned in the Qur'an, by the Prophet, and by many others.

METHOD OE LEARNING THE MAJOR PRINCIPLES. In learning the major principles of religion, everyone is free to investigate the facts and to try to discover the principles which they reveal. In this way man comes to recognize the truth of the unity of God and the truth of God's justice. God has endowed everyone with wisdom, which makes it possible for everyone to use his reason to discover that he did not exist previously but now he does exist. Therefore, man must have a cause which brought him into existence, and that cause is either himself or someone else. If he is the cause of his own existence, then he was either a cause when he did not exist, or he existed before he caused his existence. Yet each of those is an impossibility, for one who has no existence cannot be the cause of existence, and if one exists already, he does not need to cause his existence. And if someone else caused a man's existence, then the same impossibilities apply to that person, as to every other possible cause for existence. Therefore one must conclude that all things which did not exist and then came into being resulted from one cause which is self-existent, which is therefore the essence of existence. Such a being did not come into existence from non-existence, from the void—therefore such a being is eternal; it is God.

The manifestations of that Creative Being—life, knowing, power, will—are evident in the creation of this universe, which is intelligently based on established principles with everything put in its proper place and every deed performed at its proper time. The secret of the universe, the mystery of creation, the beginning and the end of every creature are all arranged with such care that no one can call the order of the universe accidental. Therefore, the Eternal Being has knowledge of this creation, and the attributes revealed in creation are as old as His entity.

This way of knowing the principles of the unity and the justice of God is open to everyone. Therefore everyone should follow this path of investigation and should know where he comes from and should recognize that an Eternal Being who is omniscient, omnipotent, all will, all wisdom, and all justice created him.

To know the major principles of religion the believer must discover the two principles of the unity and justice of God through learning and through contemplation. Then, since he seeks happiness, he will continue to discover what he should do to gain happiness, for he is assured that the all-wise Creator did not create him in vain. At this point he discovers that God has sent prophets and endowed them with the knowledge and ability to guide others toward happiness and perfection, the purpose for which God created them. In this way, the need for prophecy and the truth of prophecy becomes known to everyone, and the third major principle of religion is accepted.

Then, following the words of the Prophet and guided by reason, man will search for the principles of the Imamate and of the Day of Resurrection; and since on the basis of reasoning he accepts the words of the Prophet and of Imams as the basis for truth, he will acknowledge the truth of the Day of Resurrection. It is by this method that man learns the truth of the five major principles of religion.

Disagreement on the principles of religion. Generally speaking, there is disagreement between the Shi'as and the Sunnis concerning the fourth major principle, the Imamate, for none of the other sects of Islam consider it to be a major principle of faith. The Shi'as believe that the Imamate was established by prophecy and is essential for guiding the people; just as God appoints prophets to protect the religion, he also appoints Imams. The Sunnis, on the other hand, believe that the selection of the successor of a religious leader is the direct responsibility of the people, who are free to choose whomsoever they like. For them, the one they elect replaces the Prophet; it becomes his responsibility to protect the religion, and the people should obey him.

There are also disagreements between the Shi'ites and some of the sects of the Sunnis, particularly the Ash'arites and the Mu'tazilites. The Ash'arites have denied that God has the attribute of justice. On the basis of the principle of justice God should give rewards to the doers of good and punish the sinners, but the Ash'arites maintain that God may give rewards to sinners and atheists and may torture the good, the virtuous, and those who are believers in God. God may do whatever He wills; all that can be known is that He is accustomed to reward good and punish evil. This does not mean, according to them, that He possesses the inherent attribute of justice which is expressed in all His actions, or that He considers individual cases. According to their belief, there is no causal relationship between happenings. Whatever exists is only a succession of events which follow one another according to God's custom and will, with no necessary causal relationship.

The Mu'tazilites agree with the Shi'ites that justice is an essential attribute of God and everyone will receive his appropriate reward.

According to Shi'a, all the attributes of God are within Him; they are not accidental but are a part of His entity. God is one entity, which is manifested as omniscience, omnipotence, power, will, and the like. The Ash'arites maintain that there are eight attributes: life, knowledge, power, will, speech, hearing, sight, and being. The attributes have always coexisted and cannot be separated from the being of God; nothing existed before God. They say that the opposite is true of human beings, for in man knowledge—as an attribute—is added to his being, and is not even given to him, for he has no knowledge other than that which he learns.

There are other points on which Shi'a is not in general agreement with the Ash'arites. For instance, the Ash'arites believe that Paradise is as old as eternity, that it has been in existence from the first day of creation, but Shi'ites do not accept this point.

Concerning determinism and free will the Shi'ites differ from both the Ash'arites and the Mu'tazilites. From the beginning of man's existence he has been faced with the paradox of freedom and determinism. There is no doubt that man passes through some stages of life without freedom of choice, as when he was hidden in the potentiality of the father, then in the womb of the mother, and then attained his existence in the world. But when he is mature, is he then free? The followers of Islam have faced the paradox of determinism and free will and have cited evidence for their conclusions on the basis of reason, verses of the Qur'an, and the words of the Prophet. The Ash'arites have accepted determinism and the Mu'tazilites believe in free will, but the Shi'ites believe that the arguments of both sects are inadequate. Shi'a takes the middle position and believes that there is neither complete determinism nor complete freedom of choice, but there is something between these two.

Particular requirements of religion. The particular requirements of religion are embodied in the rules and regulations which are given as guides to personal and social welfare. There is not a single deed, not a moment in a man's life, for which Islam has not issued a rule, and all Muslims are required to accept the regulations of Islam with faith and to obey them. Man's duty toward himself and his duties toward others have all been explicitly mentioned. Even when man exists potentially in his father's sperm, and in the fetal stage in his mother's womb, there are rules of behavior prescribed for the parents.

For instance, the father must not drink alcohol, and he is taught how to have intercourse for the sake of having a child; it is the father's duty to protect the fetus. When the baby is born the parents should follow certain rules for upbringing until he becomes spiritually and physically mature; then he should follow the rules of Islam himself. The regulations of Islam specify the proper procedure concerning food, clothing, sleep, awaking, friendship, hostile behavior, silence, talking, and how to benefit one's self. Even when the individual departs from this world there are codes covering the proper forms for his burial which must be followed by his survivors.

The particular requirements of religion are concerned with worship, contracts, unilateral agreements, and practical rules of conduct.

Worship includes those religious deeds which aim to reach God, deeds which should be performed to achieve perfection, not out of passion or personal desire. Worship, in this sense, includes praying, fasting, almsgiving *(khums)*, giving away one-tenth *(zakat)*, pilgrimage, holy war, preaching righteousness, and prohibiting bad deeds. Generally speaking, all rules of Islam take into consideration all of those eight requirements, for they are the means of achieving happiness. All of these rules are supported by reason, and whatever fits reason is acceptable to religion. But often reason and common sense fail to understand the advantages or disadvantages of an act; therefore, there is need for an authority, someone to lead. That is why the Prophet made the rules for Islam.

Prayer is required five times during the twenty-four hours of the day of every mature individual (according to Shi'a a girl is mature at ten years and a boy at fifteen) who is intelligent and able. These prayers should follow certain prescribed rituals. For example, the clothes and the body should be clean; one should observe the washing of the hands, arms, and face before praying. The place of praying should not be a usurped place that is being taken by force. During the prayer one should face Mecca, pray in the prescribed way, and submit himself to Allah. One prayer should be given at dawn before sunrise, the second at noon, the third in the evening, the fourth after sunset, and the fifth should be given when one goes to bed.

The requirement of the five prayers is designed to make one attentive, to enlighten one's spirit, and to cause one to seek happiness and perfection in drawing near to God. If a man's body is clean and his spirit enlightened through the regular practice of worshiping God five times a day, he will behave according to the rules of Islam and accomplish good deeds and avoid bad ones. Such a man's body and spirit will make progress in this world and the next, and a society full of such individuals will follow the path to perfection.

Fasting during the month of Ramadan is obligatory in Islam for every intelligent, mature, and able Muslim; from dawn to sunset he is forbidden to eat, drink, or have sexual intercourse. Fasting offers both bodily and spiritual advantages—advantages for the individual and for society in this world and in the world to come. For example, the man who fasts develops strength of will because he decides not to eat or drink; he becomes more considerate of his fellowmen; he becomes pious and virtuous; his spirit is enlightened and his body becomes clean of sin. If he is rich he will find a common tie with the poor which is beneficial to society because some of his property will be distributed to the poor; and the poor will be gratified because they will see that pleasure is sometimes denied to the rich. There are many other advantages to fasting which are recognized in Islam.

Almsgiving is obligatory in all sects of Islam, but the way in which it is administered in Shi'a differs from the practice of other sects. There are two kinds of almsgiving—*khums* and *zakat*. To make up khums, Shi'a takes a fifth of one's properties, including a share of gold and silver, valuables, and property captured in a war, as well as a certain percentage of the benefits derived from business. According to Shi'a this fifth of these properties should be given to the Imam and Muhammad's descendants (or Sayyids) who do not share in zakat, the second form of almsgiving. An Imam, who is one of the grandsons of the Prophet, can use the share he receives from khums in any way he likes. Those descendants of Muhammad's family who are in need can use their share for their living expenses. The advantage of khums is that those of Muhammad's descendants who are blind, old, and unable to work are thus taken care of and they need not turn to begging and lose their self-respect. The Imam also has a free hand in using the money for educating the people, helping the poor, and improving social conditions.

The second form of almsgiving is zakat, the giving away of one-tenth of one's income if one is a person of wealth who owns gold, silver, cattle, or crops of a certain amount. Zakat should be used to help the poor and the stranger, those who are in debt, those who are not Muslims but might become believers, or those who would be able to assist Islam in some way. It should also be used for public works, such as the construction of schools, bridges, water reservoirs, and the like.

Pilgrimage to Mecca is required of every Muslim who can afford and is able to make the trip. The duties he should perform at Mecca are called *Hajj* and the man who has performed the duties of the pilgrimage is known as a *Hajji.* One of the social advantages of the pilgrimage is that every year from all over the world Muslims gather together in one place. There the rich and the learned ones exchange ideas and learn about one another's country, life, and people; they learn of the needs in various parts of the Muslim world; they discover their friends and foes; and they are able to cooperate to solve their problems. In the early days, before modern means of communication were available, the religious center was especially important, but even today it serves as a means by which Muslims learn to live together in unity and diversity. In addition to the pilgrimage to Mecca, great numbers of Shi'ites make the pilgrimage to Karbala, Najaf, Meshed, Qum, and other such centers where they honor Ali or the other Imams. Such pilgrimages are not obligatory but the people go out of respect for Ali and his descendants and as a means of strengthening their faith. Many more people can afford to go on these pilgrimages than could make the long trip to Mecca.

Holy war is obligatory on Muslims under certain circumstances. It is every Muslim's duty to fight against unbelievers, idol worshipers, and pagans; to defend Islam; to extend the borders of Islamic countries; and to scatter Islam to other places. According to Shiʿa when the Imam is not present and there is no special substitute for him, a holy war is not obligatory. However, if an enemy attacks and an Islamic country is in danger, it is everyone's duty to fight in defense of his country.

Worship in Islam also includes preaching righteousness and preventing people from performing bad deeds. One is responsible for others as well as for oneself; therefore, each individual has the obligation to encourage others to do good and to prevent others from doing evil deeds.

In addition to worship, as we have said, the particular requirements of religion include contracts, unilateral agreements, and practical rules of conduct. The contracts are written or verbal agreements between two persons, and are governed by certain prescribed regulations and verbal forms which must be followed. When the dealers have uttered the required phrases, the contract is binding and everyone is obligated to fulfill his promise except under certain clearly defined conditions. Contracts in Islam cover many aspects of human relations, such as renting, marrying, buying, and the like.

The unilateral agreement is a relationship between two persons but its fulfillment depends upon the words of one person, as in a divorce, confession, and taking an oath.

The practical rules of conduct cover personal and social actions such as inheritance, giving evidence, political activities, and many other aspects of life. They include the areas of Islamic jurisprudence not covered in the other three categories of religious requirements.

METHOD OF LEARNING THE PRACTICAL REQUIREMENTS. There are two ways of learning the particular requirements of religion: by truth-seeking *(ijtihad)*, or by imitation. Those who use the method of ijtihad seek the truth by individual interpretation through discussion, investigation of the evidence, and the use of reason. The second method is that of learning the truth from learned men who are worthy of confidence; it is also valid because those who follow it imitate an authority. By these methods it is possible to understand the rules and regulations of religion and to discover their proper application in particular instances.

These two ways of learning are valid for learning the particular requirements of religion, but not, as we have seen, for belief in the major principles of religion. The principles of religion must be discovered by each person through his own knowledge and contemplation, and no one should imitate another person blindly in worshiping God, recognizing His attributes, believing in His Prophet, or believing in the Imams and the Day of Resurrection. It is necessary for everyone to discover the truth and believe it himself.

On the other hand, it is not important for the individual to contemplate the laws and regulations of Islam and act according to his own understanding. Rather, if a religious authority has studied and understood the laws and regulations, the rest of the people may follow him without having gone through the process of study. The laws and regulations of Islam have come to the people through the Qur'an, the words of Muhammad, and Imams. Therefore, one who has potentialities for becoming a religious leader strives to gain knowledge of these three sources and derives specific laws from them; he follows those laws and sets an example for the people. Such a man is known as a *Mujtahid*, and those who accept his leadership are called imitators.

The religious leaders believe in the five major principles of religion and in the Twelve Imams, accepting the twelfth one in absence, but they may differ in their interpretation of religious laws. One group of the mujtahid bases its understanding and interpretation of the religious laws on the Qur'an, on major authorities, and on reason, while another group bases its rules and procedures on Tradition. The first group has clearly worked out principles of jurisprudence as a guide, with accepted procedures for legal actions, while the second group uses only testaments and Tradition as guides for their actions.

According to Shi'a there are four sources for the particular requirements of religion, for religious law: the Qur'an, Tradition (Sunnah), general agreement, and reason. The first source for guidance in formulating a religious law, for determining what would be a good action in a given situation, is the Qur'an, whether its teaching is explicit or implicit. If guidance is not found in the Qur'an, then one turns to the Traditions. If a basis for the ruling is not found in the Qur'an or the Traditions, then it should be sought in the general agreement (ijma) of the religious leaders, and that general agreement should be followed by all the people. Sometimes, however, even such an agreement may not be reached; in such a case one's reason must serve as a guide. Reason as a means of forming a judgment is included in religious doctrine because whatever reason favors, religion agrees to. All Shi'as accept these four sources of religious law, but those who derive religious laws from scriptures and Traditions define reasoning as the use of analogy, or parallels from Tradition, rather than deductive and inductive reasoning; those who follow the principles of jurisprudence do not accept reasoning by analogy as valid.

When the practical regulations or laws of Islam are inferred from the four sources—the Qur'an, Traditions, agreement of leaders, or individual reason, in that order—there is always the possibility of misinterpretation because of differences in intelligence and understanding. Many of the differences between Shi'as and Sunnis are due to differing interpretations of the four sources. Even during the governing of Ali as Caliph there were differences of interpretation of the same sources; at such times not all Muslims followed Ali, but at least the Shi'ites did. During the early centuries of Islam there grew up five schools of law in the Muslim world: the four Sunni schools of Hanbali, Maliki, Shafi'i, and Hanafi, and the Shi'a school which is sometimes called Ja'fari after the sixth Imam.

Shi'ites believe that in formulating the laws governing practical affairs it is essential to follow strictly the words of Muhammad when he said, "I leave two things with you, the Qur'an and my descendants, which will lead you to the true way." Shi'a received Muhammad's own teachings, actions, and sermons as transmitted by his grandchildren, not by others. Under the Umayyads the Imams were not allowed to teach publicly, but when the Abbasids came to power the sixth Imam was free to explain the particulars of religion, the laws of Islam. He educated a large number of people who collected his teachings in book form and laid the basis for Islamic law as interpreted by Shi'a. From his teachings and the teachings of the other Imams, four hundred principles have been handed down to present-day Shi'ites; these principles are, next to the Qur'an, the fundamental principles of Shi'a.

The four hundred principles were too many for everyone to learn and were in danger of being lost, so it was appropriate for the reliable learned religious leaders to summarize the principles in a more readily available form. In the fourth and fifth centuries the four hundred principles were outlined in four books which serve as the basis for the rules of Shi'a. This is fortunate, since almost all of the original four hundred principles have been lost. At the beginning of the fourth century of Islam and before the long absence of the twelfth Imam, there lived a learned man named Muhammad Ibn Ya'qub al-Kulaini (died 329; A.D. 940) who was known as the "guardian of Islam" and who became famous as the compiler of the first book, known as *Kafi*, or *The Sufficient*. The second book was written by another great man, Muhammad Ibn Ali Ibn Babawaih al-Qummi (died 381; A.D. 991), known as the "truth-teller"; his book is *Man la Yahduruh al Faqih*, which means *Self-Study Jurisprudence*. The third and fourth books—*Tahdhib al Ahkam*, or *The Best Selection of All Principles*, and *Istibsar*, or *Enlightening the People*—were written by Muhammad Ibn Hasan al-Tusi (died 460; A.D. 1067), known by the title "The Great Man of Shi'a."

These four books, written by great religious scholars, are the basis for Shi'a jurisprudence; after the Qur'an, they are the sources of law for religious leaders in Shi'a.

Disagreement on the requirements of religion. Although there are differences in interpretation between the five schools of law in Islam, it should be noted that Shi'a differs more sharply from the four Sunni schools in the codes it derives from the Qur'an, the Sunnah, the consensus of the religious leaders, and from individual interpretation. For instance, as was mentioned, although some sects consider reasoning from analogy to be a valid method for deriving laws, Shi'ites do not accept inferences from analogy as conclusive.

Shi'a recognizes Tradition as a source of religious rules, but it does not find all kinds of Traditions acceptable. Only those Traditions are accepted which were revealed to the family of Muhammad and interpreted by Imams and learned men who follow the authority of the family of the Prophet. The books of Traditions gathered by the Sunnis are not accepted as authoritative by Shi'ites.

Shi'a, that is, the followers of the twelve Imams, differ from other sects in Islam in that it allows ijtihad; that is, it allows everyone to become an authority for himself in religion. The believer can study the rules and regulations and by referring to the sources and using his reason can infer their application in specific cases. He is able to act according to his understanding of the rules of Islam without obligation to follow other authorities. Everyone, under certain clearly defined conditions, can derive a code of conduct from the Qur'an, from Tradition, from the consensus of authorities (ijma), and from the use of reason.

In the four schools of Sunni law ijtihad is not permitted; the follower must adhere strictly to the orders of the religious leaders. Hanafi followers, for instance, must be guided by what was said by Abu Hanifah who lived twelve hundred years ago; whether he was right or wrong, there is no recourse to studying such primary sources as the Qur'an or Tradition. Abu Hanifah lived a hundred years after Muhammad and thus was not present to hear Muhammad's teachings; nor did Muhammad ever say that Abu Hanifah was to be the sole interpreter of matters of jurisprudence. No one before or after him had any right to check his words and guide the people according to a revised doctrine, and even if someone more learned than Abu Hanifah were to appear, the disciple of that sect must still follow what Abu Hanifah has said. The same criticism applies to the other sects.

By contrast, the door of personal responsibility in religion, ijtihad, is open to every Muslim, according to Shi'a doctrine. Every eligible person who can make an intelligent judgment can derive particular applications of religion from the sources. This is a major point of disagreement between Shi'a and Sunni in the area of the particular requirements of religion.

Islam in society. In its laws, Islam tries to establish a foundation for equality, brotherhood, and friendliness among men. According to Islam, no individual has an advantage over another except through virtue and knowledge. Through its major principles of religion Islam expects everyone to seek his own happiness through recognizing that God is omnipotent, omniscient, infinite, all-living, and eternal. Whatever a man is, it is because of God, and whatever a man has obtained, it has been given to him by God.

Islam demands moral virtues from everyone, everywhere, always. It wants everyone to love his fellow beings, to search for the truth, to be brave, faithful, honest, noble, true, just, and reliable. He must avoid immorality, must not be cruel, must not lie, or be a traitor, or deceitful, or jealous, or aggressive; he must not harm animals. Islam does not make distinctions between men, is not in favor of class distinction; Arab, Turk, occidental, oriental, a man of the north or of the south—they are all alike. All people are brothers and Islam wants people from all over the world to be kind to one another and to help one another so they can achieve their own perfection and happiness in a brotherly way. The only superiority of one man over another which is recognized by Islam is that which is gained by virtue and knowledge, for the virtuous and learned man has a superior place in the eyes of God.

Islam tries to make people understand that this world is not the eternal world, that it is a place we pass through as an introduction to the other world; it is a field that we cultivate, but we will have our harvest in the other world. Man must not be charmed by the façade of this world. He must recognize that real happiness is not available in this world—it can be achieved only in the Other World. To improve this world is not the ultimate aim of man, nor is it to make contributions to civilization or to build up the physical aspects of this world. The real aim of man is to work for the perfection of the Other World. Unless a man realizes this he will spend all his time in this world receiving hardship and troubles and will leave this world bare-handed and despondent, feeling at the moment of departure that he has wasted his life and has not gained anything worthwhile. An intelligent man knows that he is a traveler in this world on his way to eternal perfection. There is no doubt that the life required of a follower of Islam is planned so that it takes a man to that end.

In truth, if a man saves himself from the danger of the illusions of this world and breaks away from the difficulties which he has spun around himself like a spider in a web, if he considers his true nature and that which is good for man, he may occasionally catch a glimpse of the Other World and be inspired to find the true godly way to his foreordained goal. If, then, he will consider the lives of the great religious leaders and discover how they reached their goal, he will, without doubt, pursue Islamic doctrines, and he will heartily follow the Prophet of Islam and his true descendants.

CHAPTER SIX

Islamic Culture in Arab and African Countries

Ishak M. Husaini

The culture of Islamic countries has grown through the interaction of groups of Islamic peoples of widely varied ethnic and geographic backgrounds and through strong cultural influences from the non-Islamic civilizations of Greece, Persia, and India in the early days, and of western Europe in modern times.

Ancient Islamic culture of the golden age of the Abbasids attained a high level of development before it fell into a period of decline similar to the decline of the Greek, Chinese, and Persian cultures. Contemporary Islamic culture is bound to the ancient Islamic culture with very close ties, but the decline between the ancient and the modern period was so apparent that contemporary Islamic culture is looked upon as a renaissance rather than a continuing growth, a renaissance which has been shaped in many ways by modernism and westernization. Unfortunately, this renaissance of the past century and a half has been seriously restricted because most of the Islamic countries have been held down by alien political and economic controls which did not permit the creative participation in cultural activities which had been characteristic of Muslims in their glorious days in the past.

Our concern in this and the subsequent chapters is not, however, with the total Islamic culture but with the specifically religious culture which originates almost exclusively from the Qur'an, the Traditions of the Prophet of Islam, and the various interpretations of these two fundamental sources. Although we are dealing here with the Islamic culture of the Arab and African countries, it is our contention that the diversities found in Islam are not due to variations in geographic environments or to different civilizations, but are due only to recognized sectarian differences. The Druzes of the Levant differ from the Sunnis of Egypt because of differing interpretations of the Qur'an and the Traditions of the Prophet, not because they live in different cultural or geographical environments. There are sectarian differences in Islam, but the Arab Muslim and the non-Arab Muslim are not separated by geographic or cultural differences.

The African Arab world includes Egypt, Sudan, Libya, Tunisia, Algeria, and Morocco, with an area of about three million square miles, and containing some forty-nine million Muslims. The rest of Africa has twenty-eight million Muslims who are sometimes a majority of the population and sometimes a minority; all of them, except in Ghana, are ruled by a colonial power.

The Asiatic Arab world is made up of the Arabian Peninsula, Iraq, and the Levant. The Kingdom of Saudi Arabia includes almost four-fifths of the area, with about six million Muslims; south and west of it is the Yemenite Kingdom with four million Muslims, and to the south and east are a number of small Amirates and Sultanates with two million Muslims. The Levant includes Jordan, Palestine, Syria, and Lebanon with five million Muslims, and there are five million more in neighboring Iraq.

Thus in the Arab and African areas there are more than one hundred million Muslims occupying a zone of highest strategic importance and possessing oil and water resources of great consequence to the future welfare of this region and of the entire world.

The Arabian Peninsula

Islam first appeared in the western area of the Arabian Peninsula, known as the Hijaz, at Mecca and then at Medina. The Hijaz is called the Holy Land, for there stands the

Ka'ba, which is the goal of thousands of pilgrims every year, and nearby is Arafat where pilgrims slaughter their sacrifices at the great Feast of the Sacrifice ('Id al-Qurban) which terminates the pilgrimage. Many pilgrims go on to Medina to pay homage before the tomb of the Prophet. Although the pilgrimage is compulsory only for those who have the means to accomplish it, Muslims exert every effort to attain the heights of happiness by making the pilgrimage and often thereafter proudly add the title *Hajj* to their name. For the whole Muslim world this small area of the Arabian Peninsula has a religious significance not equalled by any other place.

When the Umayyads moved the capital from Medina to Damascus the political and intellectual center of gravity left the Arabian Peninsula. The isolation of the Hijaz was even more pronounced when the more distant Baghdad became the home of the Abbasid Caliphs and the center of political, intellectual, and literary activity. If it were not for the pilgrimage, the Hijaz would have lost its religious power as well.

Nothing much of consequence seems to have happened in the Peninsula after the capital was moved until the rise of the Wahhabi movement which, after only a few years, became in 1157 (A.D. 1744) the official sect of the Muslims of the central plateau of the Peninsula, as it has continued to be ever since. As was explained in Chapter Two, the Wahhabi movement was inspired by the teachings of Ibn Taymiyya, the great reformer who sought to save the Muslim world from doctrinal divisive forces so it could be more powerful in withstanding foreign aggression. He opposed doctrinal fanaticism and Sufi innovations, and advocated a restoration of the original purity of doctrine and daily life which were manifested in the Qur'an and Traditions of the Prophet.

The prevailing conditions in the Arabian Peninsula and surrounding regions drove Muhammad Ibn Abd al-Wahhab to lay greater emphasis on some of Ibn Taymiyya's teachings than on others. He sought first of all to purge the faith in Allah of what he called polytheism, typified by the practice of venerating the tombs of prophets and saints in ways indistinguishable from worship. The Wahhabis considered such veneration equal to idolatry and worship of the stars, which are condemned by Islam as acts of infidelity, the most serious of all sins. Therefore, they destroyed sacred tombs and prohibited excessive prostrations in front of the Prophet's tomb in Medina.

Ibn Abd al-Wahhab also held that the recital of the creed—*I testify that there is no God but God and Muhammad is the Messenger of God*—is not sufficient testimony of one's faith in Islam but must be accompanied by other devotions such as prayer and almsgiving. Willfully to neglect prayer and almsgiving is an act of infidelity. On the basis of this belief there came to be a group of Wahhabis known as Compellers who considered it their religious duty to see that people performed the prayers at the prescribed times, basing their action on the injunction "to command the good and prohibit the bad." They were also rigid in enforcing the Islamic prohibition of wine and gambling, and went so far as to condemn smoking.

Ibn Abd al-Wahhab held that the Qur'an as the word of God is primordial and uncreated; it is from God and returns to God; it was transmitted to the Prophet by Gabriel as he heard it from God. It was also held that Muslims must believe in the Messenger's Traditions concerning the Resurrection, punishment, reward, and walking on the path to Heaven. No genuine Tradition may be disregarded in preference for a logical deduction, and no opinion put forward by a Mujtahid is acceptable unless it is supported by evidence from the Qur'an and the Sunnah. No new idea or saying may be advocated unless it was given by the four Imams, the first four Caliphs. And finally, the Wahhabis believe that God's names as given in the Qur'an must be accepted without interpreting them as symbols or in an anthropomorphic sense. The Qur'an states that God will be seen in Paradise in person.

Such are the Wahhabi teachings concerning the fundamentals of the faith, but concerning the consequences, the particular requirements of religion, they follow the orthodox teachings of the school of Hanbali, which follows the Qur'an and the Hadith (Tradition), and refuses deduction—although they do not forbid the code of practices of any of the other Imams. The Wahhabis renounced Shi'a jurisprudence and regarded any preference for tribal laws as an act of infidelity. They vigorously opposed all innovations introduced by Sufis and extremist Shi'ites, even refusing their testimony in courts and refusing intermarriage with them.

A group of the Wahhabis who went to great lengths in enforcing these doctrines and in standing adamant against any innovation, even including useful contributions of modern civilization, were suppressed by King Abul Aziz Ibn Sa'ud who believed in a wise, moderate policy of modernization. Although the Wahhabis demanded at the outset of their mission that every Muslim should accept their teachings, they later adopted a more moderate attitude and permitted their Muslim dissenters, especially in the Hijaz, to hold their own views, and even to smoke if they wished—thereby avoiding a new schism in Islam. They are therefore looked upon, not as a separate sect, but rather as a group of conservative, orthodox Muslims whose belief is centered around the Qur'an and the Hadith, who seek to express their faith in word and deed, and whose object is the reestablishment of the Muslim state on the basis of Muslim jurisprudence.

The majority of Muslims of the Arabian Peninsula are Sunnis, whether they be Wahhabis or not, with two main exceptions—the Zaidis in Yemen and the Kharijites in Oman.

In pre-Islamic times Yemen was known as *Arabia Felix* because of its prosperity in comparison with the rest of the arid peninsula. The irrigation dam of Ma'rib, which is one of the most ancient in the world, is evidence of the high standard of prosperity and civilization attained in Yemen. Its rainfall is bountiful, it abounds with mountainous regions with rivers, valleys, springs of water, and numerous wells—all exploited for agriculture. It is famous for its many-storied buildings. Except for a Jewish community by the walls of San'a, all of the inhabitants of Yemen are of pure Arab origin and followers of Islam with the large majority belonging to the Shi'a Zaidi group. The rest are Sunnis who belong to the school of Imam al-Shafi'i. The Zaidis live in the mountainous regions where they have been able to maintain their purity of origin, while the Sunnis live along the coast where they have intermarried with Africans.

Yemen embraced Islam in the days of the Prophet. In the third century of the Hijrah the Zaidi sect penetrated Yemen through an Imam who came from Iraq. Dynasties succeeded each other at a great pace because of the Zaidi doctrine that the Imam had to be a warrior who seized power by his own strength as did Imam Zaid their founder. Through the centuries, Yemen has been ruled by governors appointed by the Hijaz government, by successive Zaidi Imams, by the radical Shi'a Qarmatians, by the Turks, and finally by the present dynasty, founded by the grandfather of the present Imam, who is a descendant of the first Zaidi Imam who came from Iraq. For a long time the Imams had held only spiritual authority, but when the Turks withdrew in 1336 (A.D. 1917) they seized temporal power. Modern Yemen is, therefore, barely forty years old, a state which, like Saudi Arabia and Afghanistan, depends upon Muslim jurisprudence for its constitution and legislation.

The Zaidi sect is named after Imam Zaid, the son of the fourth Imam of Shi'a. The Zaidis claimed that the fourth Imam forfeited the Imamate when he failed to fight against the Umayyads, and the succession continues through his son Zaid who was killed in battle against the Umayyad forces. Zaid studied Muslim theology under the leading Mu'tazilite of his time and taught his views concerning the major principles of Islam. Concerning the consequences—worship and jurisprudence—the Zaidis follow the Shafi'i school, which makes them the Shi'ites nearest to the Sunnis. They also differ from most Shi'a sects in believing that the succession of the Imamate continues to this day.

The Yemenites are well known for their fondness for knowledge within the carefully defined limits of their faith, for their religious zeal, for their pride in their language, and their distrust of foreigners. Their policy has been one of gradual progress for fear of falling into the hands of imperialist powers. Although the ancient Yemenite civilization which found its stimulus in its favorable climate and trade is no more, the latent human and natural resources of the country are still there and will come to the fore when they have security from foreign invasion and can introduce modernization and democratic rule.

The inhabitants of the coastal regions from the Persian Gulf to Yemen are Muslim Arabs, with a Sunni majority and a small percentage of Shi'ites. They are ruled by amirs and sultans, all of whom are under British influence. There is little civilization or advanced culture in this region because of the poverty, ignorance, and fanaticism which flourish under an imperialist power. There is, however, the beginning of a renaissance in Kuwait and Bahrein because of the wealth brought by oil royalties. Excellent schools have been developed there and if education continues at its present pace a general reform is inevitable.

In addition to the Sunnis and Shi'ites in this area, the Kharijite sect is found in Oman. The Kharijites go back to the time of Ali when a number of his followers turned against him because he consented to the arbitration of men rather than the Qur'an in his dispute with Mu'awiya. Although Ali defeated and dispersed them, it was a Kharijite who assassinated him and they continued to rebel against all authority for some time. It is believed that two of the Kharijites escaped to Oman where they established the sect which is thriving today.

The Kharijites believe that the Imamate need not be given to descendants of the Prophet or of the early leaders at Mecca or Medina. The Imamate is determined by elections, not by heredity. Government must be based on Muslim jurisprudence. If the Imam does not comply with the Sunnah it is the moral and religious obligation of a Muslim to rebel against his authority. It is even conceivable and permissible not to have an Imam at all. They also hold that to commit a major sin is an act of infidelity. In the succession of Imams, they reject Ali because he accepted arbitration and Uthman because he misused his authority.

Within the Kharijites there is a moderate sect known as Ibadis. Ibadis believe that Muslim dissenters are infidels, but not polytheists; and that dissenters from their sect still belong to the body of Islam. It is permissible for them to intermarry among their own dissenters, to leave them legacies, and to inherit from them. For the Ibadis, faith includes action; the person who commits a major sin is still a monotheist, but not faithful. They follow Muslim jurisprudence in marriage, divorce, and inheritance, but resort to the judgments of wise men in questions of war, tribal solidarity, and trade.

The Arab Muslims of the Peninsula are extremely tolerant of each other. In Oman, for instance, the mosques are used without differentiation by Sunnis, Shi'ites, and Kharijites; and in Yemen the former Imam often led Zaidis and Shi'ites in prayer without distinguishing between them. The differences are regarded by these tribes as merely doctrinal variations within a community which is united in its customs and ways of thinking. Tribal customs and antecedents are more important than sectarian beliefs in maintaining unity among the people of the Arabian Peninsula.

The Levant

The Levant includes the Arab countries north of the Arabian Peninsula, except Iraq—that is, Syria, Jordan, Palestine, and Lebanon. The Arabs in this area form a homogeneous group with a Sunni majority except in Lebanon which, like a Persian carpet, is made up of a colorful mixture of all the creeds and sects to be found in the Middle East.

The Arabs completed the conquest of the Levant within a few years of the death of the Prophet, their surprising success made possible by the inspiration of their new faith which filled their souls with confidence, and by the decline of the power of Persia and Byzantium as a result of their perpetual wars against each other. Since the population of this region was chiefly of true Arab stock they received the Muslim forces as kinsmen rather than foreigners. The Christians did not find Islam a strange religion for it upheld the mission of Christ and urged the following of his Book. The Qur'an says,

"And thou wilt find the nearest of them in affection to those who believe (to be) those who say: Lo! We are Christians. That is because there are among them priests and monks, and because they are not proud." (Surah V, 82).

For almost a century after the death of Ali the Umayyads ruled from Damascus, giving to the Caliphate a royal character which was not found in the earlier years when the power centered in the Arabian Peninsula. Then the Caliphate moved to Baghdad under the Abbasids for five centuries and the Levant was ruled by a succession of dynasties—the Ayyubids, the Mamluks, the Turks, and in 1339 (A.D. 1920) came occupation by Western powers which continued until the end of the second World War.

The majority of the people of the Levant are Sunnis who are united in their beliefs concerning the fundamentals of Islam and the consequences. City-dwellers usually follow the school of Imam Abu Hanifa in their interpretation of the consequences—the code of laws—while the rural population usually follows Imam Shafi'i. However, the distinction between the schools is so subtle that most Muslims of today hardly know which of the four schools of law they follow and are content to be known as Muslim Sunnites. In religious courts the judge usually passes judgment according to the canonical interpretation of the school of law which the suitors follow. In civil courts, however, the judge applies the civil code without making any distinction between citizens because of their religion or sect.

Syria is a parliamentary republic with its capital at Damascus, where it has been since the rule of the Umayyads. The great mosque at Damascus is still called the Umayyad Mosque after the dynasty which established it. Syrians are noted for their strong Arab nationalism, their religious zeal, commercial ingenuity, intelligence, and love of knowledge. Their university at Damascus has faculties of letters, sciences, medicine, pharmacy, and law; the university at Aleppo has a faculty of engineering, and at Salamiya they have a faculty of agriculture.

In the Hamah region near Salamiya is a group of the Isma'ili sect with about twenty-three thousand followers, all paying allegiance to the Agha Khan as their spiritual leader. Salamiya has been one of the main centers of the Isma'ilis since the early days and is still important for that sect even though the Agha Khan does not use it for his headquarters.

In Jabal ad-Druz there are some thirty-one thousand followers of the Druze sect, of the same beliefs as the Druzes of Lebanon. At Latakia there are some 356,000 Nusairis who at one time were an extremist branch of Shi'a but are now returning to a more moderate position.

The Isma'ilis trace the continuing succession of their Imams from Isma'il, the son of the sixth Imam of the Shi'ites. The believe that the Qur'an is God's revelation but they interpret it in their own way, which is not secretive and allegorical as with the Druzes, but is philosophical according to the reasoning of their leaders. Second in importance to the Qur'an is the book *Brethren of Serenity*, which they recite as part of their prayers. Their living Imam is infallible and is aided by a number of missionaries who lead the faithful and explain their religion to them. They keep the five pillars of Islam but emphasize deep philosophical contemplation in prayer, fasting, and pilgrimage as did the Mu'tazilites with whom they agree in considering God far above having any limiting attributes.

The Druzes parted company with the Isma'ilis in the time of al-Hakim-bi'amr-Illah the Fatimite (died 411; A.D. 1020) when they claimed that the Imamate ended with him, while the rest of the Isma'ilis believe that the Imamate continued. The differences between the Druzes and Isma'ilis have increased since that time, with the addition of a mixture of Greek, Persian, and Indian philosophy and mysticism to Druze beliefs. The Druzes believe that God was incarnated in the Imam just as He was in the prophets, that the Imam is infallible, that creation came about through a series of emanations, that after death souls are reincarnated in other bodies, and that holy jurisprudence changes with the succession of the prophets. They accept the Qur'an as inspired but have their own secret commentaries on it, which they received from their Imams. They tend to overlook most of the Muslim devotional practices and to emphasize the ethics of love and truthfulness. It is interesting to note that once when a number of young Druzes who had moved to America asked a Druze scholar what they should study to understand their religion he replied that they should go back to the Qur'an which is the source of all Islam.

An obscure sect found in Syria is called Nusairi after Muhammad Ibn Nusayr who was originally a follower of the eleventh Shi'a Imam but later dissented and proclaimed the doctrine that the Imam is a divine incarnation. The series of Imams continues to the present, according to the Nusairis. They perform all of the Muslim devotions, but it is said that this is only a veil hiding their true convictions, which are flagrant contradictions of Islam, even including belief in a trinity made up of the spirit of God (Ali), the outer form (Muhammad), and the propagator of the shari'a (Salman al-Farisi).

Many of these sects have recently tended toward a critical study of their beliefs and a concern for the spiritual life of their followers. There are hopeful signs of an attempt to bridge the differences between the sects by means similar to those encouraged by the Society for the Reconciliation of Muslim Sects which was established a few years ago in Cairo. Since the differences between Sunnis and Shi'ites are political rather than doctrinal, and all of these sects were originally Muslim, it can be expected that as the fanaticism and racial antagonisms of the ages of degeneration disappear there will be even stronger tendencies toward reconciliation of their differences.

In Jordan and Palestine the Muslims are Sunnis who hold the same convictions and follow the same devotions and practices as do the Muslims of Syria. Their many family ties and common customs bind these people closely to the people of Syria. The Bedouins here, as in Arabia, tend to follow tribal customs rather than Muslim jurisprudence and know little of religion beyond the recital of words they have memorized but scarcely comprehend. They are chiefly concerned with deriving a scanty living from the desert; for them, water is often more important than religion.

The Arabs of Palestine are mostly the descendants of pilgrims, visitors, and refugees who sought a haven in the sacred land which is the home of the Mosque of the Rock and the Aqsa Mosque which is venerated by all Muslims as second only to the Ka'ba as a sanctuary. Under the Ayyubids and the Mamluks, Palestine attained a high degree of prosperity which made possible the creation of numerous schools. The remnants of the schools which once surrounded the Aqsa Mosque still stand today with their huge ornate iron gates. Just before the first World War the Ottoman governor of Palestine brought in teachers from all over the Muslim world to create a university designed to be a small Azhar, but it did not survive the Turkish withdrawal. During the mandate after the first World War a number of schools and colleges were established, raising the cultural level of the country, but the budget for education was limited and attempts to introduce technical and industrial training were curtailed, forcing students to go to Cairo, Beirut, and the West for advanced education. Students of religion went to Al Azhar in Cairo, the foremost Muslim university.

Iraq

When the Caliphate moved to Baghdad in the second century (eighth century A.D.) one of the most outstanding cultural centers of the world was created. Baghdad became the melting pot where Muslim culture was mixed with the ancient Greek culture and with the cultures of Iran, India, and China. In this atmosphere of stimulating cultural interaction was laid the basis of Muslim theology, philosophy, linguistics, and letters as well as chemistry, mathematics, medicine, architecture, and astronomy. For five hundred consecutive years the flourishing of Muslim culture made Baghdad the lighthouse of knowledge for the whole world. Two of the greatest universities in the history of education were established there and all branches of knowledge grew from the study of religion and flourished in the service of religion.

In the Abbasid period Muslim culture became society-oriented, with emphasis on such subjects as the sciences and engineering and architecture; but no contradiction was felt between these fields and religion, for all scholars combined religious knowledge with mastery of other fields of learning. During the same period, Muslim culture, although it did not initiate the tendency, turned toward the development of the arts which are dependent upon the existence of a wealthy leisured class, as has happened in the West recently. Muslims became engrossed in the study of music, the art of story-telling, and exerted great efforts to perfect the art of writing prose and poetry. They revelled in performance of shadow plays, imported from China. Since religion did not demand austerity such pleasure-seeking was tolerated. It was not to be wondered at that such a religious figure as al-Jahiz should write about singing, wine drinking, and jokes.

In the field of religious research new questions were raised concerning matters which had formerly been blindly accepted without rational analysis. Questions about the nature of God, the nature of the Qur'an, the Other World, punishment and reward, predestination, and the whole realm of metaphysics were fervently disputed everywhere.

This tremendous intellectual energy which was released under the protection of religion was brought to a disastrous end by the Mongol invasion in the seventh century (thirteenth century A.D.) when Baghdad was destroyed, its books burned, and its inhabitants slaughtered. The Caliph moved from Baghdad to Cairo and the glory of Iraq was irretrievably lost. Under the later Ottoman rule the Muslim culture in Iraq reached its lowest level. It is only since the first World War that there has been a revival in Iraq. Today there is a university in Baghdad with faculties in the sciences and letters, and religious schools similar to the old Azhar exist in Najaf and Karbala for Shi'ites and in Baghdad for the Sunnis.

The inhabitants of Iraq are divided today about equally between the Shi'a and Sunni sects, with most of the Shi'ites in the south and the Sunnis in the north. Every effort is made by the government to persuade the younger generation to disregard their sectarian differences.

The Iraq of today is far behind the Iraq of the past. Young men who have graduated from the modern civil schools, and those who have gone abroad for study, are interested in modern sciences and accept the modern scientific outlook, while those who studied in the old style religious schools are still mainly engrossed in traditional religious learning. There has rarely been a thinker who had familiarity with both fields and could attempt a synthesis which would open up new intellectual horizons as happened during the Abbasid age.

The fundamental problem in Muslim culture, not only in Iraq but in the whole Muslim world, is that the political and social conditions which are necessary for the development of a culture have not existed. The social insecurity, which results from foreign rule and the foreign pressures which are effective so long as the Arab world is broken into small states with an average population of one to five millions, makes it impossible for Islamic culture to flower as it did in the days of the Abbasids.

Egypt

The Arabs invaded Egypt early in the first century of the Hijrah, starting a gradual process of Arabization and the spread of Islam which continued until Arabic became the language of the people and Christians became a minority. The Islamic culture of Egypt was similar to the culture of the rest of the Muslim world. For about a century Egypt was under the Umayyads; then the Abbasids ruled the country. The Fatimids held the power in Egypt in the fifth and sixth centuries of the Hijrah (eleventh and twelfth centuries A.D.), giving way to the Ayyubids for more than a century; the Mamluks then seized the power and held it until the Ottoman Turks established their rule in the tenth century (sixteenth century A.D.). For the past century and a half until quite recently Egypt was dominated by Western powers.

During the rule of the Fatimids, Shi'a doctrines were spread in Egypt and the Druze sect came into being. The Ayyubids were Sunnis whose strong opposition to the Druzes drove them out of Egypt to their present settlements in Syria and

Lebanon. Since the time of the Ayyubids Egypt has been entirely Sunni.

The most important event during the Fatimid rule was the founding of Al Azhar University in 362 (A.D. 972) in Cairo. Azhar, the oldest university in the world, has played a decisive part in the history of Muslim civilization, not only in the Arab countries, but throughout all the non-Arab Muslim world as well. For centuries it has served as the main center for the study of Islamic doctrine and as a meeting place for Muslim students from all over the world who come to receive training for careers as judges, jurists, and scholars; above all, it is a great mosque where prayers are said, and Friday sermons are preached to the assembled worshipers and to the thousands who hear them over the radio. The Azhar's traditional pattern of instruction was for the students to choose their teachers according to their inclinations and the standards they had achieved, continuing their studies for an indeterminate time with no examinations until they were ready to graduate. Recently it has been divided into two departments with the general department continuing the old system and a special department which is composed of faculties of theology, jurisprudence, and the Arabic language, to each of which is attached a number of primary and secondary schools. In the special department students are taught modern subjects with a defined curriculum, given annual examinations, required to specialize and submit a dissertation, and awarded academic degrees. Some of the teachers have studied in the West, notably the present Rector, who is a graduate of a French university with a high degree. The present enrollment at Al Azhar University includes several thousand students from foreign countries.

Although Egypt is entirely Sunni and most of the people are followers of the Hanafi school, Azhar teaches the four schools without distinction, and the religious courts pass judgment according to the religious school of the defendant.

During the Ottoman rule Muslim culture declined in Egypt because of the belief of the rulers that the study of philosophy, geography, mathematics, and related fields would lead to heresy. In the beginning of the last century a modernist movement emerged, encouraged by the Egyptians' desire to attain independence of the Ottoman Empire, and by their new ties established with the West as a result of the opening of the Suez Canal. During this time Egypt continued to be a center for continuing cultural and commercial emigrations from neighboring Arab countries as well as a crossroads for the infiltration of Western culture—an infiltration which remained within the bounds imposed by the desire to maintain the Arabic and Islamic character of the culture of Egypt.

During the last century two men appeared who were destined to change the direction of Islamic culture—Jamal ad-Din al-Afghani (died 1315; A.D. 1897) and Muhammad Abduh (died 1323; A.D. 1905). Jamal ad-Din was the man who awakened spiritual consciousness wherever he went in the Muslim world. He directed attention to the Muslim legacy in philosophy and to the impact of Western culture. Political problems, however, dominated his thinking. His disciple, Muhammad Abduh, followed in his steps by beginning his career with an interest in politics, but soon turned to cultural concerns.

Muhammad Abduh was a true genius whose talents extended to almost all spheres of life and whose activities touched many countries of the Muslim world. In the spiritual sphere he attempted to rejuvenate Islam by a clarification of its fundamental principles and an elucidation of its doctrines in modern terms. He refuted the attacks of Western scholars against Islam by showing that there is no contradiction between Islam and reason; rather, that for Islam reason is the key to faith in God. In literature he delivered Arabic style from its ornate redundancies, setting the literary form which was followed by newspapers and essayists from that time on. He encouraged the revival and printing of old Islamic manuscripts and the introduction of some of the literary classics into the scholastic circles of the Azhar. In the social sphere he persuaded the people to establish and use organized charities instead of relying on haphazard private acts of charity.

In politics he advocated the democratic system. No man of his stature and talents has since come to the fore.

Another influence of great importance in the cultural life of Egypt was the establishment of the Egyptian University shortly before the first World War. This university has grown to include faculties of medicine, pharmacy, engineering, agriculture, commerce, law, and letters. The growing desire for education which it has stimulated led to the establishment of another university in Alexandria and later a third, Ein Shams, in Cairo. The establishment of these universities has introduced modern culture into the stream of Arabic culture without the least resistance or protest, with the result that Egypt is now being pulled in two directions—the scholastic path by the Azhar and its subsidiary religious institutions, and the modern scientific way by the system of modern secular education. These two great forces maintain in Egypt a remarkable equilibrium without either destroying the other—perhaps because of the deep-rooted faith in religion which has been growing in the hearts of the Egyptians for hundreds of years—and education in Egypt continues to rest on the dual foundation of religious and secular studies. It is not likely that Egypt will give up either of these two foundations, but it is expected that they will draw closer together to form one firm base for Egyptian culture. Religious fanaticism as well as scientific monomania are both giving way at present, while the Sufi orders which used to exert great influence are waning as a result of the spread of education among the middle classes. Many intellectuals who were at first intrigued by secularism are becoming genuinely interested in religion.

Some Western scholars lament that Muslims, especially in Egypt, have closed the door to free interpretation, ijtihad, in the fundamentals. Ijtihad has been denied in Egypt because Egypt is the leader of all Muslim countries—in spite of the fact that it is smaller than some of them—and since it has been subjected, together with other Muslim countries, to imperialist invasion it has had to direct all its energy toward deliverance from imperialism and the protection of its own and its neighbors' safety. Ijtihad in religion at such a time could easily have led to such schism that only the imperialist powers would have profited. This is the reason for the silence with which Islam has met the double challenge from the atheist East and the Christian West. A primitive, naïve faith with safety was felt to be better than a rationalistic faith with the peril of disintegration and confusion. Ijtihad, however, remains inevitable and will come as soon as the Muslim world is secure from the evils surrounding it and can attain respite and tranquillity.

Nationalism in Egypt has taken an unprecedented turn since the people won their independence. Formerly, nationalistic movements set aside religion in order to maintain unity among all citizens, whether Muslim or Christian, while religious movements tended to exclude Arab nationalism. In this new nationalism the two movements meet in unison and harmony without secular nationalist opiniativeness or religious rigidity. This internal harmony is the basis for the desire of Egypt to be neutral in relation to external nationalistic conflicts between the East and the West. If there were any tendency for Egypt to favor one side, it would be toward the countries which still cling to religious values, if it were not for the antagonistic stand adopted by the West toward the Arab cause, especially in Palestine and North Africa.

North Africa

This section on North Africa is based on material written by Shaikh Muhammad al-Fadil Ibn Ashur of Tunis.

The Muslims invaded North Africa in 22 (A.D. 642) after Amr Ibn al-As had concluded the occupation of Egypt, but the effective invasion came some forty years later under the Umayyads who established a Muslim Arab garrison town at Qairawan near Tunis. That invasion was steadily extended westward until it reached the shores of the Atlantic, bringing into Islam great numbers of Berbers—remnants of the Romans and Vandals—who soon attained equal civil status with the invaders and became recruits in the Arab armies. It was with the help of the Berbers that the Umayyad forces were able to push on from Morocco to conquer Spain.

The city of Qairawan became the capital of the Maghrib, as North Africa is commonly called, governing the five states of Tripolitania, Tunisia, Algeria, al-Maghrib al-Aqsa (Morocco), and Andalusia. From Qairawan were exerted the efforts to spread Islam and the Arabic language among the Berbers. In the year 100 (A.D. 718) the Caliph stationed there the missionary delegation, better known as the Mission of the Ten Scholars, which receives the credit for persuading most of the Berber tribes to embrace the Arabic language and Islam. By the second century of the Hijrah many of the Berbers were contributing to theological discussions and Arab literature.

The Kharijites appeared in the Maghrib after they were scattered by their struggles with Ali and Mu'awiya, but they were successfully resisted by the Umayyads and confined to certain regions in the center of the Maghrib and in Africa, where societies of a special social and political character were established. The people of North Africa adopted Sunni Islam and followed the intrepretation of the Maliki school since most of their students went to study at Medina, where the school of Malik held sway. Their loyalty to Sunni doctrines and the Maliki school was consolidated at the end of the third century of the Hijrah by their opposition to the Fatimid dynasty of Egypt. The resistance to the Shi'a forces of the Fatimids centered in Qairawan and Tunis, where most of the Maliki scholars gathered forces.

At the beginning of the sixth century of the Hijrah, Muhammad Ibn Tumart—known as the Mahdi, that is, the Imam who is to come—appeared as a reformer and established a new state with the avowed purpose of reforming dogma and the social order. His new dynasty was able to unite the whole Maghrib for a time, and the four succeeding dynasties, although they struggled for political power, did not renounce his spiritual leadership.

At the end of the ninth century (fifteenth century A.D.) Arab rule over Andalusia finally collapsed and its Muslim communities took refuge in the Maghrib. Parts of North Africa were seized by the Spaniards and held until the coming of the Ottoman Turks, who delivered Tripolitania, Tunisia, and

Algeria. Morocco was spared the Ottoman rule and continued to be governed by sultans who traced their ancestry to the Prophet. After the Ottoman rule, in more recent times, France and Italy seized control of North Africa and held it until in the past few years, Libya, Tunis, and Morocco were able to establish their own governments, leaving only Algeria struggling for emancipation from French imperialism.

In modern times the population of North Africa is composed of Arabs and Berbers who have intermarried. Arabic is the common language, although it is spoken in various dialects, influenced chiefly by geographic conditions. The Berber influence is obvious in customs and in language, especially among the Berbers of the mountain regions in the Atlas, and in Morocco. It is least obvious in Tunisia where less than one per cent of the people are Berber. There are about two million Berbers in Morocco, one million in Algeria, and only about fifty thousand in Libya. All the inhabitants of North Africa are Muslim except for a million and a half Christians and Jews, of whom a million live in Algeria.

Most of the Muslims of the Maghrib are Sunnis of the Ash'arite school, following the interpretations of the Maliki school in matters of jurisprudence. In Morocco all the people follow the school of Malik, while in Algeria and Tunisia a limited number are Hanafis. Those who follow the school of Hanafi are descendants of families who came to North Africa with the Ottoman army and are found chiefly in cities which used to be army headquarters.

There are still about one hundred thousand Kharijites in Algeria, Tunisia, and Libya; they are members of the Ibadi sect, with their headquarters in Ghardaia where they have schools and shari'a courts which follow their doctrines in deciding issues brought before them.

Among the Sunnis there are many Sufi orders, all tracing their origin to the famous mystic al-Junayd (died 298; A.D. 910). The three main orders are Qadiri, Shazili, and Tijani, each having many subdivisions. These orders work through lodges (*tekkes*)—organized communities which seek to spread their Sufi teachings and practices. There are more than seven hundred such lodges in the Maghrib. Although the influence of these orders has declined during the present century, there are still important lodges in Algeria and Libya whose influence extends into central Africa.

The Senussi order was started in 1253 (A.D. 1837) in Mecca, somewhat influenced by the Wahhabi movement but tracing its origin back ultimately to the Shazili order of Sufis. It advocated the prohibition of music, dancing, and smoking, but discouraged exaggerated forms of asceticism. It placed great emphasis on the establishment of lodges for communal living; each member of the lodge would engage in a useful community activity such as cultivation, education, or commerce which would make the lodge self-sufficient. They are opposed to the use of force, and although they are a bridge between Wahhabi and Sufi practices, they follow orthodox Sunni doctrines, rather than the usual Sufi teachings, and accept the school of Malik in the particular requirements of religion. They rely upon the Qur'an and the Traditions of the Prophet and reject consensus (ijma) and individual interpretation (ijtihad) as sources of legislation.

Like the Wahhabis, the Senussi order began as a religious reformation and ended by establishing new Muslim states. Because of their closeness to the Wahhabis they were permitted to establish a lodge in the Hijaz. In North Africa the Italians made a special effort to destroy the Senussi lodges in the years before the second World War. Today the Senussi order exists in Libya as a spiritual movement led by the present sovereign.

Education in North Africa is provided through religious schools associated with the mosques and lodges and through secular schools supported by the state. Half a century ago the Tunisians modernized their schools by opening them to boys and girls alike and offering instruction in arithmetic, natural science, geography, and French—a pattern of secular education which has been followed in varying degrees by other North African countries. The teaching of Arabic and the Islamic religion in these schools was formerly very meagre but it has received greater emphasis in some countries in recent years with the growth of nationalist governments. Opportunities for higher technical and professional training are still lacking in North Africa, making it necessary for doctors, lawyers, and engineers to get their training abroad, chiefly in France. There is no doubt that such foreign education has had a great effect on North African culture, especially in Algeria and Tunisia. In Algeria, because of the direct French control, the official schools have shown no concern for Muslim Arabic education. The only exception is the three government schools for training judges and lawyers in the shari'a, with the number of students limited to the positions to be filled.

The religious schools, which are only concerned with teaching the Qur'an, Islamic doctrines, and Arabic, have greatly declined in the cities and villages because of the spread of modern schools and are now found chiefly in the desert and the lodges of the Sufi orders. There are many more such schools in Morocco than in Tunisia, where there are a greater number of secular schools. The Algerians have taken the initiative in spreading Muslim education through the establishment of modern nongovernmental institutions which are found in most towns and villages. The Association of Muslim Ulama has been active in promoting these schools and controls some one hundred and thirty of the three hundred religious schools in Algeria.

It is worthy of note that all mosques in North Africa are not only places of worship but also popular schools where religious instruction is given to the people. Those who supervise the performance of devotional practices in the mosques also teach and are paid for their services with funds from the religious trusts—except in Algeria and Tunisia where they receive their salaries from the state because of the limited funds available from the religious endowments. In Libya, the religious education which was formerly given in the major mosques was almost entirely supported by the Italian rulers. There are still, however, three main Senussi lodges with over fifty subsidiary lodges which are concerned with the training of religious leaders who work for the maintenance and propagation of Islamic culture.

Higher education in religion is offered in Morocco at the University of Qarawiyin in Fez and the Big Mosque in Tatwan; in Tunisia the center of higher studies is at the famous old University of Zaitouna and its subsidiaries; and in Libya advanced work in religion is given at the University of Benghazi. The education at these universities is purely Muslim, in Arabic, with a nationalist orientation, and centered around a mosque. Attached to the Qarawiyin is another great mosque in the capital of the south, called the Mosque of Ibn Youssif, and the Zaitouna Mosque in Tunisia has twenty branches spread all over the country. Education in these two universities includes literary subjects, mathematics, and natural sciences at a secondary level; and at the higher level Qarawiyin trains scholars and specialists in jurisprudence and literature, while Zaitouna has faculties in jurisprudence, theology, philology, literature, and the Qur'an. There are about two thousand students at the higher level, of whom fifteen hundred are in Tunisia. Both institutions have libraries which contain many valuable Islamic manuscripts.

The Rest of Africa

Islam came to Africa in three stages. During the first four centuries it spread through North Africa and into the Sudan; from the fourth to the middle of the fifth century Islam was embraced by the Christians of Nubia, the Swahilis and the people of the Zanzibar coast, and the tribes of the desert; the third stage dates from about 1160 (A.D. 1747) to the beginning of the present century, during which time Islam was introduced by the Sufi orders in competition with the Christian missionary work of the Protestants and Catholics.

During the fifth century (eleventh century A.D.) the most active tribes in the diffusion of Islam were the barbaric tribes which had embraced Islam under a Sufi Shaikh who established a lodge—that is, a dwelling, school, and mosque—on an island near the Senegal coast. Some of his followers, who were called al-Murabitin, invaded Morocco and established the State of al-Murabitin; another group of his followers penetrated the interior of the continent and captured the Kingdom of Ghana, between the Senegal and the Niger, whose people embraced Islam. Subsequently Islam spread among the tribes living along the upper banks of the Niger. During this century Islam reached Timbuktu and was accepted by the people of the desert. Two centuries later it reached Nigeria. In East Africa the Faith was spread by the merchants who settled in Mombasa and Zanzibar and eventually extended Islam to Uganda and the Congo. In the eleventh century (seventeenth century A.D.) Islam expanded southward through the activities of Muslims from India until it reached Natal and Cape Province and spread a little into the Transvaal and Rhodesia.

Islam found its way into the African continent through three channels: through the merchants who came from Egypt, the Maghrib, and Zanzibar in the east; through followers of Sufi orders and graduates of the Islamic schools of Fez, Zaitouna, and Cairo; and through the intermarriage of Muslim merchants and religious leaders with African women.

There was a strong interest in Sufism in Africa in the twelfth and thirteenth centuries (eighteenth and nineteenth centuries A.D.) which found expression in a renaissance of the two old orders of Qadiri and Shazili and the creation of two new Sufi orders, the Tijani and Senussi. The Qadiri order was the most enthusiastic of the orders in the propagation of Islam in Africa, using education and trade as its means. The followers were distinguished for their tolerance which they inherited from their founder, who in the sixth century (twelfth century A.D.) had been known for his genuine veneration of Jesus and was accustomed to say, "We should pray not only for our own selves, but also for everyone who is created by God as we are." In Africa they established lodges with schools and even established schools in villages where there were no lodges. They sent the best of their students to the great Islamic schools in Fez, Zaitouna, and Cairo to be trained and sent home as religious leaders and missionaries.

The Shazili order was one of the first Sufi orders in the Maghrib. Its center was in Morocco, and its followers were known for their extreme obedience to their leaders, whether at home or when sent on missions abroad. The Tijani order was founded in Fez in Morocco less than two centuries ago and spread chiefly into the Sudan. The Senussi order, which has been discussed above, also spread in the Sudan and western Egypt and into mid-Africa in the vicinity of Lake Chad.

These Sufi orders resembled each other in their extreme love of the Prophet, their strictness in observing their religious duties, their application of the shari'a in as far as possible, their respect for their leaders, and their guidance of followers of the order until they could be promoted to the highest ranks. At the same time they differed in details. Each order had its own invocation; some of them made their prayer beads of a hundred beads, others used only twelve. And while the Senussis were tolerant and would perform their recitations and prayers with others, the Tijanis preferred isolation for their devotions.

There are several reasons for the success of the Sufi orders in propagating Islam among the people of Africa. Islam is a religion of ease and simplicity which charges the Muslim with no more than proclaiming his profession of faith and performing its easy religious rites. Another reason is that Islam has a social character which strengthens the morale of the group, bringing men together as brothers without discrimination in a way which facilitates travel, trade, and the struggle for a livelihood. Also, the Sufi orders have some practices which resemble those of the tribes of Africa, such as the prescribed daily recitations, the gathering around the Shaikh, or head of the order, belief in spiritual powers, and communal living.

Undoubtedly, Islamic belief among the African peoples was not safe from pagan influence and did not reach the Africans in its perfect state. Nevertheless, the spread of Islam had its distinct effects. It has spread monotheism and driven out heathenism which was based on the worship of spirits which were symbolized in the mean forms of animals and inanimate objects. The spread of Islam in Africa has helped in the encouragement of education because in every lodge there was a school which taught reading, writing, and the Qur'an. Islam has also introduced moral values higher than those of heathenism; it has prohibited adultery and wine-drinking; it has introduced cleanliness through its required ablutions; it has introduced fraternal gatherings for prayer; and it has created a spirit of cooperation in the agricultural communities of Africa.

There have appeared in Africa some people who pretended that they were the Mahdi—the saviour who is to come to wipe out oppression and fill the world with justice. One of these pretenders appeared in Senegal in 1244 (A.D. 1828) and created a revolution which failed and ended in his death. The most important of the Mahdis was the one who appeared in the Sudan in 1300 (A.D. 1882) and led a revolt against Egypt. His success in several engagements with the Egyptian army greatly strengthened his hold over his followers and made him the ruler of all of Sudan. When he died after three years he was succeeded by one of his leaders, who failed in an attempted invasion of Egypt, was faced by revolt at home, and was vanquished by Lord Kitchener in 1314 (A.D. 1896). Another Mahdi appeared on the scene in Somalia about that time. He started as a Sufi mystic and ended by claiming to be a Mahdi, which gave him influence with his tribe. At the end of the first World War the Italians exterminated his influence in Somalia. He died in 1339 (A.D. 1920).

At the present time there is a strong tendency in Africa to purify Islam of its alien innovations. This is being done by African students who study in the higher educational institutions in Cairo and North Africa and go back to their countries with new ideas acquired from the reform movements which are being advocated by enlightened Muslims. When such students see that the ceremonial practices of the Sufis have lost their power in Egypt and the other Arab countries in Asia, they have no doubt that the same thing will happen in other parts of the Muslim world. In addition to the tendency to purify Islam of its alien innovations there is today a strong movement for expansion of education among Muslims. There is nothing which can purify the Faith better than the return to the original sources of Islam—to understand them by study and meditation. Any excessive dependence of the Sufis on intuition and rites will be corrected by recourse to the Qur'an by educated men.

Conclusions

It is apparent from what has been said that when education and civilization flourished in the Muslim world the distinctively religious aspects of Islamic culture were exalted, and when the civilization was weakened and stagnated religion also suffered. During the Abbasid era, for example, Muslim culture progressed rapidly, and the religious texts were interpreted in a way which suited the spirit of the age. During the periods of eclipse, however, Muslims adhered to texts in their liberal form and closed the door against rational interpretation—ijtihad—in the fundamentals and the consequences of the Faith.

Islamic culture has been affected by the cultural, social, and political conditions in which it existed and by the challenge which the Muslims faced, a challenge which stimulated them to meditate on their Faith and to present it in its genuine form, free of alien interpolations. Because the cultural, social, and political conditions were favorable and their religion was being challenged, the Islamic culture in Iraq and Egypt reached a high level. Among the primitive tribes which were isolated from civilization and from any challenge to their religion, Islam has stagnated.

Sufi orders prevailed among the illiterate and naïve tribes of Africa because illiterate people rely completely on others for an understanding of their religion, while an educated Muslim would turn to the Qur'an to know what Islam really is. Because of the tendency of the illiterate to want religion presented to him in a way which suits his imagination, we find that educated Muslims today disapprove of the innovations invented by the Sufi orders, such as veneration of saints, seeking blessings from tombs, seeking the mediation of religious leaders, and excessive asceticism.

At the time when Muslims were not keeping up with the course of civilization, and illiteracy was so widespread among them that the educated class became an exclusive minority, they thought that religion was everything in life, determining their situation. But religion is only one factor in civilization.

There are other effective factors, such as education, scientific thinking, legislation, politics, social and economic institutions, and the like. Had the Muslims thought more objectively about the causes of their backwardness they would have seen that it was not due to their religion. Some Western scholars have made the same mistake of attributing the backwardness of the Muslims to their religion. But it is apparent that if religion were the real cause, Muslims in every time and place would have been in the same condition of backwardness, and this is not the case; there was a great difference in Islamic culture in the time of glory and the time of eclipse. At all times, there is a vast difference between the educated and the uneducated Muslims. Those who observe that modernization in Islam in recent times was carried out by the secular Muslims should be aware that this was because they are the ones who had acquired some degree of education.

The scholars who study Islamic culture today point out that the chief factors which have influenced contemporary Arab Muslim society are: the Western ideas which penetrated Arab society through education and increased contact with the West, socialist concepts which have spread throughout the world, communist doctrines which challenge religion in general, the expansion of university education, the admission of Muslim women to higher education, the study of ancient and modern philosophy in the universities, and the modern Muslim movements which have been so influential. As a result of all these factors we find the following tendencies in Islamic culture in the Arab world: there is a movement calling for the re-evaluation of religion; methods of philosophical research are being embarked upon as preparation for consideration of religious studies which deal with the fundamentals of Islam; a new study of the shari'a is being made to clarify its relation to civil legislation; a dissolution of the Sufi orders is taking place; reconciliation among the Muslim sects is progressing with increasing success; Muslim sects are reviving, and their views, which have remained concealed for a long time, are being reconsidered; a study of genuine Islam is being made in order to purify it of alien ideas; religious controversy between Muslims and Christians is disappearing; the enthusiasm for translating the Qur'an is increasing; the issuing of religious verdicts (*fatwas*) is decreasing, a step toward confining religion to its own area so that civilization may be adopted without hindrances.

Finally, we must remember that although some of the Islamic people of the Arab and African countries have attained their independence, only after all of them have become free can they proceed to the next stage of security, peace, and prosperity which is so necessary for the growth of Islamic culture. Then they will be able to meditate on the relation between God and man. Then they will turn back to religion with a view to understanding it in the light of the new ideas and knowledge that will be brought forth in the world. Then we can expect Islamic culture to flourish again.

CHAPTER SEVEN

Islamic Culture in Turkish Areas

Hasan Basri Çantay

In the Name of Allah, the All Compassionate, the Merciful

Turks are spread from the Balkans to the coast of the China Sea. In addition to Turkey, they are found in Greece, Yugoslavia, Albania, Romania, Bulgaria and Cyprus. In the Soviet Union there are large numbers of Turkish Muslims in the Caucasus, Azerbaijan, the Volga Basin, Turkmen, Kazakh, Uzbek, Tadzik, and Kirgiz. They are found in northern Iraq, in Iran, Afghanistan, Pakistan and India, Sinkiang, the Mongolian Republic, and China. Almost all of these Muslim Turks are Sunnis who look to Turkey as the center of their culture. In all, there are almost seventy-five million Muslim Turks, making up slightly less than one-fifth of the Muslims in the world.

As one of the oldest and most widely dispersed peoples of the world, Turks were followers of many religions before they finally adopted Islam forever. They followed shamanism, Manichaeanism, Zoroastrianism, Confucianism, and Buddhism at one time or another, with shamanism and Buddhism the most popular among them. Never, however, did they fight among themselves about religion, for the Turks, as distinct from some fanatic races—Slavs, for instance—have always been tolerant of all religions. But none of those religions ever really satisfied the Turks. As a people who never accepted slavery, were loyal to their friends, respectful toward their elders, fair to their equals, and affectionate to their children, nurturing the highest ideals and aspirations of mankind, the Turks could not remain content within the rather narrow confines of those religions. They longed for a religion suited to their magnanimous hearts.

No religion could be close to the hearts of the Turks if it condemned reason and relied on myths and superstitions, favored laziness and lethargy instead of encouraging action and enterprise, made man the slave of man, and forced him to worship nature as god. The Turks were yearning for a religion able to take the whole of humanity into its fold, to elevate man to the highest moral and spiritual levels, and to be an unswerving guide to the straight path which leads to happiness in this world and the hereafter. It may be that when they were adherents of different religions before Islam, they were tolerant of other religions because they did not believe wholeheartedly in any of them; they followed them only for lack of a better religion. It is in Islam that the Turks have found the true religion for which they were yearning so long. So, when they were confronted with Islam, they almost rushed into the faith and are to this day its most loyal followers and impetuous defenders.

Since they left their motherland and spread out in search of new homelands, the Turks have founded many states and even several empires. They have invaded many lands and have been invaded themselves; but in victory or defeat they remained loyal to their chiefs and faithful to their traditions and culture. The Turks have been fearless pioneers, courageous but humble in success and failure, loyal to friends, terrible to foes but magnanimous to the defeated. They have been jealous of their own ideals, religion, and country, but respectful of the rights and beliefs of others. Turks have always been ready to defend their country and to give a hand to a friend even if it cost them their lives. Those have always been, and are today, the characteristics of the Turks, as is testified to by legends of ancient times, by the Crusades, the defense of Dardanelles, and many episodes in the long history of this people.

Many writers have praised the Turks. Early in the third century of the Hijrah an Arab writer, Jahiz, said, "The Turk is shepherd, coppersmith, veterinarian, and artist. His arts are varied and so perfect that he does not need anyone's help. He does not know flattery, hypocrisy, tale-bearing, mischief-making, spying. He does not care for pomp and ceremony. He loves his country, he loves best independence and sovereignty." Another Arab writer at about the same time, Yazid Ibn Mazid, said, "A Turk is no weight for the horse he mounts or the earth he walks on. While our cavalrymen do not see what is in front of them, the Turk is aware of what is behind. He thinks of us as a game, of his horse as a gazelle, and of himself as a lion." Sumama Ibn Ashras said, "The Turk does not fear, he frightens, he dares to do things above his powers; he does not sleep unless very tired and when he sleeps he does it as if one of his eyes were open." And the great Sufi poet Rumi said, "The Turk is one under whose protection the peasant is saved from paying tribute to the foreigner."

Turks are also mentioned in the Hadiths of our Prophet Muhammad (the Peace and Mercy of Allah be upon him), "If you do not fight with the Turks, Doomsday will never happen." And at another time he said, "Unless they attack, do not fight with the Turks." In obedience to this tradition Umar, the second Caliph, ordered that the commander of the Muslim army which captured Iran should not pursue the Iranian Shah who had taken refuge with his Turkish neighbors. The Muslims obeyed the Hadiths and followed a policy of living on good terms with the Turks before and after they accepted Islam. The Turks, in turn, respected this policy of nonaggression and as they discovered Islam, adopted it as the answer to their heart's longing and were converted in masses.

Islam saved the Turks from wrong beliefs and superstitions, strengthened their characters, and taught them the true ideals for mankind. In return the Turks became the most sincere champions of Islam. They strove for its glory and expansion with their schools, learned men, and saints; they lived as persuasive examples of their faith; they spread Islam by pacific means. The expansion of the Turks by the sword was for economic or military purposes and not in order to force Islam on non-Muslims. They used the sword only in the defense of Islam, not for its expansion, but then they defended it with all their strength and when necessary with their lives. The highways and byways of Islamic countries have been strewn with the bodies of heroes who fell in defense of Islam. If it were not for the Turks, Islam would have been pushed back into the Arabian desert by the unscrupulous and fanatic invaders from Europe.

Three centuries after the Hijrah the events in the Islamic world of the Middle East were being determined more by the Turks than by the Arabs. But the Turks never assumed the title of protector of Islam. They adhered to Islam, they made it their own, they defended it, they glorified it with deep attachment and veneration, but they did not claim to be its protector. Their attitude was expressed by the great Ghaznavid King Mahmud when, as he lay on his deathbed, one of his attendants in great sorrow cried, "O Majesty, who will protect Islam if you will not be with us?" The dying King reproved him by saying, "Who am I to protect Islam? God Almighty is its protector." And again, when the first sermon was being given after Sultan Selim became Caliph in 923 (A.D. 1517), the Imam in the course of his remarks referred to Selim as the owner of the two Holy Cities, Mecca and Medina. Sultan Selim stopped the Imam at that point and told him to say that he was the servant of the two Holy Cities, a title which was given to the Caliphs from that time until the end of the Caliphate. Allah is the Protector of Islam to the end of time, as is said in the Qur'an: "We send down the Qur'an, We, and undoubtedly We, are its Protector" (Surah XV, 9).

The union of Islam with the Turks was so complete that the people of the West often used the word Turk as synonymous with Muslim. There is no doubt that the former supremacy of the Ottoman Turks in Europe and the Middle East was due to the closeness with which they held to their Islamic faith. Islam, before everything else, is a spiritual bond, a bond which no material force can break. Without organized efforts to convert, Islam has kept on gaining strength among the Turks despite many threats, invasions, and injustices committed by Europeans and non-Muslim neighbors. Islam assimilates; it is not assimilated. One embraces Islam; but one does not, cannot leave it. The spreading and taking root of a religion among a people is a clear proof that such a religion fulfills their ideals, aspirations and spiritual needs, as was the case with the Turks.

It is misleading to attempt to describe Islam as a product of Arab civilization and culture. Islam is not the property of the Arabs, nor of the Turks, nor of any nation—it is a foundation of God addressed to the whole of humanity. The Qur'an says, "Those whom you worship other than Allah are but names which you and your fathers attached (to them). Allah has sent down no sanction for them. The decision is no one's but Allah's. He has commanded you that you worship none save Him. The true and right religion is this, but most men do not know" (Surah XII, 40). And again, "Say (O Muhammad): O Mankind, I am the Messenger sent to all of you by Allah to Whom undoubtedly belongs the sovereignty (and possession) of heavens and earth, and there is no God save Him Who gives life and death" (Surah VII, 158).

The sun of Islam rose first above the horizons of Arabia but it found hearts most open to its ennobling and life-giving rays in Turkestan. As soon as the Turks realized the nature of Islam they embraced it and became its champions and true defenders, as they have been for twelve centuries. Islam has become their true and natural religion, as it is for all people who sincerely love the Truth.

The Growth of Turkish Influence in Islamic Culture

After the passing away of Muhammad (the Peace and Mercy of Allah be upon him) in the eleventh year of the Hijrah, the armies of Islam moved eastward during the time of the Four Great Caliphs, and Arab vanguards advanced beyond the Oxus river in Turkestan. Islam had changed the life of the Arabs. They were no longer a desert people; now they had a new, a universal religion, new horizons for their aspirations, and new ideals in their hearts. Since these ideals and aspirations were akin to those which Turks had nurtured during the centuries since their origin, conversions soon began to take place.

The relations between the Muslims and Turks increased during the Caliphate of Mu'awiya when he sent an army which crossed the Oxus and conquered Turkestan and Afganistan and went as far as India. In the year 88 (A.D. 706) Amir Qutaiba captured Bukhara, Samarkand, and the surrounding territories. This had fortunate results for the Western world, for in Samarkand the Arabs learned how to make paper and passed their skill on to Spain and Europe. The conquered territories were incorporated in the province of Transoxiana. Some two centuries later the governers of Transoxiana declared their independence and founded the Samanid dynasty which ruled an area beginning with the Oxus river and extending eastward with indefinite boundaries. Non-Muslim Turks were attacking Muslim Turks at that time. It was during the reign of the Samanids that Islam spread through Central Asia, for the dominant religions of Buddhism and shamanism could not hold their own when faced with Islam. Soon Islam was supreme and the Turks became its sincere and loyal followers. Many schools for Islamic learning were opened in Transoxiana a full century before similar institutions were created in Baghdad, the capital. Through these schools the Turks trained learned men who hold high places in Islamic history.

The conversion of Turks to Islam began within the first century after the Hijrah and gained momentum until great masses were coming into the fold, a movement which continued for hundreds of years until all Turks became Muslims. Their influence in Islam was notable quite early. When the Umayyad dynasty became corrupt and was oppressing the people, it was a Turk from Khurasan, Abu Muslim, who had a hand in its overthrow. During the reign of the Abbasid Caliph Mansur, early in the second century, Turks began to enlist in the armies of Islam. Since they were good soldiers, they were received in the army in preference to others.

During the time of the Abbasid Caliph Mu'tasim (died 227; A.D. 841) the influence of Turks increased a great deal because the Caliph was not sure of the loyalty of the Arabs and Iranians and needed a dependable bodyguard. When he had built up his Turkish forces to seventy thousand men, the presence of such a large number of soldiers in Baghdad was causing discontent among the people of the city so the Caliph ordered new housing built especially for the army. The city built for them was so beautiful that the Arabs named it *Sarra Man Raa*, which means "who sees it rejoices," and the words were by usage elided to become Samarra.

Turks who came as soldiers began to fill administrative posts in Baghdad and soon so much power in the government passed into their hands that they could dethrone Caliphs. Not only were they able to determine policies in Baghdad, but they could give the lands taken from the Byzantines to Turks who were defending the frontiers and pushing them still farther west. Their occupation of commanding ranks in the army and administrative posts in the government made it possible for them to open new trails for the western migrations of the Turks who had formerly been compelled to take the difficult northern routes. Now they were able to move much faster toward the southwest through Azerbaijan, Anatolia, Syria, and Byzantium. Unending streams of Turkish tribes were flowing into what we call the Middle East today. There seemed to be inexhaustible sources of Turks in Central Asia between Turkestan and the Chinese borders. Those who came first moved onward and their places were taken by others who were in their turn pushed on westward. Later that movement continued into the Balkans, up to Vienna, down to the Hijaz, Egypt, and the Maghrib.

Conversion to Islam enhanced the qualities and virtues of the Turks, making the record of their history a fascinating study. In the new lands where they settled they continued to found states and build empires; they even furnished rulers in several non-Turkish countries. During the more than thirteen centuries since the time of the Four Great Caliphs hundreds of states and kingdoms, large and small, appeared and disappeared in the Middle East, and Turks had something to say in most of them. An appreciation of the role of the Turks in Islamic culture requires some understanding of the part played by the different Turkish empires during these centuries.

The Turkish Empires

The Seljuq Empire takes its name from the chief of a powerful tribe which settled near Bukhara and Samarkand after they had followed their leader in accepting Islam. The Empire was established by Seljuq's grandson Tughrul in the first half of the fifth century (*ca.* A.D. 1040) and extended from the Mediterranean to Afghanistan. Later it was divided into several states, of which the one with its capital at Konya in modern Turkey survived until it was included in the Ottoman Empire. The Seljuqs' most important contribution was the reaffirmation and strengthening of Sunni doctrines in the Abbasid times when Shi'a was increasing its influence. And it was a great Seljuq military leader, Alp Arlsan, who defeated the Byzantine emperor Romanus Diogenes and opened Anatolia for settlement by Turks.

Seljuq rulers were great patrons of the arts, sciences, and literature, and showed in many ways their appreciation for learned men. The buildings and works of art which remain today show the high level attained in art and architecture under the Seljuqs. As rulers, the Seljuqs were true to the traditions of their ancestors, democratic in their relations with the people and always ready to listen directly to their grievances. They were sincere followers of Islam who strove to be just and tried not to overburden their people. They knew how to surround themselves with able and wise men. Alp Arlsan and his son chose as their Vizier the illustrious Nizamul Mulk (died 485; A.D. 1092) who built a university in Baghdad which was famous for the great learning of its teachers. He gave a chair to al-Ghazali, the great mystic and philosopher, and paid a monthly salary to Umar Khayyam which freed him to write his poetry.

It was in the time of the Seljuqs that the Turks took the leadership of Islam from the Arabs. It was a Seljuq king who brought Rumi, the great Sufi poet, to Konya; and it was in Seljuq times that Ahmad Yesevi (died 562; A.D. 1166), another great Sufi, lived and taught. The influence of those two remarkable teachers has continued to the present. In the times of the Seljuq Turks Islam flourished wherever their rule was established.

In Egypt the first dynasty ruled by a Turk was the Tulunid dynasty established by Ahmad Ibn Tulun in 255 (A.D. 868), which lasted for only thirty-seven years. It was renowned for its public works of which the beautiful Tulun Mosque in Cairo remains today as an outstanding example. There was an interval after the Tulunids in which Egypt was ruled again by the Abbasids, and then a second Turkish ruler seized power and the Ikhshidids ruled Egypt from 323 until 359 (A.D. 934–69), when the Fatimid dynasty was established. Ikhshid was the title of the rulers of Farghana, a Turkish city beyond the Oxus river. The father of the founder of the Ikhshidid dynasty in Cairo had come to Baghdad to serve the Caliph and had been appointed governor of Damascus.

After more than two hundred and fifty years of rule by the Shi'a Fatimid dynasty, Egypt was once more governed by a Turkish ruler, Salah-al-Din Ibn Ayyub (known as Saladin), the founder of the Ayyubid dynasty which lasted from 565 to 650 (A.D. 1169–1252). His rule extended from the Nile to the Euphrates, except for the fortified places held by the Crusaders, and after 583 (A.D. 1187) when he captured Jerusalem only the fortifications at Tyre remained in Crusader hands. Europe sought to regain its power through the Third Crusade, led by Richard I of England and Philip Augustus of France in 586 (A.D. 1190); but after two years of fighting a peace treaty was signed without loss of rights by Saladin. Saladin died in 589 leaving a great record which even Christian historians have praised as matchless in the annals of chivalry. Even though he was occupied with fighting against the Crusaders, this Muslim Turkish ruler found time to strengthen Sunni faith in his territory, bringing the people of Egypt back from the Shi'a doctrines favored by the Fatimids.

At the time that the Seljuqs were extending their empire another Turkish leader, Ahmad Gazi Danishmand (died 477; A.D. 1084) established his kingdom in Cappadocia in the neighborhood of Caesarea (modern Kayseri). The Danishmands were distinguished for their successes against the Crusades and for their efforts to spread Islam. After less than a century of independent rule their territory was absorbed in the greater Seljuq Empire and many of the people from that area spread throughout Anatolia and European Turkey, as is shown by the large number of Turkish villages bearing the name of Danishmand.

There were also, in Seljuq times, many small dynasties headed by Atabegs, that is, Seljuq officers who as regents created independent dynasties. They were found, to mention only a few of them, at Damascus, Mesopotamia, Anatolia, Azerbaijan, and Luristan (in Iran), some lasting for about a century and some as long as four centuries. The largest of the independent dynasties was that of the Khwarizm which at one time controlled almost all of Iran, Khurasan, Afghanistan, Transoxiana, and Ghazna, extending from India to the borders of the Seljuq Empire. The Khwarizm dynasty lasted from 470 to 629 (A.D. 1077–1231), when it was destroyed by the invasion of the Mongol hordes of Genghis Khan. A branch of the Khwarizm dynasty ruled at Delhi from 612 to 801 (A.D. 1215–1398).

The Ottoman Empire was created by descendants of the tribe of Bozok and Kayi, one of the noblest tribes of the Turks which settled for a time in Iran and then began its westward migration at the beginning of the fifth century (eleventh century A.D.). Two centuries later, pressed by the Mongol invasions, the tribe moved on westward under their Bey, Sulayman Shah, intending to settle in Seljuq territory near Aleppo. Sulayman was drowned as they crossed the Euphrates in 626 (A.D. 1228), but under his son Ertugrul the tribe received from the Seljuqs a grant of land for settlement in Anatolia. As the tribesmen were moving to their new home, they came upon a battle in progress. Since it is one of the national characteristics of the Turks to help the weak, they joined with the losing side, which happened to be the Seljuqs, and helped them secure the victory. In return for their help the Seljuqs awarded them better lands near Bursa, which bordered on Byzantium. Ertugrul extended their holdings.

This was the beginning of another Turkish Empire which would take the leadership of Islam from the Seljuqs and continue for six centuries. For the five hundred years of its strength it brought peace and security to the people living within its boundaries, which spread over three continents. There were fierce battles on faraway frontiers between giant armies, but the people living in the interior, Muslim or non-Muslim, Turk or non-Turk, were able to go about their business in peace and safety.

The name Ottoman comes from Othman Bey, Ertugrul's son, who ruled from 699 to 727 (A.D. 1299–1326), but it was his son Orkhan Bey who laid the foundations of the Ottoman Empire by conquering the cities in the vicinity and then crossing the Dardanelles to begin seizing control of the Balkans. It was in his time that the corps of janissaries was formed and the administration for the new state was organized. The janissaries were the special guards of the Sultan, recruited from Christian youths who were given special privileges and free education which inculcated in them absolute loyalty to the ruler.

The successors of Orkhan were as sagacious as he was. The early Ottoman sultans were devout Muslims and good commanders who knew how to surround themselves with men of merit and learning—which is perhaps the main reason for their success in building an empire. They were astute in diplomacy and were able administrators who created an efficient military and civilian organization by training men and putting them in the right positions with authority and responsibility. They patronized the arts, sciences, and literature, honored men of learning, and showed great respect to the ulama and often sought their advice. Thus they were far ahead of their contemporary rulers in the numerous neighboring feudal kingdoms and were able to bring them sooner or later, willy-nilly, under the Ottoman banner.

As the early Ottoman sultans succeeded each other, the frontiers of the new kingdom were pushed farther and farther eastward in Anatolia and westward in Europe. Although the Popes organized Crusades, victory followed victory until the whole Balkan Peninsula—except for Constantinople—became Ottoman territory, part of an empire which extended from the Dardanelles to the Euphrates.

Timur (Tamerlane) invaded Anatolia in 805 (A.D. 1402). The gallant Bayazid, surnamed the Thunderbolt because he was as quick as lightning and could strike a blow like a thunderbolt, rushed to meet him, but he was defeated and taken prisoner at Ankara due to the treason of some of his officers who deserted to the enemy. Bayazid died of grief. This tragedy shook the new empire to its foundations and gave respite to Byzantium for at least fifty years. It was followed by a period of useless civil wars, after which Sultan Mehmed I restored the power of the dynasty. His son, Sultan Murad II, was forced to defend his country against the attacks of Hunyad, the White Knight of Wallachia, but at the battle of Varna in 848 (A.D. 1444) he won a decisive victory against the Crusaders. After that the Turks were comparatively free from European attacks for two hundred years, and did not have to face another Crusade until about the beginning of the fourteenth century (the latter half of the nineteenth century A.D.).

After Constantinople was taken in 857 (A.D. 1453) by Sultan Mehmed II—who was known as Fatih, the Conqueror—many more Christians and Jews came to live there. Fatih reinstated the Greek Orthodox Patriarch and granted him privileges which later were used against the Turks. Under Fatih Mehmed II Serbia, Bosnia, and surrounding territories of the Balkans were added to the Empire, Anatolia was unified, and the independent princes of Asia Minor were subdued. He also reorganized the administration of the Ottoman Empire along more efficient lines, which were followed with little alteration for over three hundred years. Fatih was a generous patron of learning who endowed many educational foundations, and was himself a serious student who used eight languages and showed his keen interest in the Renaissance by inviting many famous scholars and artists to come and work in Istanbul.

Ottoman influence continued to expand, notably again under Sultan Selim, who, in eight years between 918 and 926 (A.D. 1512–20), conquered Kurdistan and then moved southward to include Arabia, with its Holy Cities, and Egypt, where the last Abbasid Caliph was living. He brought the Caliph to Istanbul and there received the title of Caliph for himself and his successors.

Selim's son, Sulayman the Magnificent, captured Belgrade and Rhodes, and in 933 (A.D. 1526) won a decisive victory over the King of Hungary. For over a century and a half Hungary was a Turkish province, one in which the social and national structure was left intact. Sulayman's army laid siege to Vienna and forced Archduke Ferdinand to pay tribute. His famous sea captains—Barbarossa, Piyale, and Dragut—made the Mediterranean a Turkish lake by chasing the Spaniards from Libya and defeating the armada of the Pope, the Emperor of the Holy Roman Empire, and Venice. Famous admirals such as Drake and Doria did not dare to leave Mediterranean ports. In the age made famous by the successes of Charles V, Queen Elizabeth, Leo X, of Cortez, Christopher Columbus, and Raleigh, Sulayman the Magnificent could hold his own against any of them. The Ottoman Empire was at its greatest height, extending from the Euphrates to Gibraltar, from Budapest to southern Egypt.

The decline of the Ottoman Empire started, although it was not immediately apparent, during the rule of Selim II, son of Sulayman the Magnificent. The defeat inflicted by Don Giovanni of Austria was a heavy blow to Turkish sea supremacy. Even though this was a period in which Turkish forces captured Cyprus and Crete, were victorious over Austria, and conquered Baghdad, their successes did not check the Empire's decline. The defeat at St. Gotthard in 1075 (A.D. 1664) was the first step toward the expulsion of the Turks from Europe, and the trend continued with the complete loss of Hungary in 1098 (A.D. 1686). By 1131 (A.D. 1718) the Turks had been pushed back across the Danube in Wallachia.

Within its boundaries the Empire continued to decline. The janissaries, who for two centuries had been models of discipline and obedience, got out of hand and began to revolt. Their barracks became veritable inns of hoodlums. There was no dependable national army. The governors of far-flung corners of the Empire were often ignorant, inefficient, and sometimes corrupt. Viziers and loyal officials of high rank tried to check the decline by reforming the governmental and military systems, but they were opposed by established interests who screened themselves behind fanatics. The first step toward progress came in 1241 (A.D. 1826) when Sultan Mahmud II abolished the janissaries. But the dismemberment of the Empire continued. Greece gained her independence in 1244 (A.D. 1828). The Crimean War in 1271–72 (A.D. 1854–56), in which the Ottoman Empire was aided by England and France, put a temporary stop to the Russian advance. Romania became independent in 1283 (A.D. 1866) and Serbia a year later. However, the Ottoman Empire stayed intact until the Russian War of 1294 (A.D. 1877). It was at that time that Cyprus was given as a hostage to England in exchange for possible future assistance. In 1300 (A.D. 1882) England occupied Egypt.

New reforms were attempted; the constitution of 1293 (A.D. 1876) was amended and Sultan Abdulhamid II deposed in 1327 (A.D. 1909). Italy attacked Turkish forces in Libya, and the Balkan countries declared war against Turkey shortly before the first World War—all of which hastened the collapse of the Ottoman Empire. Faced by these threats, the Turks showed that they were still inspired by the spirit of their ancestors. The admiration of the whole world was aroused by their success in stopping the Anglo-French armada. They gave up over four hundred thousand men in the flower of their manhood at the Dardanelles. When Allied forces occupied Turkey after the armistice, and Greeks, armed by England, invaded Anatolia, the Turkish nation rose overnight in defense as men, women, and children, the old and the young, all rushed to save their homeland. The army organized under the leadership of Mustafa Kemal Ataturk threw the invaders into the sea.

The Turks turned then to the reconstruction of their ravaged country. The Sultanate was abolished in 1341 (A.D. 1922) and the Caliphate, considered to be essentially embodied in the government of the Republic, was abolished two years later. From the ruins of the Ottoman Empire emerged a new and dynamic Turkish state—The Republic of Turkey.

Looking back over the long history of the Turks since they became Muslims it is clear that they have made a great contribution to Islam. The Turkish people brought a new vitality into a Muslim world which had become lifeless in the hands of the Arabs and other Muslims. Turks, with their philosophic interests and more reasonable thinking, have given to Islam great men and great scholars in the fields of literal and mystical interpretation. They have for centuries accepted the duty of keeping Islam alive and maintaining security within Muslim lands, protecting them from the invasions of Europe and Russia. If it were not for the Turks, the Arab lands would long ago have become a part of the Communist colonial empire. Islam, because it was founded by Allah, is neither Arabic nor Turkish. Throughout this long history the Turks have simply sought to serve the Faith which Allah has given, even with the supreme sacrifice if necessary.

The Fundamentals of Islam

The true religion with Allah is Islam

There are eleven requirements of belief in Islam which are prescribed by divine ordinance, by definite orders of Allah, and are therefore obligations which must be fulfilled in order to be a believer and a Muslim. All Muslims in the world adhere to these eleven requirements with not the slightest disagreement among them on these points. The apparent differences between Sunnis and Shi'ites and other Islamic sects do not touch the fundamental precepts; they are concerned only with minor details.

The basic precept of Islam is expressed in the Word of Witness: *I attest and affirm that there is no God but Allah and that Muhammad is his creature and Prophet.* The core, the essence of belief in Islam is to believe in the Unity of God and that Muhammad (the Peace and Mercy of Allah be upon him) is the true and last Prophet.

The six requirements of belief in Islam are: to believe in the existence and unity of Allah; to believe in God's Angels, the sinless creatures of Allah who perform His orders; to believe in Allah's books, the Old and New Testaments and the Qur'an; to believe in all the prophets of Allah; to believe in the Day of Judgment with rewards and punishments; to believe that destiny belongs to Allah, recognizing that although every creature's destiny is in Allah's power, each one must use his reason and accept responsibility for his conduct. In those six requirements the heavenly religions of the Christians and Jews separate themselves from Muslims by not believing in the Unity of God and in Muhammad (the Peace and Mercy of Allah be upon him) as God's rightful and last Prophet. The Trinity is totally contrary to the tenets of Islam.

In addition to the six requirements of belief there are five requirements of action by which Islam is put into practice by Muslims: praying five times a day in the prescribed form; fasting during the month of Ramadan; pilgrimage to Mecca, when health, wealth, and the safety of the roads permit; zakat, the yearly almsgiving of one fortieth of one's movable property and wealth; and pronouncing the Word of Witness by word of mouth and with true intent in the heart.

These eleven requirements have been the fundamentals for the Turks ever since the first tribes in Central Asia accepted Islam, as they are for all Muslims. The Turks are Sunnis and followers of the school of interpretation of Hanafi. In the other chapters of this book the verses from the Qur'an which are the basis for Muslim belief everywhere have been quoted. Here are some of the Hadiths—verified Traditions—of Muhammad (the Peace and Mercy of Allah be upon him) which have been treasured as guides to belief and practice among all Muslims.

> All human beings are like the teeth of a comb. Only by worship do they become superior to each other.
>
> What you wish for yourself, wish also for all mankind.

A wise man is one who takes his example from what happens to others. The unwise man is the one who gives an example from what happens to him.

Don't exaggerate in praising me as is done for Jesus, Son of Mary. I am only a creature. Therefore call me Allah's creature and messenger.

Unless you love one another, you are not true believers. Shall I tell you how you will love each other? Salute each other (by showing love and respect). I swear by Allah, in whose power is my soul, that you will not enter Paradise unless you show affection and mercy to each other. The mercy I am talking about is not a mercy for any one of you, limited and personal, but a general mercy for all people (humanitarian and social), mutual assistance, loving each other, and having pity for all creatures of god.

Allah's bringing a man to the straight path through your efforts is the most blessed of the things that may happen between sunrise and sunset.

Leave the thing that fills you with doubt for the one that does not fill you with doubt.

The beauty in a Muslim's belief is his ability to leave things which are useless to him.

How fortunate is the one whose life is long and his conduct, deeds, and worship are beautiful.

Don't hold hatred or ill-will toward each other. Don't break your connections (with relatives or friends), don't turn your backs on each other, don't be jealous of each other, don't raise prices artificially, don't cheat, O God's creatures. Be brothers as Allah orders you. For a Muslim to stay on non-speaking terms with his brother in religion for more than three days is not legitimate.

The true believer lives in harmony with others and he himself is easy to get along with. No good comes from one who lives not in harmony with others and with whom it is not possible to get along easily.

These are only a hint of the Traditions of Muhammad (the Peace and Mercy of Allah be upon him) which have been treasured as guides for conduct by Muslims everywhere.

Sufism in Turkey

Sufism has always played an important role in Islam, especially among the Turks. The whole substance of the teaching of Sufism is the love of Allah and the love of the Prophet (the Peace and Mercy of Allah be upon him). Love for one's family, one's nation, and all mankind comes naturally from that love. Sufism seeks to strengthen that love by showing the disciple the means by which he can purify his actions and thus purify his character, and then elevate his soul to sublime heights—which is accomplished under the continual supervision of spiritual educators who are true mystics following the rules and precepts of Islam. The true sources of Sufi mysticism are the Qur'an and the Sunnah, the words and actions of Muhammad (the Peace and Mercy of Allah be upon him).

In order to be a Sufi, or a disciple who is learning how to become a Sufi, one must be attached to a religious teacher, a Shaikh, and work under his supervision and guidance. The Shaikh who understands the task of directing souls must be enlightened and perfect. His instruction takes two forms: teaching, which deals with specific subject matter and results in the attainment of knowledge; and enlightenment, which means to bring to maturity and is accomplished by counsel, by inspiration, by assigning work to be done, or just by a glance—some would call it a kind of telepathy. The Shaikh is one who has been authorized by a sage or religious leader *(Pir)* to teach and enlighten. The Sufis and disciples who gather around a Shaikh usually form a religious order *(tariqa)*, of which there are many in Islam, and sometimes center their activities in a *tekke*, an organized residential community. There are, of course, many Muslims who follow special religious practices without the guidance of a Shaikh; they are called worshipers or ascetics, but not Sufis.

As the name of Allah is mentioned in all kinds of prayer and worship, all worship in Islam may be summarized in the word *dhikr*. Literally it means mentioning or reciting and is commonly used to refer to all kinds of prescribed worship—the daily prayers, fasting, pilgrimage, almsgiving, and repeating the Word of Witness. Reading and reciting the Qur'an is also dhikr. In Sufism dhikr includes the commonly accepted worship of Islam and also means to recite orally or in silence the names of Allah, certain prayers and invocations recommended by the Shaikh, and also extra prayers, voluntarily performed, according to the method taught by the Shaikh. Such voluntary prayers are called *nawafil*, which means extras. Muhammad (the Peace and Mercy of Allah be upon him) said in one of his *kudsi* Hadiths (a Hadith in which Allah's meaning is expressed in the Prophet's words), "[Allah speaking] O my creatures! It is with nawafil that one can approach me (with my approval). Thus at the end I love him, and when I love him I almost become his ear, eye, hand, foot, and his tongue, so that he hears with Me, sees with Me, holds with Me, and speaks with Me." According to this kudsi Hadith, the continued practice of such voluntary prayers turns human beings into Angels, makes them spiritual forces in their community, nation, and the whole world. They become models of the highest and purest morals.

There are many verses in the Qur'an and many Hadiths which make it clear that Islamic Sufism started with the birth of Islam. The practice of being attached to a Shaikh and accepting him as a guide is based on such verses as this from the Qur'an: "O Believers! Fear Allah. And be together with the right ones (those who are right in their belief, action, words, and pledge, and do not separate from the truth)" (Surah IX, 119). The Qur'an also says, "O Believers! Remember Allah frequently in dhikr (recite with your tongue and remember always with your heart)" (Surah XXXIII, 41). "Know that with dhikr of Allah hearts reach the highest maturity" (Surah XIII, 28). "Woe to those whose hearts are (empty and) hardened against remembrance of Allah. They are plainly deviating (from the straight path)" (Surah XXXIX, 22).

Muhammad (the Peace and Mercy of Allah be upon him) has said among his Hadiths, "The highest degree of belief is your knowing that Allah is certainly always with you." "There is a polish for everything. The polish of hearts is dhikr of Allah." "The creatures who are at the highest rank (in the opinion of Allah) are those who dhikr Allah frequently." "Those who dhikr Allah frequently save themselves from hypocrisy and mischief."

In all of the religious orders the goal is to please and satisfy the Prophet (the Peace and Mercy of Allah be upon him) and to win God's approval of one's conduct. As one sets out toward that goal the point of departure is the struggle with one's self, one's body and mind. The Qur'an says, "(When it comes to) those who strive in Our cause We surely guide them to Our paths. Without doubt Allah is in any case with the people who do their duty toward God well" (Surah XXIX, 69). Our Prophet Muhammad (the Peace and Mercy of Allah be upon him) has explained that "the people who do their duty toward God well" means "worshiping Allah as if you were seeing Him. Even if you do not see Him, He is seeing you." According to this verse from the Qur'an, the striving must be absolutely for Allah's sake. When it is, Allah gives to the believer some insights (or openings, or uncoverings) which enlighten him concerning things he did not know.

According to the followers of Sufism there are seven stages along the way as one strives to reach the goal of Allah's approval. In the first stage man's physical nature, his carnal mind, is dominant. At this stage the self is the self that commends the tendency toward evil. In the Qur'an this first stage is pointed out in the fifty-third verse of the twelfth Surah, "Surely the self orders with utmost force the doing of evil." The vices of this stage are sometimes described as pride, cupidity, lust, envy, anger, avarice, and hatred. At this first stage the self tends toward the pleasures of the senses, the animal pleasures, which pull the heart toward baseness. This first stage is the nest of evils, the source of bad habits. Every religious order seeks to arouse its followers to struggle against this first stage of the self and to wipe out all traces of this level of existence.

In the second stage the self begins to awaken from its former blindness to the Truth, its ignorance of God's mysterious purposes, and its preoccupation with selfish hopes and fears. It is the stage of the self-reproaching self, for when man does an evil deed under the influence of his base nature the self reproaches and blames himself at once and repents of the evil he has done. In the second verse of the seventy-fifth Surah, Allah swears to the importance of the blaming, or accusing, soul. And in the twenty-second verse of the fourteenth Surah, the Qur'an says, "Blame yourselves." At this stage of awakening and self-reproach the self is separated from its old depravity and wickedness, and as it is awakened it takes the road of obedience and piety. If the self does not persist in its progress, it returns to the first stage and improvement becomes extremely difficult.

The third stage is the first step toward saintliness, the stage in which Allah reveals truth to man by inspiration, as is pointed out in the seventh and eighth verses of the ninety-first Surah of the Qur'an. "And a soul and Him who perfected it And inspired it (with conscience of) what is wrong for it and (what is) right for it." Inspiration is that which is suggested to the heart by divine blessing; it may be regarded as knowledge which invites to action even though it was not gained by deduction or evidence. In this third stage the self leaves sin but cannot forget it, just as a cigarette smoker who gives up smoking still finds in his heart a desire to smoke.

The self which reaches the fourth stage leaves behind all material desires and forgets them completely. He is free of all desires, even the desire to progress to higher levels which are now open to him, and turns only toward Allah's approval and blessing. The self at this stage is a thoroughly subdued and pious spirit which neither rebels nor murmurs. Through the inspiration given generously by Allah the self has been adapted, harmonized to Allah's will, and acquires tranquillity and religious certitude. The Qur'an says, "Allah conducts to the straight path those who turn their hearts to Him. These are believers. It is through dhikr of Allah that hearts come to serenity and peace. Know that only with dhikr of Allah do hearts find rest and satisfaction (do hearts ripen)" (Surah XIII, 27–28). At this stage the self is freed from bad qualities and endowed with good habits, freed from anxiety, hesitation, and doubt.

In the fifth stage the self never complains about anything that happens to it, it is indifferent to everything except Allah and finds everything equal that comes from Him, whether good or bad, affliction or blessing. The mystic Turkish poet Yunus Emreh has explained this stage in a quatrain,

> What comes from You is good to me
> Be it roses or thorns which pour down
> Or robe of dignity or shroud
> And pleasant is Your blessing and pleasant Your affliction.

If the self persists in remaining in the fifth stage of uncomplaining acceptance he progresses to the sixth stage and attains Allah's approval and blessing. This stage is described in the Qur'an (Surah LXXXIX, 27–30), "O selves who are certain and free of desires! Return unto your Lord, you content with Him, He content with you. Now then, enter among My (beloved) creatures, enter My heaven." Or, as Arberry translates the verse,

> O soul at peace, return unto thy Lord,
> Well-pleased, well-pleasing!
> Enter thou among My servants!
> Enter thou My Paradise!

The seventh stage is reached by those who keep on progressing, leaving behind all egotism, pretensions, or even claims to have reached a perfect stage. They become heirs to the prophets, gain the knowledge of divine Providence, and understand the Truth. This is the final stage of saintliness.

These seven stages are the educational system and discipline common to all Muslim religious orders. The differences between the religious orders are only in details of their practices. For instance, some orders do their dhikr silently while sitting alone or in a circle, while others follow open rites which may include chanting, music, and dancing. According to the followers of Sufism the Prophet Muhammad (the Peace and Mercy of Allah be upon him) taught Abu Bakr the secret, or silent, dhikr and taught Ali the open dhikr. That is why the Naqshbandi order, which comes from the Prophet (the Peace and Mercy of Allah be upon him) through Abu Bakr, perform the silent dhikr and the orders which come through Ali use the open dhikr.

The rites of the open dhikr orders became too animated and

frenzied. They used to start to dhikr loudly all together under the direction of their Shaikh, then stand up and, holding each others' hands, turn around in a circle, at the same time leaning forward and backward or to the right and left, keeping up this movement in an intermittent and harmonious rhythm. Singers with beautiful voices used to lead the men in singing as they turned about, thus encouraging them to more enthusiastic activity. Some of the orders used a tambourine to beat time; Mevlevis used to use a flute. There were many tekkes belonging to different Sufi orders in the cities and towns of Turkey, some following open dhikr and others insisting on silent dhikr. In the Sha'bani order in Istanbul, Shaikh Ahmed Amish early in this century forbade his disciples to assemble for dhikr together; they were taught to do their dhikr privately, reading the Qur'an frequently and reciting phrases and words of love and attachment to the Prophet (the Peace and Mercy of Allah be upon him) and his Companions. Many such variations in practices were common among all the orders of Sufism.

The spread of Sufism among Eastern Turks began with Ahmad Yesevi (died 562; A.D. 1166), who was a native of Turkestan. He took the name Yesevi from the city where he was teaching, after he had become famous for his great knowledge and Sufi-like deeds and was commanded by the ruler to bring honor to the city by adding its name to his own. After the death of the Shaikh under whom he was studying, Ahmad Yesevi went to Bukhara where he became a Shaikh under the most famous Shaikh of his time. Many Sufis who later became famous studied under Ahmad Yesevi. His influence was not restricted to Eastern Turks, for it spread into Anatolia and over into the European part of the Ottoman Empire. The famous Turkish traveler Evlia Chelebi, who wrote in the eleventh century (seventeenth century A.D.), tells in his ten volumes of travel notes of many saints belonging to the order of Ahmad Yesevi and describes one tekke capable of housing two hundred men.

There were many Shaikhs among the Turks who fled from the invasions of Genghis Khan. Thus the Sufi orders were established wherever the Turks settled, and Sufis from other countries also settled in the Turkish lands, until several tekkes could be found in every community. There were always scholars and Shaikhs in the armies of the Ottoman Empire wherever they went. The scholars taught the tenets of Islam and the Shaikhs were busy in the education of souls and assisting in the establishment of Sufi orders and tekkes throughout the Empire.

In addition to Ahmad Yesevi there were hundreds of famous Sufi leaders in the long history of Turkey. Mevlana Jalal al-Din Rumi (died 672; A.D. 1273) was one of the greatest poets and saints of Islam, and father of the founder of the Mevlevi order. He was born at Balkh in a Turkish family of the Khwarizm, the son of a scholar who was known as the Sultan of the Ulama. Father and son migrated to the Hijaz, then to Damascus, and finally to Konya at the invitation of the Seljuq Sultan. There at Konya he succeeded his father as a teacher and won great fame for his intelligence and knowledge. Later, when he became better acquainted with the Sufis, he renounced his teaching and plunged into the ocean of Sufism. After that he began to write, beginning with his *Mathnawi*, which is one of the masterpieces of the Orient. That book of thirty thousand couplets and his other mystical writings are widely studied in modern times by the intellectuals of Turkey, Pakistan, Iran, and Afghanistan. Mevlana was buried at Konya where his tomb has been made a national monument and is visited by a constant stream of people who come from all over Turkey and from many other countries. On the anniversay of his death elaborate memorial ceremonies are held at Konya, and the broadcasting stations of Istanbul and Ankara give special programs devoted to his life and writings.

The writings of Mevlana Jalal al-Din contain stories, anecdotes, moral instruction, and mystical insights, often in lyrical and symbolic passages. They were written in Persian and have been translated into Turkish and many other languages. Here are a few favorite lines from Mevlana:

> O Love! You are the physician of all our ills.
>
> Who has not the fire of Love, let him perish.

Whether you be a stone, a rock, or even a marble, in the hand of a mature and perfect educator who is a man of soul you will become a jewel.

Your inclination is toward thorny and sandy places. In that thorny and sandy soil how can you find and gather roses?

The end of every weeping is without doubt laughter. The man who sees the end of the affair is a holy man.

Mevlana is a title given to the greatest Shaikhs, meaning our Chief, our Lord, our Great One. It is merited by Jalal al-Din Rumi, not because he is a great philosopher, for he scorned philosophy, but because of his great mystical insight. In the *Mathnawi* he says, "The philosopher busies himself with ideas and opinions and denies things above them. Go and tell him to knock his head against the wall. The philosopher also denies Satan but at that moment he becomes his fool." He goes on to say that reason, which is the source of philosophy, cannot get outside of its rational limitations and cannot taste the pleasures of the Love of God which is above reason. "Reason in commenting on Love has become helpless, like an ass sunk in mud. It is Love which will say the Truth of Love and being in Love."

The followers of Mevlana Jalal al-Din Rumi formed the Mevlevi order, with its headquarters at Konya. The administration of the order was in the hands of the presiding chief at Konya who was appointed or removed from office by the Sultans during the time of the Ottoman empire. Many Mevlevi tekkes were built in Turkey and as far away as Hungary and India. In Turkey the Seljuq and Ottoman Sultans and high-ranking officials revered Rumi, and in every generation great numbers of learned men have been students of his *Mathnawi*. But when Sultan Mahmud II abolished the janissaries he also abolished the Bektashi order which had been influential among them, and many Bektashis saved their lives by entering Mevlevi tekkes. As a result, the Mevlevi order lost its former position; it was even accused of following Shi'a doctrines, due to the activities of Bektashis disguised as Mevlevis. That could not be true, for Mevlevis recited every morning "I am willing and consenting to have Allah as my

God, Islam as my religion, Muhammad as my Prophet, the Qur'an as my Book, Abu Bakr, Umar, Uthman, and Ali as my Imams," which shows how they cared for the first four Caliphs.

After the Republic of Turkey was founded all Sufi tekkes in Turkey were closed by decree, and since that time there have been no Sufi orders in the country.

Once when Jalal al-Din Rumi was asked what was the dhikr in his tekke he replied, "Our dhikr is Allah, Allah, Allah, because we are Allah's. We have come from Allah, we go to Allah. My father always heard of Allah, spoke of Allah, and always recited the name of Allah. God Almighty has manifested Himself to all prophets and saints with a different name. The manifestation to us Muslims is the name of Allah which contains all the names and attributes."

According to the Mevlevis, Mevlana encouraged his followers to use the ritual dance to arouse emotion which leads to ecstasy. He spoke of ritual dance as enlightening and adorning the hearts of the seekers, as being illegitimate for those who deny religion and legitimate for the lovers of Allah. Mevlevis base the legitimacy of the ritual dance on the tacit approval of the Prophet (the Peace and Mercy of Allah be upon him) when he saw people dancing. Once when the Prophet (the Peace and Mercy of Allah be upon him) met Jafar Ibn Abi Talib he embraced him and kissed him on the forehead and said, "In regard to birth and character you resemble me." When Jafar heard this he was so happy that he unconsciously started to dance, and he was not reproved for this joyful action. Another argument relied upon by Sufis is that one day when the Prophet (the Peace and Mercy of Allah be upon him) was looking out from his room he saw some Ethiopian Muslims playing and dancing and did not reprove them.

The Mevlevis argued in favor of the ritual dance that dancing and rejoicing is common to all living beings; even animals jump, run, and play when they are happy. Man, as a superior animal, has this feeling and a natural tendency to perform rhythmic movements, especially when he hears exhilarating music. The rising and turning of men of God, of *darwishes*, in rhythmic movements during the ritual dance were the result of the rejoicing in their hearts; when done with pure sincerity of heart it led to ecstacy.

As the ceremony of the ritual dance used to be performed, it began with the eulogy, which starts out, "O Beloved of Allah, you are the Messenger of the Only Creator." When the sound of this eulogy filled the air, heads were bent down, eyes closed, and the souls would fly to the world of melody. After the eulogy, the chief flute player would play a solo according to his mood, and then a prelude would be played. When the tambourine started to beat the darwishes would get up and then turn in a circle three times in time with the beats. Then the ritual dance would begin.

The men of Sufism imagine the circle of the ritual dance as representing a circulating flame which symbolizes the universe. Half of the circle is the Arc of Descent, showing how things get away from their origin; man, being the last created thing, is the lowest of the low. The other half of the circle is the Arc of Ascent, showing the approach of creatures to their original source. Man who is the lowest of the low progresses up and up by grades until he returns to his original source. "And you will return to Him," says the Qur'an. The descent in the Arc of Descent was referred to as from Allah and the ascent was to Allah. The basis of the ritual dance was a human being's desire above all else to keep progressing on the Arc of Ascent, to return to Allah.

We have discussed the Mevlevi order at some length because there is much in its history and organization which is typical of other Sufi orders. Another order which had many followers before the banning of the orders by the Republic was the Bektashi order which had considerable influence because of its association with the janissaries. The order was founded by Hajji Bektash Veli who was born in Khurasan and came to Anatolia in 680 (A.D. 1281), where he established his order. His father had been attached to one of the Shaikhs of Ahmad Yesevi. His tomb, which is open for visiting, is in the town to which he gave his name, and many people go there to pray to Allah, to recite the Qur'an, and to ask assistance of the saint.

Another order which formerly had large numbers of followers in Turkey and has spread even to Indonesia is the Naqshbandi, founded by Muhammad Baha-ud-din Naqshbandi who was born at Bukhara and spent most of his life there (died 790; A.D. 1388). He wrote *The Book of Life* and the *Guide to Lovers* (of Allah), and had a great many followers and disciples. Because he received instruction from a follower of the Yesevi order, the Naqshbandi order is often considered to be a branch of the Yesevi.

The people of Turkey are well-acquainted with the names and teachings of dozens of other famous Sufis, but space does not allow a detailed discussion of them all. The influence of their teachings has been very great in the history of Islam among the Turks. In Turkey today all the Sufi tekkes are closed and all Sufi orders and their rites are forbidden. The old purity and sincerity of the orders had long ago deteriorated in some of the tekkes. The impact of Sufism has not disappeared completely, however, since everyone is free to pray as he pleases, to follow his own dhikr in seclusion, and to obey the commands and teachings of Allah and the Prophet (the Peace and Mercy of Allah be upon him). Today in Turkey there is no conflict between Sunni and Shi'a or between those who follow a literal interpretation of Islam and those who prefer a mystical interpretation. All people are free to do as they please.

Government in Turkey

The Grand National Assembly, made up of elected members who are ninety-nine per cent Muslim Turks, makes the laws concerning secular affairs and punishments which govern the country. All rules and commandments of shari'a concerning beliefs, prayers, and morals are in force and observed by the people. The official and legal authority on Islam in Turkey today is the office of the Director of Religious Affairs and the Muftis attached to it. However, because there is no clergy in Islam everyone with religious authority can speak about the Faith.

The national policies of Turkey are not racist, for Islam forbids Muslims to think only of one's own race or to despise or discredit other races. There are many verses in the Qur'an and many Hadiths which forbid racism. From the beginning Islam has sought to establish brotherhood among men and nations.

The fundamental requirements for a true Islamic state—mutual deliberation, knowledge and ability, justice, responsibility, and control—have been stated in many places in the Qur'an, "The conduct of affairs of those who answer the call of their Lord and who do their *salat* [prayers] is always by mutual deliberation" (Surah XLII, 38). "(O Muhammad) We set you on the way (shari'a) of religion. You follow it and do not follow the whims of those who do not know" (Surah XLV, 18). "Without doubt Allah commands you to entrust (public functions and services) to the hands of qualified people, and when you judge among mankind judge with justice" (Surah IV, 58). "O Believers! Be of (judges) holding erect the right and of men witnessing in justice. Do not let your hatred for a people seduce you into dealing with injustice. Respect justice because it is the nearest to piety, fear, and respect for Allah" (Surah V, 8). These, according to Islam, are the requirements of a government.

Because the Turks have conquered many lands and established large empires, the question is often raised as to the place of jihad, holy war, in Turkish thought. Jihad is for Turks just what it is for all Muslims.It is in one sense an interior war, a fighting against bad inclinations in oneself. As many verses and Hadiths bear witness, this is the most important sense of the holy war. Between nations Islam accepts war as a last resort for defense of Islam, and only for defense. Rulers may have gone to war for their own secular purposes, but Islam has never justified a war except for defense of the faith. The expansion of Islam through the centuries has not needed the use of force or compulsion. Islam is like fresh air to breathe. Everyone with common sense will welcome it. At the time of the Crusades many Christians embraced Islam by their own free will. The people of Turkey will defend their faith with their lives, but as good Muslims they cannot use compulsion to bring others to accept their religion.

Education under the Republic is supported by the government. There are primary and secondary schools which give secular education and optional religious instruction. The Faculty of Theology at the University of Ankara and the Institute of Islamic Studies at the University of Istanbul have become centers for teaching and research in Muslim history and literature. Instruction in Islam is also given by the religious leaders of the community—the Mufti, who gives canonical opinions on matters concerning Islamic law; the Imam, who leads the prayers in the mosque; and the *Hatip*, who preaches at the weekly services and on special days. One man may be both Imam and Hatip, with responsibility for leading the prayers and for giving instruction through preaching and teaching. There are now Imam–Hatip schools in seventeen provinces of Turkey, created to train religious leaders in Islam.

The governmental office of the Director of Religious Affairs has published books on Islam and is responsible for general supervision of Islam in Turkey. The next steps would seem to be for the government to expand its publishing activities and especially to publish small, inexpensive books on Islam written in simple language for popular circulation; to take steps toward training an adequate number of Imams and Hatips by increasing the number of schools and making them residential; and to open public courses for religious teaching and schools specializing in religious instruction, reinforced by general cultural subjects.

During the Ottoman rule there was a minister of shari'a called Shaikh-ul-Islam, and also a minister of waqfs (religious endowments). When the Republic was formed the Grand National Assembly gave authority over both shari'a and waqfs to the Minister of Shari'a but when the religious orders were abolished all matters concerning shari'a were put under the care of the Director of Religious Affairs and all matters related to the waqfs were put under the Director of Waqfs, with both Directors attached to the office of the Premier. A *waqf* is property or a fund given as a perpetual endowment to provide income for a religious or public service—for some purpose which will be pleasing to Allah. There have been waqfs in Islam from the earliest times and in all countries. In all Turkish areas waqfs have played a great role in the service of mankind and in spreading learning, culture, and the arts. Most of the learned men were trained in institutions supported by waqfs and most of the monuments and mosques which are admired today are the product of waqfs. The Turkish waqfs were born of the devotion of the people, created for the good of the people, and stand as symbols of the humanitarian ideals of the Muslim Turks.

The waqfs were created for a great variety of services, such as the building and upkeep of water conduits, fountains, wells, roads, sidewalks, bridges, kitchens for the distribution of free meals, guest houses, homes for widows, schools, libraries, mosques, tekkes, cemeteries, open-air places for prayer, caravansaries to lodge full caravans of men and animals, clock towers for telling time, bakeries for distributing bread and cakes to the poor, dispensaries, hospitals, public baths, shaded land on the roadside. Waqfs were established to furnish trousseaux for orphan girls, for paying the debts of imprisoned or bankrupt businessmen, for clothing for the aged, to help pay village and neighborhood taxes, to help the army and the navy, to found trade guilds, to give land for public markets, to build lighthouses, to help orphans and widows and the destitute, to care for the needs of poor school children and to give them picnics, to pay for the funerals of the poor, to provide holiday gifts for poor families, to build seaside cottages for holidays for the people, to distribute ice-cold water during the summer, to create public playing fields, to distribute rice to birds, and to give food and water to animals.

It is thanks to the waqfs that most of the monuments, works of art, and educational institutions were built in Turkish lands. Everyone, rich or poor, wanted to leave a waqf. It was a social must for a rich man or a man who had attained a high rank in the government to build a mosque with a school in his home town or to leave a waqf in the city. The poor also sought to do their part. Although they could not build a mosque, they could give a small waqf to support the teaching of Hadiths in a mosque. A widow once left a waqf for replacing a well-bucket and its rope; another woman left a waqf for the care of storks which broke their legs. All of these waqfs were intended to last forever under management which was regulated by religious law.

The income from the waqfs was decreased steadily by continued wars, loss of territories, and the inevitable disruption of management of the properties in such times of stress, and many monuments and mosques fell into disrepair. The Republic of Turkey has recognized that the waqfs constitute a great part of the national fortune of the country and has undertaken a careful administration of waqf funds, even founding a bank to care for the funds and use the income for the care and preservation of historical mosques and monuments, many of which are now being restored. Under the Director of Waqfs a staff of architects and civil engineers are freeing national monuments from their slum-like surroundings and restoring their original beauty. New endowments are being given today by the rich to support schools, the Red Crescent, and charitable institutions.

The Turkish Area Today

Fifty years ago religious teaching in the Turkish area was following about the same methods which had been used for centuries. There were Sufi tekkes in most communities and madrasas (schools for religious instruction) everywhere. The madrasas followed a scholastic pattern which had not changed for centuries, emphasizing memorization and repetition. The teachers were men who got their certification from local Shaikhs; the best of the teachers went to Istanbul, Baghdad, or Cairo. At the beginning of the present century a movement of reform started in the Ottoman Empire and in the Turkish areas under the yoke of Russia, but unfortunately the successive wars and defeats in Turkey and the rise of Communism in Russia prevented the accomplishment of the reforms.

TURKEY. After the defeat and destruction of the Ottoman Empire the Republic of Turkey was formed under Kemal Ataturk, who as the commander of the Turkish National Army had repulsed the invasion of the Greeks. The new constitution was on a secular basis. The Sufi orders and tekkes were abolished soon after the new government was formed. Most of those orders which had played an important role during the growth of the Seljuq and Ottoman Empires, contributed so much to the sciences, arts, and literature in Turkish lands for a thousand years, and provided for the religious needs of the intellectuals had lost their spirit and deteriorated into asylums for good-for-nothings. The religious orders had become ghostly remnants of their splendid past and deserved to be closed.

It is a mistake, however, to assume that because the orders have been abolished the devotion to Islam is declining in Turkey. In place of beliefs full of superstition and meaningless fanaticism, a sincere and genuine revival of Islamic faith is taking place among the people of Turkey. In almost every mosque there is a course in the Qur'an. Islam is being taught in the primary and secondary schools and special schools have been created for training Imams and Hatips. Islam is taught at the University of Ankara. Books on Islam are published by the Director of Religious Affairs and by private publishers. Three interpretations of the Qur'an have been published recently. A nine-volume commentary on the whole Qur'an and several commentaries on particular Surahs and Hadiths have appeared. There are also several monthlies and weeklies which deal with Islamic beliefs and practices. Those who question the vitality of Islam, those who think that the Turks could ever be without religion and without Allah, should come and see the crowded mosques of Turkey, the new mosques being built today, and the devotion of the Turks to Islam.

THE BALKAN PENINSULA. The diverse religions, nationalities, languages, and cultures of the Balkan Peninsula make it one of the most complex areas of the world. Islam came to the Balkans with the Arabs even before the Ottoman Empire, and for over five hundred years Bulgaria, Romania, Yugoslavia, Greece, and Albania were parts of the Ottoman Empire.

Bulgaria became an autonomous principality in 1295 (A.D. 1878) and an independent state in 1326 (A.D. 1908). After its independence Islamic affairs were under the direction of a Mufti appointed from Turkey, and assisted by an Islamic Community Organization. The larger towns had their own Muftis and councils which administered the funds for religious teaching in their madrasas and schools, many of which employed Turkish teachers. They were able to train their own Muftis, Imams, and Hatips and to give instruction in science, languages, literature, and the arts. It was the graduates of their schools who struggled against the Communists when they closed the schools and appointed Muftis whom they could control. Most of the teachers were forced to join the refugees who fled Bulgaria in order to save their lives. Today there are over eight hundred thousand Turks in Bulgaria under Communist oppression.

Romania had a Muslim community quite similar to the one in Bulgaria but today there are only about fifty thousand Muslims who have not migrated to Turkey. There are also about one hundred and twenty thousand Christian Turks in Romania under the Communists.

Yugoslavia has almost two million Muslims whose lot is little better than that of the Muslims in Bulgaria. They still are allowed to have their madrasas which fare as well as any non-Communist school may fare in a national state ruled by Communism.

Albania has been independent since 1329 (A.D. 1911), but the small, mountainous country has been the scene of continuous revolts and civil wars. The people of Albania are descendants of Turks who left Anatolia to settle there four centuries ago. Almost seven hundred thousand of the one million people in Albania are Muslims who now live under a strict Communist regime which has closed all madrasas and tekkes and forbidden the expression of their religion.

In Greece the eighty thousand Muslim Turks are under a systematic and fiendish oppression. The Muslim population of Crete and the Aegean islands and all parts of Greece except western Thrace have been driven out or exterminated. In western Thrace there are still madrasas but only the most ignorant teachers are allowed to teach and no Muslim community can bring teachers from Turkey even though Greek schools in Turkey can freely bring teachers from Greece. In Greece intensive efforts are made to limit the educational and commercial opportunities of Muslims, and relations with the Muslims of Turkey are prevented whenever possible. Except for Soviet Russia Islam is persecuted and oppressed in Greece more than anywhere in the world.

CYPRUS. Cyprus was first taken by Muslims in the twenty-sixth year of the Hijrah (A.D. 648). After a time the island was ruled by several kings, but never was held by the Greeks. Sultan Selim II conquered Cyprus in 978 (A.D. 1570), and it was Turkish territory until it was put in the custody of England in 1295 (A.D. 1878) in return for British help against Russia. At that time the population was about one hundred and ten thousand people, today there are half a million residents of the island of whom one hundred thousand are Muslim Turks. After the arrival of the British a great many Cypriots moved to Turkey, where today there are three hundred thousand descendants of the people of Cyprus. Such a large number of Greeks migrated to Cyprus that the Greek government has sought to annex the island, even though it is only forty miles from Turkey and a vital strategic point for Turkish defense. Muslims in Cyprus are under a Mufti whom they elect and Islam is taught in religious and secular schools and through publications in Turkish. Muslims of Cyprus come and go freely between their island and Turkey.

THE SOVIET UNION. The story of Islam in the Soviet Union is, to say the least, the saddest that one can imagine. Conditions were bad enough under the Czars but under Communism they have become worse because the Russians, whether White or Red, have always looked upon Islam with hatred. Communists have learned that Islam is the greatest obstacle to the spread of Communism and use against the Muslims in the Soviet Union all the diabolical devices that the mind can devise.

To understand the present situation in the Soviet Union one must give up the erroneous idea that it is a unified nation. Russia, like Great Britain and France, has for centuries been an imperialist and colonial power. Great Britain and France—and Holland should be included—resorted to colonialism chiefly for economic reasons, but Russia sought colonies to satisfy its passion for conquering and dominating the world. While the colonies of the European countries were overseas, the colonies of Russia are its neighboring countries. And just as the colonies of the British and French and Dutch are alien peoples, so also the nations in the Russian colonies are alien to Russia. At a time when the European countries are freeing their colonies, the Russians are tightening their hold and expanding their colonial empire.

The story of Islam in the Soviet Union is the story of four hundred years of struggle against Russian tyranny and oppression, a resistance which has been as tenacious as the oppression has been merciless. From the reign of Ivan the Terrible until the accession of Catherine the Great, Muslims were subjected to a program of Russification and suppression of their mosques and madrasas. Even so, Muslims prayed in secret behind closed doors and secretly performed the last rites for their dead. Their teachers studied in Bukhara, Istanbul, and Cairo and returned to teach secretly. Under Catherine the Great some mosques and madrasas were permitted and there was a religious tribunal which was headed for years by puppets of the Russians who were devoid of Islamic understanding and devotion. Under those circumstances Islam was given some respite and mosques and madrasas increased; but Turkish language and literature were forbidden and books and magazines dealing with Turkish subjects could not be circulated.

For a few years before the Russian Revolution the attitude toward the Muslims became quite tolerant, which made it possible for the Muslims to obtain from the government a decree for the opening of primary schools in which religion and courses in Turkish language, literature, and history could be taught. Famous madrasas for higher learning were opened at Ufa, Kazan, Orenburg, and Troiski. They also were able to develop publishing centers in Crimea, at Kazan, Tashkent, and Baku, and to interchange books, magazines, and newspapers with Istanbul. Educated men were permitted to move freely between the Muslim centers of Russia and Istanbul.

These new developments brought about an awakening of religious and national aspirations among the Muslims of Russia. Turks in Russia had for some time participated in the fields of commerce and industry; now they entered the fields of the liberal arts and science. They even had theatres which played the works of Turkish writers. They began to modify the old scholastic system in the madrasas and sought to bring the some twenty-six different dialects of Turkish closer to the language as it is spoken in Istanbul, where it is used in its most refined and articulate form. Through contributions from Muslim merchants and landowners new madrasas were started and new mosques built until there were over forty thousand mosques under Russian rule. Of course, the Russians did not like this expansion and the beginning of solidarity among the Muslims in Russia, but the first World War came about that time and the Muslims were not molested since the government was enlisting them in the army.

As soon as the Communists gained control they launched invasions of the lands where Muslim Turks were living. Some of those territories had declared their autonomy and the Muslims there resisted the Communist occupation fiercely, but in the end they were all subdued and enslaved. The Communists stopped the efforts to teach the Turkish language and took control of all schooling. Today there is only one Islamic religious school, at Bukhara, with eighty students for the whole of the Soviet Union. Over eighty thousand religious leaders were either sent to Siberia or shot. Mosques were turned into stables. Today there are only a few dozen mosques, and they are heavily taxed. Muslim men of religion are not allowed to have ration cards. It is impossible to know the exact number of Muslims in the Soviet Union but estimates range from twenty to fifty millions. Four and a half million Central Asians have fled from Russia and are now living in neighboring lands. No one knows how many Muslims have been sent to Siberia. Islam behind the iron curtain is in a desperate situation unequalled anywhere except possibly in Spain at the time of the Inquisition.

IRAQ, IRAN, AND AFGHANISTAN. In Iraq there are about one million Turks, chiefly in the northwestern regions and in Baghdad. Most of them are Sunnis, followers of the school of Hanafi, and a few are Shi'ites.

About six million of the people of Iran are Turks, including all of the people of Iranian Azerbaijan who speak a Turkish dialect of their own. They are both Sunni and Shi'a, with the majority Sunnis of the Hanafi school.

Afghanistan, which for centuries has been a crossroads for Asia, has a population made up of Afghans, Iranians, Turks, Mongols, and Indians who through intermarriage have become one people. They are an independent folk with a remarkably strong attachment to Islam. Almost all of the people of Afghanistan are Sunnis of the Hanafi school; a few are Shi'ites. The old type of madrasas and Sufi tekkes still flourish there, but new types of schools are being opened and Afghanistan is moving toward a new era of progress.

CHINA AND SINKIANG. It is estimated that there are over a million Muslims in China of Turkish descent, but it is not possible to get accurate information. Estimates as to the number of Muslim Turks in Sinkiang vary from three to eight million. They are Sunnis who have kept in touch with Islam in Turkey. Their chief madrasas were at Kashgar, Khotan, and Turfan. Sufi tekkes have been very important in Sinkiang. Today they are subjected to restrictions similar to those which the Muslims in Soviet Russian have had to endure, and information concerning their sad fate comes out only occasionally when refugees escape to Pakistan.

Why Is Muslim Culture So Backward Today?

Muslims assert that Islam is a religion with the best standards and ideals, giving to its believers high moral principles and guiding them to a deep spiritual life which brings peace and comfort in this world and the next. Anyone who studies the history of Islam knows that the Middle Ages were a time of splendor in Islamic civilization, when arts and sciences flourished and Islam brought new vitality to the Muslim world. But anyone who is introduced to Islam for the first time will ask why Muslim culture is so backward today, and he will be right in asking.

The great Pakistani poet, philosopher, and patriot, Muhammad Iqbal, gave a general answer to this question when he said, "Nothing is wrong with Islam. All the wrong there is is in our way of being Muslims." Islam itself cannot be responsible for this decadence for it is well known that culture has both flourished and declined under Islam. Nevertheless, the fact that Muslim nations are backward today is a reality which is recognized by thoughtful Muslims who are seeking to correct this situation. The reasons for this backwardness are manifold. Some of the reasons may be found in the Muslims themselves; some are found in the economic, political, and historical circumstances of the Muslim world.

One of the first causes of the backwardness of Muslim culture today is the negligence and disobedience of the precepts of Islam on the part of people who have called themselves Muslims. As Islam spread to many countries the newly converted people often did not fully understand the teachings and practices; others who embraced Islam were actually only disguised as Muslims and introduced beliefs in contradiction to the Truth. Unfortunately, sects and religious orders grew up which claimed to be Islamic but in reality they were not—and some even exist today. All of these factors tended to encourage deterioration of Muslim culture.

Much of Western civilization has been introduced to the Muslim world by haughty merchants who were assisted by the military forces of colonial powers, causing the people of the

East to draw back into their own world. The devout Muslim believes that anyone can be without modern comforts of the industrialized West and still be a superior being. As one expressed it, "Western civilization is a circle which widens its radius all the time, having no depth or height." For a true Muslim, richness resides not in material wealth but in spiritual and moral values. Western civilization had spiritual values, but they were for home consumption, not for export. It exported material goods and brutal treatment which were not neutralized by the self-denying work of a few missionaries.

The loss of the trade routes because of the discovery of the sea route around the Cape of Good Hope was an economic blow of great importance in the Muslim world. Up to that time all the goods of the Orient were brought by caravans which created prosperity along their routes. The prosperous commercial activities along the trade routes provided endowments for schools and mosques, but when the trade was lost cities became villages or disappeared, schools closed, scholars and artists were without support. Soon after this the Europeans gained a stranglehold on the economic life of the area which did not begin to be broken until after the first and second World Wars.

The rise of colonialism, like an octopus, clasped under its tentacles an unsuspecting and indolent Orient. When it awoke it found itself tightly in the grip of the invaders. To the struggle with the Western Powers has been added the conflict with the Communists of our own day. In this struggle it was the Turks who led the fight against colonialism and first threw off the yoke of the invaders, thus setting an example in the Muslim world. That is one of the reasons for the antagonism often expressed in the Western press against the Turks and Islam. It is also paradoxical but true that under Western colonialism Islam continued to spread, for the peace and order maintained by the colonial powers prevented tribal and racial conflicts which could have sapped the strength of the East.

The rise of industry in the West was scorned by the whole Orient, Muslims included, partly because of their disdain for the West, and partly because of their pride in their handicraft and their attachment to their guilds. Muslims were so bound to their own ways that they abhorred anything which came from the nonbelievers. At first this was not fanaticism but a loyalty and pride in their own things, but as it became exaggerated in the hands of the ignorant it was turned against themselves. The printing press, for instance, was not introduced into Turkey for a century and a half after its invention because of the opposition of those who wanted to preserve the fine art of calligraphy and feared that the scribes would lose their jobs.

Another factor in the backwardness of the Muslims was their neglect of the Renaissance. The Renaissance was in part due to the Muslim scholars who at the height of Muslim culture had translated, interpreted, discussed, and made their own the writings of ancient Greece which had been long forgotten in Europe. One important aspect of the Renaissance in Europe was that by freeing their learning from the scholastic system, by taking teaching and learning from the monopoly of the clergy and making it available to other classes, the way was opened to new knowledge and new sciences which secured for Europe progress which the Muslims did not, or would not, recognize. It was unfortunate that Islam did not recognize this aspect of the Renaissance. Of course, if the Muslims had held truly and sincerely to their Faith, they would not have had any need for a Renaissance.

In Turkey the Muslims neglected the Renaissance because of their pride in their brilliant past and their no less brilliant present, and because of their contempt for anything Western which remained indelibly in their minds from the times of the destruction and havoc of the Crusades. Another factor in the Turk's scorn for the Renaissance was the ignorance and fanaticism which crept up on the ulama and contributed to the backwardness of the Muslims.

The Situation Today

Today there is an unmistakable change in the Muslim world and its relations with the West. In the past many Western writers ridiculed and belittled Islam. Today there are many intellectually honest and impartial Western scholars who are trying to study Islam without bias or preconceived ideas. The attitude of Muslims toward the West is changing, too. They recognize that they are behind the Western peoples in many ways and have much to learn from them, especially in technical fields. The prospects for better understanding between the East and West are good.

The attitude of Muslims toward themselves and their religion is changing also. For the past fifty years Muslim young men have been studying in the universities of the West and coming home with new knowledge and new conceptions of life. Although some come back infected with skepticism and unbelief (it is next to impossible to adhere to any other religion after having been even loosely attached to Islam), the majority come back with renewed interest in their own religion. They are no longer satisfied with the mere observance of the outward form of their religion but are looking for spiritual and moral guidance in Islam compatible with modern civilization.

Until the beginning of this century the Muslim intellectual could find the spiritual life he craved in the religious orders, but the orders and other religious institutions degenerated into the observance of outward forms which did not satisfy the intellectuals. For a time the intellectuals loosened their ties with Islam, but this did not last long and reaction has already set in. The recent publication of books on Islam of a high level and addressed to intellectuals is evidence of this revived interest. Also, there is continual improvement in the quality of the instruction in the higher religious schools by many teachers who have received their training both in the East and the West. All of this is evidence of the promising and vital interest of intellectuals in Islam in Turkey today.

It is often pointed out that Islam spreads among primitive people, but not among intellectuals. It is true that Muslims have for a long time known the way in which primitive people come to understand Islam and have been able to teach them the Faith. Today the way to explain Islam to intellectuals is being worked out in Turkey as well as in other Muslim countries, and as that is done there is no doubt that Islam will spread among the intellectuals of the world.

CHAPTER EIGHT

Muslim Culture in Pakistan and India

Mazheruddin Siddiqi

The Arabs had commercial relations with southern India long before Islam, and their commerce by sea continued—along with missionary activity—after the appearance of the Holy Prophet. The Muslim Arabs first settled on the Malabar coast about fifty years after the Hijrah, toward the end of the seventh century A.D., at a time when South India was agitated by religious conflicts and political instability. Islam, with its simplicity of faith and clarity of doctrine, made a tremendous impression on the Hindu mind, and within the first twenty-five years many of the people, including the King of Malabar, had accepted the new religion.

Although the commerce by sea continued, the main route by which Islam came to India was overland through Iran and Central Asia. During the Caliphate of Umar the land approaches to India were explored, but Umar's policy did not countenance expansion into India. It was under the Umayyads that the first efforts were made to invade India.

For convenience in discussing the rise of Muslim culture in Pakistan and India we may divide the history into four periods: the period before the Mughals; the Mughal rule of almost two centuries; the period of disintegration; and the past century, which includes the British rule and the creation of Pakistan.

Before the Mughals
To 933 (A.D. 1526)

The first Muslim invasion of India took place during the reign of the Umayyad Caliph Walid (87–97; A.D. 705–15) who sent Muhammad Ibn Qasim on an expedition into Sind, the area which then included most of what is now the Punjab. Although Sind was at that time governed by a Brahman family, the religion of the common people was Buddhist. The Buddhists were suffering serious religious, social, and economic disabilities under the Brahman rule, as is shown by their petition to Qasim for the right to worship in their Buddhist temples as they used to do. Muhammad Ibn Qasim treated the Hindus very generously, keeping Hindu ministers and police inspectors in his service, but he was soon recalled and after his departure many of the Hindu feudal princes revolted against the Caliph's authority.

The first Abbasid Caliph sent an army into Sind to oust the Umayyad governor, and the second Caliph, Mansur, sent another expedition which founded the garrison town of Mansura. During the time of the Abbasid Caliph Mamun (198–218; A.D. 813–33) many Arab families migrated to Sind, founding a large Arab colony. Later, as the power of the Abbasid Caliphs declined, Sind became a neglected province governed by petty princes who acknowledged the Caliph only as their spiritual head. The two principal Muslim kingdoms of Sind were at that time Multan and Mansura.

The real history of Muslim India begins with Mahmud of Ghazna, ruler of a small Turkish kingdom in Afghanistan which had become independent when the Samanid Empire collapsed. Mahmud led seventeen expeditions into India from 391 to 417 (A.D. 1000–1026). The rule of the Arabs in Sind came to an end in 396 (A.D. 1005) when Mahmud of Ghazna sent an army of Turks and Hindu mercenaries under Abdu'r Razzaq to uproot the power of the Qarmati Ima'ilis, who seem to have gained considerable influence there. The Punjab was annexed to the Ghaznavid Empire and ruled from Ghazna, but Mahmud's successors, faced with the rising power of the Seljuq Turks, could not hold it.

The dynasty which laid the permanent foundations of Muslim rule in North India was that of the Ghorids, rulers of a small mountainous state in Afghanistan. Ghori conquered Multan in 572 (A.D. 1176), defeated the last Ghaznavid king of the Punjab, and in 588 (A.D. 1192) gave a crushing blow to the remnants of the Rajput Hindu princes. His Turkish slaves who served as leaders of his armies carried on his work and consolidated the Muslim power with the conquest of Banaras and Bengal, carrying Muslim rule to the east coast of India. After the death of Ghori, one of the Turkish slaves, Qutbuddin Aibak, assumed supreme power and became the first real Indian Muslim Emperor and the founder of what was called the Slave Dynasty.

The Slave Dynasty was an oligarchy of Turks which jealously kept the doors shut against the non-Turks. They were replaced by the Khilji Turks who came to power in Delhi in 689 (A.D. 1290). Under the Khiljis the distinction between Turks and non-Turks vanished, and all avenues to power and office were open to Indianized Muslims, converts and nonconverts. They extended Muslim power much farther into southern India than ever before. The farthest southern extension of Muslim rule came under the Tughluqs, who held power from 720 to 815 (A.D. 1320–1412) and pressed their invasion almost to the southern tip of the continent. It was during their dynasty that Timur invaded northern India in 801 (A.D. 1398) and created chaotic conditions which weakened the control from Delhi. The Sayyids ruled for a time after the Tughluqs, only to be supplanted by the Lodhis, an Afghan tribe which exercised authority until they were ousted by the Mughal invader, Babar, who defeated the last of the Lodhis at the famous battle of Panipat in 933 (A.D. 1526).

The Muslim culture in Sind did not receive much influence from its Arab rulers since the center of the Arab Empire was in Damascus and then in Baghdad, so far from the Sind that the Arabs paid little attention to their distant eastern provinces. The chief Arab influence centered in the garrison towns established after the departure of Qasim in an effort to retain some measure of control over the local rulers. The Arab tribes which settled there left some influence on the language of Sind, but little is known about them. After the establishment of the Fatimid rule in Egypt, toward the end of the third century (A.D. 909), Isma'ili preachers began to enter Sind and established a particularly active following. A family of these Isma'ilis, perhaps of the same blood as the Druzes of Syria, founded a separate Kingdom near modern Thatta. Later the Isma'ilis gained a foothold in Multan, which had long been under Sunni rule. The name of the Fatimid rulers was recited in the Friday addresses at Multan and in other centers of Isma'ili influence.

There were several Sindhi Muslim scholars of note in this period, men whose influence extended to Iraq where the people thought highly of their learning. Their judges were also noted for their mastery of Hadith. The school of Hanafi came to dominate the whole province of Sind to the exclusion of all other systems of jurisprudence. Two Sindhi poets, Abul Ata and Abu Zila, attained great fame. The Arab poets were generally bilingual, writing in both Sindhi and Arabic. Some of the poetic compositions of the Sind were transmitted throughout the Arab Empire, and it is related that famous Arab poets visited Sind or sent their poems to the governors there. The development of literature and poetry in India was quickened by the coming of many scholars who were driven from their homes in Iran and Transoxiana by the Mongol invasions. Outstanding among the immigrant scholars was the famous historian al-Biruni, author of the epoch-making *Kitabul Hind*.

Under the Arabic rule the official language used for governmental and commercial dealings in Sind was Arabic. The educated classes used both Arabic and Sindhi, but the common people spoke only their own mother tongue. With the rise of Persian power, the Persian language gained a firm footing in Sind along with Arabic, with the result that modern Sindhi, written in Arabic script, contains more than fifty per cent Arabic and Persian words.

Since no schools are mentioned in the accounts of travelers of that time, it is assumed that there was no regular system of education in Sind other than the mosques which served as centers of learning, as they did in other parts of the Muslim world. Uchh, however, seems to have been a busy center of educational activity, for when it was conquered in 614 (A.D. 1217) it is recorded that the conqueror carried away to Delhi a large number of Sindhi scholars.

The kings of Delhi before the advent of the Mughals were absolute autocrats. Some of them even defied the shari'a which placed limitations on the absolutism of rulers. Most of them, however, respected the religious law and some, like Firuz Tughlaq, went to unreasonable lengths in their orthodoxy. Their relations with the Abbasid Caliphs varied according to the inclinations of individual rulers. Even when the power of the Abbasid Caliph was reduced to a shadow the Indian rulers maintained their allegiance, as is shown by the fact that the Caliph's name was struck on the coins and prayers were offered for him in the Friday services in the mosques.

There were usually two religious departments under the pre-Mughal rulers, each of them headed by an officer of the highest rank whose authority came directly from the monarch. One department dealt with the administration of mosques, the supervision of waqf funds, and financial aid to schools and Sufi lodges. The other was the department of the judiciary, in which the judges followed the provisions of Islamic law with complete freedom from the encroachment of executive authority.

The Sufis generally were favored over the ulama because they kept aloof from politics, while the religious scholars sometimes could set limits to the authority of the rulers. Most of the kings of Delhi were ardent devotees of the Sufis. Two great Sufis, Salar Masud Ghazi and Shaikh Isma'il, came to India in the fifth century (eleventh century A.D.) and won thousands to Islam in spite of the fact that there was as yet no Muslim ruler in India. Another great mystic was Moinuddin Chishti who was born in Samarkand and came to India sometime before the establishment of the Ghorid dynasty. There he laid the foundation of the Chishti order of Sufis, which is even today the most popular Sufi order in Pakistan and India. His tomb in Ajmer is visited annually by hundreds of thousands of Muslims and many Hindus.

The Suhrawardi order of Sufis which was founded in this period differed from the Chishtis in laying greater stress on the observance of religious law. It disapproved of the particular type of music and dancing usually sanctioned by the other Sufis. Two other orders, the Qadiri and Naqshbandi, also gained widespread influence in India in pre-Mughal times.

The impact of Islam on Hinduism made itself felt in the reform movements it inspired among the Hindus in the third to the sixth century (ninth to twelfth century A.D.). These movements, associated with the names of Sankara and Ramanuja and their followers, appeared first in South India as a result of early contacts with Muslims who came to India as travelers and merchants, before there were any Muslim conquests in southern India. It was only later that the reform movements spread to the north where the rulers were Muslim. The early influence of Islam on Hinduism seems to have come chiefly from observing the Sufi practices and the rites and customs of Muslims in their daily life.

The Mughal Period
933 to 1119 (A.D. 1526–1707)

The Mughal period begins with the battle of Panipat in 933 (A.D. 1526), in which Babar's decisive victory over the Lodhis made it possible for him to establish his rule at Delhi. Babar, who was descended from Timur, was a Turk and proud of his lineage. He spoke both Persian and Turkish, but since the Mughals were already saturated with Persian culture before they came to India, it was Persian rather than Turkish which was the vehicle of literary expression. Many scholars and poets from Khurasan and neighboring lands settled in India after the invasion of Babar, and soon the Mughal court became the center of intense literary and cultural activity.

When Babar died in 937 (A.D. 1530) he was succeeded by his son Humayun, a man of taste, of learning in astronomy and mathematics, and the founder of the first schools and colleges in Mughal India. But Humayun's rule was brief, for he was driven out by Pathan forces and compelled to take refuge in Iran. He later returned and reconquered northern India with the help of the Iranian monarch.

The real history of Mughal India begins in 963 (A.D. 1555) when Akbar, son of Humayun, came to the throne. His Persian teacher and guardian, Bairam Khan, consolidated Mughal rule in India while Akbar was still in his teens. Akbar had the genius to attach to himself many native Hindus of administrative experience, one of whom created the Mughal revenue system which continued with some modifications under the British rule. At the beginning of the eleventh century (seventeenth century A.D.) the territory governed by Akbar was one of the best administered in the world and cultural pursuits flourished as never before.

After fifty years of rule Akbar was followed by Jahangir, who reigned from 1014 to 1038 (A.D. 1605–28). Shah Jahan, famous as the builder of the Taj Mahal, was emperor from 1038 until 1070 (A.D. 1628–59), when the control of the government was taken over by his son Aurangzeb, the last of the great Mughal emperors, who died in 1119 (A.D. 1707). Although the Mughal rule continued after Aurangzeb, it was a prolonged period of disintegration, which lasted until the Mutiny of 1274 (A.D. 1857).

It was under the Mughals that Muslim rule in India was finally consolidated. Although some fresh conquests were made in southern India, the main center of Mughal power remained in the north. Since they came from Central Asia, where they were within the range of Turko-Iranian culture, the Mughals had imbibed many Iranian influences. Babar called himself *Padishah*, an Iranian title for king which implied that he was not the democratic chief of a few Turkish tribes but was an autocratic Iranian sovereign. The Mughal power structure rested on a heterogeneous Muslim aristocracy composed of newcomers from Transoxiana (where Bukhara and Samarkand had long been centers of Arabic Islamic culture), of Iranian noblemen seeking careers in the newly conquered country, and of the Turkish and Afghan aristocracy who were already entrenched in India but now removed from supreme power. The Mughals themselves were a microscopic minority, but were able to maintain their control. For a long time immigration from Central Asia and Iran continued—until the foreign Muslim aristocracy in India became Indianized, and then foreigners were no longer welcome.

The Muslim aristocracy was feudal in character, depending on levies enlisted from the middle and lower classes of Muslims, usually of the same nationality as the feudal leader. Thus Afghans would never enlist themselves in the feudal levies commanded by the Iranian Shi'a nobles. In this way separatist and sectarian trends were fostered among the other members of the Muslim minority of India, the people on whom the Mughal power ultimately depended. The Mughal emperor who ruled over this mixed population was an autocrat bound by no law and admitting only the slight restraint imposed by the Islamic shari'a, which was never allowed full sway. The emperor could take the life and property of his nobles whenever he was displeased with them, a thing which would never have been possible under the rule of the shari'a. Thus the Mughal state was in no sense an Islamic state. It was primarily an Iranian autocracy with a few Mongol and Turkish features added.

The Mughal system of administration was patterned on the Abbasid government as adapted to Indian needs. The emperor was the spiritual as well as the temporal head of the state. He had a Vizier, or Chief Minister, aided by secretaries, but no cabinet of ministers. The chief of the religious department occupied an important position as the guardian of Islamic law. He awarded lands and stipends to religious scholars, schools, and colleges and was charged with the duty of helping the needy. The chief judge was the highest judicial officer, overseeing the Qadis and Muftis who tried and decided the civil and criminal cases of the Hindus and Muslims. They were chiefly concerned with the administration of sacred law based on the interpretations of the four Muslim schools of law.

Literature and poetry were assiduously cultivated under the patronage of the Mughal court. Mughal rulers such as Babar and Jahangir were themselves literary men of high distinction, and their courtiers included men of great learning and collectors of large libraries. Persian poetry under the Mughals reached a high degree of perfection with famous Indian poets who could stand comparison with the best poets of Iran. The use of the Persian language has left a permanent influence on Indian languages and gave birth to Urdu, one of the great languages of India and Pakistan today. Historians of this period wrote works which are immensely valuable sources of information to scholars of modern times. Many translations from Indian languages into Persian were made under the patronage of the Mughal emperors, notably the translation of the Mahabharata and Ramayana under Akbar. Akbar's interest in religion was so extensive that he had the Bible translated into Persian for the first time.

The Mughal period was marked by the rise of new religious movements in Islam. At the time when the Hindus were taking to new ways of religious thought, the Muslims were shaken out of their lethargy by the Mahdavi and Roshni movements. Sayyid Muhammad of Jaunpur, who was born about 982 (A.D. 1574), claimed to be the Mahdi, the Expected One. The followers of this movement organized a brotherhood in which all members enjoyed equal rights. At the same time the Roshni movement arose in Afghanistan. Although both of these movements created militant groups in which the leader claimed temporal and spiritual power, they did not leave any appreciable marks on Muslim religious thought. The Mahdavi sect still exists in India and Pakistan as an insignificant minority group.

Much more important were the consequences of the religious controversy created by the emperor himself and some of his courtiers. Akbar believed that he needed closer social contacts with the Hindus, for he was of the opinion that Mughal rule in India could not rest for long on the strength of the Muslim minority unless it had the active support of the Hindus. This led him to adopt many Hindu customs and abolish the customary poll-tax on non-Muslims. Muslim orthodoxy, however, was firmly entrenched and Akbar's new policy started a religious struggle whose effects outlasted him.

After about 983 (A.D. 1575) Akbar began to show unusual interest in religious discussions, largely as a result of association with some of his courtiers who were free-thinkers. Akbar erected a special hall where religious discussions were held with scholars of all views and schools. The controversies could not, of course, be restricted to the differing views of the Sunnis and Shi'as, or the conflicts of the various schools of law. Soon the fundamentals of religion came under discussion and Akbar felt dissatisfied with the existing state of religion. He then began to invite people of all religions to take part in the discussions. Even the Christian fathers from Goa, represented by Aquaviva and Monserrate, came to join this debate, but they failed to influence Akbar. Gradually he was led to assume the mantle of a religious leader. He issued a decree of infallibility which made him the supreme arbiter in matters of religion and then went a step further by promulgating a new religion compounded of Muslim, Hindu and Christian elements. In the new religion Akbar required the followers to prostrate themselves before the emperor and forbade circumcision, prohibited the use of beef, and discouraged the growing of beards. Eighteen of his courtiers joined the new religion but all the rest kept aloof. In the end, Akbar achieved only the exasperation of the ulama.

Akbar's religion died with him, but some of its ideas lived and found an echo during the next two generations. Dara Shikoh, the son of Shah Jahan, was in his early life influenced by the liberalism of the Sufis, as distinct from the orthodoxy of the ulama, and later began to take increasing interest in the Hindu religion. Under his inspiration, several of the Hindu scriptures were translated into Persian, and he was himself the author of many books on religion, including a biography of Sufis and saints, and a treatise on the technical terms of Hindu pantheism and their equivalents in Sufi theology. He also tried, under the influence of the Sufis, to arrive at a synthesis which would reconcile the opposition between Islam and Hinduism. The Sufis, though many of them were orthodox in their practices, verged more and more toward pantheistic ideas congenial to the Indian mind. Their theology provided a common ground between Islam and Hinduism.

Such tendencies spurred the orthodox party to muster enough strength to play a leading role in the defeat and assassination of Dara Shikoh at the hands of his brother Aurangzeb, who was his rival for the throne. Aurangzeb was largely influenced by the religious ideas of Shaikh Ahmad of Sirhind, who played a prominent part in reestablishing Muslim orthodoxy and combating Sufi deviations from Islam. Shaikh Ahmad's son was a close associate of Aurangzeb. The reaction which set in following the appearance of Shaikh Ahmad inspired Aurangzeb to order a codification of Muslim law by bringing together the scattered elements of Hanafi law found in the legal decisions of the Muftis. This stress on the juristic aspect of Islam is plainly a reaction against the deviating Sufis and Muslim free-thinkers whose attitude toward Muslim law had loosened the bonds of social and religious discipline.

The ideas and teachings of Shaikh Ahmad Sirhindi are important in the history of Islam, for he has left a permanent impression on Indian Muslim thought. Shaikh Ahmad, now called the Twelfth Renovator, was born in the Punjab in 1002 (A.D. 1593). After completing his religious education he joined the Suhrawardi and Chishti orders of the Sufis, but later he became a member of the Naqshbandi order. Shaikh Ahmad was quick to perceive the spiritual degeneration which had overtaken his contemporaries, the Sufis as well as the ulama. While the Sufis, under the influence of Ibn Arabi's philosophy, had come to believe in the doctrine of the unity of existence and were prone to abolish all distinction between God and man, the ulama were under the spell of a narrow legalism which led to interminable disputes on minor points of law. Both, according to Shaikh Ahmad, had lost the moral fervor of Islam.

Shaikh Ahmad regarded the Sufis as more dangerous than the ulama for he clearly perceived that all the commandments of religion are based on a distinction between God and His creation. If creation were unreal and God alone had existence, as Ibn Arabi maintained, then the need for religion and law would vanish, and, what is more important, life and existence would become matters of little moment. No wonder that the Sufis sought refuge in the doctrine of annihilation in God, leaving mundane matters to be attended to by worldly-minded men. Therefore, Shaikh Ahmad set himself to disprove the philosophy of Ibn Arabi and put forward the contention that the mystic experience of the unity of God and the world is an illusion. He affirmed the existence of the world as a separate entity which is the shadow of a Real Being. This philosophy was directed against the pantheistic ideas of the Sufis, which were influenced by Ibn Arabi and drew largely upon Hindu sources.

Shaikh Ahmad's writings gained for him a considerable following, both at the Mughal court and in the army. Jahangir for a time took strong steps to check his pervasive influence but, faced with an uprising by one of his army chiefs who was an adherent of Shaikh Ahmad, came to terms with him. It was agreed that all of the non-Islamic practices adopted by Akbar, such as prostration before the emperor and the prohibition of beef, should be stopped at once. Jahangir afterward became a devoted follower of Shaikh Ahmad, and thus Muslim orthodoxy was able to reassert itself after a brief eclipse.

Under the Mughals education depended on private initiative. The emperors and their nobles encouraged education by grants of land and money to mosques, to lodges which served as residences for religious training, and to individual saints and scholars. The mosques invariably had primary schools attached to them. Jahangir promulgated a regulation that whenever a rich man or traveler died without heir his property would go to the crown to be used for repairing madrasas and lodges. Shah Jahan founded an imperial college at Delhi and Aurangzeb founded numberless colleges and schools. He gave extensive grants of land and money to develop a flourishing center of learning at Lucknow. Female education under the Mughals seems to have been confined to rich and learned families, especially the ladies of the royal house, some of whom were famous for the high literary quality of their writings.

Babar brought with him the Byzantine architectural style, for the Turks and Turkish offshoots of the disintegrated Timurid Empire had long been in touch with the Greek states and the Balkan Peninsula. The pupils of Sinan, the Albanian architect famous in the Ottoman Empire, found their way into the kingdoms of the Timurid rulers. But Babar employed Indian stonemasons chiefly. Akbar adhered to the Persian ideas of art which he inherited from his mother and his father, who had lived in Persia, but his Rajput marriages attracted him to Hindu art traditions. Thus the Jahangir Mahal in Agra Fort and many of the buildings of Fatehpur Sikri, his projected capital, show unmistakable blending of Persian and Indian art types. Since craftsmen even from the Far East are said to have been drawn to the Mughal court and some acquaintance with Indonesian architectural styles through overseas pilgrim traffic and trade survived in the time of the Mughals, it is not improbable that Indian and Indonesian Buddhist survivals left their stamp on Mughal architecture.

The palaces and forts constructed by the Mughals are a mixture of Indian and Muslim styles, but the mosques and mausoleums are chiefly Islamic in conception and execution, with the dome and the pointed arch as their most characteristic features. Of all the Mughals, Shah Jahan holds the preeminent position in the history of Muslim architecture. His Special Hall (Diwan-i-Khas) and the Taj Mahal, which is the mausoleum of his wife, are the finest achievements of Mughal architecture. Among the characteristics of this architecture are the lavish use of marble and the decoration of walls and roofs with multi-colored carved and inlaid lacework.

The art of calligraphy received great encouragement from the Mughals, who had many famous calligraphers attached to the court. Even greater favor was shown to painters. When Babar conquered India, the popularity of the great Persian painter Bihzad was at its zenith. His style of miniature painting was the standard which Mughal painters chose to follow. After the return of Humayun from his enforced exile in Persia, the Mughal nobles took the Persian style of painting for their model, thus making Bihzad and his school the example as Persian art was engrafted on Indian painting.

Miniature painting is characterized by its intense individualism which shows no interest in masses and crowds or the interrelation of forms in their infinite multiplicity. It looks at every detail of the individual figure. Since this art form was born in the courts of Genghis Khan and Timur it naturally depicts scenes of battles and the hunt—but chivalry and romance, youths and maidens dallying in gardens, and gorgeous receptions in princely courts are also represented, and of piety and mysticism there is no lack. The king and the beggar were the two poles around which the individual moved. The Sultan of today may be the darwish of tomorrow—hence the frequency of the scenes showing the darwish living in the wild forest or the lonely cave, the darwish as the miraculous master leading fierce animals as if they were lambs, and the darwish dancing in the ecstacy of mystic joy. The supernatural was represented in the figures of Jinn, goblins, monsters, and fairies.

Period of Disintegration
1119 to 1274 (A.D. *1707–1857*)

After the death of Aurangzeb in 1119 (A.D. 1707) the Mughal Empire went into a sharp decline. The various provincial governors became semi-independent, and the extent of Mughal rule shrank to Delhi and the adjoining areas. The anarchic conditions created by warfare among the provincial governors were further complicated by the rise of the Maratha power in the Deccan. The Marathas were militant Hindus in the Bombay province, led at first by the able Hindu leader Sivaji, who formed a small kingdom along the coast. During the period of anarchy following Aurangzeb's death their kingdom was extended by a succession of able Maratha rulers until it became a formidable empire in the Deccan and threatened to engulf the warring Muslim leaders and their nominal sovereign, the Mughal emperor himself. Their power was crushed by the Afghan invader Ahmad Shah Abdali, in 1175 (A.D. 1761).

Meanwhile the English, along with the Portuguese, the Dutch, and the French, had entered India as traders and obtained many commercial concessions from the Mughal emperors. As the Mughal authority declined, the Europeans' factories became fortified settlements to protect their trading operations from the prevalent anarchy and disorder. The acquisition of Bengal by Clive after the battle of Plassey in 1171 (A.D. 1757), in which the independent Mughal Governor of Bengal was defeated, transformed the position of the British in India. They became then one of the many local powers contending for ultimate sovereignty. After the Mutiny of 1274 (A.D. 1857), in which the remnants of Muslim nobility rallied under the last Mughal Emperor of Delhi and suffered total defeat, the British rule was firmly established. The East India Company then gave way to the direct exercise of control by the British Parliament, and India became the brightest jewel in the British crown.

The disintegration of the Mughal Empire after the death of Aurangzeb went on rapidly, but the Muslim literature of this period shows no consciousness of the fate that was overtaking the Muslims. Age-old methods of education and the cultivation of established sciences went on as before because of the large endowments which learned scholars had received at the hands of the Mughal emperors. A significant feature of this period was the rise of the Urdu language and the creation of Urdu literature which took its place side by side with Persian literature. The new language was a combination of Hindi, Arabic, and Persian, its grammar and syntax being based on Sanskrit while its vocabulary was largely Arabic and Persian. Persian still retained its predominance as late as the period of the last Mughal emperor, when Ghalib, one of the most brilliant Urdu poets, still prided himself on his Persian odes and looked upon his Urdu poetry with shame.

Although it was a time of disintegration, the age of decline produced one thinker and scholar of great profundity, Shah Walliyulla (died 1180; A.D. 1766), rated by some as superior to Ghazali and Ibn Rushd (Averroes). Shah Walliyulla left an abiding impression on the development of Muslim thought. Both politically and intellectually the idea of Pakistan owes much to him because from his theories and practical activities arose the tides which were to lead to the Muslim struggle for independence. Alone among his contemporaries Shah Walliyulla was conscious of the period of disintegration through which Muslim culture was passing and recognized the need for a mental transformation to cope with the changing situation. He was quick to realize that the age of kings and monarchs had passed and the age of masses and democracy was within sight. He was conscious of the economic breakdown in Muslim society caused by the luxurious living of the rulers and upper classes among the Muslims. His writings contain unmistakable hints of his antimonarchical and socialistic tendencies.

His first work was the Persian translation of the Qur'an with commentary. Up to that time the Qur'an had not been accessible to the average educated man in his own language. This was a daring innovation in the light of the ultraconservative temper of the times and Walliyulla had to face the full brunt of the public fury excited by the ulama. He followed his translation of the Qur'an with a work on the principles of Quranic exegesis, the first attempt made at the scientific study of the Qur'an. In an attempt to popularize the scientific study of the Hadith, Walliyulla wrote two commentaries on the works of Imam Malik, choosing him because in his opinion Malik's work was the foundation on which the superstructure of Hadith had been reared. His object was to simplify the unwieldy and complex material of the Hadith and thus reduce the conflicts among the recognized schools of Muslim law. Since Malik's writing takes account only of the traditions which bear on legal matters, Walliyulla seems to confine genuine Hadith to purely legal traditions and to treat the rest of the corpus with all its complexities as of subsidiary importance.

In the realm of jurisprudence, Walliyulla's main work was concerned with reconciling the conflicts and differences among the four recognized schools of jurisprudence. In a tract on *The Differences Among the Jurists* Walliyulla shows that the supposed differences are more apparent than real if they are referred to the main source of Muslim jurisprudence, the science of Hadith. In drawing attention to Hadith as the source of Islamic jurisprudence he not only initiated a departure from the accepted modes of juristic deductions, but also gave a new impetus to the science of Hadith and paved the way toward the formation of a new school of thought, known as the People of the Hadith, a school which rejected the authority of the jurists and sought direct guidance from the Hadith in matters concerning Islamic law.

At the same time Walliyulla attempted to reconcile the two rival schools of mysticism, the one pantheistic under the influence of Ibn Arabi and the other which followed Shaikh Ahmad Sirhindi in maintaining the transcendentalism of Islam. The pantheistic school believed in the identity of the Creator and the created, while the rival school held to the generally accepted view that the relation between the two was one of opposites. Walliyulla showed that these differences were trivial and at a deeper level there was much in common between the two schools. It is obvious that he was distressed by the growing disunity of the schools, both juristic and mystical, and by the sectarian conflicts to which Muslim society had fallen prey. He was in search of a unity that could make the Muslims what they were intended to be—a compact body of believers inspired by the unity of spiritual ideals.

The same urge for unity led Walliyulla to write a work in which he deals with the political theory of Islam and refutes the doctrines of the Shi'a sect. The significance of the book lies in its insistence that Islam is not a matter of personal loyalties but a movement in which loyalty to ideals is the decisive factor. This point was emphasized because Walliyulla seems to have felt that the Shi'as had from the outset given a highly personal turn to religion by taking their stand on loyalty to the house of Ali, which logically involved a condemnation of all those members of the Islamic community who did not believe that the succession to the holy Prophet was an exclusive privilege of his family.

Shah Walliyulla's most important work contained, for the first time, the germs of a theory of natural religion which was to be developed later by Sir Sayyid Ahmad Khan, and the beginnings of a revolutionary socialism which was to be used by Ubaidulla Sindhi, who was a tireless commentator on Walliyulla and a great revolutionary leader at the time of the Pakistan movement. Here for the first time is presented an evolutionary concept of Islam. Walliyulla begins with the primitive social organization as the primal unit of social life and goes on to develop four stages of civilization, each rising upon the other and growing out of it. In the first stage man rises above animal life by adopting the use of tools to provide for his basic needs. When he has learned to provide for his primary economic needs he rises to the second stage of social organization, with markets and villages. The third stage is that of city life, which requires a higher form of social organization and brings into existence law and order and government which applies moral and legal sanctions to protect the social organization. Thus morality replaces custom. But the growth of independent cities and small kingdoms leads to frontier disputes, intercity rivalries, and warfare. This leads to the fourth stage, when man is forced to develop international law and international agencies to solve his difficulties.

It is in the fourth stage that religion comes into prominence because city life exposes men to all kinds of temptations arising from the ample leisure and wealth of the richer classes. As the social evils multiply and the exploitation of the lower classes increases, the need for religious morality is recognized and the penal laws of religion come into force. According to Walliyulla, Islam made its appearance in the fourth stage of human evolution at the opportune moment, when the Roman and Persian civilizations had crushed the natural equality of mankind and the exploitation of the poorer classes by the rich had become almost unbearable for large masses of mankind. The entire life mission of the Prophet of Islam was the destruction of the Roman and Persian ways of life and the substitution of a juster social and economic order.

Thus Walliyulla builds his concept of Islam on ideals rather than on personalities. In his writings Islam becomes a social and religious movement arising out of the natural needs of man. At the same time he shows signs of a universalism remarkable for a man of his times and surroundings. He says that the permissible and the forbidden in Islam are equally matched by similar commands and prohibitions in all other societies, for the innate moral sense of man is the same in all religions and societies. He also explains the penal laws of Islam as arising from the needs of Arabian tribal society, and as based on the national sentiments of the Arabs. He repudiates the common misunderstanding that the laws of religion have nothing to do with man's natural reason or needs. Walliyulla likens a moral and religious preceptor to a physician who enforces restrictions in diet on his patients to cure them of their maladies.

Walliyulla's political and intellectual outlook bore fruit in what is incorrectly known as the Wahhabi movement. The leader of this movement was Sayyid Ahmad of Bareli (died 1246; A.D. 1831) who started as a disciple of the Walliyulla family and soon assumed the role of spiritual and temporal leadership. With members of the Walliyulla family as his supporters he toured northern India and attracted large masses of Muslims. Although he traveled to Mecca he does not seem to have made contact with the Wahhabis there, for they were under a ban at that time. He fought against the prevailing practices among the Muslims, such as the worship of saints and other social customs which had no religious sanction. The Punjab was then under the rule of the Sikhs who made life impossible for the Muslims there. Sayyid Ahmad and his follower, Shah Isma'il, who was a prominent member of the Walliyulla family, fired the Muslims of northern India with a burning zeal to overthrow the Sikh power which was suppressing the Muslims and interfering with their religion. After some phenomenal successes with the help of the frontier tribesmen of Peshawar and adjoining districts, the movement suffered a serious defeat due to the betrayal of Sayyid Ahmad by his tribal followers and the disunity of the party caused by minor religious and juristic differences. He and his disciples were killed in 1246 (A.D. 1831), but the movement spread to other parts of India, particularly to Bengal where it led to a clash with the British. Though suppressed by force of arms and economic pressure, the memory of this great upsurge lived for a long time.

After the Mutiny, when the Muslim freedom movement was finally crushed by the British, the remnants of the defeated party sought to revive the Walliyulla tradition and build up a fresh movement for the freedom of Islam. They established the famous religious and educational institution at Deoband which produced many distinguished religious leaders and scholars and still carries on a precarious existence in India. Deoband was really the recruiting ground for a new movement for freedom, with educational activity secondary to their main purpose. In later years it served as a center of Muslim orthodoxy, but it also created religious leaders who did not hesitate to make common cause with the Hindus in an effort to wrest power from the British. Muslim orthodoxy, in general, remained so firmly anti-British in outlook that it could not reconcile itself to the Muslim League politics which it suspected of being pro-British. However, under the growing menace of Hindu communalism a not inconsiderable section of the religious leadership came forward to support the Pakistan movement.

While the Walliyulla school gravitated more and more toward religious conservatism in sharp contrast to its original stand—largely because of its anti-Western bias—and soon became merged in the general Muslim conservatism, a pro-Western group of Muslims was taking shape under the leadership of Sir Sayyid Ahmad Khan.

The British Period and Partition
Since 1274 (A.D. 1857)

Throughout the early British period, the Muslims of India suffered a terrible economic, educational, and political loss, as they were suspect in the eyes of their new rulers and much too conscious of their erstwhile political, intellectual, and cultural superiority to be able to accept their new position. While the Muslims lost in the economic, political, and educational spheres, the Hindus made corresponding gains all around due to their realistic acceptance of the new order and their freedom from a false sense of pride. The British also favored the Hindus at the expense of the Muslims.

A new era of Muslim cooperation with the British was inaugurated by Sir Sayyid Ahmad Khan, the founder of Aligarh Muslim University. Muslims began to turn increasingly toward Western education and the acceptance of Western ideas, even though they had to face the full opposition of conservative Muslims, to whom modernism was anathema. The Hindus, who had become by this time economically very powerful and educationally much more advanced than the Muslims, were not slow to enlist the support and sympathies of the Muslim conservative classes in the political struggle which they were beginning to launch against the British with the aim of gaining political power for themselves. But a large majority of the Muslims, under the leadership of Sir Sayyid, were suspicious of Hindu motives, particularly because of their communal and revivalistic outlook. Sir Sayyid, for that reason, discouraged Muslim participation in the Indian National Congress which was agitating for home rule under the British.

The Balkan wars, the invasion of Tripoli, and the dismemberment of Turkey after the first World War, however, dealt a severe blow to the concept of British–Muslim cooperation envisaged by Sir Sayyid. Muslim feeling was so embittered by the British attitude toward the Turks and Arabs that they increasingly turned away from their own political organization, the Muslim League, and joined the Hindu National Congress in large numbers. With the support and sacrifices of the Muslims, the Indian National Congress emerged as the most powerful political organization and was able finally to obtain self-government in the provinces. In 1937 the Congress formed its own ministries in seven of the eleven Indian provinces, but the Muslim supporters of the Congress were so disillusioned by the short period of Congress rule and its attempts to destroy Muslim culture and the separate sense of nationhood that they began to support the Muslim League.

When the Muslims found that the constitutional safeguards against the encroachment of the majority on the minority rights were of no avail against the formidable power of Hindu communalism, they became vigorous supporters of the Pakistan idea, which envisaged separate homelands for the Muslims in the northeast and northwest of India where Muslims had a clear majority. From the idea of Pakistan to its realization the way seemed difficult, but the justice of the claim was based on such strong grounds that when the British left India they were forced, despite the opposition from all Hindu parties and their own unwillingness, to accede to the demand for Pakistan, which became a reality on the fourteenth of August, 1367 (A.D. 1947).

The appearance of the West on the Indian scene some two centuries ago brought a new force with which both the Hindus and the Muslims had to reckon. Hinduism had already been influenced by Islamic monotheism, giving rise to such eclectic schools as the Sikh religion which sought to unite the Hindus and Muslims. To the impact of Islam was now added that of Christianity and the West. Among the Hindus this led to the rise of the Brahmo Samaj school led by Ram Mohan Roy. Like the Hindus, the Muslims also felt the impact of the new forces. Ram Mohan Roy had his Muslim counterpart in Sir Sayyid Ahmad Khan. Just as Ram Mohan Roy had established a Hindu college in Calcutta, Sir Sayyid established a Muslim college at Aligarh in 1292 (A.D. 1875) which played a prominent role in the struggle for Pakistan. Free-thinking had its start at both institutions. Again, like Mohan Roy, Sayyid Ahmad entered into controversy with Christian missionaries and writers and developed in the process a naturalistic view of religion which earned for him the accusation by conservative Muslim leaders that he worshiped nature rather than God. Sir Sayyid gathered around him at Aligarh some leading Muslim intellectuals who sought to defend Islam not only against Christian missionaries but also against the conservative Muslim outlook which provided the occasion for Christian attacks on Islam.

Sir Sayyid's chief work was his series of addresses written in reply to Sir William Muir's *Life of Mohammad*. In his first address he says that some scholars have likened religion to the prescriptions of a doctor who does not create any properties in the medicines but only points to such as nature has put in them. Shah Walliyulla, he regrets, has rejected this view, but he himself believes in the truth of this simile. He also expressed the opinion that the term Islam should not be applied to those juristic decisions which have been accepted by the Muslim community. Real Islam consists of those clear and specific injunctions of the Holy Prophet which do not admit of differing interpretations. These injunctions are of two kinds—those which constitute the inner core of religion and are in full accord with the laws of nature, and others which form a protective cover to the original commands.

In the sixth address Sir Sayyid clarifies his stand concerning Hadith. He says that authentic Hadith is of three kinds: that which accords well with the Qur'an, that which explains Quranic verses, and that which consists of commands which are not mentioned in the Qur'an. Concerning the last category he says that the Prophet himself made it clear that except for the Qur'an no part of his speech should be treated as a divine inspiration. The divine inspiration, he says, is limited to those matters which relate to the Prophet's religious mission, such as ethical rules and descriptions of Heaven and Hell. Lest this should be taken as a wholesale rejection of Hadith, Sir Sayyid advocates closer scrutiny of the Hadith relating to the personal habits and social circumstances of the Holy Prophet, as well as the Hadith bearing on political and administrative matters. He says that unless there is sufficient reason for the acceptance of such Hadith, we are not bound by any of them.

Sir Sayyid urged the Muslims to develop a new science of dialectics to counter the atheistic trends produced by Western civilization, and in 1292 (A.D. 1875) he wrote a commentary on the Qur'an in which he rejected the conception of Islam as a code of rules and regulations which, he said, cannot stand the test of scientific scrutiny. He claimed that the Qur'an cannot be disproved by any fresh development in the field of knowledge. His commentary produced a sharp reaction from the conservative sections of the Muslim community and spurred them to produce their own rival commentaries.

Sayyid Ahmad Khan was also involved in a controversy with the Christian missionaries which led him to write a commentary on the Bible, in which he showed that many Muslim religious scholars, such as Bukhari, did not believe that the words of the Old Testament and the New Testament had suffered from interpolation at the hands of the Jews and the Christians. This again produced a storm of indignation among the conservatives, who held to the dogma that the words of the Bible had been changed. They were particularly antagonized because Sayyid was attempting to prove that true Christianity did not differ materially from true Islam. But the Christian missionaries also did not like the book because it repudiated the doctrine of the Trinity and condemned the Christians for their rejection of the Prophet of Islam.

Thus Sir Sayyid created a trend in Muslim thought toward the rejection of Hadith and toward a theology based exclusively on the Qur'an, a trend which ultimately resulted in the formation of the school of thought which rejects all other sources of authority than the Qur'an. Walliyulla had already turned Muslim attention to the Hadith as the real source of Islamic jurisprudence as opposed to the decisions of the jurists. Sayyid went further and brought Muslims direct to the Qur'an. He also made a great contribution toward understanding between Muslims and Christians by writing articles which dealt with the lawfulness of Muslims taking Christian food and associating with them in social affairs. It was rather bold on his part to indulge in such writing at a time when the Muslim sense of pride had been so deeply wounded by Western supremacy.

Although Sayyid could not prevail against Muslim orthodoxy, he set in motion a trend of thought which produced free-thinkers like Ameer Ali, whose *The Spirit of Islam* expresses similar sentiments. It is significant that Ameer Ali calls himself a neo-Mu'tazilite, one who believes that there is no inherent conflict between reason and revelation.

Among the colleagues and disciples of Sir Sayyid one of the most outstanding was the historian Shibli, who wrote scholarly biographies of the Holy Prophet and of several other religious leaders such as the Caliph Umar, Abu Hanifah, and Ghazali, thus awakening the Muslims of India to a sense of their glorious past. He laid the foundation of the Nadva, a rival educational institution at Lucknow, because he felt that Sir Sayyid was taking the Muslims much too far from their proper religious outlook, and because he felt that religious education should be combined with secular education. Although it was a religious institution, English and some modern subjects were also taught at Nadva, but it could not rival Deoband which was founded earlier by Walliyulla's followers. It was much less conservative than Deoband, because of the slight secular bias of its curriculum.

Among the disciples of Shibli was Abul Kalam Azad, who soon rose to prominence as a writer of great power. He was a profound scholar of Arabic and Persian who developed a highly ornate style of Urdu prose and edited two weekly papers from Calcutta. This was the period of the Balkan Wars and the invasion of Tripoli by Italy, before the first World War. The atmosphere was charged with anti-Westernism due to the attitude of the European powers toward Turkey and the crusading zeal of the Christian powers. It was natural, therefore, for the Muslims of India to turn away from the pro-Western attitude fostered by the writings of Sir Sayyid and his colleagues. Even Aligarh, the center of Muslim free-thinking, succumbed to the religious frenzy of the day. In Azad, the Education Minister of the Government of India until his death in 1377 (A.D. 1958), the Muslims found an exponent of the pan-Islamic doctrine. Azad's early writings exercised great influence on the minds of Indian Muslims. He created a lively interest in the study of the Qur'an and became the earliest exponent of political concepts based on it. He was also responsible for the later anti-intellectual trends in Muslim thought and the religious emotionalism of the Muslims of India which was not always healthy in its effects. Although he later abandoned his pan-Islamism and became a vigorous champion of Indian nationalism and secular politics, his earlier writings had so deeply influenced the Muslim mind that he could not turn the Muslims away from the paths into which he had led them.

Azad's last work was an incomplete commentary on the Holy Qur'an in which his literary style bloomed in full vigor. But unlike his previous writings, the commentary added further to his unpopularity because he attempted to find a common ground between Islam and other religions. This was offensive to Muslim sentiment because it brought Islam to a level with other religions.

Among those who came under the influence of Abul Kalam Azad was Sir Muhammad Iqbal (died 1357; A.D. 1938), the only philosopher of modern times produced by the Muslim world. It is strange that while Azad, the product of religious education, became an ardent nationalist and moved toward a secular outlook, Iqbal, the product of Western education, grew to be a fiery pan-Islamist and advocated a return to the religious and political ethics of early Islam. Iqbal's poetry is full of the religious emotionalism which characterized the Muslim thought of this period. He wrote his poems both in Urdu and Persian, particularly in Persian because he sought to address his appeal to the entire Muslim world. Among his Persian poems, *The Secrets of the Self* and *The Mysteries of Selflessness* are the most thought-provoking. In these two poems he presents a theory of the self which is plainly a reaction against the doctrine of self-annihilation developed by Muslim mystics under the influence of non-Muslim religious thought.

Iqbal seemed to attribute the decline of Muslim culture to the enervating philosophy of self-annihilation which had led the Muslims to despise the conquest of material forces. He argued from the Qur'an and early Muslim history that Islam is a doctrine of self-assertion which teaches man to work for the attainment of worldly power and to attempt the conquest of the self and the non-self. This power philosophy led him to formulate the ideal of the superman. His idea of the superman is obviously derived from the philosophy of Nietzsche, but it is given a new form by Iqbal who called his superman the Man of Belief. This Man of Belief was armed both with spiritual and material power. Iqbal stood for the fusion of the material and the spiritual and criticized Nietzsche because his superman accepted no moral or spiritual limits to his power. The same union of the spiritual and temporal characterizes Iqbal's concept of the state and, on the same ground, he opposed the concept of Indian nationalism and the secular philosophy of the state associated with it.

Iqbal's thesis was that the spirit is dynamic, not earth-rooted. The spiritual view of life, therefore, repudiates nationalism for nationalism is earth-rooted and is opposed to the principle of movement which is one of the fundamentals of Islamic teachings. The migration of the Holy Prophet to Medina typifies to Iqbal the dynamic nature of Islam, with its freedom from geographical and racial limitations.

Iqbal's only prose work is a series of lectures entitled *Reconstruction of Religious Thought in Islam.* This book shows how much Iqbal had been influenced by Western philosophy. From Bergson and Nietzsche he derives much of his anti-intellectualism, giving primacy to will and conation over reason, while his philosophy of the self is largely based on McDougall's psychology. In giving primacy to love over reason, Iqbal follows in the footsteps of the Muslim Sufis whom he nevertheless opposes for their self-denying and self-annihilating trends. In claiming for intuition a higher place than reason, Iqbal defends revelation, on which all religion is based. However, Iqbal does not repudiate reason in its entirety and even criticizes Bergson for his anti-intellectualism. He stands for the fusion of the heart and mind.

Iqbal was not unaware of the fact that the Muslims of his age were going through the same process of mental transformation that had taken place in Europe during the Age of Reformation. He therefore welcomed the advent of liberal ideas but warned that "Liberalism has a tendency to act as a force of disintegration." In the same lectures he cautioned the Muslims against the rising tide of Muslim protestantism. "A careful reading of history shows that the Reformation was essentially a political movement, and the net result of it in Europe was a gradual displacement of the universal ethics of

Christianity by systems of national ethics." He also moderated his anti-nationalistic views in those lectures when he said, "It seems to me that God is slowly bringing home to us the truth that Islam is neither nationalism nor imperialism but a league of nations."

Iqbal not only prepared the necessary intellectual atmosphere for the Pakistan movement but also played a leading role in the agitation for Pakistan. He was the first leader to realize that no amount of constitutional safeguards would avail against the menace of Hindu communalism and that the only solution of the Hindu–Muslim problem was the partition of India into predominantly Muslim and Hindu areas. Mr. Muhammed Ali Jinnah, hitherto a nationalist, was so much impressed by his discussions with Iqbal that he took up the cause for Pakistan and made it a live issue from then on.

While thinkers like Sir Sayyid and Iqbal were dealing with the problem posed by the impact of the West, a religious conflict was in progress because of the activities of the Christian missionaries and militant Hindu movements like the Arya Samaj, both of them trying to win Muslims to their own faith. Out of the religious and theological discussions between Muslims and the Christian and Hindu missionaries was born the Qadiani movement, founded by Mirza Ghulam Ahmad, who was born in 1251 (A.D. 1835) at Qadian in the Punjab. He proved his mettle in discussions with the Christian and Hindu Arya Samaj missionaries and as a result gained many followers and admirers. Emboldened by his success he claimed at first to be the double of the Christian Messiah, and later—about 1311 (A.D. 1893)—he said that he was the Christ whose second coming had been promised. At the same time he maintained that he was still a follower of the Prophet of Islam and a non-lawgiving prophet, and since he brought no new law and adhered to the law of Islam as interpreted and codified by the jurists, he claimed to be a good Muslim. He also denied that Muhammad was the last prophet, a basic article of faith with the Muslims. As he gained a strong and well-organized following he went further and claimed that a true Muslim must believe that he, Mirza Ghulam Ahmad, was a prophet.

Among the doctrines which caused conflict between the Qadianis and the general body of Muslims was Ghulam Ahmad's rejection of jihad, holy war, as one of the principles of Islam. He stood for cooperation with the British power and would not countenance any attempt to undermine in the name of Islam the British hold on India. The doctrine that the holy war was not necessary was, of course, pleasing to the British since those were the days when the Indian Muslims were carrying on agitation to restore the Caliph of Turkey to his temporal power. Because Britain was considered to be responsible for the dismemberment of Turkey and the overthrow of the Caliphate, the Muslims of India were calling for jihad. But the pro-British attitude made the Qadiani movement unpopular and its adherents remained largely a local group confined to the Punjab.

The opposition to the Qadianis was often most virulent. Even Dr. Muhammad Iqbal joined the fray in his last days when Pandit Jawaharlal Nehru, the leader of the Indian national movement, entered the lists and sought to defend the Qadianis. Iqbal wrote a long letter to the Pandit in which he made out a case against the Qadianis, the main charge being that the Qadianis did not look to Mecca as their spiritual home but to Qadian. They were, therefore, opposed to the spirit of international Islam and belonged to a purely Indian religion. The growing unpopularity of the Qadianis resulted in their social segregation, which led them to adopt an increasingly exclusive attitude toward Muslims in general, sometimes even declaring them pagans. The moderate Qadianis, however, treat Muslims as people of the book, just as Muslims look upon the Christians and Jews. They are now a minority of less than half a million people.

The unpopularity of the movement led to a split among the Qadianis when a group called the Lahoris seceded under the leadership of Maulana Muhammad Ali and Khwaja Kamaluddin. Those two men founded the Ahmadiyyah Association to preach Islam, an organization which is still active. The Lahoris do not believe in the prophethood of Ghulam Ahmad, maintaining that he was a Renovator—but the general body of Muslims do not notice much difference between the Qadianis and the Lahoris, both of whom refuse to intermarry with Muslims. The main service of the Qadianis to Islam consists of their defense of Islam against Christians and the Arya Samaj Hindus and their vigorous missionary activity in Western countries. The Lahoris had a mission in Berlin before the second World War. The mosque in London also achieved some notable results. In the United States the Qadianis have succeeded in getting a few Negro converts. The Qadiani organization is at present controlled from Ribwa, a small town in the Punjab which is peopled exclusively by the followers of Ghulam Ahmad, whose successor, known as the Second Messiah, is the head of the organization.

In the triangular conflict between Muslim modernism, Indian secular nationalism, and communism, another religious and political movement was born, led by Maulana Ab'ul A'la Maudoodi (born 1322; A.D. 1904). Islam was being subjected to the two-pronged attack of the communists and the Indian secularists. The communists prophesied the downfall of all religions; the secularists reduced religion to a few private beliefs and rituals and denied that any social order could be built on the basis of religion. In his autobiography Pandit Nehru declared that there is no such thing as a Muslim culture distinct from modern international culture. What distinguishes the Muslim from the Hindus, he said, is a particular kind of dress and a few remnants of Mughal refinements which will soon be swept away by the scientific and international culture of the modern age. At the same time a few Muslim freethinkers, led by one Niaz Fatehpuri, were attacking traditional Islam and concentrating their criticism on the Hadith and medieval jurisprudence.

Maudoodi took up the cudgels on behalf of Islam. He had been an editor of a Muslim Congress magazine and was recognized as a polished writer, even though he had neither the formal scholastic training of a religious seminary nor the Western training of an English school. He began by publishing a monthly Urdu magazine from Hyderabad in the Deccan. Hyderabad, under the Muslim dynasty of the Nizams, had become a center of Muslim culture and Urdu literature and poetry after the establishment of Usmania University, the first institution to use Urdu as the medium of instruction in higher education. In his magazine articles Maudoodi developed a dialectic which, though it could not silence the triple attack of communism, secularism, and modernism, was yet able to meet them face to face. None of those three schools had produced as able an exponent of their doctrines as Maudoodi. His articles over a period of years exercised great influence on youthful minds and made many converts from the modernists and Muslim communists—but very few from the Muslim nationalists, since they belonged to religious orthodoxy and were not inclined to listen to the young Maudoodi.

Iqbal himself was impressed with the dialectical ability of Maudoodi; it is said that he called him to the Punjab, where Maudoodi settled in 1357 (A.D. 1938). Soon after he arrived Iqbal died and Maudoodi moved to Lahore where he continued to edit his magazine and write books and pamphlets in his popular, lucid style. While still in Hyderabad he had written a book on *Holy War in Islam*, a comparative study of Islamic laws on war and modern international law. He also had written a series of articles on Islam and nationalism in which he denounced nationalism as contrary to Islam, maintaining that the Muslims are not a nation but an international party with a universal creed and a definite social and economic program.

Maudoodi entered the lists against the Muslim wing of the Indian National Congress by writing a book on *Muslims and the Present Political Struggle*, in which he argued so forcefully against the stand taken by the Muslim Congress that the Muslim Leaguers hoped he would come over to support the Pakistan movement. But Maudoodi maintained his opposition to all kinds of nationalism, whether Indian or Muslim. He wanted a true Islamic state, not a mere displacement of Hindus by Muslims. He maintained that unless the Muslims developed a truly Islamic outlook and underwent a great mental transformation, Pakistan would not be Islamic in the real sense of the word. He charged that the program of the Muslim League did not differ from that of the Indian nationalists except that the Muslim League stood for the material uplift of the Muslims while the Indian nationalists worked for the uplift of the Hindus. Muslim nationalism, he said, was no better than Hindu nationalism because its values, outlook, and program were drawn from the Western concept of nationalism and had nothing to do with the international creed of Islam.

In a tract on *The Process of Islamic Revolution* Maudoodi said that a true revolution must be preceded by a great mental transformation and be led by men who believed and practiced Islamic ethics and stood for equal rights for all human beings, who did not exploit the basic emotional side of man's nature for their immediate ends, who did not preach national hatred and economic rivalry, who exemplified in their daily lives the Islamic virtues of piety and God-consciousness. He charged that the Muslim League leaders were utterly lacking in those virtues and that their outlook was purely nationalistic and Western. The Muslim League made the fight with the Hindus a struggle for power, office, and economic and commercial interests. But Islam requires preaching, suffering, and struggle. Unless the issues at stake were ideological and spiritual, rather than territorial and political, the Hindus would feel no attraction for Islam.

A considerable number of Muslim intelligentsia, particularly those who had no deep acquaintance with Western civilization, were so much influenced by Maudoodi's writings that he was able to form a party of his own in 1360 (A.D. 1941). Only those were admitted who fulfilled the minimum requirements of Islamic doctrine and practice, and they had to go through a probation period. Not many joined, but a considerable number came forward as sympathizers.

During the last years of the British rule in India another religious thinker, Maulana Ubaidulla Sindhi, came into prominence. He was born in 1289 (A.D. 1872) in a Sikh family, but early in life he left his birthplace in the Punjab and accepted Islam. He received his education at Deoband and then was sent to Kabul, where he founded the Kabul branch of the Indian National Congress and maintained contacts with Indian fighters for independence who had gone into exile in Moscow and Berlin. He spent some time in Russia and then moved to Turkey, where he greatly admired the work of the Turkish revolutionaries. For a considerable time he lived in Mecca, devoting himself to the study of Walliyulla. Through the intercession of the Indian National Congress he was permitted to return to India while the British were still in power, but he was not popular with the Congress because he objected to the Hindu revivalism which characterized the work of Mr. Gandhi. He believed that India should be a multinational country in which the people should be given the largest possible amount of cultural, linguistic, and political freedom. This was contrary to the one nation creed of the Indian National Congress and its policy of centralization.

Ubaidulla's main contribution lies in popularizing the philosophy of Shah Walliyulla, whom he believed to be the greatest thinker of Islam. Ubaidulla did not gain much following because he was torn between opposing forces and tried to reconcile too many conflicting doctrines. By nature a revolutionary, by training an orthodox Muslim, he yet admired international communism and Turkish secularism and tried to combine them with Walliyulla's program of a religious revolution based on the true teachings of the Qur'an, a revolution which would follow the model of the international revolutionary party built by the Prophet of Islam.

A significant movement which came into prominence some time before the partition was the Khaksar movement led by Inayatulla Khan Mashriqi of Lahore. This was a militant organization which seems to have been influenced by Iqbal's philosophy of power. Its object was to create military discipline among the Muslims, looking back to the early Islamic tradition when every Muslim was a soldier of God. The movement was very popular because of its religious color, military discipline, the habits of simple living it inculcated, the unconditioned obedience to leaders which it enjoined upon its followers, and its utter disregard of rank and riches in the enforcement of its discipline. But the leader, Mashriqi, seemed to have no clear objectives.

The Khaksars first interfered in the conflict between the Sunnis and Shi'as at Lucknow. Lucknow had long been the seat of a Shi'a ruling dynasty before the coming of the British and was noted for Shi'a fanaticism which was much more pronounced than that found among the other Indian Shi'as. Some of their practices, such as their public condemnation of the first two successors of the Holy Prophet, injured the feelings of the Sunnis. The Sunnis retaliated by publicly praising the deeds of the first four Caliphs. This agitation, known as the praise of the Companions, created much Shi'a–Sunni bitterness. The Khaksar leader threatened both parties, urging them to stop the senseless agitation, and pitched his semimilitary camp at Lucknow, whereupon the Congress government of the province put Mashriqi in jail for a time. After he was released it was discovered that a member of the Khaksar party had been involved in an attempted assassination of Mr. Jinnah, which caused a great wave of resentment among the Muslims. The British government suppressed the movement because of their suspicion of its Nazi affiliations, and thereafter the movement died a natural death. Mashriqi passed into obscurity for a time but recently has staged a comeback in Pakistan as leader of a small party which is shorn of all militant aspects.

One of the most influential religious leaders in Sind today is the present Pir Pagaro, head of a branch of the Qadiri order of Sufis. In the past century, when Sayyid Ahmad led his followers against the Sikhs in the Punjab, the Pir Pagaro of that time offered him men and money. This party of warriors came to be known as the Hurs and developed martial traditions. Originally they were staunch followers of the shari'a, but later they developed heretical tendencies—they believed that their leader was divinely inspired, that his word had the same authority as the Word of God. The rest of Pir Pagaro's followers remained true to the shari'a. There are about a quarter of a million followers of Pir Pagaro in Pakistan today.

Pakistan and the Islamic State. Pakistan was created by the Muslims of India who believed that they should form a separate nation because of their history, religion, and culture.

To the Hindu objection that religion could not be the basis of separate nationhood the Muslim League replied that Islam is not a religion in the usual sense of the word but it is at the same time a religion and a social order with a distinct culture of its own. Those of the religious leaders among the Indian Muslims who supported Pakistan did so on the understanding that it would be an Islamic state where the social and economic principles of Islam would be implemented.

The party of Maudoodi at first opposed Pakistan on the ground that the Muslim League leadership, since it was composed of people who accepted Western concepts of social and political life, could not create a true Islamic state. After the establishment of Pakistan, however, they joined with some of the leading conservatives of the ulama and took up agitation for the promotion of a state which they could recognize as truly Islamic. The Maudoodi school by and large agreed with the time-honored concept of Islam as a complete social system with detailed rules and regulations which do not allow legislative freedom to the Muslims except in such matters as were not expressly touched upon by the Qur'an and the Hadith. The Muslim League and Mr. Muhammad Ali Jinnah, the founder of Pakistan, were not altogether clear in their statements as to what an Islamic state should be in the modern world. Sometimes they spoke in purely secular terms and sometimes they expressed the view that Pakistan was created in order to enable the Muslims to live according to the Islamic principles of life.

The Objectives Resolution of the Pakistan Constituent Assembly, passed in 1368 (March, A.D. 1949), stated that all sovereignty belongs to God and that the Constitution of Pakistan would be framed in accordance with the principles of democracy as enunciated by Islam. The Resolution promised that the Muslims would be able to live their lives in accordance with the principles of the Holy Qur'an and the Sunnah, and the religious minorities would enjoy full and equal rights of citizenship.

The Islamic concept of the state has been defined and interpreted in various ways, not all of which are easily reconciled. The religious classes, and particularly the followers of Maudoodi, seem to have a clear idea of the kind of social structure the Islamic state would create, but the secular elements raise several objections to their interpretation. They say that the Islamic state would be a theocratic state dominated by the Mullahs—the conservative religious leaders—and that the shari'a cannot be enforced under modern conditions because the very attempt to enforce it would undermine the economic structure of the state based on modern finance and banking. They object that such an Islamic state would reduce the non-Muslims to a secondary position in the society and would introduce sectarianism in the body politic. It would also, they object, lead to a highly complicated and unwieldy legal system, since not only each religious community but also each sect within the community would have to be allowed full freedom to follow its own laws.

The initial popularity of Maudoodi's party was greatly lessened when he said that the war in Kashmir could not be a jihad, a holy war, because no specific declaration of war against India had been made and all treaties with that country were still unabrogated. A considerable section of the Muslims was alienated from the Maudoodi group when he came forward in support of feudalism. He quoted the Qur'an and the Hadith in support of his contention that Islam never tampers with the rights of individual property in land or industry and therefore the state was not allowed, on religious grounds, to appropriate the lands of the big landholders. His opponents charged him with feudalism. Maudoodi, however, stuck to his concept of a highly individualistic capitalist economy and opposed all tendencies toward the nationalization of property as being against Islamic principles.

Meanwhile the communists had given up open attacks on Islam and encouraged many writers to vindicate socialistic and communistic principles on the basis of quotations from the Qur'an and the Hadith and the actions of the Companions of the Holy Prophet.

Although progressive Muslims in Pakistan differ from Maudoodi, only one group has emerged with a clear-cut school of thought. This group is led by Ghulam Ahmad Parvez, a retired Under-Secretary of the Government of Pakistan, who before the partition published in Delhi a monthly magazine dedicated to popularizing the philosophy of Iqbal. Parvez rejects the Hadith, claiming that it is binding only on those who lived in the time of the Prophet but not on other Muslims. The Qur'an is the final and only authority after the time of the first four Caliphs. The interpretation of the Qur'an must be made by the ruler of the state. "The revival of Islam," says Parvez, "would mean the re-establishment of a central authority, a ruler, who would deduce detailed regulations from the Qur'an in accordance with modern needs and conditions and would enforce the collective obedience of the people."

Parvez combines with this concept of the Islamic state the principles of a socialistic state. He denies that the Qur'an sanctioned individual rights in property. According to him, the Qur'an expressly declares that all land and property belongs to God, and God, in Islamic terminology, is the state.

The denial of Hadith exposes this school to the charge that it breaks up the historical continuity of Islam. By giving the ruler the sole authority to interpret the Qur'an it would bring Islam under an infallible leader who would be, in effect, a Pope. This runs counter to the popular conception of Islam as a democracy in which ijma, or the consensus of opinion of the leading religious scholars, is the final authority on all questions. The Maudoodi school, on the other hand, accepts only the Qur'an and the Hadith as the infallible sources of law and does not regard the decisions of the medieval jurists as binding in all cases. Such legal decisions were, after all, made by fallible men and the community can revise them in the light of the Qur'an and the Hadith. The other ulama and conservative scholars, while accepting the Qur'an and the Hadith, retain their allegiance to the legal schools to which they belong and are guided by the legal decisions handed down by recognized jurists. They do not believe in the right of ijtihad, that is, of individual judgment.

In addition to these influential schools in Pakistan there are prominent individuals who have their own interpretations of Islam which are accepted by their admirers scattered over the whole country. Among them is Dr. Khalifa Abdul Hakim, Director of the Institute of Islamic Culture at Lahore. The Institute has published many books on Islamic ideology and the Islamic solution of the economic and social problems of the country. Dr. Khalifa holds that only the fundamental principles of Islam are eternal, while its specific commands are subject to readjustment. Islam has only set certain goals and pointed the direction for mankind to follow. In the modern world Islamic principles will have to be applied in new ways. The social and economic structure of the Muslim world was largely conditioned by the stage of social development in which it appeared. He also believes in the coexistence of religions.

Another such individual is Vice-Chancellor Allama I. I. Kazi of Sind University, a man of profound learning who spent a large part of his life in England. He has written a very good book on comparative religion called *Adventures of the Brown Girl in Her Search for God.* He believes in the evolutionary concept of religion. Islam, as the latest product of religious evolution, he says, has displaced all other religions, which exist today only as fossils. He also holds very firmly that Western civilization is essentially Islamic since the West has adopted most of the leading principles of Islam and made them an integral part of the structure of modern civilization. He is opposed to nationalism because Islam is, in his opinion, outgoing and expansionist, unconfined by geographical, natural, or racial frontiers.

The clash of Islam with modern secularism is replete with big consequences out of which may come a new synthesis. In Pakistan secularism lacks the attraction which it possessed for the Western mind for it has not grown from within; it has not produced any thinker or intellectual school with a clear-cut secular philosophy. The past hundred years have been the years of secular rule and the religious classes have been out of power. There is no organized church or religious order in the Muslim world which could inspire men with the fear of a religious priesthood. There is much dislike of conservatism and dogmatism in the Muslim educated class, but none of that hatred which led to the Protestant revolt in Europe. Secularism is, therefore, unable to harness the emotional loyalties of the people.

At best, secularism is a negative doctrine in Pakistan which can offer freedom from the possibility of the Mullah Raj, the rule of the Mullahs, and liberation from sectarian feuds. Beyond that it has no positive content comparable to that offered by either Islam or communism. In a country where the last hundred years of foreign rule have destroyed the concept of social equality and intensified class stratification, where a foreign system of education has created a wide gulf between the educated class and the masses, the prevailing mood of the people is to recover their lost dignity and equality. Islam or communism, with their positive programs, can attract them, but secularism cannot.

Even so, the future of Islam is beset with difficulties. Unless the religious leadership gives up its medieval ways of thinking, its rigidity and conservatism, it is difficult to see how the modern educated class will accept its conception of Islam. The conflict must continue until the secular and religious groups arrive at a compromise which accepts the best in both points of view, but this will require a sustained effort to liberalize the popular concept of Islam.

Islam in Pakistan and India Today

In East Pakistan, where the average Muslim is more religiously inclined than in West Pakistan, the influence of Islam has been very strong. The political-religious movement led by Sayyid Ahmad of Bareli lasted much longer in Bengal than elsewhere, but with the consolidation of the British power things began to change. The Muslims of Bengal suffered economically and educationally even more than other Muslims, and the influence of the Hindus increased until they practically monopolized all education, culture, government services, and respectable means of livelihood. The Bengali language also was infiltrated more and more by Hindu mythology and all art and literature was deeply permeated with Hindu ideas. When the Muslims began to develop political consciousness some forty years ago, they attempted to Islamize their language and literature, aided by such leaders as the poet Qazi Nazrul Islam, who popularized Islamic ideas. However, these attempts could not change the literary and artistic trends overnight. It needed the creation of an independent Pakistan to rouse the consciousness of Bengali Muslims. The progress of liberal Islamic ideas is impeded in East Pakistan today by the presence of a powerful minority of the Hindus, the existence of communist fifth columnists, and, above all, by the hold of the conservative ulama, who are wedded to medieval scholastic notions about Islam.

The Muslims of India, after the initial frustration and demoralization which followed partition, have recovered their poise and are gradually gaining in self-confidence. Some competent observers even hold the opinion that Islamic religious life has better prospects in India than in Pakistan. Certainly the religious life of the people has become more intensified. There is a feeling among the Indian Muslims that they have not lived up to Islamic ideals and this has been the cause of their suffering and persecution. Their persecution has created new energy, but it is regrettable that they are still in the grip of narrow orthodoxy.

The agitation for the recognition of Urdu as a regional language in India has so far met with little success. It was once hoped that Urdu might become the national language of India, but since it was a product of Muslim culture the Hindus, under the leadership of Mr. Gandhi, took their stand for Sanskritized Hindi as the future national language. This alienated a large number of Indian Muslims and added force to the Pakistan movement. With the partition of the country, the cause of Urdu naturally suffered a great setback, but the Muslims of North India are very active in popularizing their language and have been able to secure for it at least a regional status. Urdu still serves as a social link between Indian and Pakistani Muslims; poetic competitions are held both in India and Pakistan and Urdu poets from both countries take part in them.

Of the various religious movements in India mention should be made of the Indian counterpart of the Maudoodi school in Pakistan. This party has been very active in post-partition India. Recently its activities aroused the suspicion of the Indian government, leading to a few arrests.

The Tabligh movement was started before partition by Maulana Iliyas and continues to be very active in India. By his exemplary life and preaching the Maulana converted many Hindus to Islam, and today his followers concentrate on preaching Islamic virtues and urging their followers to observe prayers, fasts, and the other injunctions of Islam. They organize preaching groups which visit the villages and go from door to door asking the people to become God-conscious and to offer their prayers with a spirit of inner devotion. One of the most prominent leaders of this group is Abul Hasan of Lucknow who is an able writer and head of the Nadva, the educational institution founded by Shibli.

There is a small group of religious leaders who regard Ashraf Ali, a man with mystic leanings, who was a prominent religious figure before partition, as their spiritual progenitor and the foremost renovator of Islam. This group defends mysticism and is opposed to the Maudoodi school for its anti-mystical attitude.

The Ferangi Mahal school at Lucknow, which was originally founded by Qutbuddin in the time of Aurangzeb and which produced many distinguished ulama, is losing its influence, but the Deoband continues its precarious existence. Many of the ulama of Deoband were vigorous supporters of the Indian National Congress and arch-opponents of Pakistan. Their leader, Maulana Husain Ahmad Madani, is still alive but is no longer as active and influential as before. Some of the post-partition policies of the Indian government have antagonized a large section of those Muslims who supported the Indian national movement against Pakistan.

The Association of Ulama of India, originally a political organization of the religious leaders and firmly wedded to

Indian nationalism, is the most active religous party in Muslim India. It has lately come forward with a definite program for the economic uplift of the Muslims, realizing that a healthy religion can exist only on sound economic foundations. Through its leadership it wields great influence in the Indian government.

It is estimated that about ten per cent of the Muslims of India and Pakistan are Shi'as and the rest Sunnis. Shi'a–Sunni relations in India and Pakistan have not been uncordial on the whole. Intermarriages between Sunnis and Shi'as were usual in the past. The Sunnis are as much devoted to Ali and Husain as the Shi'as. There is even a group of Sunnis which believes that Ali was superior to all other Companions, although it holds them all in deep reverence. On most matters the Shi'as and Sunnis agree. However, the Shi'as differ on certain matters relating to ceremonial worship. For example, they consider it lawful to combine the noonday prayers with the evening and night prayers—but this is a practice which is sanctioned by some jurists among the Sunnis as well. The Shi'as have their own criteria of judgment concerning Hadith since they attach greater authenticity to the Hadith transmitted by Ali and his descendants and followers.

A distinctive practice of the Shi'as is called *taqiya*, that is, the art of concealing one's religious views, for the Shi'as hold that they can lawfully pretend to be other than what they are if they find themselves in hostile circumstances. The Shi'as' condemnation of the first three Caliphs has been a source of friction with the Sunnis, for the Sunnis believe that excellence belonged to the first four Caliphs in the order of their succession. But the majority of the Sunnis agree with the Shi'as in the condemnation of Yazid, the son of Mu'awiya and murderer of Imam Husain. It is a general Sunni accusation that on special occasions the Shi'as indulge in condemnation of the first three Caliphs, whom they regard as usurpers. The act of condemnation is a necessary religious duty of the Shi'as, but whether it is real abuse or only unfavorable comment, it is difficult to say. The more fanatical Shi'as may go to extremes, but the cultured Shi'as hold that the condemnation is no more than what it literally means, the declaration of one's total dissociation from the acts of injustice done to the house of Ali. Modern education seems to have had little effect in breaking down sectarian barriers between Shi'as and Sunnis since, as with all minority religions, the Shi'as take special interest in the religious training of their children.

Even more than Ali, Imam Husain holds the highest place in the affection of the Shi'as of Pakistan and India, while their attitude toward his elder brother Hasan is lukewarm, as he is said to have compromised with Mu'awiya. The tragedy of Karbala, where Husain and his family suffered martyrdom at the hands of the Umayyad general, is annually commemorated by the Shi'as with great religious devotion and has become the central feature of Shi'a religious practice. The celebrations take place during the first ten days of Muharram, the first month of the Muslim lunar year. While the more orthodox Sunnis refrain from participation in these celebrations, the illiterate Sunni masses join in large numbers. Wealthy Shi'a families set apart a special building for the annual performance of the Muharram celebrations, usually decorated with fanciful representations of the tombs of the martyrs, often handsome and costly structures of wood and paper on which great artistic skill is lavished.

The celebrations begin with large gatherings held in the homes of the well-to-do and middle-class Shi'a families. A preacher narrates in dramatic detail the story of Karbala, working up the passions of the audience by dwelling on the most gruesome features of the tragedy and bringing into prominence the cruelties of Yazid and his generals. The audience goes wild with lamentations and shrieks, the more sober confining themselves to shedding silent tears—for weeping is considered to be a meritorious act. This is followed by regular beating of the breasts which is sometimes done so violently that it causes bleeding. Cultured people, however, just pat the breasts with their hands. Women also take a prominent part in these lamentations.

The ten days of the Muharram celebrations are all days of lamentation, but on the seventh day there is a procession to commemorate the marriage of Qasim, son of Husain. The next day lances are paraded on the streets to represent the standards of Husain, and on the ninth day the representations of the tombs of the martyrs are carried through the streets with much drumming and shouting. On the last day the interment in the local Karbala is enacted.

The two religious festivals sanctioned by Islam and observed by the Sunnis are the Id al-Fitr, the Little Festival, which comes at the end of Ramadan, the month of fasting, and the Id al-Adha, the Great Festival, which comes after the pilgrimage. Although many Muslims do not practice fasting, public opinion is generally sensitive to the sanctity of the month. Eating, drinking, or smoking in public during the month of Ramadan is sure to bring heavy censure and in some regions, such as the Northwest Frontier and the tribal areas of Pakistan, it may even lead to physical violence. The festival which comes at the end of the month of fasting is celebrated with great pomp after the public prayers have been offered in the morning.

The festival which comes after the conclusion of the annual pilgrimage is accompanied by animal sacrifice. Recently there has been great agitation in Pakistan about the enormous wastage involved in animal sacrifice and suggestions have been made that the money spent on slaughtering animals should be spent on social and philanthropic activities, but the conservative groups remain unconvinced. On the occasion of both festivals the rich as well as the poor put on their best clothes and exchange greetings with their friends and relatives.

Another important occasion celebrated by Muslims is the Prophet's birthday, although this seems to be a late innovation. It is not sanctioned by religion and was not observed in the early centuries of Islam. However, most people observe the occasion by holding meetings in public and in private homes where poems are recited in praise of the Holy Prophet and speeches are made in praise of his life, manners, character, and work. When the speaker describes the birth of the Holy Prophet and the stories of miraculous events associated with it, the audience stands up as a mark of reverence. There has been some difference of opinion concerning the lawfulness of this practice because the Prophet prohibited his Companions from standing up when he appeared in public. Some hold that the Prophet's commands should be obeyed, but others believe that reverence is more essential.

Another recent Sunni innovation, probably as a reaction to Shi'a practices, is the commemoration of the birthdays of the Companions of the Prophet. However the Companions do not call forth the same amount of devotion as do some of the saints, notably the highest saint, Abdu'l Qadir Jilani of Baghdad, who lived in the fifth century (eleventh century A.D.). He is considered to be a patron saint by a large number of the Sunnis, who invoke his help in case of difficulty. His birthday falls on the eleventh of the month Rabi Awwal. At that time prayers are offered over specially prepared food, which is then distributed among relatives and the poor. This is not as universal a practice as the observance of the birthday celebrations of the Holy Prophet.

A large number of illiterate and semi-educated—and some of the educated—Muslims are also great believers in prayers for the souls of dead ancestors. On the anniversary of death special food is prepared, and after the recitation of prayers it is distributed within the family, to relatives, and to the poor. Preoccupation with the dead is a marked social phenomenon among the general body of Muslims. Those who can afford it build costly sepulchres for their dead relatives and observe the fortieth day of death with great ceremony, preparing rich food and inviting friends and relatives to partake of it. Some of these practices are falling into disuse with the spread of modern education.

While the emphasis on the external observances and rites of Islam is palpably decreasing, Western culture seems to have had little effect on the cult of saints. Even highly educated people, persons who are otherwise skeptical of religion in general, are devoted admirers of saints and believe literally in the miracles ascribed to them. The saints are believed to retain effective power after their death and are credited with the power to heal diseases, to avert calamities, and to bring material prosperity and promotions to their devotees. Most, but not all, of the worship of saints is associated with Sufism. Among the tombs of great saints which attract large crowds are those of Shah Abdul Latif Bhittai in Bhit Shah in the Sind, Data Ganj Bakhsh in Lahore, Khwaja Moinuddin Chishti in Ajmer, Hajji Waris Ali Shah in Dewan in Uttar Pradesh, Yousuf Sharif Shah in Hyderabad, Deccan, and Nizamuddin Auliya in Delhi—as well as those of many other famous saints and thousands of lesser local saints. It is interesting to see skeptics who ordinarily laugh at the externals of religion offer their homage to saints in the hope and expectation of rapid success in their worldly ventures.

There is usually an annual function held at each of the tombs of the saints, sometimes accompanied by fairs. At these functions a number of ceremonies are carried out, such as laying wreaths on the sepulchres, covering them with costly drapes, and burning candles before them. A particularly interesting feature of these functions is the musical party in which professional singers perform to the accompaniment of drums and other musical instruments. Female singers are not excluded, but only one type of music is allowed—music which is considered lawful in Sufi circles.

The people visit the tombs of the saints and invoke their help in their daily needs. Sometimes written requests are hung by the side of the sepulchre, and some extreme devotees offer prostration at the grave—and religious authority is not wanting to support such practices. The more orthodox Muslims, however, condemn such practices as non-Islamic and limit themselves to offering prayers for the dead; and the extremely orthodox Muslims would never visit a tomb, for they believe that once a man is dead his connection with the living is ended forever. Those Muslims who lack devotion to the saints are dubbed Wahhabis by the large mass of the people.

The mosques have ceased to attract worshipers. Only the poor and the illiterate among the people frequent the mosques at the daily services. The educated people, if they pray at all, offer their prayers at home. This is because the religious leadership of the Muslims has passed into the hands of people whose knowledge even of the purely religious sciences is highly inadequate. The educated classes find their age-old arguments and preaching dull, insipid, and unconvincing. The prayers and addresses are conducted in Arabic in a stereotyped form and can no longer provide inspiration to a generation which has no knowledge of Arabic and the traditional sciences. The Imams and religious preachers do not discuss the problems which are agitating the minds of the educated people; they are even ignorant of the very existence of such problems. For them the world is still the old medieval world with its scholasticism.

Muslim youth also is sceptical and finds no guidance from the Imams and the mosque preachers. It is only on the occasion of the two great annual festivals that the people visit the mosques in large numbers and offer their prayers there. It has been suggested from time to time that the mosques should be converted into centers of social and educational activity guided by properly trained and educated Imams, but so far these ideas have not been put into practice because there is no proper organization to look after the mosques and their keepers. At present the mosques exist on purely private contributions and the Imams are paid by the local community—and very poorly paid, with an income less than that of the lowest paid clerk.

Still, the mosques hold great possibilities. No social reform of the future can dispense with the need for this institution where prayers can be combined with instruction. Left to themselves the mosques will remain centers of fanaticism and obscurantism. The government has been afraid to touch this problem lest it be exposed to the criticism of the people who distrust official activity in this area, but some means must be found to organize the support of the mosques and to give proper education to the Imams who are responsible for their care. The strength and vitality of Islam springs from its social and institutional ideals. Islam started as a social order with a definite social and economic structure, but it has become a highly individualistic religion. At this time, when the people are moved by a strong urge for social equality and economic and political justice, there is a great need for a country-wide agency to look after their religious needs and to guide them to an understanding of the principles of Islam.

CHAPTER NINE

Islamic Culture in China

Dawood C. M. Ting

Historians are not agreed as to when Islam came to China. There is no record of the event in Arab history and only a brief mention in Chinese annals. *The Ancient Record of the T'ang Dynasty* notes that in the second year of the rule of Yung-wei (31; A.D. 651) an emissary from Arabia came to the royal court bearing gifts. The emissary claimed that his state had been established thirty-one years before, which would mean that he reached the T'ang court during the Caliphate of Uthman. According to the traditions of the Muslims of China this is considered to be the first time that Islam was brought to China. The leader of this delegation was Said Ibn Abi Waqqas, one of the noted Companions of the Prophet. His party included fifteen persons who had traveled together by way of the Indian Ocean and the China Sea to the port of Kwangchow in south China, going overland from there to the capital city, Ch'ang-an, where they paid their respects to the emperor.

The emperor, after searching inquiries about the religion of Muhammad, gave general approval to the new religion—which he considered to be compatible with the teachings of Confucius—but he felt that five daily prayers and a month of fasting were requirements too severe for his taste, and he was not converted. He gave Said and his delegation freedom to propagate their faith and expressed his admiration for Islam by ordering the establishment of the first mosque at Ch'ang-an, an important event in the history of Islam. This mosque still stands in excellent condition in modern Sian after ages of repairs and restorations.

Years later when Said was advanced in age and in ill health, he received permission to return to his homeland, but unfortunately he died on the way and was buried at Kwangchow. The mosque built at the site of his grave, in memory of the holiness of Muhammad, is still preserved today, the second historic mosque in China. Some of his followers died in China and others returned to their homeland. There is no agreement between Chinese and foreign historians as to whether Said Ibn Abi Waqqas died in China or Arabia. Chinese historians of Islam believe he died in Kwangchow, pointing to his grave as evidence, while Arab historians insist that he died in Medina and was buried there. Chinese pilgrims who visit Medina after the pilgrimage to Mecca are shown the reputed grave of Said there. This point is still in doubt and all that can be said is that one grave is real while the other is only symbolic.

The first Muslim visitors to China came by the sea route, following the example of the visit and preaching of Said and his party which laid the foundation stone of Islam in China. Many Arab and Persian visitors came to China for commercial and religious reasons, both under the Umayyads and the Abbasids. The Arabians who came in the time of the Umayyads were known in China as the *White Robed Tashi* and when relations between China and the Muslim empire further improved under the Abbasids, their emissaries were known as the *Black Robed Tashi*. The Umayyads and Abbasids sent five or six delegations to China, ranging from a few to a score of persons in each party, bringing precious gifts to the Chinese emperors. These delegations were cordially received by the Chinese and laden with gifts to carry back to the Caliphs, indicating the continuing friendly relations between China and the Muslim rulers.

In the century and a half between 31 and 184 (A.D. 651–800) a considerable number of Arab and Persian businessmen came to China by the sea route. Initially they settled in Kwangchow but slowly began to push their way along the coast to the main cities and even as far north as Hangchow. Wherever they went they gathered contributions and built mosques as centers for their religion, mosques which were relatively large and well-built, attesting to the substantial economic position of the traders. Many of those historically important mosques are still preserved, but in some places the converts have dwindled through the ages and the mosques remain today as historical ruins. During this period a growing number of Arab and Persian businessmen settled down in the southern provinces of China, many of them marrying Chinese women. Because of the differences in religion and customs, these people lived apart in their own communities where they could follow the religious injunctions of Islam in their living habits, marriage and funeral rites, and other ceremonies. They had their own courts in which they handled cases concerning marriage, divorce, inheritance, and other problems of Islamic law, evidence of the influence and power of Islam in China at that time.

The Arabs and Persians who came to China by sea exercised great influence in trade with a virtual monopoly of the import and export business. By the time of the Sung dynasty (349–678; A.D. 960–1279) a foreign quarter and bazaar had been established in Kwangchow. The office of Director General of Shipping was created to take charge of the movement of commodities through the port and to supervise customs and other commercial matters—a post which was always held by a Muslim, further evidence of the strength and social position of Muslim merchants of the time.

While the Muslims who came by sea were settling in the south along the coast, Islam was introduced into northwest China by the overland route. For some time the Hsiung Nu tribes of northwest China had caused constant border disturbances. After they were conquered by the Arabs these tribes were gradually converted to Islam. During the T'ang dynasty, in 138 (A.D. 755), Emperor Hsuan Tsung was faced with a rebellion which forced him to take refuge in Szechwan. He sent emissaries to ask for assistance from the Muslims of northwest China and they sent eight thousand soldiers who aided him in his struggle with the rebels. In recognition of their valuable services Hsuan Tsung gave the soldiers the choice of returning to their homes laden with gifts or of remaining in China. When they all elected to remain they were settled on farm land and given eight thousand young women in marriage. Thus they were provided with land, homes, and an opportunity to live in peace and happiness. These new settlers became the founding fathers of the Muslim communities of northwest China.

The improved relations with the Hsiung Nu tribes brought greater numbers of their people into China proper for business, many of whom chose to settle there. Still later Iranian and Afghan traders came through the northwest to Ch'ang-an, continuing the introduction of Islam to China by the overland route.

The Rise and Fall of Islam in China

During the T'ang dynasty (ended 295; A.D. 907) and the Sung dynasty (349–678; A.D. 960–1279) foreign trade grew steadily as Arabs and Iranians took silk, art objects, Chinese porcelain, and other commodities to the Middle East and to Europe, returning with herbs, spices, pearls, and other products of those areas. They became middlemen in a most profitable trade which attracted ever greater numbers for commerce and the propagation of their faith, and as the new traders came to China many Muslim communities were established in the southeast and northwest parts of the country. These Muslim communities became a strong force in Chinese society. Because the Muslims were law-abiding and self-disciplined citizens of high economic status they were received with respect and friendship by the *Han* (Chinese) people and were given the confidence and protection of the government. During the T'ang and Sung dynasties there was no anti-foreign feeling on the part of the government, and the Muslim population was able to increase steadily and move inland. Thus the Chinese and Islamic cultures lived together in harmony and tolerance.

The Yuan dynasty was considered a foreign dynasty because it started under Genghis Khan, whose Mongol forces occupied China, Central Asia, Iran, Arabia, and parts of Eastern Europe. When these areas were divided into various kingdoms, Kublai Khan became the ruler of China and Mongolia, and the founder of the Yuan dynasty. Of the other areas which were for a time under Mongol control, the kingdoms of Central Asia were converted to Islam. Throughout the whole area the freedom of travel maintained by the Mongols encouraged great crosscurrents of peoples and cultures—the Chinese into Central Asia and the Arabs, Turks, and Iranians into China—which brought an influx into China of Muslim merchants and also Muslim doctors, scholars, astronomers, astrologers, and high-ranking warriors who were attached to the Mongol army as advisors, military aides, and staff officers. Although the Yuan dynasty was Mongolian, Muslims enhanced their standing by holding positions of military and civil power, and the propagation of the faith was greatly facilitated. According to the eminent Chinese historian Professor Ting-hsueh Wu, over thirty Muslims were high officials at the royal court in Peking, and the governors of nine provinces were Muslims.

Of the many important Muslims at the royal court of the Mongols, Sayyid Edjell was the most prominent. Rising through a series of high offices, he became Commander-in-Chief of the Mongolian Expeditionary Forces in Szechwan and was appointed the governor of the province in 671 (A.D. 1272). Two years later he was transferred to the governorship of Yunnan where his enlightened and glorious rule spread Chinese culture into the southwest, bringing the people Chinese law, education, and improved agriculture. He did this without prejudice as to race or religion and without forced conversion of the people to Islam—on the contrary, he was the first to establish Confucian temples in Yunnan. Many of the cultural patterns of the present day are due to this great governor whose name is still revered by the people of Yunnan. Were it not for his religion, he would long since have been worshiped in the temples.

The great Iranian historian, Rashidu'd-Din Fadlu'llah, in his remarkable history *Jami'u't-Tawarikh*—the first volume of which deals with the history of the Mongols—tells us that

"China during the Mongolian dynasty of Kublai Khan was administered in twelve districts, with a governor and vice-governor in each. Of these twelve governors, eight were Muslims. In the remaining districts, Muslims were vice-governors." Thus we can imagine the status and importance of Muslims in China during the Yuan dynasty.

The Yuan dynasty lasted for roughly ninety years (678–770; A.D. 1279–1368) until it was overthrown and the Ming dynasty was established. During the Ming dynasty—which ruled almost three centuries, from 770 to 1054 (A.D. 1368–1644)—the Muslims made many great contributions to the life of China, and Islam gained its rightful place as a popular religion.

By the beginning of the Ming dynasty Islam had been in China for seven centuries. The considerable number of Muslims who had settled in China had laid a secure foundation for Islam, but during those seven hundred years the Muslims had retained their alien status as a special class which preserved its own language, customs, and manners and was never fully integrated with the Han people. Under the Ming dynasty, however, with the retreat of foreign influence and the cessation of the migrations, the Muslims in China slowly lost their alien status and became Chinese citizens, and their manner of living was gradually Sinicized.

The most striking example of this process of integration was the adoption of Chinese surnames. Many Muslims who married Chinese wives adopted the name of the wife. In most cases Muslims picked Chinese names which sounded closest to their original names. For example, the surname Ma belonged to a prominent Chinese family and many historical figures were named Ma. Many Muslims whose names started with the letter *M* took the name Ma, partly because of the similarity in sound, and partly because the Muslims loved horses and the character *Ma* stands for horses. Thus so many Muslims of northwest China bear the surname Ma that there is a common saying, "Nine Ma in ten Muslims." The Chinese surnames Mo, Mai, and Mu have been adopted by Muslims whose names were Mohammed, Mustafa, Murad, Masoud. Many Muslims who found no existing common Chinese surname sounding like their names simply used the Chinese character sounding closest to their name—Ta for Daoud and Tahir; Ha for Hassan; Ho for Hussein; Ting for Jelaluddin, Shamsuddin, Ghamaruddin; Sai for Said and Saad; Na for Nasser and Naguib; Sha for Salem, Salih, Sabih; Ai for Issa and Amin.

Muslim customs concerning food and clothing were also Sinicized, but these changes in food did not involve the breaking of religious admonitions concerning the use of pork or wine. In education, Muslim children started speaking Han dialects and reading Chinese books. In a relatively short time the Muslims in China became almost totally Sinicized so that, except for those religious tenets which were retained as necessary to their Islamic faith, the Muslims could not be distinguished from other Chinese. Hence the Muslims were respected and accepted without prejudice and enjoyed equal treatment and opportunities in government, business, and agricultural life. There was very little conflict or friction.

The Ming dynasty may be called the golden age of Muslims in China, for long years of peace and prosperity brought a flowering of art and culture in which the Muslims participated. Prominent Muslims had taken part in the establishment of the Ming dynasty, and later, in the reign of Yung Lo from 808 to 836 (A.D. 1405–32), the eminent Muslim statesman Cheng Ho was sent by the monarch to establish friendly relations with the countries of the South Pacific and with India, Arabia, and East Africa. During the Ming dynasty Muslims continued in positions of power, some historians even going so far as to say that the Ming was a dynasty of Muslims. There is even evidence for the claim that Ming T'ai Tsu, the founder of the dynasty, was a Muslim. It is pointed out that the wife of T'ai Tsu, Empress Ma, was a Muslim, that many of his responsible officials were Muslims, that he never worshiped in a temple after his accession, that he forbade the drinking of wine, that he composed the hymn of praise of one hundred words to Muhammad which may still be found inscribed in the main mosque in Nanking, and that historians mention his strange facial features, which may have been due to foreign blood as a descendant of a Persian or Arab. At any rate, Muslims were well treated during the Ming dynasty and there was harmony between the Muslims and the Han people.

The Ch'ing dynasty ruled from 1054 to 1329 (A.D. 1644–1911). This last imperial dynasty of China was not a dynasty of the Han people, but of an alien minority, the Manchus. The Manchus established by force the Ch'ing imperialism which ruled over the majority of Han, Muslim, Mongolian, and Tibetan people. Their ruthless policy of divide and rule, setting off one group of people against another, meant the beginning of trouble for the Muslims of China. The Ch'ing dynasty, jealous of the influence of the Muslims and fearful of a counterrevolutionary attempt to restore the Ming dynasty, created many incidents to foment anti-Muslim feeling. The Chinese Muslims reacted with violence several times and the Ch'ing dynasty retaliated with their army. Since their armies were led and manned by Han soldiers, these incidents led to Muslim enmity toward the Hans. There were four major rebellions between 1236 and 1293 (A.D. 1820–76).

The loss of life and property as a consequence of these events was severe, and the spiritual and psychological reactions of the Muslims were unfortunate. They developed a hatred for officialdom and the Han people and forbade their own people to study Han books or work for the government. They developed a passive attitude toward life, did not participate in government, took no interest in politics, and derived their chief comfort and satisfaction from their religion. This led to their gradual disappearance from the national political scene and represents the low ebb of the fortunes of the Muslims in China.

With the downfall of the Manchu dynasty and the establishment of the Republic of China, the status of Muslims in China entered a new era because the founder of the Republic, Dr. Sun Yat-sen, in his wisdom and foresight, proclaimed that the Republic belonged to the five races of China—Han, Man (Manchu), Meng (Mongol), Hui (Muslim), and Tsang (Tibetan)—the five great components of the Republic, with equal status. They were like five brothers of a big family, with the Han peoples acting as the elder brother in leading the others.

Under the Republic the Muslims of China once more regained their former eminence. The passing of the Manchus and the tolerant policies of the Republic led the Muslims to regain their faith in the people and to participate actively in the affairs of the country. The Muslims made great contributions both in money and manpower in the revolutionary wars, the anti-Communist wars, and the Sino-Japanese war. Now that China has unfortunately fallen under the yoke of the Communists the Muslims of China are struggling hand in hand with their Han brethren to regain the freedom of the people. When the mainland was lost the Muslim leaders followed the government to the island of Taiwan. The Chinese Islamic Association, spiritual heart of the fifty million Muslims of China, also moved to Taiwan to continue its struggle. The unfortunate Muslims forced to remain in China are, with few exceptions, still loyal to the Republic even though they cannot openly defy the Communists. Their reasons are not hard to find, for the Communists are anti-religious, denying the existence of a Creator, and the Muslims in China have had personal experience of the deceit and brutality of the Communists. When they have an opportunity they will certainly rise in rebellion, but inferiority in numbers and lack of arms make the Muslims an easy prey to the oppressors. At present the Chinese Communists are following the peaceful offensive of the Kremlin, the policy of conciliation of the Muslims as a strategy to obtain the friendship and sympathy of the Islamic countries—but these sly maneuvers will not deceive the Chinese Muslims.

The Muslim Community

There are many conflicting figures as to the number of Muslims in China. The 1948 *China Year Book*, published in Chungking, states the population of Muslims in China as 48,104,000. That official estimate of the government is close to the figure of fifty million which is considered by Chinese Muslims to be the most accurate and reliable figure. Thus, if the total population of China is taken as five hundred million, the Muslims constitute about ten per cent of the people. This makes the Muslims the second largest of the five races comprising the Chinese nation; following the Han race are the Hui (Muslim), Meng (Mongolian), Tsang (Tibetan), and Man (Manchu) minorities, in that order. The recent claim of the Communists that the Muslim population is ten million may be dismissed as pure propaganda. The largest concentration of Muslims is found in the provinces of the northwest and the northeast, followed by Honan, Hopei, and Shantung provinces. In the southwest, Yunnan and Szechwan lead; while in the southeast, in the Yangtse valley Anhwei province leads in the number of Muslims. The coastal provinces of Kiangsu, Chekiang, Fukien, and Kwangtung contain the smallest number of Muslims in modern times, although formerly they had the largest Muslim population. The size of the former Muslim community in that area is indicated by the fact that when the Ming Dynasty established its capital in Nanking there were thirty-six mosques in the city.

According to recent investigations, there were very old Muslim communities in Taiwan, but today only five or six thousand Muslims can be found, mostly fishermen living along the west coast of Central Taiwan. Their forebears presumably came from Fukien. Time, lack of religious leadership, isolation from the Chinese mainland, and Japanese control have reduced this group to apathy. Like sheep who have lost their way and await their shepherd, the only remnant of their religion is their refusal to eat pork.

In the early days the Chinese Muslims were mostly rich merchants; in Yuan times they were high government officials; and in Ming times they were leading intellectuals. In the north they almost monopolized transportation with caravans of donkeys, horses, and camels. Along the Yangtze river and the Huai Ho, and in the provinces along the canal where rice was produced, the Muslims controlled the grain trade and transportation. Evidences of this may be found even today in those areas where Iranian commercial terms and numbers are used in the grain trade, even though the present grain merchants are not Muslim and use the terms without understanding their meanings.

During the Ch'ing dynasty the Muslims lost their grip on commerce and finance. At present the principal trades of the Muslims are the jewelry and curio business, leather-working, the tea business, raising and butchering animals, the operation of restaurants, and agriculture. The collecting of precious pearls, jade, antiques, calligraphy, and paintings is a highly specialized business which caters to royalty and wealthy merchants and requires great skill and experience. At the end of the Ch'ing dynasty Muslims owned nearly all the curio business in Peking and many other cities in China, and even today they are leaders in the field. Recently the Chinese government in Taiwan invited Muslim experts to study the quality of the jewels possessed by the treasury.

In the northwest and northeast of China the Muslims deal in a great variety of furs and leathers. In Yunnan the Muslims are tea planters and carry on a large business with Tibet and Sinkiang as well as with Burma, Thailand, Nepal, and Bhutan. Tea is transported by donkey and horse caravans to neighboring countries over a difficult and tedious route which serves as a channel of trade on the return journeys. The great plain of the northwest is a good place to raise cattle, sheep, horses, and camels, and since that is home ground for the Muslims they have been deeply involved in raising animals. Because of Muslim rules governing butchering, Muslims have become involved in the butchering business not only in the northwest, but in many other provinces as well. But they do not raise and kill pigs.

In addition to those trades which are restricted to limited areas, Muslims have engaged widely in restaurant-keeping throughout China. Their cooking methods are slightly different from those of the Chinese since they use no pork or lard, and their restaurants are always identified by special signs. Many Muslims are farmers, and in the cities there are many Muslim merchants as well as doctors, engineers, lawyers, teachers, and public workers. Due to their interest in brave deeds, Muslims frequently join the army and follow careers as soldiers and officers. A Muslim will not take a job as a barber, or perform other personal services such as cutting toenails or massaging. Nor will Muslim girls become prostitutes. If a Muslim girl should fall into bad company the local service committee of Muslims would buy her freedom right away and remarry her—an evidence of the well-organized and closely cooperative Muslim community.

CHINESE MUSLIM CUSTOMS. Chinese Muslim customs are very different from those of the Han, Manchu, Mongol, and Tibetan peoples. This is due to the special ideals of Islam which result in customs different from those of people who come close to believing in no God—such as Confucianists and Taoists—or of those who believe in many gods, as do the Buddhists. Although other religions pay no attention to such matters, the rules of Islam forbid the eating of pork, certain sea foods, dead animals, blood, or anything not killed according to the Islamic method, and Muslims must obey. Special customs naturally developed under such circumstances.

To solve many living problems, separate residential areas for Muslims and for Hans were created in large cities where Muslims were dominant. Whether or not the Muslims live in separate quarters there are differences in the homes which are recognizable. At the Chinese New Year the Hans decorate their homes with a pair of door gods on each side of the door and paste posters by the door frames. Muslim residences do not have anything on their doors; they are well-kept, clean, and natural in appearance. In Han homes, you find the gods, the ancestors, and the Heaven and Earth Emperor in their proper place in the living room, with incense burning all year round. There is no such thing in Muslim homes. At the four seasons festivals the Han people hang certain herbs in their homes, but the Muslims never do. Most Muslims have had bathrooms in their homes in order to perform their religious rites, but few Han people had bathrooms; they usually used wooden tubs for bathing. Modern construction and living customs have brought bathrooms to the Hans, so outward differences seem to be decreasing.

The clothing of Chinese Muslims is similar to that of the Chinese except for a few tribes like the Uighurs of Sinkiang and the Kazakhs of the northwest. There are still some differences, however. In the northwest Muslim women wear a face veil when they go out, and in some provinces women wear a turban. Muslim men in the northwest provinces wear flat white hats and men in Sinkiang have colorful embroidered small hats. Some wear white cotton or yellow silk turbans. Muslims in other provinces put on a flat white hat when they attend the weekly service in the mosque. Men, especially religious leaders, generally do not wear silk since it was forbidden by the Prophet as a means of preventing luxurious habits and maintaining the heroic nature of men. Women are allowed to wear silk. Muslim children do not wear a necklace or the "one hundred families" locket which is used in the superstitious belief that it protects children from the devil. Instead of the prayer for longevity around hats, Muslims decorated hats with the Word of Witness in Arabic. Since white stands for purity the Muslims love to use white material for clothing, and because Muhammad's favorite color was green the Muslims like to use green also. Muslim men did not wear the long hair of the Manchu period and Muslim women did not bind their feet. Muslims in the interior parts of China, where they are in a minority, tend to follow the common practices of their communities.

Islam, for hygienic reasons and in order to form kind and good habits, forbids Muslims to eat pork, animals dead by themselves, animals not killed by Muslims, blood, food given to gods, snakes, poultry which eats meat, and sea food not shaped like a fish, and forbids smoking, drinking, and the use of narcotics. Because of these laws concerning food, Muslims are very careful at home and when they are traveling. It was customary for local governments to provide a certain ratio of cows and sheep monthly to the Muslim community and Muslim butchers prepared the meat. Even chickens and ducks must be taken to the mosques to be killed unless there is someone in the family who knows how to do it properly.

In Muslim restaurants there is no trace of pork, of course, but wine is tolerated because of the many non-Muslim customers. The wine is always served in special cups which can be kept separate. Because Han Chinese love to eat pork and lard the Muslims are very careful not to eat anything cooked by Hans, such as candy, bread, and pastries. In a Muslim community the Muslims have their own stores, bakeries, and restaurants where vegetable oil is used for cooking so everything is pure and fragrant. Non-Muslims also like the foods prepared by Muslims. Fried dumplings are a very common and popular form of dessert. They are made of flour shaped into a ball, flavored either salty or sweet, and fried in vegetable oil. They are served on many occasions in the home—to remember dead relatives, to treat friends after worshiping in the home, and to give to friends. No one knows the origin of this food, but it is very popular.

When traveling in the northwest and Yunnan, Muslim traders customarily formed caravans for mutual help and for convenience in cooking food and worshiping together, but in China proper there was no need to form groups for travel. There are no superstitious preparations before traveling among Muslims, such as the custom of choosing a lucky day to travel by the use of diagrams or by drawing lots. Many Muslims take their own cooking utensils with them to prepare their own food. When they come to a town the first thing they do is to locate a mosque to decide where to stay for the night, for the mosques serve as service centers where the traveler always gets help no matter who he is or where he comes from. Timely aid and brotherly cooperation help to solve difficulties and serve as consolation and inspiration to travelers.

Two kinds of Muslims live in China, the so-called Turbanded Muslims of Sinkiang and the Han Muslims of China proper. In Sinkiang they speak Turkish and most of them can also speak the Kansu dialect. The Han Muslims speak Mandarin and local dialects. But Arabic and Iranian terms, especially Iranian, are used for religious purposes in a mixture which is hard for non-Muslims to understand. There is another secret dialect which is used by some Muslims. Some Muslims who speak Chinese but do not write it use Arabic letters to spell Chinese words.

Muhammad said to his followers, "Teach your children riding, archery, and swimming." All three were necessary for military training in the old days and are still useful as exercise and for sport in modern times. In the Chinese northwest where the Muslims are good at riding and archery because of their surroundings many of the Muslims recruited for the cavalry learned these skills. Chinese Muslims also like swimming, wherever water is available, and for generation after generation they have participated in boxing as a favorite sport.

Islam and Confucianism, Taoism, and Buddhism. China did not produce any religion of her own. Confucianism and Taoism are schools of philosophy and political theory, not religions. The religions of China—Buddhism, Islam, and Christianity—were imported and allowed to grow freely and peacefully.

Confucius, the great politician, great philosopher, and great educator, did not claim to discover his teachings but said that his ideas came from good and wise scholars of ancient times. "I teach but do not invent," he said. "I believe in the ancients." Confucianism is concerned with the principles of human relations but not with the universe. Confucius taught that to develop good relations between man and man one must start with oneself—therefore he emphasized self-sacrifice, good manners, cultivating oneself, and trust and reconciliation in relations with others. He stressed loyalty to the ruler and the nation as the path which would lead to utopia. Confucianism has a perfect ethical system based on the five human relations; it teaches that man should faithfully search for reason for human actions and should refine and control himself; should carry on his ancestral traditions and teach them to succeeding generations; should die to preserve his virtue; and should be just without partiality. There are eight virtues, with filial piety ranking first, followed by the subordination of younger to older brothers, loyalty, sincerity, propriety, morality, modesty, and a sense of shame. All of these principles of Confucianism go very well with Islam but they are insufficient because they are related only to material human existence, and Islam goes further and searches the universe. Confucius refused to answer any questions concerning the future. "Since you do not know life," he said, "how do you know death?" Thus we see that he had an ethical philosophy, but not a religion.

Originally Taoism was also a body of philosophical ideas and political theories but not a religion. In Lao Tzu's *Tao Te Ching* the fundamental theory in political relations is "to follow nature in order to obtain perfection," and to follow the principle of "noninterference." Everything is to be allowed to follow its own course. Proper relations between man and man can be attained only by suppression of self and abolition of hatred—which can be achieved by eliminating desire. Lao Tzu says, "To stop competition, do not honor virtues; to halt stealing, do not value rare objects; and to obtain a peaceful mind, do not develop craving." The philosophy of Lao Tzu is quite similar to Sufism in Islam. Islam agrees with his doctrine of the suppression of self and of enmity. In Islam the purpose of the five daily prayers and the month of fasting is to purify oneself and to decrease desires as a means to the practice of self-control.

Confucianism and Taoism both created temples where images are worshiped—which is contrary to Islam, for Islam believes in only one God, without form or likeness. So Islam has no intercourse with Confucianism and Taoism but has great respect for Confucius and Lao Tzu as Chinese prophets. In the Qur'an God says, "I have sent native prophets to each race to influence and to teach." Lao Tzu and Confucius were before the Prophet Muhammad, therefore they were prophets sent by God to the Chinese race.

When Buddhism came to China it was easy for the people to accept it because many of its teachings coincided with Confucianism and Taoism. It gained the confidence and protection of the ruling class for generations, and the great books of Buddhism were carefully translated by many first-rate scholars. Buddhism also penetrated to the Chinese public and profoundly influenced the literature and art of China. Its contribution to Chinese literature and art has not been equalled by either Islam or Christianity. There was no relation between Buddhism and Islam because the Buddhist belief in passiveness, in idols, and in rebirth is absolutely contrary to Islam. True Muslims studied the books of Confucius and Lao Tzu, but very few touched the Buddhist classics.

The Muslims of China lost connections with other Muslim countries for a long time and were influenced unconsciously by Confucianism and Buddhism in several ways—for instance, they call the worship place *shih*, the Buddhist word for temple, rather than *mosque* as in Islamic countries. The mosques constructed in China look exactly like Confucian and Buddhist temples from the outside. The responsible personnel in the mosques held ranks similar to those of the head priest, priest, and monk in Buddhist temples and lived in the mosque and received alms and performed all religious duties. At a wedding or a funeral the religious leaders of Islam were asked to say prayers and recite passages, just as the Buddhist monks did in the temples. Just as the Buddhists emphasized silence and meditation, so also the Sufis among the Muslims stressed similar practices and shared the belief that meditation would finally give power to perform miracles. The men who gained such powers were called Shaikhs by the Muslims. The Shaikhs and Buddhist monks often had contests in magic, which the Muslims frequently won.

The good characteristic of the Chinese, summarized in the phrase "to let live," paved the way for all religions in China. In recent years the four great religions of China—Buddhism, Catholicism, Protestantism, and Islam—founded a "Religious Friends Association" to unite in the fight against communism.

Religious organization of Chinese Muslims. Mosques in China, as centers for spiritual inspiration and social activities, are used as a place of worship, prayer, and chanting—and also used as a meeting place, a school, a place to perform Islamic ceremonies, a funeral home, and a judicial court. In former times there were women's mosques in some parts of China, used as religious and charitable centers for women and led by women religious teachers. Now both men and women share the same mosque but meet in different rooms for praying and religious rituals, coming together for discussions and conferences. In appearance the mosques look like Confucian or Buddhist temples because during the monarchic period no foreign-style buildings were allowed. The graceful domes and pointed minarets which characterize the stone mosques of other countries are not found in the wooden mosques of China. The interior of Chinese mosques is divided into a lecture hall, a dormitory, conference rooms, the office of the leaders of the mosque, a bathroom, and the "dead man's room" for washing the deceased. The endowments of the Chinese mosques are held chiefly in real estate. The yearly income of some mosques is more than enough to support a technical college or a light industrial factory, but because there is no central organization—such as a Ministry of Waqfs—to look after the budget, much that could be done to advance the cause of Islam is not accomplished.

The chief religious leader in the mosque is called the Ahund (or Ahung), which means scholar, or teacher of religion. He is assisted by the Imam whose duties are to lead the congregation in worship and in prayers. The Khatib preaches at the Friday service, which is usually of a religious nature but is also sometimes political, and is also responsible for religious ceremonies in engagements and weddings. The mu'ezzin gives the call to prayer five times a day. There is also in some mosques an "unclassified Ahund" who knows some Arabic and has a little training in religion but is not sufficiently educated to be a real Ahund. He is responsible for chanting, praying, and arranging funerals. The educational activities of the mosque are cared for by the Ahund. The administration of the income and property of the mosque is the responsibility of a committee of from three to seven members who are elected for a year and serve without pay.

The Muslims of China are all Sunnis and followers of the school of Hanafi in jurisprudence. They differ from other

Muslims in some details—notably in the chanting of the Qur'an—because Chinese Muslims lost contact with other Muslim countries due to difficulties of communications. During the long period of isolation when few of the Ahunds could read either Chinese or Arabic, the practice of handing down the teachings orally led to misinterpretation of doctrines and the development of different circles in the Muslim community. With the coming of the Republic it became possible to take the water route to the Middle East, and many Muslim scholars made the pilgrimage to Mecca and visited the educational organizations in Egypt and Turkey. They were inspired by what they learned and brought back many books which served as the basis for careful studies of the fundamentals and consequences of Islam. As a result a great cry for reform was raised. The Muslim community was divided, with one side favoring reforms and becoming known as the New Sect, and the other opposing changes and known as the Old Sect. Each side suspected the other and accused it of heresy. It was a shame to have such a break develop.

The New Sect was limited to a few large cities while the Old Sect was dominant throughout the rest of China. As communications improved and the number of pilgrims to Mecca increased, many more Ahunds and intellectuals recognized the differences between Chinese and other Muslims and the New Sect grew in strength. Before the end of the Sino-Japanse war the Old Sect died a natural death and the problem of half a century was solved without a break. The struggle between the Old and New Sects made Islam a laughing stock in China, for the differences were not over fundamentals but over trivial matters. A listing of some of those differences gives an illuminating picture of the problems faced by Chinese Muslims after the restoration of communication with the rest of the Islamic world.

It was customary in the old days to give a Qur'an to those who attend a funeral, as atonement for the deceased, but the New Sect said that only cash should be given; actually, only God can forgive and neither the Qur'an nor cash should be given for atonement. The Old Sect followed the Chinese tradition of wearing white mourning garments, while the New forebade wearing special clothes of mourning; Islam has no rules governing this custom. During Ramadan, on the twenty-seventh night, the Old Sect bowed one hundred times, but the New Sect did not. It was formerly the custom to give money to the leader after chanting and praying, but the New Sect opposed the custom. The New Sect introduced the custom of pointing the forefinger in the middle of worship to indicate that God is One. The New Sect also insisted that the style of chanting the Qur'an should conform to the standard of other Muslim countries. There were also differences as to the proper way to kill poultry, and the New Sect insisted that on the basis of the Hadith it is permissible to eat crabs but not seals or dolphins. These are indicative of the differences between the sects.

Except for those minor differences, there was only one sect which was a disturbing element in China, the *Jahriyah*, a word which means to pray aloud. The Jahriyah was originally a Sufi sect whose ritual included the practice of praising God aloud in a high voice. The members of the sect gather in a circle, holding hands and praying so loudly that they can be heard outside the mosque. Following their leader, they start by turning the body to the left, then to the right, with their feet moving lightly, their eyes closed, their heads shaking as they walk and chant. The chanting goes faster and faster with the bodily movements keeping pace with the tempo of the chanting. Finally they are chanting only one phrase—Allah, Allah, Allah, Allah—and they keep on until they are too tired to continue. Some even faint. That is why the Chinese call the Jahriyah the "shaking head" religion.

The headquarters of this sect was originally in Kansu province under a leader whose position was hereditary. In the great earthquake of 1338 (A.D. 1919) their leader was killed, and his followers spread to Sinkiang, the northwest provinces, Shantung, and Yunnan. Because of the peculiar customs of the Jahriyah sect, which are judged to be superstitious, they are regarded as heretical by the other Muslims. The result has been bad relations between the Jahriyah sect and other Muslims which have caused frequent conflicts and have even led to killing. The members of this sect are striving for virtue, but not many have arrived there. Beside this sect there are no other Sufi sects in China, although there are Muslims with Sufi tendencies.

Since the founding of the Republic there have been three organizations which sought to unite all the Muslims of China for the good of Islam. The first of these was the Muslim Progressive Society of China which was founded in Peking in 1332 (A.D. 1913) by Ahund Wang Hao-nan after his pilgrimage to Mecca and his visits to Turkey and Egypt. Inspired by the new ideas aroused during the Chinese revolution and by the cultural advancement he had seen in other Muslim countries, he felt deeply the need for education among the Chinese Muslims. Therefore, he founded a national organization to unite the manpower, material strength, and talents of the Muslim community to raise their standard of living and improve the level of education. His proposal was enthusiastically accepted. His first aim was to add a few hours of teaching in Arabic and Islamic interpretation to the instruction in the elementary schools in the mosques. Although his aims were purely religious, political interests penetrated the movement and the united Muslims showed strong potential political power. But three years after the movement was started the organization was ill-used by Yuan Shih-kai in an attempt to become emperor, and when he was defeated the organization disappeared.

The Chinese Muslim's Association was founded in 1357 (A.D. 1938) at the start of the Sino-Japanese war when the Central Government ordered a Muslim general in the armed forces to form a nationwide organization which would unify the Muslims of China in support of the government and obtain support from Muslim countries. This is the only Muslim organization initiated by the government in Chinese history. Its five thousand local units carried on both religious and political activities. During the war it united Muslims in the fight against the Japanese. It trained more than two thousand men in its military academy for service in the armed forces and organized visiting committees in the northwest to give medical aid and comfort to wounded soldiers and officials. In the field of education it established a religious research committee to translate the Qur'an and print religious books and pamphlets, and it established schools in the northwest and gave scholarships which enabled outstanding Muslim students to study in the universities of Turkey and Egypt. Three different times it sent delegations to Southeast Asia and the Middle East to stimulate friendship and understanding and to encourage cultural exchange. When the constitutional government was established by the Republic of China it represented the Muslim people as one of the five races of China.

A third national organization was the Muslim Literary Society of China, founded in 1345 (A.D. 1926) in Shanghai by Hajji Jelaluddin Ha Teh-cheng, a famous scholar who had studied in India and Egypt and knew Arabic, Persian, Urdu, and English. The Society was organized to encourage scholarly study of the Qur'an and Hadith, to improve and extend Islamic education, to increase cultural exchanges with Muslims of other countries, and to improve the social position of Muslims in China. It avoided politics. One of its first undertakings was the translation of the Qur'an into Chinese, using Chinese quotations and literary language—a task which is unfortunately unfinished due to the outbreak of the Sino-Japanese war. The Society published the *Chinese Muslim Monthly*—later changed to a quarterly—and gave public lectures and courses on Islam as part of its educational program. It established a normal school and a primary school, constructed a Muslim library and public reading room, assisted Muslim students in Shanghai universities, and provided scholarships for promising young men and women.

CHINESE MUSLIM RELIGIOUS PRACTICES. Muhammad taught that Islam is based on the Five Virtues, the Five Pillars, which are the repetition of the Word of Witness, praying, fasting, almsgiving, and pilgrimage. Every Muslim, man or woman, must chant the Ching Tseng Yen and Tso Chung Yen once in his or her life. The Ching Tseng Yen is, "All things are not

God. Only Allah is the God. Muhammad is God's special Prophet." The Tso Chung Yen is, "I witness that all things are not God. Allah is the only One. I also witness that Muhammad is God's Messenger and His Prophet." In the early days the Muslims of China knew Arabic and could chant in Arabic, but because of the unstable times they lost the ability and today less than twenty per cent of the people can chant in the original language. Now they chant in Chinese. Very few people in China can read the Qur'an in Arabic.

In the beginning the Chinese Muslims were very serious about practicing the five daily prayers, but in recent years, due to the influence of materialism, unsettled conditions, difficulties of obtaining a livelihood, and the distance from mosques, only the Ahunds and country people of strong faith observe the five daily prayers. Others observe only two or three prayers and make the rest up at home and others go to the mosque only for the Friday service, but the largest group go to the mosque only for the two great festivals. Some Muslims never go to the mosque except for a relative's funeral and then they disappear as soon as the ceremonies are finished; this is a large group. Not many men go to the mosque to worship and even fewer women go.

Fasting during the month of Ramadan changes the daily schedule of the people throughout the whole Muslim world, and so it used to be in China. There are several kinds of fasting observed by Muslims in China—some keep the whole month, some fast on the first ten days or the last ten days, some observe only the Gadar fast which begins on the twenty-seventh night. When Ramadan is a thirty-day month there are three full days of fasting, but when it is a twenty-nine day month there are only two days. This is not the right way, since the Holy Command is for a full month of fasting. Of course, even two or three days of fasting shows that the person has an interest in religion, but if the full thirty days is interrupted it should be made up later.

Almsgiving, zakat, is the requirement that two and one-half per cent of the total yearly income should be given to charity. It is the duty of rich people. Some Chinese Muslims are rich but most of them are poor, and some are very poor, so more people would receive zakat than would give it. Many of those who can afford to give alms lack any interest in religion and are misers so actually their giving approaches the zero point. This is true in every country of the Muslim world. Zakat is a special characteristic of Islam which encourages social cooperation, helps to balance the rich and the poor, stabilizes society, and is the best weapon against communism. Unfortunately, religious leaders do not seem to recognize the importance of zakat, and political leaders in the Muslim world do not seem to have much interest in religious teaching, especially in almsgiving. Now that we are facing the pressure of communism we ought to wake up and rethink the importance of zakat.

The pilgrimage to Mecca is such a long trip and so costly that very few Chinese are able to go. Before the second World War not more than two or three thousand were able to make the pilgrimage each year, chiefly from the northwest and Yunnan. Some went by boat from Shanghai or Hong Kong to Jidda, while others went overland to India and then by boat. After the mainland was locked behind the iron curtain Chinese Muslims were not allowed to leave the country, so the number of pilgrims in recent years has been quite small. Recently when a Muslim committee from Free China visited Mecca the first question asked by King Saud of Saudi Arabia was why no Chinese Hajjis had come from the mainland in the last few years. When he learned that the Communists would not allow them to make the pilgrimage he expressed his pity and prayed God to help all Chinese Muslim brothers to be free men. There are now about fifteen thousand Chinese Hajji refugees in Saudi Arabia, all strong anti-Communists. The Saudi government, guided by the spirit of Islam which recognizes all Muslims as one family, allows the refugees to live there and to support themselves.

Marriage ceremonies may differ in Muslim countries according to local customs, but the basic principles of Islam must be obeyed: the bride and groom must be of the same faith, consent must be given by both parties, there must be two witnesses, and betrothal money must be paid by the man's family. Chinese Muslims have been so scattered that each province adopted its own customs, with only the Muslims in the northwest able to keep close to Muslim practices. A Chinese Muslim wedding is very complex, but it avoids all superstitions such as the reading of the horoscopes of the betrothed persons. Some ask the Ahund to read the Arabic wedding rite on the wedding day or the day before. If one of the parties is not a Muslim, the Ahund admits that one into Islam one or two days before the wedding so both may be of the same faith. Betrothal money was not taken seriously since it looked like a business transaction. Now it is customary to give clothing or jewelry, or a small amount of money is given and looked upon as only a symbol. Marriage is based on love, which shows that Chinese Muslims are comparatively progressive. This change should be introduced to other Islamic countries as a means of solving the problem of the decrease in marriage due to the heavy betrothal price.

The old type of Chinese wedding ceremony is now out of date except among poor people in the country. According to the old custom the parents of the concerned parties monopolized the whole affair. The new type follows the teaching of Islam and gains the consent of both parties. Islamic wedding customs are progressive and rational and at the same time are timeless, for they follow rules laid down more than thirteen hundred years ago. Emphasis on agreement between both parties, especially the consent of the girl, shows the Islamic stress on the rights of men and the protection of the rights of womanhood.

The ceremonies of engagement and marriage are quite similar for Chinese Muslims and non-Muslims except that the Muslims celebrate the event with a religious and a general ceremony, and they do not use old Chinese music or gongs or fire crackers since they consider them to be superstitious. The religious ceremony is held a day before or just preceding the general ceremony. At present Muslims hold the marriage ceremony in the mosque. In modern times Western music has been adopted for marriages since it is not associated with the worship of other gods. Chinese Muslims obey the Civil Law of China by practicing monogamy almost everywhere except in the frontier provinces. There is no Muslim court to take care of divorce, adoption, and inheritance, as in other Muslim countries; all these matters are now handled in the general courts.

The Chinese Muslims follow Islamic rites strictly in the funeral but follow Confucianism in mourning and in dressing because of its fitness in the surroundings. When a sick person reaches his last moments of life the family ought to keep calm so there will be no disturbance of the emotions which could cause the dying person any loss of faith in the last moments. During that period the relatives stay with the dying person and remind him all the time to chant, "All things are not God. Only Allah is God. Muhammad is His special Prophet." This keeps the sick person close to his Islamic faith as he returns to his Maker. This short and delicate moment is very serious and ought to be emphasized.

Right after death it is necessary to close the mouth and eyes, to straighten the hands and feet, and to cover the face with a cotton towel. Then the family can start to mourn but must not cry aloud nor curse the Creator. The family moves the dead body out of the room to place it on the death bed and then passes the sad news around. They remove the clothing and cover the body with a white cloth, and burn incense at the feet. Experienced relatives should be around taking care of details so the burial can be carried out within twenty-four hours if possible, and not later than three days. They start digging the grave and getting the necessary articles, and then wash the body. Men wash a dead man and women wash a dead woman. Before starting the last bath they walk around the death bed seven times with burning incense. Washing is done strictly in order—the dirty parts first and then the head, face, neck, shoulders, back, and so on; the top first, the bottom later; right first, left last; front first, and back later. This is done three times. One person washes, one pours water, and a third turns the body around, then they dry it gently with a soft white cloth and put on three coverings—underwear, a small sheet, and a large sheet. There is a headdress for a man and a turban veil and brassiere for a woman. Powder with medical perfumery is used on the forehead, nose, mouth, hands, feet, and knee-cap to discourage insects. Then the body is put in a coffin and covered and a blanket spread over the coffin, which is then placed in the great hall or the yard until the funeral service. At present in China all Muslims, rich and poor, use the mosque as the center for all these procedures.

The funeral ceremony consists only of raising the hands and standing up. The men who attend the funeral stand in line and follow the Ahund in worship—they pray by raising the hands, bowing, and chanting aloud, "God is Greatest," chanting it again as they bow the head; then they shake the head right and left and say, "Salam." This funeral service is very important. If a man is not buried with a religious funeral his family is to blame, of course, but all Muslims in the locality are to be blamed as well.

According to Islamic customs the funeral march begins when four men place the coffin—head first—on their shoulders and walk slowly; every few minutes another four men take over. Everyone walks after the coffin, without music or talking, and with heads bowed in meditation, thinking that just as death has come to this person it will come to everyone. At the grave the host inspects the grave and perfumed powder is spread in the four corners. Then the body is taken from the coffin by three or four men and placed in the grave face up, head to the north, with the uncovered face toward Mecca. It is covered with a stone or a thick board and then with a rectangular mound of earth while the Ahund recites the first chapter of the Qur'an. All the mourners follow the Ahund and raise their hands and pray. The tombstone and plantings are private matters of the family, but the religious regulations forbid too much decoration on a tomb.

After the funeral the family keeps on mourning and visits the cemetery according to schedule, also inviting the Ahund or other religious leaders to pray for the dead. The prayers should be said on the funeral day, the seventh day, and the second, third, and seventh week. Some keep the seventh day, the fortieth day, the hundredth day, the first year, and the third year. After that chanting is carried out only on the anniversaries of birth and death. The best way is to pray for one's own dead relatives on Fridays and chant the Qur'an. If one invites the Ahund or religious leaders to chant at the home, the host provides food after the service, and money wrapped in red paper must be given to the Ahund and to the poor in the name of the dead.

Chinese Muslims regard the funeral as important because it relates to the everlasting happiness of the dead. At the time of funerals the whole community tries to help. Even members who are not religious ordinarily come to the mosque to help at this time and often they are impressed by the greatness of religion and the closeness of friendship among Muslims and are brought back into the community. In weddings Chinese Muslims have modified their practices according to local customs, but in funerals everything is done by the Islamic method with no single trace of change, for they recognize its importance.

There are three important festivals, one at the end of the month of Ramadan, one when the pilgrimage at Mecca reaches the peak of Arafat, and one on the birthday of Muhammad. Id al-Fitr, the feast at the end of the fast of Ramadan, is celebrated throughout the Muslim world as the Little Festival. Id al-Adha, also called Id al-Qurban, the festival at the end of the pilgrimage, is the Great Festival at which Muslims from all over the world gather at the mosques to worship and then kill animals to memorialize the story of Abraham and Ishmael and their willingness to obey the authority of God. According to Muslim rule five men kill one camel, three one cow, and one person kills one sheep; then they divide the meat among the poor and their relatives, saving a small portion for themselves. Chinese Muslims turn the two festivals around, making the Ramadan feast the large festival and the pilgrimage festival the small one, which shows wrong teaching.

The Holy Birthday of Muhammad follows the Arabic lunar calendar, which means that every three years it is advanced one month, so it can be at any season. On this day every Muslim dresses in his best clothes and gathers with the others at the mosque to chant the Qur'an and the praises of Muhammad under the leadership of the Ahund. Then they listen to the Ahund speak about Muhammad's good deeds and teachings, and are inspired by what he says. Soon after the worship sweets are distributed to adults and children, and some mosques even have banquets. In recent years Muslims have broadcast inspirational talks about Muhammad on his birthday and have even distributed leaflets by chartered airplanes.

There is also a Fatimah memorial day which is a festival for women.

Education and Culture of Chinese Muslims. The old style of religious education in China was patterned after the Arabic and Iranian methods of the Middle Ages in which there were several specialists who lectured and the students chose their lectures according to their inclinations. But in China there were only special schools of this kind in three centers and there one Ahund would handle all courses. There was no schedule, no definite standard, and no required length of schooling since everything depended on the will of each Ahund. Such a system had serious drawbacks because the teaching materials were several centuries old, the study of Arabic—and no Chinese—was inadequate, so the students could read only a limited amount and could not speak the language, there was no general educational background for the religious courses, and the freedom allowed to the students often led them to form bad habits.

After the founding of the Republic, in response to the progressive demands of the period, several new style schools were founded for religious education, of which the three best were the Cheng-tai Normal School at Peking, the Islam Normal School at Shanghai, and the Ming-teh High School at Kunming. Unfortunately, the schools at Peking and Shanghai were forced to move inland during the Sino-Japanese war, and although it was hoped that they could be revived after the war, there has been no news of them since the Communists took over the mainland. Before the war these three schools had sent twenty-eight students to study at Al Azhar in Cairo, the first time in its thousand years that it had received students from China.

Under the Republic the Muslims also founded more than a thousand primary schools and several well-known high schools for general education. They lacked the funds to found colleges and universities, but there were special classes in Islam and the Arabic language at Peking University, the Central University, Yunnan University, and Chung San University. At present in Taiwan the Taiwan University and Tsun-Chi University also give such courses for Muslims and others who are interested.

In the short period of just over thirty years between the founding of the Republic and the Sino-Japanese war Chinese Muslims did their utmost to advance the culture of their people. Several local magazines and papers were published, both of a political and a religious nature, but there is still need for national publications which will reach all Muslims in China. As a means of reaching a wider group the Chinese Islamic Association obtained permission after the Sino-Japanese war to broadcast Islamic lectures once a week. Many scholars broadcast on these programs, which were well received by the public. Their talks were also published as pamphlets and distributed widely. The Taiwan broadcasting station continues this practice.

For more than a thousand years after Islam came to China there was no translation of the Qur'an or the Hadith, nor were there books which touched on Islam's philosophy, history, science, and literature. The work of providing such literary and historical materials began to be accomplished shortly before the war but then suffered serious interruption; however, a new translation of the Qur'an was recently published in Taiwan. The Education Bureau of Taiwan has recently invited Arabian, Iranian, and Turkish scholars to become members of a World Literature Committee to translate Arabian, Iranian, and Turkish books into Chinese. This is a most significant development.

The majority of Chinese Muslims were descendants of Arabian, Iranian, or Turkish parents who intermarried in China and adopted Han customs. This led to a mixture of both cultures, which is shown in their appreciation for the cultures of both areas, and led also to some interesting cultural contributions in China. During the Ming dynasty Muslims began to make cloisonné vases, plates, and bowls covered with colorful blues and with delicate Arabian and Persian designs or with writings from the Qur'an and the Prophet's Tradition. They are found today among the Chinese national treasures and in museums and the homes of wealthy collectors.

Chinese artists of Muslim background also made contributions to the art of calligraphy by forming first the outline of a Chinese character and then filling it with the Muslim creed, or proverbs, or poems. At a distance it is a big Chinese character meaning "tiger" or "long life" but on careful examination it is seen to be filled with Arabic phrases. Another form of calligraphy was the writing of Arabic words in the Chinese running hand; in appearance it is Chinese writing, but it can be read only by those who know Arabic. In painting, also, Muslim artists made their contribution, but they painted only vases, water containers, or flowers, and never mountains, water, birds, or animals. Art of this kind is a combination of Arabian and Chinese forms, a new contribution to art which symbolizes the contribution to Chinese culture made by the Muslim people who settled in China.

CHAPTER TEN

Islam in Indonesia

P. A. Hoesein Djajadiningrat

Before the coming of Islam to Indonesia the culture of the islands had been greatly influenced by many centuries of acceptance of Hindu and Buddhist culture. Today, Indonesia has one of the largest Islamic populations in the world, more than seventy million Muslims.

The earliest reliable information concerning Islam in Indonesia is found in Marco Polo's report that, when returning to Venice in 692 (A.D. 1292) after his years in the service of Kublai Khan in China, he stopped at Perlak on the north coast of Sumatra and found that the people of that city had been converted to Islam by "Saracene" merchants. In the neighboring principalities, according to his account, the population was made up of wild heathens. At Samara, where Marco Polo waited five months for favorable winds, he had to protect himself and his traveling companions against the cannibal peoples of the area by building a fortified stockade. The Samara of Marco Polo's account, and the nearby Basma to which he refers, have been identified as Samudra and Pasé, two towns separated by the Pasé River, a short distance above Perlak.

The grave of the first king of Samudra-Pasé has been discovered in a burial place near the village of Samudra. The epitaph tells us that the king, al-Mulakkab Sultan Malik al-Salih, "the upright king," died in 696 (A.D. 1297). There is also a Malay tradition which relates that the first king of Samudra was a heathen who adopted the Islamic faith between 669 and 674 (A.D. 1270–75) and assumed the title of Malik al-Salih.

If the identification of Samara with Samudra is correct, then this must have been the first Muslim kingdom in Indonesia when Marco Polo visited it at the end of the seventh century (thirteenth century A.D.). The influence of the little kingdom of Samudra ultimately gave the name Sumatra to the whole island.

The famous Moroccan traveler Ibn Battuta (died 779; A.D. 1377) visited Samudra on his way to China in 746 (A.D. 1345) during the reign of Sultan Malik al-Zahir, who was the grandson of the Sultan of Marco Polo's time. Ibn Battuta says that Islam had been established there for almost a century and tells of the piety, humility, and religious zeal of the king who, like his people, was a follower of the Shafi'i school of jurisprudence. Malik al-Zahir held meetings with theologians for discussion of religious matters and the recital of the Qur'an, went to Friday public worship on foot, and from time to time went to war against the unbelievers in the interior regions. Ibn Battuta's description of the wedding of one of the king's sons gives details concerning the ceremonies and public worship which give an impression of considerable pomp and splendor at the royal court of Samudra.

In a village near Gersik, northwest of Surabaya on the island of Java, a loose headstone from a grave has been found which bears an Arabic epitaph in Kufic script saying that the grave held the remains of a woman who died in 475 or 495 (A.D. 1082 or 1102)—the uncertainty is due to the difficulty in deciphering one word which may be either seventy or ninety. This would be the earliest date for a Muslim in Indonesia but doubt has been expressed, supported by very strong arguments, as to whether or not this headstone actually belonged there. There is, however, in Gersik the grave of one Malik Ibrahim who probably hailed from Iran—the epitaph does not make this clear—and who died in 822 (A.D. 1419). A marble mausoleum found in a graveyard near Pasé is, according to the complete genealogy given in the epitaph, the resting place of a descendant of the Abbasid Caliph al-Mustansir, who was Caliph from 623 to 640 (A.D. 1226–42). The epitaph says that the man buried in the mausoleum, who died in 810 (A.D.

1407), was the great-grandson of one of the princes who managed to escape the slaughter when the Mongols under Hulagu destroyed Baghdad in 656 (A.D. 1258).

Ma Huan, a Chinese Muslim traveler who accompanied a high dignitary from China on an official journey, visited Tuban, Gersik, and Surabaya—all on the north coast of Java—in the ninth century, at the earliest in 855 (A.D. 1451). He describes the population as made up of Muslims who had immigrated from the west, of Chinese—many of whom had embraced Islam—and of natives who were still heathen and believers in demons. Other than the epitaphs mentioned above, and the brief report by Ma Huan, there is no existing information about earlier Islamic settlements on the island of Java.

The Sultanate of Samudra-Pasé, probably weakened by the rising rival sultanates in northern Sumatra, fell to the Portuguese in 928 (A.D. 1521). After the city had been conquered by the Portuguese, a resident of Pasé—called Falatehan by Portuguese historians—went to Mecca where he studied for two or three years. When he returned to Pasé and found that the presence of the Portuguese did not make the territory favorable for further spreading of Islam, he left for Demak on the north coast of Java. Demak was the capital city of the first Islamic kingdom on the island of Java, founded by Raden Patah (died 924; A.D. 1518).

When Falatehan arrived in Demak it was ruled by the third Sultan of Demak, Pangeran Trenggana, who reigned from 928 to 953 (A.D. 1521–46). He was well received, not only as a scholar who had studied in Mecca but also because he was, according to tradition, a Sharif—a descendant of the Prophet. He was even given a sister of the sultan in marriage. From Demak he proceeded to propagate Islam westward. With troops mustered from Demak he took possession of Banten and then in 933 (toward the end of A.D. 1526 or beginning of 1527), conquered Sunda Kalapa, the port of western Java, which he rechristened Djayakarta—now Djakarta—which is probably a Javanese translation of the first word in the phrase in the Qur'an, *fathan mubinan*, which means "obvious victory."

Contemporary historians identify Falatehan with Sunan Gunung Djati, "the saint buried on the hill of Djati," who is known traditionally as one of the nine saints who converted Java to Islam. Most of the nine saints are known either by the name of the place where they lived or the place where they were buried, to which is added a title such as Susuhunan—abbreviated to Sunan—meaning "the worshiped," or Maulana, "our Lord," or similar titles expressing the high regard in which they were held. The existing traditions about these saints, together with some established historical data, give an idea of the Islamic doctrines which were taught in Indonesia in the early days of Islam.

Tradition speaks of one of them, Sunan Kali Djaga, as a saint who concealed his devoutness by making it appear as if he were not leading a pious life. In order to spread Islam he made use of the *wayang*, the shadow play performed with leather puppets representing figures from the Hindu epics Ramayana and Mahabharata. Performances were accompanied by the *gamelan*, an orchestra of copper and wooden percussion instruments, drums, a flute, and a two-stringed instrument. Sunan Kali Djaga was an excellent performer of these plays based on the Hindu epics, and as a reward for a performance he did not ask for anything but that the audience should repeat after him the Islamic creed. Thus he easily led many along the road to Islam, according to the traditional account.

It is said that when the mosque in Demak was being built the saints were supposed to contribute their manual labor and Sunan Kali Djaga was delegated to provide one of the lofty main wooden columns. He produced it at the last moment by tying together some chips of wood to piece it out. This column can still be seen in the mosque—at the top where one of the four planks spanning it does not extend to the end one can see something resembling chips of wood. This mosque was later regarded as so sacred that participation seven times there in the ritual worship of the Id al-Qurban, the festival associated with the annual pilgrimage, was believed to be equal to one pilgrimage to Mecca. This belief is probably connected with the extraordinary holiness ascribed to the nine saints of Java. It is an indication of the degree of holiness assigned to these saints that their miracles are described by the Arabic word which in Muslim dogmatics is used only for miracles performed by God's messengers, rather than by the word customarily used to refer to the miracles of saints.

Two Javanese Islamic documents which give some idea of the Muslim thought of the tenth century (sixteenth century A.D.) have been preserved. One was the work of Sunan Bonang whose period of activity may be assigned to the years between 880 and 932 (A.D. 1475–1525). His document was written in opposition to heretical mystical doctrines such as the assertion that what is, is God, and what is not, is God; that the not-being of God is not-creating, and this explains the high purity of the Lord, for God is alone and lonely and can be known only by the not-being which surrounds Him. Sunan Bonang argues in opposition that God is above all such talk. He is the Most High, the Immaterial, the High, who is neither preceded by not-being nor accompanied by not-being, nor even surrounded by not-being. This brief reference should suffice to show that from the very beginning of Islam on Java mystic contemplation existed in both its orthodox and its heretical, pantheistic forms.

The other tenth-century Islamic document in Javanese is from an unknown author—unknown because a number of pages are missing at the beginning and the end of the manuscript. It is the kind of document later called *primbon* in Javanese, that is, a heterogeneous collection of notes on religion, prayers, exorcisms, physiognomy, interpretation of dreams, prophesying from symbols, and the like. This tenth-century manuscript contains mostly religious notes, except for one page at the end on ominous body vibrations. The religious notes are chiefly ethical in nature; for instance, they place special emphasis on the intention before performing the ritual purification or the salat, the ritual worship. In its comments on mysticism, the orthodox character of its ethical comments and the orthodox interpretation of innovations—and warnings against them—create the impression of a document written to oppose pantheistic mysticism in the community. This document also mentions a Shaikh Ibrahim Maulana and his exhortations. This is probably the Malik Ibrahim who died in 822 (A.D. 1419) and whose grave was found at Gersik.

There is a well-known tradition, which is appropriate to the mystical atmosphere of these two tenth-century documents, that the founding saints of Java unanimously condemned one of their number, Seh Siti Djenar, who taught the hidden knowledge and neglected the performance of the Friday public worship, and also asserted that he and God were identical. This doctrine of Seh Siti Djenar reminds one of the claim of the famous Sufi of Baghdad, al-Hallaj, who said, "I am Reality," that is, Allah. Al-Hallaj was executed in Baghdad in 310 (A.D. 922), but the mysticism which he taught was carried on by many of his followers, especially in Iran where their mysticism flowered in Persian poetry.

The striking similarity between the Sufism of Seh Siti Djenar and the Iranian al-Hallaj could probably not be accepted in itself as convincing evidence that Islam came to Java by way of Iran, but it is a significant part of the evidence for believing that Islam as it was known in Java came through Iran and from there through western India and Sumatra.

For instance, on the tenth of the month Muharram—the day the Shi'as remember the martyrdom of Husain—many families prepare a special dish which they call *bubur sura* from the Iranian word *Ashura*, which means the tenth of Muharram. The month Muharram is also called *Sura* in Javanese. Reminiscences of Shi'a influences are also found in Atjeh, north Sumatra, where the month Muharram is called "the month Hasan-Husain." In Minangkabau, on the west coast of central Sumatra, Muharram is called "coffin-month," a reference to the Shi'a custom of commemorating Husain's death by carrying a symbolic coffin through the streets and throwing it into a river or other body of water. According to tradition, Islam was first introduced to Minangkabau by a Sufi who belonged to the Shattari order, which is still found in India and Indonesia. Another convincing clue to the conclusion that Islam came to Indonesia by way of Iran is the practice of using Iranian—not Arabic—names to designate the vowel signals of the Arabic script when learning the proper way to recite the Qur'an. There are other easily recognizable evidences of Iranian influence in the written language used in Islamic studies.

Relations with the west coast of India are indicated by the tombstones found in north Sumatra, and the tombstone of Malik Ibrahim in Gersik, which came from Cambay in Gujerat, where they made tombstones to order with any inscription desired. Another strong indication of relations with western India is the acceptance by Indonesian Muslims of the Shafi'i school of the law, which was the dominant school in Malabar. The evidences cited here are typical of the clues which have led historians to accept the theory that Islam came to Indonesia through Iran and the west coast of India.

Once Islam had arrived in Indonesia the further dissemination of the faith took place chiefly through the activities of Muslim merchants who married women from the places where they settled either temporarily or permanently. Before marriage the women had been converted to Islam, and such a marriage often led to the adoption of Islam by members of the woman's family. This is a process which can be found even now in many parts of the world not yet completely Islamized. The forming of new Islamic families naturally gave rise to the need for religious instruction for the children, and for adults as well. Traditional religious instruction which originated in the early days still exists today in a form which has been little altered through the years. It is this system of education, combined with intermarriage, which accounts for the peaceful spread of Islam throughout the islands of Indonesia.

The instruction in its elementary form is instruction in Qur'an recital, given today on the basis of a booklet in which the Arabic characters are printed with and without vowel and other symbols; it customarily includes the first Surah of the Qur'an and the last section, which includes Surahs LXXVIII through CXIV, arranged in reverse order, from short to long. Instruction is given to children of distinguished families by a teacher—called a guru—who visits them at their home; children from ordinary families of the common people go to the guru's home or to a place of worship. The place of worship is called a *langgar* in the Javanese language of central Java; a *tadjug* in the Sundanese language of western Java; a *surau* in Malay, the language nearest to Indonesian which is used throughout the islands; and a *meunasah*—from the Arabic *madrasa*—in the language of Atjeh in western Sumatra. It is used only for the communal performance of the five daily salats, for religious meetings, and for religious instruction, but not for the Friday public worship since it does not meet the requirements for a mosque.

After the student has mastered the introductory studies he goes on to learn the rest of the Qur'an and finally demonstrates his competence in reciting the Qur'an at a festive gathering of his parents and friends, followed by a special meal—called a *slametan*—which is considered to have some religious significance. The basic religious instruction also includes instruction in ritual purification and in performance of the salat, the daily ritual prayers, and in the proper way to formulate the intention to fast the following day, an intention which should be expressed every evening during the month of Ramadan. For such instruction there are booklets, often illustrated, to clarify the actions which must be carried out in performing the rituals of purification and daily worship. Such booklets are usually called a "collection of the pillars," or essential constituents of Islam, and are published in inexpensive format in Malay with Arabic characters, or in Indonesian in Latin script, with translation of the Arabic formulas. Instruction in the principles and essentials of Islam is also given to men and women who have had little or no opportunity for it in childhood or who have forgotten much of what they once learned. Such instruction is available for women in the morning, given by a woman, and for men in the evening after work.

Those who want to penetrate deeper into the study of Islam go to a *pesantren*, a residential school for Islamic studies. Such institutions can be very large, and the subjects they offer may include all branches of Islamic theology from elementary Qur'an recital up to the three constituents of Islamic science—law, creed, and Sufism—as well as the accessory sciences such as instruction in the correct way to recite the Qur'an, Arabic grammar, exegesis of the Qur'an, and the study of the Hadith. Some students go from one pesantren to another to hear famous teachers, and some are able to continue their studies in Mecca or Cairo. In Sumatra the pesantren is called a madrasah, the Malay name which comes from the Arabic, while on Java that name is used to designate a religious school where the subjects are taught according to modern methods along with instruction in secular subjects.

Among the books used in these studies, the most widely used in the field of shari'a is *The Ship of Salvation* by Salim b. Sumair al-Hadrami, who died in Djakarta in 1271 (A.D. 1854). This book gives a concise survey of the five fundamentals, or pillars, of Islam. There are four editions of this booklet, one in Arabic only and three with interlinear translations in Malay, Javanese, and Sundanese. More detailed studies of the Traditions, Arabic works of law, and the regulations of the shari'a concerning problems usually submitted to Islamic courts of justice—such as appointing the time for the beginning and end of the fast, matrimonial law, hereditary law—are available in Malay for students in the pesantrens. For the study of theology and jurisprudence the classical work by al-Sanusi is available, with interlinear translation in Malay, and other works which follow the Shafi'i school of law chiefly, although the Hanafi school is also represented in some writings. For the study of mysticism al-Ghazali is available in a Malay translation.

In recent years there has been a considerable increase in the number of religious schools, religious instruction has been introduced in public elementary schools, and modern madrasas have been founded. These new developments have encouraged the publication of many books in the field of Islam in Indonesian in Latin script, with or without Arabic texts. New Indonesian translations of the Qur'an have been published, and new editions of the Qur'an have been printed with—and this is very useful—a supplement covering the major rules governing the right way to recite the Qur'an. It is remarkable to note that during this generation there have been books published on Islam in the Sundanese language, sometimes with Arabic text and interlinear translations. Instruction in the Sundanese pesantrens has traditionally been given in Javanese because the teacher had received his instruction in that language, but evidently it is now more effective to use the mother tongue. The extensive work of Indonesian theologians as translators and writers of textbooks has had great influence in the dissemination of Islam throughout the islands.

The Shari'a

In judging the religion of a people one should consider not only their knowledge of their religion and their practices in living up to it, but also their disposition, their sentiments toward their religion. The Javanese speak of the "white people," those who live religiously, and the "red people," or those who do not live religiously but nevertheless are Muslims. The number of white people, or those who have knowledge of Islam and are living up to Islamic principles, is increasing through the expansion of religious instruction, the activity of Islamic political parties, and the increasing significance of Islam in international affairs. Intellectuals especially are attracted to Islam through its political significance.

The shari'a, as was made clear in earlier chapters in this book, stresses the five basic principles of Islam: the acceptance of the Word of Witness—that is, the confession that there is One God and Muhammad is His Messenger—and the four obligations of prayer, zakat, fasting, and pilgrimage. In Indonesia, ritual prayer, *salat*, is probably given most consideration. Throughout Indonesia at any of the five times appointed for the daily prayers believers can be seen in any mosque or langgar performing the salat together. The compulsory Friday public worship in the mosque is observed by a far larger number of people, so many that the mosques are usually overcrowded and often have more worshipers than can get into the building. The special services at the time of the fast at the end of Ramadan are even more crowded. It is further evidence of the concern of the people of Indonesia for salat that as the population increases new mosques are built to accommodate them.

The traditional mosque in Indonesia has as its characteristic style what is known as a broken roof, consisting of two or three layers with an independent, curved roof line. If there is a minaret it is a tower which stands apart from the mosque. In the new mosques a new architectural style is being introduced, influenced somewhat by the mosques of western Islamic countries. In Indonesian mosques the time for prayer is announced by powerful beating on a great drum made of a thick, hollow tree trunk covered with buffalo skin; then the call to prayer is usually chanted either from the mosque itself or from the roof of the mosque.

Most Indonesians—not only those who have made a special study of religion—are aware of the significance of the intention at the beginning of the ritual worship as well as during its performance. They recognize the significance of humility toward God, of devotion in all worship, an attitude which is almost inevitably developed by the positions of the body, the bending, kneeling, and prostration which are a part of salat. The sense of humility and devotion is especially strong when the ritual prayer is repeated in a congregation.

It is interesting to note that among the people of Lombok, the island just beyond Bali, there is a sect which teaches that the ritual prayers are to be performed only three times a day. This sect is known as the "people of the three times" in contrast with the "people of the five times," or the orthodox Muslims. They are also notable as a sect which holds to many of the traditional customs, known as *adat*, together with the religious law of Islam. Their adat, customary law, holds that no woman can inherit a rice field, for instance, while Islamic law does not exclude women from such inheritance.

Concerning zakat, the fundamental principle of almsgiving, in Indonesia most consideration is given to the obligation to give to the poor at the time of the festival at the end of Ramadan. The gift, in accordance with the shari'a, should consist of rice but in practice is also given in the form of money.

The donor buys the amount of "wheat of the country"—rice, in this case—which is determined for each person and presents it as zakat to a religious teacher, usually the teacher of his children. In the big cities today committees are organized which send circulars to heads of families requesting them to send their zakat in money to these committees which take responsibility for its distribution in gifts to the poor. The regulations in the shari'a concerning the categories of people among whom the zakat should be distributed are, however, only applied to the collectors of zakat, and to the poor and destitute, among whom are also included religious teachers because their activity is not considered to be a means of living. The other categories of people having a right to a share of zakat do not exist in Indonesia.

The fast during the month of Ramadan is only observed by devout people. Others may begin the fast, but give up after a few days either because they are physically or mentally unable to live up to the heavy strain of the fasting obligation, or simply because they are not able to generate the will power required for the fast. Some deliberately fast only on the first day—the Javanese mockingly call this "fasting like the bedug," which is a drum covered only on one side. Others fast on only the first and the last day—mockingly referred to as "fasting the way a kendang is covered," that is, a drum with skins on both sides. Some fast on the first, the middle, and the last day; and some do not fast at all. During Ramadan religious meetings are held every night in the mosque, the langgar, or private homes for the performance of communal ritual prayers and for reciting the Qur'an, or listening to the recital of the Qur'an. Such meetings are attended also by people who are not fasting.

According to Shafi'i teaching, the descent of the Qur'an took place on one of the uneven dates of the last ten days of Ramadan; therefore, the nights of the 21st, 23rd, 25th, 27th, and 29th of Ramadan have a special holiness. Those nights are usually spent in performing acts of devotion such as salats, dhikrs, Qur'an recital, and the distribution of alms in order to make sure that they will be done on the correct night which commemorates the descent of the Qur'an. People living near a mosque or langgar send food to it as a contribution for a slametan, a meal of well-being, a ceremonial meal which seeks a blessing either for the participants or for other specified persons. In former times there was an adat celebration on those nights with fireworks and Chinese lanterns.

At the end of the fast, after the final ritual of prayers has been performed, people dressed in their new clothes go to visit relatives and acquaintances. This is a general festival day throughout Indonesia. In some parts of the country the people visit the graves of their relatives on this day.

The number of Indonesians who make the pilgrimage to Mecca is some indication of the vitality of Islam among the people of the islands. In 1349 (A.D. 1930) thirty-three thousand pilgrims went from Indonesia in a year when the total number of pilgrims from overseas was eighty-five thousand; the next year the figures were seventeen thousand and forty thousand respectively. The ordinary citizen has to save for years in order to carry out this religious obligation, so the determination to make the pilgrimage must be very strong. Sometimes it happens that when a deceased relative could have made the pilgrimage but did not, another is asked to go as his representative and is given a reward in money for making the trip. Under the present government the Ministry of Religious Affairs supervises the travel of the pilgrims to Mecca. It receives from the government an allocation of foreign exchange which allows some ten to twelve thousand pilgrims to make the journey and then allocates quotas to different parts of the country and supervises the selection of those who will be permitted to go, for from two to ten times as many apply as can be cared for. The government charters ships and supervises the journey to Saudi Arabia.

The shari'a is concerned not only with the regulations governing the four basic requirements—salat, zakat, fasting, and pilgrimage—but also with matrimonial law, family law, inheritance, business, and political activities. In these fields an important role is played by *adat*, that is, the pre-Islamic conceptions, customs, and habits which have persisted even though they have not always been reconciled with religious law.

The recommendation given in the law books in favor of sanctioning the marriage in the mosque is not generally followed. In distinguished families the marriage is usually contracted at the home of the parents or relatives of the bride; among ordinary folk the marriage is contracted at the office of the official in charge of overseeing contracts of marriage. After contracting the marriage, it is adat—all over Java and in a number of the other islands—that the groom make a conditional declaration of divorce, that is, a declaration of divorce which becomes effective if certain conditions are met. All kinds of conditions may be included, provided, of course, they do not contravene Islamic prescriptions. In Djakarta, the usual conditions are: if the husband deserts his wife for six months in succession, or does not provide sustenance for her for three months, or does her bodily harm, or ignores her for six months —then the divorce takes effect. To prevent automatic divorce every time these conditions are met, another condition is added—that the wife must be unwilling to put up with the situation and brings the matter before the appropriate authorities, and her complaint is considered justified.

According to Javanese tradition the conditional declaration of divorce was introduced by a sultan when several of his soldiers returned from an expedition after a long absence and found that their wives had married other men. Religious judges had dissolved their marriages on the grounds that their husbands had deserted them without any provision for sustenance. That led to the additional condition that the divorce does not occur if the absence is caused by the command of the ruler.

The well-known modernist Rashid Rida, a pupil of Muhammad Abduh who became a leader of modernism in Egypt after his master's death, declared in a fatwa, a religious edict, that the conditional declaration of divorce is an unjustified innovation. However, legal authorities who are familiar with circumstances in Java have supported this adat as a means of preventing legal insecurity.

When the husband and wife practice a profession together, as is the case in some parts of Java, there is the adat that when the marriage is dissolved the jointly acquired goods are distributed between them either equally or in a proportion of two parts for the husband and one for the wife—this provision varies in different parts of the country. The goods brought into marriage remain the property of their respective owners. In the case of death of either husband or wife, ownership naturally falls to the heirs of the deceased. Sayyid Uthman, a great scholar who had an open eye for what is good and just in adat, brought this adat into line with the religious law—which knows no community of goods through marriage—by tacitly assuming existence of partnership between husband and wife.

In the field of hereditary law there is the adat, deviating from religious law, that daughters and sons of the testator receive equal shares of the inheritance. If harmony prevails between them, they first inquire from a religious judge how the inheritance should be divided according to religious law—the sons should receive twice as much as the daughters—and afterwards the sons give their sisters enough of their inheritance to make the shares equal. In this way both the customary law and the religious law are satisfied. In order to prevent a dispute among the heirs and at the same time to satisfy one's own sense of justice, sometimes the property is distributed among the future heirs as gifts. Another device is to make a donation in the form of a trust which becomes irrevocable only in case of the death of the donor; in this case the parties concerned are made to sign a written document as proof of their consent. These methods are used to satisfy the adat sense of justice without coming into conflict with the shari'a.

There are, however, adat conceptions which are definitely contrary to shari'a, such as the adat, mentioned above, that among the "people of the three times" of the island of Lombok women are not allowed to inherit rice fields even though there is no such restriction in shari'a. Among some fishermen the son inherits the boat and the daughter the house. In other places the inheritance is not distributed as long as the widow is still alive, and she may go on living in the house. In Minangkabau the shari'a hereditary law is not followed; there, since their laws governing kinship are matriarchal, the privately acquired property of the individual goes after death to his relatives on the mother's side as family property.

Among the Javanese the auspicious month, day, and hour for a wedding ceremony are of primary importance. The auspicious times must be found both for the actual contract of the marriage and for the ceremonial encounter, which may take place some hours after the making of the contract. The chronology followed by the Javanese, introduced by Sultan Agung when he became sultan in 1043 (A.D. 1633), was based on the usual Hindu-Javanese Saka era. On this basis the Hijrah Era year 1377 (beginning in July, A.D. 1957) corresponds to the Javanese-Islamic year 1889. It is a complicated system based on a period of eight years which includes three leap years, with the total number of days divisible by both seven and five. With this system, each year starts with the same day of both the seven-day and the five-day week. Since this chronology runs ahead of the actual lunar year, it must be corrected once every one hundred and twenty years. Certain months are considered to be positively unfavorable for initiating activities, and others are generally regarded as favorable. The month Shawwal, recommended in the Islamic law books as favorable for weddings, is regarded under the Javanese chronology as not very favorable. Nowadays more and more deviation from these conceptions concerning favorable and unfavorable times is evident.

Religious Doctrine—The Fundamentals

The six fundamentals of Islam—belief in God, in Angels, in the scriptures, in the messengers of God, in the Day of Resurrection, and in God's disposition for good and evil—are taught to all Muslims, but those who receive only simple religious instruction have only superficial knowledge of religious doctrine.

Concerning the first fundamental, belief in God, only the twenty attributes are taught—God exists, He is without beginning, infinite, unique, and so on—and possibly the ninety-nine beautiful names of God. Later, some of the twenty attributes may be remembered and some of His ninety-nine beautiful names, such as the Merciful (al-Rahman). These names of God are remembered as part of proper names, preceded by *Abd* (meaning the slave, or servant, of), but often their full meaning as names of God is not recognized. Non-Islamic sources often give a one-sided picture of the Islamic conception of God as a potentate who is far-distant from man and does what He pleases to do. Indeed, it is written in the Qur'an more than once that God forgives whom He pleases, and punishes whom He pleases. But it is also written in the Qur'an that God forgives readily, accepts repentance readily, is full of grace and mercy, and is charitable. The Indonesian Muslims, including those who do not adhere to any mystic doctrine, are well aware of these aspects of the Islamic conception of God.

The belief in Angels, in the Devil *(Iblis)*, and Jinn (Djin in Indonesian) understandably gives pre-Islamic belief in invisible beings, in good or evil spirits or powers, the opportunity to continue in existence among the people. Among the Javanese there is, for instance, belief in the guardian spirit of the village who dwells in a tree. Among the Sundanese there is a belief in Lady Sri, the personification of the rice kernel, for whom all kinds of things are done or avoided in order to insure a rich harvest. Among both the Javanese and Sundanese there is belief in the good or evil power residing in an ancient kris, sword, or pike.

The third fundamental belief of Islam, belief in the Scriptures revealed by God, holds significance for the ordinary believer only insofar as it concerns the Qur'an. He knows at least that the Qur'an consists of Surahs and verses and is divided into thirty similar parts. In Atjeh it is also known exactly where the midpoint in the Qur'an is because when during instruction in Qur'an recital a child has progressed to the midpoint it is adat that the parents send a dish of yellow rice with certain side-dishes as a gift to the teacher. In the Qur'an editions used—originally printed in India, now from

Pakistan or published in Indonesia—the middle word of the Qur'an, found in Surah XVIII, 19, is printed in large or red letters.

The central point in the fourth fundamental belief of Islam, the belief in God's messengers, is, of course, belief in the Messenger of God, Muhammad. The ordinary believer is also familiar with several of the names of the twenty-five prophets mentioned in the Qur'an, not only because almost all of these names are used as proper names, but also because there are more or less complete descriptions of the lives of the prophets written in Malay, in Arabic script, and now also available in Indonesian in Latin characters, and in Javanese in Javanese script. The deep reverence of the Indonesian Muslim for his own Prophet is evident from the way in which the Prophet's birth is commemorated. This commemoration, which is celebrated on the twelfth of the month Rabi Awwal and every day after that for the rest of the month, is so important that the whole month is given the name for the festival, *Mulud*, and generally throughout Indonesia the months before and after are given special names such as "the brother of Mulud" for the preceding month and "the younger brother of Mulud" for the succeeding month.

According to tradition the Prophet was born on a Monday. When the Javanese-Islamic calendar was introduced, the twelfth day of the month Rabi Awwal fell on a Monday in the fifth year of the eight-year cycle; when the correction is made in the one hundred twenty-year cycle it is always done in such a way that the twelfth of Rabi Awwal in the fifth year of the eight-year cycle will be a Monday—and that particular day is a great ceremonial occasion. Even in the other years the commemoration of the Prophet's birth is ranked equal to the two major festivals of Islam in importance. In Surakarta and Jogjakarta on Java it starts on the sixth of the month with the opening of a fair which is announced by the playing of the holy gamelan in the yard of the mosque. The religious part of the commemoration of the Prophet's birth is a recital by the leader from one of the well-known biographies of the Prophet—written either in verse or in rhythmic prose—interspersed with songs of praise sung by the leader or by the leader and congregation together.

There are certain practices associated with the commemoration which give evidence of the belief that special blessings are conferred by the celebration of the Prophet's birth. In Atjeh, during the singing of the songs of praise, the singers tie knots in pieces of black thread which are then given to the children to wear around their necks as amulets. In West Java, the tying of knots in threads to be worn as amulets is done during prayer after the recital. There is also a practice in West Java associated with the final prayer which is associated with the passage "and receive it [that is, our recital] from us . . . in good . . . acceptance." When the word "acceptance" is pronounced the participants take a handful of rice which has been served at the ceremony and this "acceptance-rice" is then dried in the sun and stored away to be used when a special blessing is needed, such as when a long journey is to be undertaken. Because of the Prophet's blessing associated with the commemoration ceremonies, people in West Java used to start important work during the recital, such as making the first knots in a fishing net.

Commemoration recitals take place not only on the birthday of the Prophet but also on other occasions such as the annual commemoration of the death of one's parents, or at the time of the hair-sacrifice of one's child, or on the night before a boy's circumcision, or the night before a marriage ceremony. Sometimes only the prayers for well-being suffice, for in Central Java at the feast for well-being—the slametan—the kind of food served is of greater importance than anything else.

In Tjirebon, during the season of commemoration of the birth of the Prophet, the people come from near and far to visit the grave of Sunan Gunung Djati, one of the nine saints of Java. The grave, which is on top of the hill, is accessible only to the sultans of Tjirebon. Ordinary visitors can go only so far as the first terrace. At the time of these celebrations the dishes which, according to legend, were used by the nine saints when they held a meeting on Mount Tjereme are exhibited at the residence of the oldest branch of the descendants of Sunan Gunung Djati, and the public can deposit money near them, for a blessing.

In a mosque in the village of Kasunjatan, near ancient Banten, where the old mosque of the sultans of Banten still stands, some hair of the Prophet's head is kept in a little box which is placed on a small bedstead which in turn rests on a larger bedstead. According to legend the Prophet left the hair in Banten during a visit, to mark it as a good Islamic country for the future.

The fifth fundamental belief in Islam is belief in the Day of Resurrection. Associated with this belief there is in Indonesia widespread belief that on the "plain of gathering" one is given as a mount the animal one has offered as sacrifice at the Great Festival, Id al-Qurban. The dead are commemorated on the third, seventh, fortieth, hundredth, and the thousandth day as well as annually on the day of death. The month Sha'ban is known as the month for commemoration of all souls, during which it is customary to have a meal for well-being in commemoration of the dead—sometimes held in the graveyard—and to visit the graveyard and clean the graves.

The belief in the disposition of God for good and for bad—the sixth fundamental belief of Islam—finds expression especially in the night in the middle of the month Sha'ban which in the law books is counted among the six most important nights of the year. As elsewhere in the Islamic world, people in Indonesia believe that during that night God determines human fate for the year to come, or—according to popular conceptions, at least among the Sundanese—that God looks into the good and bad deeds of the people, which have been recorded in their books. Devout people perform a special kind of salat that night, the salat of praise, and say prayers in which they beg God for forgiveness and protection from disaster. The ordinary believer also speaks of fate, using it in the sense of recorded predestination, when he has in mind an unfavorable lot accorded to a person.

Deviations from the fundamentals of Islam and from the required consequences, which are ordinarily the basis for the formation of sects, practically do not exist in Indonesia. Sectarian differences have not arisen. The only Indonesian sect of Islam is the minor group on Lombok who believe in prayer three times a day instead of five. Not native, but originating in India, is the Ahmadiyyah sect which had a representative in Indonesia before the second World War and acquired some followers among the intellectuals. In general it was met with reserve because a doctrine which recognizes Mirza Ghulam Ahmad as a prophet after Muhammad, the Messenger of God, was regarded as being contrary to Islam.

Sufism

Sufism, or mysticism, and particularly pantheistic mysticism, found fertile soil in Indonesian spiritual and emotional life from the very beginning because of the nature of the Indonesian mind and because of the age-old influence of Hinduism and Buddhism. Moreover, Islam was introduced in Indonesia by Indians. Mention has already been made of the influence of Sufism at the time of the introduction of Islam when Sunan Bonang opposed heterodox Sufism, and the nine saints of Java were involved in a controversy concerning the identity of God and man.

Similar Sufi doctrines were taught in northern Sumatra in the tenth and first half of the eleventh century (sixteenth and seventeenth centuries A.D.) by Hamza Fansuri and Shams al-din al-Samatra'i (died 1040; A.D. 1630), followers of the famous pantheistic Sufi, Ibn Arabi. Hamza, who was a member of the Qadiri order of Sufis even though he emphatically counted himself a follower of Ibn Arabi, traveled widely throughout Java and Sumatra expounding his mystical conceptions in symbolic and esoteric poetry. Shams al-din enjoyed the patronage of Atjeh's greatest monarch of all time. Shortly after his time, Nur al-din al-Raniri, a scholar from Gujarat in India, succeeded in persuading the following sultan to consent to the persecution of teachers of heretical mysticism. There were other famous Sufis of that period who had great influence in Indonesia, some of whom had studied in Arabia.

The Sufi orders which found acceptance were the Qadiri, Rifa'i, Naqshbandi, Sammani, Qushashi, Shattari, Shazili, Khalwati, and Tijani. The Qadiri order of Sufis did not have many followers but its founder must have enjoyed deep reverence, for in the opening lines of the document for recognition of the most important holders of hereditary offices and titles when blessings are invoked from God, the Prophet, and the saints, express mention is made of the founder of the Qadiri order, Abdul Qadir Jilani. The Rifa'i order of Sufis was known for the self-castigating performances connected with their activities. In the Indonesian language they are referred to by the word for iron dagger because members of this order, after having reached a state of ecstacy by reciting dhikrs and making all kinds of bodily movements under the leadership of their teacher, tried to stab themselves in the chest or shoulder with the iron dagger. If a wound were inflicted the teacher used to heal it with a little saliva, while invoking the name of the founder of the order. In the area of ancient Banten such instruments for self-injury are still kept in the outer buildings of the mosque, and are used, in sport, during celebrations such as circumcision celebrations. Such a game of self-injury, using a big kris, exists also among the non-Islamic Balinese.

The Sammani order is distinguished by the loud clamor with which the dhikrs, the praises of God, are shouted by the participants in its meetings. In Djakarta the life history of the founder of the Sammani order of Sufis, Shaikh Muhammad Samman, is popular. It has been edited by Hadji (Hajji) Muhammad Nasir in the form of the story of the saint's miraculous qualities and the miracles performed by him, followed by a prayer. It is concise enough to be read aloud during small feasts of well-being (slametans). The recital of the life history of the founder of a Sufi order, or just listening to such a recitation, is considered to be a good work in religion, and it actually does have an edifying effect on the believer. There are also similar booklets concerning the lives of other founders of Sufi orders, particularly one on the founder of the Qadiri order, which is available both in Malay and Javanese.

The Shattari order, which is considered to be the first Sufi order introduced on Java, believes in the Javanese doctrine of the seven stages of God's being, the science of true reality. In the first stage only the being of God existed and nothing had been created; the seventh and last stage is the sphere of man, or the sphere of the perfect man. Joined with this is the conception in which the Messenger of God is allegorized as the perfect man, who reflects divine powers as a mirror reflects light, and the belief that the souls of other human beings possess those divine powers as copies. The Javanese mystics started their contemplations from the belief that every human being carries within him the seeds of the perfect man and must therefore try to live up to that ideal. Connected with such ideas are speculations concerning man's relation to God as similar to that of a servant to his master.

Heterodox mystical ideas continued to exist in certain circles in Indonesia in spite of the influence of the many orthodox Sufi orders and in spite of the influence of orthodox Sufi writers such as al-Ghazali, who introduced a synthesis of the fundamental doctrines, the law, and Sufism. The pervasive influence of Sufism in Indonesia is shown by the frequency with which the names of the founders of the orders, and of famous mystics like Ghazali, are used as proper names for the sake of the blessing ascribed to them. In the Indonesian language, Ghazali becomes Gadjali or Godjali, and similar modifications may be made of other Sufi names.

Al-Ghazali's works have been known in Indonesia for almost two centuries in Malay translations and are now available in modern Indonesian. His mysticism has strong ethical tendencies which are evident in Islam in Indonesia. Through the study of al-Ghazali in the religious schools, several Arabic terms from his ethics have become common property, such as the words for self-love, hypocrisy, pride, patience, and gratitude toward God. Also commonly known is his concept that a Muslim should abstain from anything doubtful, even though it may be permissible. These Arabic terms have been adopted in several Indonesian languages, sometimes changed in form and somewhat altered in meaning. In Javanese, for instance, *udjub* (self-love) and *riya* (hypocrisy) were combined and shortened to *djubria*, meaning overestimation of oneself, especially in relation to God.

Reformist Tendencies

Indonesia was naturally not left untouched by the influence of the Islamic revival and reforms in Egypt. Young Indonesians studied at the Azhar in Cairo and learned there of the teachings of Muhammad Abduh and his students, especially Rashid Rida. They returned to their own country more or less influenced by the modern ideas acquired during their years of study in Egypt. The Arabs who had settled in Indonesia were also influenced by the reformist currents from Egypt, especially through the paper of the Egyptian reformists which became known in Indonesia. To these tendencies from Egypt were added the general modern conceptions of the period. The Islamic revival in India, which occurred earlier than in Egypt, became known in the intellectual circles of Indonesia later than the revival in Egypt because it used the medium of the English language.

In Djakarta in 1323 (A.D. 1905) Indonesian Arabs founded the Organization for the Good which aimed at establishing Islamic schools which used modern methods of instruction and taught general as well as religious subjects. The work of the Organization for the Good was open to Indonesians and their children as well as to the Arabs. It brought from Mecca a Sudanese scholar, Ahmad b. Muhammad Surkati al-Ansari (died 1363; A.D. 1943), who, it turned out, held very radical ideas. Among other things, he opposed in a pamphlet the idea that marriage between a non-Sayyid man and a Sayyid's daughter should be forbidden; he opposed the custom of regarding Sayyid as a hereditary title, like Sharif, for descendants of the Prophet, for the word does not mean anything more than *gentleman*, or the title *Mr.* Of course such a pamphlet caused a break with the Organization for the Good, for it included several Sayyids. With supporters from among the non-Sayyid Arabs he founded another organization called Guidance and Improvement, which founded schools for Arab and Indonesian children in several parts of Java.

In Jogjakarta in 1331 (A.D. 1912), Kiai Hadji Ahmad Dahlan (died 1342; A.D. 1923), founded a social and religious organization called the Muhamadiah (Muhammadiya) on religious principles similar to those of the reformist movement in Egypt. They held that the basic authority of Islam is the Qur'an, together with the Hadith—both interpreted in a modern manner. The acceptance of the pronouncements or actions of another as authoritative was rejected. With the activities of the Catholic and Protestant missions in mind, the Muhamadiah founded schools based on Islamic principles but similar to the public schools of the Dutch-Indonesian government, and the schools were granted a government subsidy when they could satisfy the subsidy regulations. Like the Catholic and Protestant missions, Muhamadiah also founded orphanages, homes for the poor, clinics, and a hospital in Jogjakarta. In the religious field Muhamadiah trained propagandists, both men and women. It also founded a special department for women, called Aisjiah after the wife of the Prophet. Through the activities of this organization special mosques for women were built in Jogjakarta and Garut, and in another mosque a small part was partitioned especially for women. Thanks to the activities of the Aisjiah even at mosques which did not have a special compartment for women the Friday public worship was attended more and more by women.

In the field of religious ceremonies the new ideas of the reformists were opposed to what they regarded as objectionable novelties. The followers of Ahmad Surkati said that it was an objectionable novelty to prompt the deceased person, after the grave had been closed, by telling him the answers he should give in reply to the questions asked by the Angels of Death. They also considered it an objectionable novelty to rise when the birth of the Prophet is mentioned in the recital commemorating his birth. The Muhamadiah disapproved of all burial practices other than those made compulsory by religion on the ground that they were superfluous and expensive—such as the slametan on certain days after a person's death.

As a reaction against reformist tendencies an organization known as the Rising of the Ulama (Nahdlatul-Ulama, abbreviated to N.U.) was founded in Surabaya in 1345 (A.D. 1926). This organization sought to encourage the following of one of the four schools of law. It recognized as the authority for Islam the Qur'an, the Hadith, consensus (which included the clothing with authority in matters of religion), and reasoning from analogy. When it met in 1372 (A.D. 1952) it seceded from the Masjumi, the largest Muslim political party in Indonesia, and founded a political party based on Islamic principles called the Partai Nahdlatul Ulama. It seeks to preserve shari'a in accordance with one of the four schools of law and to promote the observance of Islamic law in society.

Several of the political parties which are represented in Parliament have basic aims and principles which characterize them as Islamic parties, even though their political programs also include many points which have no specific Islamic connotations. The Masjumi party, whose name is a contraction of the Arabic words meaning Council of Indonesian Muslims, was founded in Jogjakarta in 1364 (A.D. 1945). The Masjumi includes individual members, and organizations, such as the Muhamadiah, which are nonpolitical Islamic groups. Masjumi has made its objective the preservation of the sovereignty of the state and of the Islamic religion, and the actualization of Islamic principles in state affairs.

The oldest Islamic political party is the Partai Sarikat Islam Indonesia (P.S.I.I.). In 1329 (A.D. 1911) Hadji Samanhudi, a batik merchant of Solo who died in 1376 (A.D. 1956), founded the Islamic Trading Organization as a social and economic organization of Muslims. A year later this became a political organization known as Sarikat Islam. The organization, which quickly became popular and expanded throughout the country, had only local organizations at first, but later they were united into a single political party. The P.S.I.I. seeks to bring unity among Muslims and to encourage friendly relations between Muslims and other groups in Indonesia.

In Minangkabau in 1348 (A.D. 1930), the religious leaders founded the Islamic League Organization for Islamic Education. Its original objectives were to improve education and religious instruction and to aid the poor. Fifteen years later it was changed to a political party called Partai Islam PERTI. (PERTI stands for the three Indonesian and Arabic words meaning Organization for Islamic Education). The basic aim of the party is to establish the religion of Islam according to the Shafi'i school of law as it applies to the ordinances for worship and the shari'a, and to establish the interpretation of the fundamentals according to the teaching of al-Ash'ari and al-Maturidi—whose teachings form the basis for the theology of the Sunnis.

Similar aims are expressed in the statement of aims of the Partai Politik Tharikat Islam (P.P.T.I.), which was also founded in Minangkabau in 1366 (A.D. 1945). It seeks to establish the observance of the Shafi'i school of law and the interpretations of al-Ash'ari and al-Maturidi, and also the observance of Sufism through one of the Sufi orders. Its Islamic character is affirmed in its expressed aim to make the laws of God the laws of the Republic of Indonesia and in its basic principle, which is "Fear, Love, Hope, and Shame toward God." It is interesting to note that in the field of international politics the P.P.T.I. seeks to obtain peace for humanity by preparing itself for the coming of the Imam Mahdi, the Expected One, whose coming is near.

The Union of Ulama of Atjeh (P.U.S.A.) is not represented in Parliament but is active in politics. It was founded in 1358 (A.D. 1939) as an orthodox counterbalance against the reformist teachings of the Muhamadiah. The members of the P.U.S.A. joined in the fight for independence, but when the fight was won they turned against the Indonesian Republic and tried to secede from it.

Darul Islam, the Abode of Islam, is another party with almost the same history as the Union of Ulama of Atjeh. It aims at making Indonesia the domain of Islam in an orthodox sense. Its leader and his closest associates were originally members of the Sarikat Islam and joined in the fight for independence, but when independence was won they turned against the Indonesian Republic.

Characteristics of Islam in Indonesia

From this survey of Islam in Indonesia it is evident that from the beginning mysticism, both orthodox and heretical, appealed most to the Indonesian mind. This was due to a variety of factors, but the primary reason for the preference for Sufism is the innate disposition of the Indonesian toward mysticism. Heretical, pantheistic mysticism continued to exist even though orthodox Sufism became more widely known through the Sufi orders. Nowadays even a political party is based on mystical principles. Even the people who do not belong to any Sufi order, chiefly the intellectuals, busy themselves with the study and practice of the science and disciplines of the inner life, of mysticism.

It is also interesting to note that where customary law—adat—deviates from religious law and cannot be reconciled to it even in a formal way, it is often customary law which is observed, and such observation is not derogatory to religious sentiment nor to the conscientious observance of the religious obligations and practices of Islam. In Indonesia, customary law has been able to hold its ground with religious law.

Reformist tendencies in Indonesia, as has been noted, are fanned by influences not only from Egypt, but also—through the intellectuals—from India, Pakistan, and other Islamic states. In addition, there are local institutions for religious instruction which breathe a modern atmosphere.

However, the reformist tendencies will always be counterbalanced by orthodoxy in Islam, an orthodoxy which is kept alive by influences from Mecca, by pilgrimages, and by local educational institutions.

CHAPTER ELEVEN

Unity and Diversity in Islam

Mohammad Rasjidi

No one can claim to speak with final authority concerning the diversity found among the more than five hundred million Muslims who seek to follow the straight path of Islam. One can only record some observations concerning the variations in practices among the Muslims from Morocco and the Balkans to China and Indonesia. It is possible, however, to be much more explicit about the basic unity of Islam, for throughout the Muslim world there is general agreement concerning the sources of Islam, the fundamentals of the faith, and the particular requirements which are the obligations of all believers.

The Sources of Islam

There is general agreement that the sources of Islam are the Qur'an, the Sunnah, and reasoning about them. Of these, the primary source is the Qur'an. Concerning matters not explicitly clear in the Qur'an, the Sunnah is the secondary, supplementary source; and when the answer to questions needs further clarification the third source for Muslims is reasoning about the intent of the Qur'an and Sunnah by those men who are recognized as having the training and experience which qualifies them to reason properly.

The miraculous revelation of the Qur'an has been fully discussed in earlier chapters of this book. It is the final revelation, the Word of God given through His Prophet as a guide to all men everywhere, regardless of race, or color, or nationality. Within two years of the death of the Prophet it was compiled in book form and has been the primary source of Islam for almost fourteen centuries, without question and without variant versions. Since it was revealed in Arabic it has necessitated knowledge of Arabic, and this has been a unifying cultural factor throughout the Muslim world. It was recognized, however, that the people in the various countries often read the Qur'an in Arabic without understanding its meaning. The uneducated people even thought that it was sufficient to pronounce the words correctly, and that such repetition—even without understanding the meaning—would bring them blessings from God and save their souls. Some even used verses of the Qur'an as amulets against dangers and diseases! Half a century ago the orthodox Muslims believed that it was forbidden to translate the Qur'an, fearing that translations would supplant the original Arabic version and that versions in different languages would cause disagreements and misinterpretations of the revelation of God. While it is true that because of its very high literary style it is difficult, if not impossible, to translate the Qur'an into any other language without losing the beauty and vigor of the original, translations in the languages of the people are necessary in order that they may understand the meaning of this book which is the source of Islam. Today the Qur'an is available in translation in most of the languages of the world.

Sometimes people ask why the Qur'an was revealed in Arabic if it is intended to be the Holy Book for all human beings. This question cannot be answered definitely, for if the Qur'an had been revealed in any other language—for example, in English—the question would still remain as to why that one language was chosen. Thus we have to content ourselves with the fact that, regardless of any possible reasons, the Qur'an was revealed in Arabic.

The second source for Islam is the Sunnah. During Muhammad's lifetime, Muslims could ask him to guide them in solving any problem when they did not find a clear answer in the Qur'an. For instance, once a man asked him if it would be proper to perform a pilgrimage on behalf of his deceased mother. The Prophet replied that it would be proper since such an act could be compared to a debt which she owed and the son was obligated to pay. When the Prophet was dying, and knew that he would not be present to give such advice, he told the people that they would not go astray so long as they held to the two guides he was leaving for them—the Qur'an, the Book of God, and the example of his own way of life, the Sunnah. The Qur'an, in Surah XXXIII, verse 21, establishes the Sunnah as the second source of Islam: "There is a good example in the Apostle of Allah for those who wish to meet God and the Day of Judgment, and to remember God much."

The Sunnah is made up of the deeds, speech, and approbation of the Prophet. His deeds include the way he prayed, or washed his hands, or took a bath, and the like. His words have been preserved for us, as for example when he said, "I am sent to perfect high morality." By approbation is meant that when Muhammad saw something done, or heard words uttered in his presence and did not object, such actions or words are approved. Approbation was applied chiefly to customs of the Arab society which were not in contradiction to the spirit of Islam. For example, when Muhammad saw a man dancing with a sword he smiled and showed his pleasure, so later jurists concluded that dancing with the sword is permitted. Such approval has been applied to customary practices and laws in all Islamic countries where such customs do not contradict the spirit of Islamic laws—for example, in the marriage ceremonies.

The codification of the Sunnah, the Traditions, began a century and a half after the Prophet when Malik Ibn Anas wrote a compilation of the Traditions concerning Islamic laws. The compilation of the Traditions took final form at the hands of Bukhari and Muslim in the third century (ninth century A.D.), and today most Muslims recognize their work as the two correct books on Traditions. Those two compilers established conditions for determining which Traditions would be accepted as authentic, conditions which related only to the persons who narrated the Traditions. Such persons must be of good moral character, pious, honest, of sound discretion, and blessed with a good memory; and the series of such transmitters must be continuous from generation to generation. The first generation was called the Companions, the second was known as the followers, and the third as the followers of the followers. Thus a tradition narrated by the followers only would not be accepted by Bukhari because there would be a gap of a generation from the time of the Prophet.

It must be explained, however, that those conditions for the correctness of a Tradition did not touch the subject matter, for internal criticism was unknown at the time. Consequently we find in the two compilations some Traditions, such as those about the signs of the approaching of the Day of Judgment, which we do not understand even yet. The lapse of two and a half centuries between the death of the Prophet and the compilation of the Sunnah has resulted in many differences between Muslims which continue in our time. In the civil war and struggle for power in the time of Uthman, the third Caliph, irreligious elements among the Muslim people did not refrain from fabricating traditions concerning the merits of some political figures. Accurate judgments concerning the narrators of Traditions became difficult because the political feuds sometimes made the judgments far from objective. A knowledge of the way in which the Traditions were compiled and transmitted facilitates an understanding of the various attitudes toward the Traditions which are found in Muslim countries today.

The Qur'an, which was revealed almost fourteen centuries ago, and the Traditions concerning the Prophet who lived that long ago exclusively in a desert society cannot serve as explicit guides for every situation which might arise centuries later, and especially in the complex societies of the present day. This was recognized by the Prophet himself. Once when he was sending one of his Companions to Yemen to serve as governor, he tested the man by asking him what principles he would follow in his new position. He answered that he would hold to the teachings of the Qur'an. The Prophet asked, "And if you do not find a particular guide in the Qur'an?" He replied, "I shall look for it in the Sunnah." Then the Prophet asked, "Well, what if you do not find it in the Sunnah either?" He replied, "In such a case, I shall make use of my own opinion." The Prophet was very pleased with that answer and said, "Thanks to God who has guided the messenger of the Messenger of Allah."

Thus a third basis for Islam became established, the basis of reasoning. We find in the Qur'an many verses which mention reasoning, or thinking, or knowing—verses which exhort us to make use of our brains instead of following blindly the traditions which our ancestors followed. Concerning the unbelievers of old, the Qur'an says, "Nay, for they say only: Lo! we found our fathers following a religion, and we are guided by their footprints" (Surah XLIII, 22). While exhorting us to contemplate nature, the Qur'an says, "In the creation of skies and the earth, the difference between night and day, the ships which run at sea carrying that which is useful for mankind, the rain water which Allah sends down from the sky to revive the earth after its death, and to spread animals on it, and the arrangement of winds and clouds between sky and earth, in all those things there are evidences (for the existence of God) for those who make use of their brains" (Surah II, 164). There is even a verse which says that once upon a time the people of Hell said to one another, "If we had made use of our ears or our brains we would not have been the inhabitants of this Hell" (Surah LXVII, 10).

Originally the word used for reasoning, *qiyas*, meant measure, used in the sense of thinking by comparing one thing with another—reasoning by analogy. As the third source of Islamic law it means determining the proper course of action by reasoning from the Qur'an and the Sunnah. Some men, however, speak of a fourth source of the law of Islam—consensus of opinion, or the agreement of capable men in their judgment on a specific question. This concept was introduced by al-Shafi'i, the founder of one of the schools of law. Some people have misunderstood consensus to mean simply public opinion, and have asserted that if public opinion approves an action it is therefore acceptable to Islam. For Muslim legislators, consensus is the agreement reached among qualified religious leaders in one place at one time. There has never been a means by which such agreement might be found for all Muslims everywhere. True consensus, ijma, was possible only during the time of the first two Caliphs and part of the rule of the third Caliph. Ijma now only means that some agreement has been found in some places concerning the interpretation of certain verses of the Qur'an. As a basic source for Islam, it is reasoning, not consensus which is the third source. The Qur'an, the Sunnah, and reasoning are the generally accepted sources of Islam.

There are, as has been seen, some exceptions to the position that these are the three sources of Islam, for some people hold that only the Qur'an and Sunnah can give us a solid foundation for Islam. Their attitude, however, is easily refuted for it must be admitted that the problems of the world today are very different from those of the time of Muhammad, and their attitude would make Islam a dead religion. Actually, Islam is a dynamic religion, based on the Qur'an, the Sunnah, and reasoning.

Some people confuse ijtihad with reasoning, but if used in the sense of a personal preference it is obviously not the same thing. In the sense of careful reasoning as to the implications of the Qur'an and the Sunnah, it is the same as reasoning. Unchecked, ijtihad might even lead to disagreement concerning such basic ideas as right and wrong, good and bad!

To understand the unity and diversity in Islam it is necessary to understand these three sources of Islamic law: the Qur'an, the Sunnah, and the proper use of reason.

The Creed of Islam

The unity in Islam is shown in the acceptance of the six articles of belief, the fundamentals of Islam—belief in God, Angels, revealed scriptures, prophets, the Day of Judgment, and the destiny of man for good or evil. These beliefs are held by all Muslims.

The proof for the existence of God is found in the Qur'an through meditation on the beauty and order of nature. The harmony of the natural world shows that there is one benevolent Allah who created the universe and all human beings. The oneness of God is His most distinctive characteristic, as is shown in Surah CXII of the Qur'an, "He is One. He it is to whom we address our demands. He never gives birth and He was never born, nothing is similar to Him." In addition, all good qualities can be ascribed to God, He is the Merciful, the Generous, the Lover, the Great, the High. Some traditions mention ninety-nine names of God, but it is probable that the number is to be understood, not literally, but only as a very great number. Thus a Muslim may choose among those names of God the one which is psychologically relevant in the circumstances, a practice which is common throughout the Muslim world.

Theological treatises mention that there are twenty attributes of God, usually listed in four divisions. The first division includes only the essential attribute of existence. The second division is made up of the five negative attributes—no beginning, no end (eternity), difference from contingent things, independence of existence, unity (uniqueness). The third division includes the seven abstract attributes of power, will, knowledge, life, and the ability to hear, see, and speak. The fourth division, which is called the correlative of the abstract attributes, is made up of present participles of the abstract attributes of the third division—powerful (overpowering), willing, knowing, living, hearing, seeing, speaking. The theologians stressed that the attributes of God are not separate from the essence of God. This division of attributes is arbitrary and not clear, but most of the people consider it to be an essential element of belief. The series of attributes is clearly an artificial reflection of a reaction to Greek philosophy; it is not found in this form in the Qur'an or the Hadith, and has made people think in an unhealthy way. It is more appropriate to understand the existence of God through contemplating nature, as is revealed in the Qur'an. The differences of opinion among Muslims as to whether or not God resembles human beings, and the opinion of some common people that God resembles a medieval absolute king, arise only from different patterns of education; they are not fundamental to Islam.

Angels are creatures who serve as liaison between God the Almighty and His apostles, bringing the Godly messages and revelations to them. Some Traditions speak of Angels who guard Hell, some who guard Paradise, some who ask dead people about their beliefs, and some who record all of a man's actions; there is also an Angel who will blow the trumpet to awaken all human beings on the Day of Judgment. Common people tend to understand such Traditions literally, while educated people prefer to understand them figuratively with an interpretation more or less acceptable to reason.

The Qur'an, the holy revealed Book of Islam, mentions three former revealed books—the Book of David, the Book of Moses, and the Book of Jesus. This does not necessarily mean that there were no other revealed books, but only that we do not know whether or not any other books were revealed. Most people believe that there were no other revealed books than those three and the Qur'an.

The names of twenty-five apostles are found in the Qur'an, beginning with Adam. Muslims depend entirely on the text of the Qur'an for information concerning those prophets since the Qur'an is the only source about which there is not the slightest doubt. It is fortunate that the career of Muhammad is well-known, that there is nothing vague in the records of his life. The Traditions picture him in a very human way—dealing in commerce, getting married, having children, losing his wife and his sons, sharing all common experiences—in no sense a supernatural being. The only difference between Muhammad and the rest of mankind is that he received the revelations of God. All Muslims recognize Muhammad as a Prophet, and the last of the prophets. They see that the proof of his revelation lies not in external miracles but in the nature of the revelation itself. When the question is asked as to whether or not the teachers of other religions, such as the Buddha or Confucius, were prophets, no clear answer can be given. The Qur'an is not explicit on that point, for it says, "I have sent many apostles before you (Muhammad). I have told you about some of them, and I have not told you about some others" (Surah XL, 78). Some people conclude that the teachers of other religions are included in the "some others" that God has not told about, but other people say that only by studying the spirit and fundamentals of those religions can one determine whether or not they are of the same spirit as Islam, and their founders might be considered to have been prophets.

The Day of Judgment is mentioned in many verses in the Qur'an. When the sky is split, when the stars collide, when the mountains are like cotton, when the earth quakes—that is the Day of Judgment. On that day all people are awakened and their deeds are weighed; those having a heavy weight of good records will live happily in Paradise and those who have light weights will go to a Hell full of fire. The descriptions of Paradise are in such beautiful language that they make a deep impression on anyone who listens to the recital of the parts of the Qur'an which refer to it. On the other hand, Hell is described in a horrible way in many passages in the Qur'an. Although the common people are inclined to understand the descriptive passages in a literal sense, educated people recognize them as figurative. When the passages which describe Paradise and Hell are meditated upon it is easy to understand what great power they have to motivate people toward good actions.

The sixth fundamental belief of Islam is the belief in destiny for good or for evil. There has been much misunderstanding of the meaning of the word destiny. Many people have thought that a belief in destiny implies that everything will happen by itself, whether we wish it or not, and that such a belief will make people apathetic and indifferent toward all progress. The real meaning of belief in destiny, however, is that one believes that God created an orderly world and one should act according to the nature of that world. Thus a man with a sense of destiny will be active in doing anything which he judges to be good, knowing that if anything bad happens in spite of all precautionary measures, then there will be no reason for regret or for blaming oneself. Then he would say that it was the destiny of Allah. This meaning was illustrated by the Caliph Umar Ibn al-Khattab when he decided not to visit Palestine while there was an epidemic there. A companion asked him, "Are you evading the destiny of God?" He answered, "Yes. I run from the destiny of God to another destiny of God."

There is no difference among Muslims concerning these six fundamental beliefs of Islam. Every Muslim believes in God, in Angels, in revealed scriptures, in apostles, in the Day of Judgment, and in destiny. The differences are only in the interpretations, as mentioned above, and these differences result primarily from the differences in standards of education.

The Pillars of Islam

The fundamental beliefs of Islam have their practical consequences in everyday life. The writers of the other chapters in this book have referred to the practical side of Islam as the consequences of religion, the particular requirements of Islam, or as worship and dealings. Tradition says that the worship obligations, or requirements, of Islam are known as the Pillars of Islam; and the guide for dealings, for the responsibilities of human beings in society, are covered by fiqh, Islamic law.

According to Tradition, Islam is based on five foundations: the confession that there is no God but Allah and that Muhammad is the Apostle of Allah; prayer; almsgiving; fasting during Ramadan; and pilgrimage to Mecca by those who are able to go. Of these five pillars, concerning the first one there is no variation anywhere in the Islamic world. All Muslims know the Word of Witness, the confession of faith in Allah and the recognition of Muhammad as His Messenger, and all Muslims repeat it as their confession of faith.

The prayers are of two kinds, obligatory and optional. The five daily prayers are obligatory, including the obligation to attend the congregational prayer on Friday in the mosque. It is impossible to estimate what proportion of the people perform the five daily prayers regularly, since women usually say their prayers in the home and men may perform the salat at the mosque, at work, or at home. There is no religious superior who checks on the performance of the prayers. It is possible, however, to observe the attendance at the Friday noon prayers in the mosque. Large number of people will be seen at the mosque on Friday in Indonesia, in Turkey, Egypt, and parts of the Maghrib, and in the Shi'a mosques of Iran, to mention only the most obvious places. The smallest attendance at the Friday service would be found in China, and in the Soviet Union.

The optional, or facultative, prayers are of many kinds, such as the additional prayers before and after the obligatory prayers, prayers on the holiday after the month of fasting, prayers at the festival which marks the end of the pilgrimage, and prayers in times of need—which are offered by anyone at any time or place when the help of God is sought. Prayer for a person who died is necessary, since the spirit of such a person continues to live. Optional prayers can be performed at any time because a Muslim is in constant relation with God.

There are minor differences from country to country in the manner of praying, differences of no importance which have grown up through varying interpretations in the schools of jurisprudence. Some people emphasize the performance of optional prayers after the Friday prayers, while others do not. There are slight differences in posture; for example, in some countries, while standing, the people put their hands one upon the other in front of the lower part of the chest, while others who follow the school of Malik or of the Shi'as bend their hands down. Such differences are of no importance, and the unity is shown by the complete harmony among Muslims as to the times of prayer, the ablutions which must be performed before prayer, and the facing toward the Ka'ba in Mecca.

The mosques are the centers for prayer, teaching, and service in the Muslim world and are recognized as the distinctive symbol of Islam even though they differ considerably from country to country. Originally the mosque was very simple, for any ground can be made a place for prayer. The first mosque built by Muhammad in Medina was a simple plot of ground with clay walls on all sides and a roof of palm branches. As Islam spread to other countries the mosques adopted the architecture of those countries. In China, for example, we find mosques which resemble pagodas in many ways; in Indonesia most mosques are built near streams which the people can use for ablutions; in Arab countries the big mosques have one section roofed for winter use and an open area for use in summer. In recent years the greatest activity in building new mosques has been in Turkey and Indonesia.

There is great variety in the minarets which are used for the call to prayer. They may be simple square or round towers, as in the Levant; or elaborate architectural designs as in Egypt; or the slender, pencil-shaped minarets of Turkey; in Iraq and Iran the minarets in Shi'a mosques are often beautifully decorated with colorful ceramic tiles; in Indonesia they stand as separate towers, or in the villages may even be a chair in a high tree; and in China the government did not permit the building of minarets. Indonesia is unique in using drums for the call to prayer.

It is generally agreed that a Muslim should give alms which amount to a tenth of the agricultural yield immediately after harvest, and a fortieth part of his wealth of goods, or of gold after a lapse of one year if it reaches the quantity of thirty-eight grams—and about the same proportion of wealth in animals. The Qur'an specifies that such alms are to be given to the poor, the needy, the collectors of zakat, those whose hearts are to be appeased, slaves, travelers, debtors, and those who are on the path of God. While the source and the recipients of zakat are generally agreed upon, there are variations in the practice of distribution, largely because most Islamic countries do not have official collectors or an official organization for administering almsgiving. Turkey has a ministry of waqfs, as a part of the government; some of the Arab countries have governmental departments which are concerned with the administration of religious endowments; but in most countries almsgiving in goods or money is a voluntary gift either to individuals or to pious foundations. In Arabia they still give animals as alms since they have official collectors, but there is no almsgiving of goods or gold. In Indonesia people pay zakat on agricultural products to the religious men in the villages, but there is no zakat on animals. It is doubtful that almsgiving in any Islamic country reaches the proportion imposed by religion.

Pilgrimage remains a very important force making for unity in the Muslim world. Each year Muslims from all over the world, Muslims of every color and race, gather in the Holy Land to fulfill their obligation to make the pilgrimage. After almost fourteen centuries the pilgrimage retains its importance for Islam in spite of the development of new means of communication, for there Muslims from all over the world, religious leaders and common folk, meet and exchange views. Such personal contact is necessary to keep the spirit of universal brotherhood alive. The minor details in practices associated with the pilgrimage are only variations which developed in the different schools of law and are not significant. In modern times the improvement in travel facilities has made it possible for large numbers of people to make the pilgrimage even from distant lands, an important factor in bringing the Muslims of the Far East into closer relations with their brothers of the Turkish and Arab areas of Islam. In recent years the major obstacles to the pilgrimage, other than the ever-present difficulty of being able to afford the expense, have been currency restrictions and the limitations imposed by the governments of the Soviet Union and China. Pilgrimage remains one of the vital pillars of Islam, wisely instituted by the Qur'an and Sunnah as a form of worship which brings Muslims closer to God and to each other.

Islamic Law

As we have seen, the practical consequences of the six fundamentals of Islam include both worship, as outlined under the five Pillars of Islam, and dealings, or the responsibilities of Muslims in their everyday life. These practical consequences, the particular requirements of religion, have been codified in the four schools of law which exist amicably side by side in the Muslim world. The Maliki school which was founded during the second century after Muhammad shows preference for the Traditions and practices of Medina where the Prophet lived for thirteen years; it is found today chiefly in North Africa, some parts of Egypt, and in the Sudan. Also in the second century there lived in Baghdad a silk merchant named Abu Hanifah, a rationalist who based his teachings concerning the consequences of religion on the Qur'an and the Traditions. He wrote no book himself, but his disciples spread his liberal teachings and founded the Hanafi school of jurisprudence which is found in Turkey, Afghanistan, Central Asia, Pakistan, India, and Egypt. Another of Abu Hanifah's disciples, Muhammad Ibn Idris al-Shafi'i, founded the Shafi'i school in the third century; he was a great systematic jurist who took an intermediate position between extreme legalism and traditionalism. The school of Shafi'i interpretation is predominant in South Arabia, South India, Thailand, Malaya, Indonesia, and the Philippines. The fourth school of law was also founded in the third century after the Prophet by Ahmad Hanbal, a resident in Baghdad; he stressed the Traditions and distrusted the use of reason. The Hanbalis are found in Central Arabia, Syria, and some parts of Africa.

These four schools of law—covering the four divisions of rites, contracts, matrimonial law, the penal codes—were worked out so completely by their founders over a thousand years ago that those who came after them found fully adequate systems of law which met all the requirements of their times. A Muslim was free to choose any one of the four systems for his personal guidance, but the prevailing practice was to choose the school of law which was followed in the place of a man's birth. Thus a man born in Indonesia is usually a follower of Shafi'i law, while a man born in Turkey will be a Hanafite.

The influence of birth was so great that many Muslims later became convinced that one did not need to look back to the original sources of the Qur'an and the Sunnah, for they believed wrongly that no one in these later days has a capacity for reasoning equal to that of the founders of the schools of law. They became imitators of their predecessors on the basis of a belief that every period since the time of the Prophet has been inferior to the earlier days. While it might be true that those who lived in the time of the Prophet could understand religion better than the people of today who must study Islam by means of documents only, we cannot ignore the considerable change in the social situation and world conditions during the past fourteen centuries. The insistence on imitating the predecessors reflects a loss of self-confidence which was at one time widespread in Islamic communities. The texts of the Qur'an are still and will always be valid, but we should understand them in the light of present knowledge. One of the great tasks facing religious scholars in our time is the re-examination of the jurisprudence of Islam in the light of reason and modern knowledge. Since Islam does not make a distinction between the secular and the religious, and since a large part of the Muslim world has but recently attained political independence and is now playing a significant role in world affairs, this re-examination of Islamic law is all the more urgently needed.

The relation between Islamic law and the law of the government is a pressing issue in modern times. In Turkey the national law is avowedly secular and even the waqf funds are administered by secular authorities. In Egypt, Pakistan, and India the problem of the relation of Islamic and national law is the subject of frequent public discussion, and in Indonesia several political parties have grown up around this issue. Another problem is the relation between Islamic law and the customary law of a country, as has been noted in China and Indonesia in particular. This will inevitably continue to be a problem as Islam spreads throughout the rest of the world.

Sects in Islam

From the beginning, the basic sources of Islam have been the Qur'an and the Sunnah. Muslims have always looked to the Qur'an as their guide and have prayed and fasted and made pilgrimages as the Prophet did. For the details governing their lives, Muslims have relied upon their reason in applying the principles of the Qur'an and the Sunnah, and this has been the cause of the different schools of law, the various tendencies, and the sects which are found in Islam.

Followers of the Hanafi school of law tend toward rationalism, such as is found among the Mu'tazilities; the Shafi'i school follows the moderate theology of the Ash'arites; the Malikites are predestinationist; and the Hanbalites tend to be literal in their interpretation of theology. These are theological tendencies, but not sectarian differences.

The two major sects in Islam are the Sunnis and the Shi'as, whose distinctive characteristics have been discussed at length in earlier chapters in this book. Among the Shi'as the three leading sects are the Ithna Ashariya, the Sab'iya, and the Zaidis. The Ithna Ashariya is the major group among the Shi'as, found primarily in Iraq and Iran; they accept the twelve Imams. The Sab'iya, sometimes called the Seveners because they broke away over the claim that Isma'il was the seventh Imam, are also known as the Isma'ilis. They have divided into several sects, of which the best known is the group which follows the Agha Khan, found in Pakistan, India, Iran, Syria, and East Africa. The Zaidis, now found in Yemen, are a small Shi'a sect which has drawn closer to the Sunnis over the years.

The Kharijites, who rebelled against Ali, were originally Shi'a and have been somewhat influenced by Sunni thought. They are found in Oman and Muscat, and in North Africa where they are known as Ibadis.

More than ninety per cent of the Muslims of the world are Sunnis, followers of the Sunnah. The only sects of any importance among the Sunnis are the Wahhabis, the reformist sect of Arabia, and the Qadiani sect of Pakistan which is generally looked upon as somewhat heretical—although its Lahori branch is not always so regarded. The various tendencies among the Sunnis have often led to differences in point of view, but not to the creation of new sects. The most widely accepted theological position is that of the Ash'arites. The rationalism of the Mu'tazilites at one time almost led to the formation of a recognizable sect, but today the rationalist point of view is only one of several tendencies among the Sunnis. Differences between the firmly orthodox and the modern reformist have not created a sectarian division.

The numerous Sufi orders cannot be classed as separate sects because they are made up of people who consider themselves to be Sunnis or Shi'as as well as Sufis. Sufi orders have been banned by the government of Turkey, but Sufism continues there as a powerful factor in the Islamic life of the country; both intellectuals and common people study the writings of their famous Sufis and continue their personal Sufi disciplines. The Sufi orders continue to be an important factor in Africa, though their influence in Egypt is declining. There is still, however, a strong interest in Sufi writings among the intellectuals in Egypt. The Shi'as have pronounced Sufi tendencies which have influenced the devotional life in Iran and Iraq as well as Pakistan and India. The Sufism of Pakistan and India has sometimes been influenced by the mysticism of Hinduism, leading on occasion to pantheistic tendencies there. In Indonesia, as we have seen, Sufism plays a major role in the devotional life of the Muslims, both as organized orders among the common people and as a study and discipline among the intellectuals. Only in China do we find that Sufism has not been an important factor in the Muslim community.

Sufism has been especially susceptible to the influences of Greek, Iranian, and Indian thought which have sometimes led it to excesses and fanaticism which were contrary to the real spirit of Islam. Some Sufis even denounced the Pillars of Islam and taught that union with God is the aim of Islam, a pantheistic doctrine which is heretical. Other Sufis have followed the teachings of Ghazali, combining the rituals of Islam with deep religious feeling. Such Sufis have made, and are making today, a valuable contribution to the religious life of the Muslim world.

Characteristic Islamic Practices

Muslims are exhorted to follow the straight path of Islam in every detail of their daily lives, guided by the Qur'an, by the example of the life of the Prophet, and by the Hadith. The life of a Muslim should illustrate the teachings and example of the Prophet.

When a Muslim baby is born, it is recommended that some one should whisper the call to prayer in his ear, "God is Most Great . . . there is no God other than Allah . . . Muhammad is the Messenger of God . . . Welcome prayer . . . Welcome good fortune . . . God is Most Great . . ." When the baby is one week old it is suggested that the parents sacrifice a sheep —one sheep for a girl and two for a boy—and distribute the meat among the poor. A baby should be given a good name on the seventh day. It is also recommended that boys should be circumcised, and girls also, for the sake of cleanliness. The parents are urged to teach the children how to pray so that by the age of nine they should know everything about the prayers, including the proper ablutions to be done before prayers.

The ablutions before prayer simply require the washing of the hands up to the wrist, washing the face and the head—a part of it is sufficent—and washing the feet up to the ankle. After any pollution or sexual intercourse, a Muslim must take an obligatory bath; in case there is no water, a symbolic action is necessary.

Muslims are required to pray five times a day, with two prostrations in the early morning before sunrise, four a little before midday, four in the afternoon when the shadow of a thing is as tall as the thing itself, three after sunset, and four about one hour later. Each prayer takes not more than five minutes, though it may be lengthened with optional prayers. It is recommended that the prayers be performed collectively, or at least with one companion. In case a person is traveling, two prayers can be performed together and shortened by half. Shi'as customarily carry a small tablet made of the clay from Karbala which they place on the ground and touch with their forehead as they prostrate themselves in prayer.

All Muslims should attend the Friday midday prayer in the mosque and listen attentively to the address given by an Imam. Women may also go to the mosque, but they must pray behind the men. In practice, women either gather at a separate place in the mosque or do not attend the collective prayers at all. At the two major festivals, the Id al-Fitr at the end of the

Ramadan fast and the Id al-Adha—or Id al-Qurban—at the end of the pilgrimage, Muslims are urged to perform additional congregational prayers, preferably in the open air, and to listen to the special address by the Imam. Before the prayers at the end of Ramadan they are urged to contribute food to the needy so no one may be hungry that day, and after the pilgrimage prayers they are exhorted to sacrifice a sheep, a cow, or a camel and distribute the meat to the needy.

There is no restriction on association between men and women in the Islamic community, the only reservation in the instructions being that there must be no occasion for misconduct. Thus, a woman must not meet a man alone, nor should a woman travel alone. She must protect her body decently but her face need not be covered. The practice of purdah, of veiling the face in public, which is followed in many Islamic countries, is only an exaggeration of the instructions enjoining modesty which has been deeprooted in Islamic communities by long centuries of ignorance.

When a young man wishes to marry he is allowed to see his prospective wife in order to assure the success of the marriage. The girl is protected by her parents, but they must ask her consent before giving her in marriage. If she is a widow, the consent must be explicit, and if she is a virgin tacit consent by silence is sufficent. The bridegroom must pay a dowry to the bride, which may be only a token. Two male witnesses are necessary for the marriage contract. A celebration after the marriage is recommended, but it should not be extravagant.

The husband must provide maintenance for the wife and children. Divorce is permitted only as a last resort. In case differences arise between a husband and his wife, relatives of both parties should serve as a committee of arbitration. Since divorce is a serious event "by which the throne of God is shaken," in the words of the Prophet, it must be delayed by two stages before it becomes final, and during that time the wife must receive maintenance. A wife can also ask for a divorce on the grounds of cruel treatment, sexual defect, contagious disease, and like conditions which make the marriage intolerable.

Polygamy is neither forbidden nor required. It may be called a necessary evil. If a man needs a son and his wife does not give birth to a male, for example, he might take a second wife. The question is still a subject of controversy among Muslim jurists, but there is general agreement that more than one wife is not permitted for the purpose of satisfying one's lust. Mut'a, a temporary marriage which may be terminated after even one day upon payment of a gift, is permitted among the Shi'as. It was originally permitted by the Prophet, but later the permission was abrogated, according to the Sunnis. The Shi'a still maintain that there was no abrogation, but even those who claim that the permission continues are against the prevalent practice, which does not differ much from prostitution. Adultery is forbidden; if the evidence is sufficient, the prescribed penalty is flogging with eighty lashes or stoning to death if the offender is married.

In case of death a man inherits from his wife or a wife inherits from her husband. The laws of inheritance are given in considerable detail but they follow the general principle that a man inherits twice as much as a woman. This is because the man must bear the responsibility for maintenance of his wife and must provide dowry for the marriage, while a woman who marries will receive both dowry and maintenance.

A dead person must be bathed and given ablution before burial and the community must pray for him. The prayer for a dead person is an obligation of the whole community. If it is neglected, the whole community is sinful, but if one person performs the prayer, the community is considered to have performed its duty. It is recommended that neighbors of the bereaved family should prepare food to be offered to the mourners and their visitors. It is also recommended that relatives should visit the grave from time to time to put flowers on it and to pray for the departed soul. Women, however, are urged not to go to the graveyard to pray for the deceased, since they are too sensitive.

Concerning food, Muslims are permitted to eat anything that is not explicitly forbidden. It is related that the Prophet said, "What God permits in His Book is permitted, and what

He forbids is forbidden, and what is not mentioned is in favor, therefore take His favor. God does not forget." According to the Qur'an, Muslims are forbidden to eat a corpse, blood, pork, a pagan sacrifice, suffocated animals, animals killed other than by slaughtering, animals which died from a fall, animals killed by other animals, remnants of food eaten by a beast, food offered as a sacrifice to idols. All fish which live in the sea may be eaten, according to the ninety-sixth verse of the fifth Surah. All animals which live in the water and on land, such as frogs, crocodiles, turtles, and the like, are forbidden as food. Of land animals, it is permitted to eat camels, cows, sheep, horses, and the like. It is forbidden to eat donkeys; beasts with claws such as lions, tigers, wolves, and bears; birds with talons, such as hawks and falcons; animals which the Prophet ordered killed, such as snakes, mice, crows; creatures which the Prophet forbade killing, such as ants and bees; animals judged to be dirty, and animals which live on dirt. In deciding what food can be eaten and what is forbidden Muslim jurisprudence accepts as guides the Qur'an, the Hadith, what the Prophet ordered to be killed and what he forbade killing, and the foods which are abhorrent to human feeling.

The verses of the Qur'an make it clear that all kinds of drinks are permitted except wine. Wine is forbidden because it is intoxicating. On this point the Holy Qur'an is so clear that no other interpretation is possible. Thus, however small the quantity may be, the drinking of wine is absolutely forbidden. By wine is meant the fermented juice of grapes. As to other fermented drinks, there is a difference of opinion among Muslim jurists. Some maintain that juices extracted from fruits other than grapes, such as apples or dates, are permitted. They base their opinion on some Traditions which say that Muhammad sometimes fermented dates for one or two days.

A Muslim is forbidden to steal, and if he steals a certain amount deliberately the punishment prescribed is the cutting off of the hands. A Muslim must not gamble nor participate in lotteries. He must not deceive concerning measures or weights; he must not break a promise or go back on his word. He is forbidden to pay or receive interest when borrowing or lending money, but a debtor may present a token of gratitude to the creditor.

These requirements and prohibitions, mentioned here only in general outline, are representative of the rules found in the Qur'an and Traditions which govern the lives of all Muslims.

Islamic Society

To understand the role of Islam in society one must first realize that Islam is a universal religion in which all Muslims are brothers, regardless of differences in homeland, race, color, or rank. This brotherhood does not divide the world into Muslims and non-Muslims, for Muslims must be friendly toward non-Muslims so long as they are friendly, so long as they do not attack Islam. Islam has retained its unity and universal characteristics in the midst of such diverse cultures as those of Arabia, Greece, Rome, and Iran in ancient times, and later in the cultures of Africa, Egypt, Turkey, Central Asia, India, China, and Southeast Asia. Once more the universalism of Islam is being shown as it comes into contact with the new culture of the West.

In this interplay between Islam and the various cultures of the world it should be remembered that Islam has no master organization which requires conformity or organizes missionary programs. The interplay is a spontaneous movement on the part of individual Muslims who seek to follow the straight path of Islam. These Muslims recognize no distinction between the religious and the secular; they try to follow in their social life the rules revealed to them in the Qur'an and the Sunnah and interpreted in Islamic law. For Islam, the present world is but a transitory existence to be followed by the Eternal World which is better by far, "And verily the latter portion will be better for thee than the former" (Surah XCIII, 4). This does not mean that we must neglect this world; on the contrary, Islam warns us against neglecting it, for the Qur'an says, "But seek the abode of the Hereafter in that which Allah hath given thee and neglect not thy portion of the world, and be thou kind even as Allah hath been kind to thee, and seek not corruption in the earth; lo! Allah loveth not corrupters" (Surah XXVIII, 77). Islam recognizes the importance of life in the community in this world, but it warns the Muslim against considering this world as the end of existence. Moral and religious values must be seen to be higher than material values.

The importance of social justice is constantly emphasized in Islam through the obligation of zakat and the distribution of gifts at the times of the great festivals. In the older Islamic countries this has been the origin of waqfs for all kinds of service to the community. The teachings concerning zakat stress the principle that the ownership of wealth is a privilege, not a right, and one which imposes obligations to the community. In the Traditions the Prophet exhorts us to give our servants the same food we eat and the same clothes we wear.

In Islam the merit of a person depends upon his deeds, not upon his words, nor his ancestors, nor his rank in the community. The Qur'an says, "there is nothing for the person but what he has done" (Surah LIII, 39), and again, "The highest among you is the most pious" (Surah XLIX, 13). The only recognized difference in rank in Islam is that which is merited by religious devotion and insight. Such recognition is accorded on the basis of deeds, not on the basis of office. Islam has no ordained clergy, no religious hierarchy with authority over their fellow Muslims. The ulama, the Shaikh, Mullah, Imam, Ahund, Mufti, Mujtahid, Hatib—all are only men like the others in the Muslim community, men who perform special services and are respected and elevated only on the basis of the Quranic principle that the highest is the most pious.

Slavery was customary at the time that Islam was revealed, but Islam prepared the grounds for its elimination. It encourages the emancipation of slaves by giving them the possibility of purchasing their freedom, it urges that part of zakat be given to slaves to help them free themselves, and it offers the possibility of atonement for certain sins, such as having sexual intercourse during fasting days, by releasing slaves.

Women are given equality with men, in principle, for the Qur'an says, "Whoever, male or female, who is a believer, performs good actions, they will enter into Paradise" (Surah IV, 124), and again, "Men have reward for what they do, and women have reward for what they do" (Surah IV, 32). But we cannot deny that in general men are superior to women and consequently men have authority over women. The Qur'an says, "Men have authority over women" (Surah IV, 34).

With the rise of nationalism in the modern world, the relation of nationalism to Islam has become a problem which is frequently discussed. Many people think that since Islam is universal it must be against nationalism, but this is not the case. Universalism can begin with national loyalty, for nationalism is simply the result of the organization of a group of people in one political body, regardless of their differences in religion. Islam does not prohibit such political organizations so long as they do not jeopardize the essentials of Islamic teachings. Nationalism can unite or divide, and when it is guided by the universal principles of Islam it can lead men to unity rather than to divisions. In this regard it should be noted that the demand for the Caliphate, in the political sense, has greatly lessened in modern times. Pan-Islamism in our day is not a movement for one super-government over all Muslims, but for cooperation between Islamic nations.

Jihad, holy war, has sometimes been misunderstood as meaning that Muslims must declare war on non-Muslims until they accept Islam. This mistake arises from a misreading of the Qur'an without knowing the context of the verses and the circumstances in which they were revealed. The verses which call for war against unbelievers were revealed when pagans were still putting obstacles in the way of the activities of Muhammad even after opportunities for reconciliation had been given. War in Islam is only legitimate when it is declared in defense of religion, property, and prestige. The Qur'an says, "Fight in the way of God those who wage war on you, and do not commit aggression. God does not like aggressors" (Surah II, 190).

Islam does not approve of hostility toward other religions. Rather, it proclaims freedom of religion and forbids coercion in religion. During his lifetime, Muhammad himself was very kind toward his neighbors and friends of other beliefs, Jews as well as Christians. He even married a Jewish woman, Safijah, and a Christian slave, Marie, who was given him by the ruler of Egypt. When the Emperor of Abyssinia died, Muhammad prayed for him in recognition of his help given to the Muslims who took refuge there in the early days of Islam.

Islamic society has been greatly influenced, and the spread of Islam has been aided, by the educational opportunities offered through the mosques and religious leaders. The Prophet encouraged education by appointing many of his Companions as teachers in Arabia when Islam spread thoughout the country. It was ruled that a poor man could marry a woman with a dowry of teaching her a chapter of the Qur'an. As Islam spread to other lands, centers of study grew up at Baghdad, Kufa, and many other cities of the Muslim world. The system of education was simple, without organized program or ceremony. Any pupil could approach a teacher and stay with him as long as he continued to learn; then he might go on to other teachers, or receive a license to be a teacher himself. In the family the parents educated their children. The teachers did not form a special class but were at the same time landowners, merchants, or government officials. This system continues today in most Muslim countries.

In addition, there have been in most countries the madrasas associated with the mosques, and special schools of higher learning. The oldest Islamic university is the Al Azhar in Cairo, founded in the fourth century (tenth century A.D.). Other centers for higher Islamic studies today are found at Fez in Morocco, at Zaitouna University in Tunisia, at Medina, at Istanbul and Ankara in Turkey, at Baghdad and Karbala in Iraq, at Tehran in Iran, at Lahore in Pakistan, at Lucknow and at Alighar and Usmania Universities in India, and at Jogjakarta in Indonesia. In some of these centers the Islamic studies are associated with government-supported universities;

there are also government universities in other countries which offer special courses in Islam, as is the case on Taiwan. Instruction in Islam is given in local languages at the lower levels, but for higher studies a good knowledge of Arabic is necessary and mastery of Persian and Turkish is required for any extensive research.

Since art and music flourish in times of peace and prosperity, there was little time for them in the early days of the Prophet. Muhammad, however, approved of the music known in his day. He forbade the art which was prevalent in his time, consisting chiefly of human figures, since it was symbolic of idols and would have spread paganism. Because of that, the literal-minded jurists deduced that Islam opposed art and music, which is not correct. The better deduction would have been that we must be careful of the consequences of any kind of art. Art for art's sake is unknown in Islam. As long as art is useful as a means of heightening religion and morality, it is permitted; but if it leads to immorality, it is forbidden.

Latest Developments in Islam

When the Mu'tazilite, or rational, movement was suppressed and the political organization of the Muslim world disintegrated, the Muslim people lost their vitality. They neglected the study of the Qur'an and the Traditions which are the original sources of Islam and instead adopted the teachings of the scholars. They thought that ijtihad was forbidden and that they must only imitate the four schools of law. Instead of making use of reason, they accepted the four schools of law as complete and unchanging and turned to mysticism and belief in the supernatural powers of saints, dead and alive. That gave rise to the worship of the graves of saints which is found today in all Islamic countries from North Africa to Indonesia.

The Wahhabi movement in Arabia was a reaction against the worship of saints, but it made use of force rather than arguments, and failed to establish a general reform. After the French occupied Egypt many scholars studied in Europe and a renaissance was started which culminated in the work of the great scholar, Muhammad Abduh, who brought new ideas to the people of Egypt. At about the same time the Muslims of India, led by such men as Sir Sayyid Ahmad Khan, who founded Alighar University, became conscious of their cultural importance and their national existence. Within the past half-century the greater ease of communication and travel has brought the peoples of the Muslim world into closer contact with each other and with the cultures of the rest of the world and made them aware of the need for a new evaluation of the ideas of the jurists and thinkers of the middle ages. This is the period in which much of the Muslim world has attained political independence and the people have been preoccupied with political and international problems.

Today the Muslims of Morocco, Tunisia, Egypt, the Levant, Turkey, Iraq, Iran, Pakistan, India, and Indonesia are vitally concerned with problems associated with the establishment of their new, independent governments. At the same time, the Muslims of Algeria and much of Africa, of the Soviet Union and of China, are struggling with political controls which are not encouraging to Islam and are often inimical. These political problems have been faced at the time when the impact of Western culture in the Muslim world has been most pronounced. More than anything else, Islam today needs a period of peace in order that favorable conditions may develop for the growth of Islamic thought. Since the time of Ibn Khaldun, more than five centuries ago, no great thinker has arisen in the Muslim world. Now more than ever there is a need for a time of peace and intellectual freedom in which devout thinkers can interpret the Qur'an in the light of the progress of human knowledge. The rituals will remain as they are, the fundamentals will remain unchanged, but the understanding of Islam will be illuminated anew for our time.

At the present time, there are four major tendencies in the Islamic world—orthodoxy, reform, Sufism, and Shi'a. The increase in communication and in education is bringing to the followers of each tendency a better understanding of the others. Significant progress is being made in Cairo in encouraging better understanding and reconciliation between

Shi'a and Sunni. Orthodoxy is becoming less reactionary and the reformers less intolerant. The Sufi orders are declining in influence at the same time that the devotional and mystical teachings of the Sufi masters are being studied more sympathetically by intellectuals. In Turkey, Egypt, and Indonesia in particular there are many evidences of a new vitality and interest in Islamic thought. Many books are being published, many students are engaged in Islamic studies, new mosques are being built.

Islam spread originally along the trade routes through North Africa, Iran, Central Asia, Indonesia, and China. As Muslim traders settled along those routes they married and established families which often became the nucleus for a new Muslim community. In spite of the diversities of cultures, they maintained the unity of Islam through the centuries. Today, with trade routes easily followed around the world, it is inevitable that the same process will be repeated and Islam will spread to new regions where it has not been known.

In this discussion of the unity and variety of Islam we have seen that divergences from the essential unity of Islam have occurred only when there is ignorance among the common people—a low level of education. It is the task of the present generation to provide training in the essentials of Islam, to know Islam deeply, for out of that knowledge of the straight path of Islam will come the unity of belief and practice which has been revealed to mankind in the Qur'an and the Sunnah.

Bibliography

ALI, AMEER. *The Spirit of Islam.* London: Christophers, Ltd., 1949.
ANDRAE, TOR. *Mohammed: The Man and His Faith.* New York: Barnes & Noble, Inc., 1957.
ARBERRY, ARTHUR J. *An Introduction to the History of Sufism.* New York: Longmans, Green & Co., Inc., 1942.
———. *The Koran Interpreted.* 2 vols. London: George Allen & Unwin, 1955.
———. *The Legacy of Persia.* London: Oxford University Press, 1953.
———. *Revelation and Reason in Islam.* London: George Allen & Unwin, 1957.
———. *Sufism.* London: George Allen & Unwin, 1950.
ARNOLD, T. W., AND GUILLAUME, A. *The Legacy of Islam.* London: Oxford University Press, 1931.
BIRGE, JOHN KINGSLEY. *The Bektashi Order of Dervishes.* London: Luzac & Co., Ltd., 1937.
BROCKELMANN, CARL. *History of the Islamic Peoples.* London: Routledge & Kegan Paul, Ltd., 1952.
BROWNE, EDWARD G. *A Literary History of Persia.* 4 vols. Cambridge: Cambridge University Press, 1951.
CHAN, WING-TSIT. *Religious Trends in Modern China.* New York: Columbia University Press, 1953.
CRAGG, KENNETH. *The Call of the Minaret.* New York: Oxford University Press, 1956.
DAWOOD, N. J. *The Koran.* Baltimore: Penguin Books, Inc., 1956.
DONALDSON, DWIGHT M. *The Shi'ite Religion.* London: Luzac & Co., Ltd., 1933.
———. *Studies in Muslim Ethics.* London: Society for the Promotion of Christian Knowledge, 1953.
Encyclopaedia of Islam. Leiden: E. J. Brill, 1913–38. (New edition in preparation, 1954–.)
FRYE, RICHARD. *Islam and the West.* The Hague: Mouton & Co., 1957.
FYZEE, ASAF, A. A. *Outlines of Muhammadan Law.* London: Oxford University Press, 1955.
GIBB, H. A. R. *Modern Trends in Islam.* Chicago: University of Chicago Press, 1954.
———. *Mohammedanism.* London: Oxford University Press, 1949.

GIBB, H. A. R., AND BOWEN, H. *Islamic Society and the West.* Vol. I, *Islamic Society in the Eighteenth Century*, Parts I and II. London: Oxford University Press, 1950, and 1957.

GIBB, H. A. R., AND KRAMERS, J. H. *Shorter Encyclopaedia of Islam.* Leiden: E. J. Brill, 1953.

GRUNEBAUM, GUSTAVE E. VON. *Islam.* London: Routledge & Kegan Paul, Ltd., 1955.

———. *Medieval Islam.* Chicago: University of Chicago Press, 1953.

———. *Muhammadan Festivals.* New York: Henry Schuman, Inc., 1951.

———. *Unity and Variety in Muslim Civilization.* Chicago: University of Chicago Press, 1955.

GUILLAUME, ALFRED. *The Life of Muhammad.* London: Oxford University Press, 1955.

———. *Islam.* Baltimore: Penguin Books, Inc., 1954.

———. *The Traditions of Islam.* London: Oxford University Press, 1924.

HAMIDULLAH, MUHAMMAD. *Muslim Conduct of State.* Lahore: Muhammad Ashraf, 1953.

HAZARD, HARRY W. *Atlas of Islamic History.* Princeton: Princeton University Press, 1954.

HITTI, P. K. *The Arabs, A Short History.* Princeton: Princeton University Press, 1952.

HOLLISTER, JOHN NORMAN. *The Shi'a of India.* London: Luzac & Co., Ltd., 1953.

HUSAINI, ISHAK MUSA. *The Moslem Brethren.* Beirut: Khayat's, 1956.

IQBAL, MUHAMMAD. *Islam as an Ethical and Political Ideal.* Lahore: Orientalia, n.d.

———. *The Reconstruction of Religious Thought in Islam.* Lahore: Muhammad Ashraf, 1954.

JEFFERY, ARTHUR. *The Qur'an as Scripture.* New York: Russell F. Moore Co., 1952.

KHADDURI, MOJID. *War and Peace in the Law of Islam.* Baltimore: Johns Hopkins Press, 1955.

LANE-POOLE, STANLEY. *The Mohammadan Dynasties.* Paris: Paul Geuthner, 1925.

LEVY, REUBEN. *The Social Structure of Islam.* Cambridge: Cambridge University Press, 1957.

LEWIS, BERNARD. *The Arabs in History.* London: Hutchinson's University Library, 1950.

———. *The Origin of Isma'ilism.* Cambridge: W. Heffer & Sons, Ltd., 1940.

MACDONALD, D. B. *Development of Muslim Theology, Jurisprudence, and Constitutional Theory.* New York: Charles Scribner's Sons, 1926.

———. *The Religious Attitude and Life in Islam.* Chicago: University of Chicago Press, 1909.

NICHOLSON, R. A. *A Literary History of the Arabs.* Cambridge: Cambridge University Press, 1953.

———. *The Mystics of Islam.* London: G. G. Bell & Sons, Ltd., 1914.

———. *Rumi, Poet and Mystic.* New York: The Macmillan Co., 1950.

———. *Studies in Islamic Mysticism.* Cambridge: Cambridge University Press, 1921.

O'LEARY, DE LACY. *Arabic Thought and Its Place in History.* London: Routledge & Kegan Paul, Ltd., 1954.

PHILBY, H. ST. J. B. *Arabia.* New York: Charles Scribner's Sons, 1930.

PICKTHALL, MOHAMMED MARMADUKE. *The Meaning of the Glorious Koran.* New York: The New American Library, 1953.

ROOLVINK, R. *Historical Atlas of the Muslim Peoples.* Cambridge: Harvard University Press, 1957.

SCHACHT, JOSEPH. *The Origins of Muhammadan Jurisprudence.* London: Oxford University Press, 1953.

SCHROEDER, ERIC. *Muhammad's People.* Portland, Maine: The Bond Wheelwright Company, 1955.

SHUSHTERY, A. M. A. *Outlines of Islamic Culture.* Bangalore: Bangalore Printing & Publishing Co., Ltd., 1954.

SMITH, MARGARET. *Al-Ghazali, The Mystic.* London: Luzac & Co., Ltd., 1944.

———. *Readings from the Mystics of Islam.* London: Luzac & Co., Ltd., 1950.

———. *The Sufi Path of Love.* London: Luzac & Co., Ltd., 1954.

SMITH, WILFRED CANTWELL. *Islam in Modern History.* Princeton: Princeton University Press, 1957.

———. *Modern Islam in India.* London: Victor Gollancz, Ltd., 1946.

TRIMINGHAM, J. SPENCER. *Islam in Ethiopia.* London: Oxford University Press, 1952.

TRITTON, A. S. *Islam.* London: Hutchinson's University Library, 1951.

———. *Muslim Theology.* London: Luzac & Co., Ltd., 1947.

VESEY-FITZGERALD, S. *Muhammadan Law.* London: Oxford University Press, 1931.

WATT, W. MONTGOMERY. *The Faith and Practice of Al-Ghazali.* London: George Allen & Unwin, 1953.

———. *Muhammad at Mecca.* London: Oxford University Press, 1953.

———. *Muhammad at Medina.* London: Oxford University Press, 1956.

WENSINCK, A. J. *The Moslem Creed.* Cambridge: Cambridge University Press, 1932.

WILBER, DONALD N. *Iran: Past and Present.* Princeton: Princeton University Press, 1955.

WILSON, RALPH PINDER. *Islamic Art*. New York: The Macmillan Co., 1957.

WOODMAN, DOROTHY. *The Republic of Indonesia*. New York: The Philosophical Library, 1955.

YOUNG, CUYLER T. *Near Eastern Culture and Society*. Princeton: Princeton University Press, 1951.

Glossary

Abbasid—Caliphate at Baghdad from 132 (A.D. 750) until the Abbasid dynasty was crushed by the Mongols under Hulagu in 656 (A.D. 1258).

adat—in Indonesia, pre-Islamic customs which persist even though not reconciled to Islamic law.

Ahmadiyyah—branch of the Qadiani sect founded at Qadian (now in India) by Mirza Ghulam Ahmad (died 1326; A.D. 1908); the Ahmadis look upon their founder as a renovator of Islam while the rest of the Qadianis accept him as a prophet after Muhammad; the general Muslim community does not recognize the distinction and regards both groups as heretical. Well-known for its missionary work in Western countries. The headquarters are now at Rabwah in Pakistan under the leadership of the founder's son.

Ahund—in China, a religious leader who teaches, officiates at ceremonies, and settles disputes; it is sometimes transliterated Ahung.

Almohad—North African dynasty, 524–667 (A.D. 1130–1269), which supplanted the Almoravids and at one time ruled Moorish Spain and all of North Africa to the borders of Egypt.

Almoravid—a Berber dynasty which established its rule in Morocco and most of Moorish Spain, ruling from 448 to 541 (A.D. 1056–1147).

amir—commander, or leader; sometimes used in the sense of ruler.

Ansar—the believers of Medina who helped Muhammad after the Hijrah.

Aoulia—Allah's constant obeyers, His favorites.

Ash'arite—follower of the theology of al-Ash'ari (died 324; A.D. 935), the theological position most widely held among Sunnis.

Ayyubid—dynasty which ruled from the Nile to the Euphrates from 564 to 648 (A.D. 1169–1250).

Bektashi—Sufi order in Turkey, characterized by the ecstatic dances of the darwishes, and the acceptance of some Shi'a beliefs; although its founder called for complete observance of the shari'a, some followers regarded shari'a as of secondary importance.

Buwayhid—Shi'a dynasty in southern Iran and Iraq, 320–447 (A.D. 932–1055).

Caliph (Khalifa)—successor to Muhammad; at first, both religious and political leader of the Muslims, but later chiefly political. At present, there is no Caliph.

Chishti—Sufi order in Pakistan and India, emphasizing poverty, contentment, austerity, no permanent home, and the repetition of the name of Allah.

darwish (dervish)—a Persian word meaning poor; the Arabic word is *faqir*. Usually used in the sense of a member of a Sufi order, sometimes means a religious wanderer; one who follows ecstatic practices in expressing religious devotion.

dhikr—to remember Allah, to speak of Allah, to recognize and acknowledge the greatness of Allah. Sometimes used in reference to the ritual prayers, more often refers to additional phrases repeated after the prayers or at other times. Sufi orders have special phrases to be repeated after the prayers and in other ceremonies.

Druze—sect found in Lebanon and Syria which follows esoteric teachings and worships the Fatimid Caliph Hakim as an incarnation of the Deity; while related to Islam, it is not considered sufficiently orthodox to be generally accepted as Muslim.

faqir—*see* darwish.

Fatimid—Shi'a dynasty which at one time extended its rule from Syria to Morocco and governed Egypt and Syria from 297 to 567 (A.D. 909–1171).

fatwa—a formal legal opinion given by a recognized religious leader; a religious pronouncement or verdict concerning a controversial question.

fiqh—Islamic jurisprudence, covering all aspects of life.

Fitna—sedition; specifically, the revolt against Uthman.

Ghaznavid—a dynasty in Afghanistan and the Punjab, 351–582 (A.D. 962–1186).

Ghorid—a dynasty in Afghanistan and India, 543–612 (A.D. 1148–1215).

Hadith—the sacred Traditions of Islam which were originated by Muhammad; specifically, the Traditions uttered by Muhammad or based on his actions.

Hajj—the pilgrimage to Mecca; the fifth pillar of Islam.

Hajji (Hadji)—a person who has made the pilgrimage to Mecca.

Hamdanid—Shi'a dynasty which ruled from Mosul and Aleppo, 317–94 (A.D. 929–1003).

Han—the Chinese people.

Hanafi—one of the four schools of Islamic law, founded by Abu Hanifa (died 150; A.D. 767); followed in Turkey, Afghanistan, Central Asia, China, Pakistan, India, and Egypt.

Hanbali—one of the four schools of Islamic law, founded by Ahmad Ibn Hanbal (died 241; A.D. 855); followed in Central Arabia, Syria, and some parts of Africa.

Hatip—altered form of Khatib, used in Turkey and Indonesia.

Hijrah (sometimes anglicized as *Hegira*)—the migration of Muhammad from Mecca to Medina in A.D. 622; the Muslim calendar is dated from this event.

Hui—Muslim people of China.

Hurs—followers of a renowned religious leader in Pakistan, Pir Pagaro.

Ibadi—a branch of the Kharijites of early Islam who have accomodated themselves to live within the community of Muslims; found chiefly in Oman, East Africa, and North Africa. They combine Shi'a and Sunni characteristics, believe in an Imam, follow Maliki jurisprudence, and have Mu'tazilite tendencies.

Iblis—the devil.

Id al-Adha—the great four-day festival which begins on the tenth day of the month Dhu'l Hijja; the pilgrimage is performed on the first three days. It is also known as Id al-Qurban, and in Turkey as Bairam.

Id al-Fitr—the little festival, held at the end of the Ramadan fast on the first day of the month Shawwal. This and the Id al-Adha are the two most important festivals in Islam.

ijma—consensus; the agreement concerning religious opinion reached by those who are qualified by knowledge and experience to form a judgment.

ijtihad—literally, striving; truth-seeking; the individual opinion or judgment of a person who has considered all the facts in the light of reason and Revelation.

Imam—in the most general sense, a Muslim head of a movement, community, or state; also used to designate a recognized religious leader. Among Shi'as, Imam is limited to the recognized successors of Ali.

irja—the doctrine that judgment on the actions of believers is postponed until the Last Day, the Day of Resurrection.

Isma'ili—Shi'a sect, which includes several sub-sects; followers of those who believe that Isma'il was the seventh and last Imam. The Fatimids believed that the succession continued through the sons of Muhammad Ibn Isma'il. The Isma'ili sects today believe either that the seventh Imam was the last and is now the Hidden Imam, or that the succession of Imams has continued in the Prophet's family from Muhammad Ibn Isma'il.

Ithna Ashariya—the major Shi'a sect which believes that there were twelve Imams and that the Hidden Imam continues as their head; sometimes called the "Twelvers."

Itrat—the family of the Prophet; belief in the Itrat implies belief that guidance in Islam comes through the descendants of the Prophet, the Imams. (In Egypt it is customary to use the phrase *Ahl al Bait* when referring to the Prophet's family).

Ja'fari—the Shi'a school of law, named after Ja'far, the sixth of the twelve Imams; comparable to the four schools of law of the Sunnis; another term for Shi'as.

Jahiliya—the pre-Islamic age of ignorance.

Jahriyah—the only Sufi sect in China; found also in Central Asia, Turkey, and Egypt.

janissaries—in Turkey, the Sultan's garrison troops made up of Christian boys who had been captured or levied at any early age and trained as soldiers.

Jinn—supernatural creatures, sometimes virtuous and sometimes wicked, who receive the revelations through the messengers of Allah and, like men, must take responsibility for hearing and believing Allah's messages.

Ka'ba—the sacred shrine at the center of the Great Mosque in Mecca; the goal of the Muslim pilgrimage.

Kaisani—Shi'a sect, no longer existing, which believed that the true succession after Ali was through Muhammad Ibn al-Hanifiyya, his son by a girl of the Hanifa clan.

Kharijite—a sect which started with those of Ali's followers who opposed him for negotiating with Mu'awiya; known to the Shi'a as "the people who have forsaken the community"; originally a warrior group, they sought to kill those who disagreed with them, and were condemned by the Muslim community. They denied the validity of the succession of Sunni Caliphs and Shi'a Imams, recognizing as Caliph only the leader elected from their own group. They exist today in small numbers in Oman, and in the moderate Ibadi sect.

Khatib—religious leader who preaches in the mosque at the Friday and holiday services.

khums—special form of almsgiving required of Shi'as to provide maintenance for and support the work of the descendants of the Prophet; it is the Arabic word for one-fifth.

Khwarizm—Muslim dynasty, 470–629 (A.D. 1077–1231), which in its last fifty years extended from the Indus almost to the Euphrates, from the Ural Mountains to the Persian Gulf; it was destroyed by the Mongol invasion.

kudsi Hadith—a Hadith which expresses God's meaning in the Prophet's words.

Lahori—sect in Pakistan which separated from the Qadianis; looked upon by the orthodox as heretical.

langgar—a gathering place in Indonesia used as a place of prayer and instruction, but not recognized as a mosque; therefore not used for Friday prayer.

Lodhi—dynasty in India, 855–930 (A.D. 1451–1526), overcome by Babar.

madrasa—school or college, often associated with a mosque, primarily for instruction in Islamic beliefs and laws.

Mahdavi—Muslim sect in India characterized by the belief that Muhammad of Jaunpur was the Mahdi.

Mahdi—the Guided One, the Expected One who is to come to set right the evils of the world; sometimes refers to the Hidden Imam who is to return.

Maliki—one of the four schools of law of Islam, based on the interpretations of the Traditions by Malik Ibn Anas (died 179; A.D. 795); found chiefly in North and West Africa and in Egypt.

Mamluk—Egyptian dynasties ruled by sultans who had been Turkish and Circassian slaves; the Bahri Mamluks ruled from 648 to 792 (A.D. 1250–1390), and the Burji Mamluks from 784 to 922 (A.D. 1382–1517). They resisted the invasions of the Crusaders and the Mongols, maintaining their power until the coming of the Ottoman Turks.

Man—the Manchu people in China.

mawali—usually translated "client." Originally a stranger affiliated with an Arabic tribe; with the expansion of Islam it was used to designate a non-Arab convert to Islam, one who in the early years was placed by the Arabs (but not by Islam) in an inferior status.

Mehmed—when the name Muhammad refers to a person other than the Prophet, it is ordinarily pronounced Mehmed in Turkey and some other non-Arabic-speaking countries.

Meng—the Mongolian people of China.

Mevlevi—Turkish Sufi order based on the teachings of Mevlana Jalal al-Din Rumi.

Mu'attila—those who insist that the divine attributes are functionless.

Mubaheleh—the ceremony at which heresy is condemned.

mu'ezzin—the man who gives the call to prayer from the minaret.

Mufti—in some Muslim countries, the religious leader who is recognized by the community as qualified to give interpretations of Muslim law; in some countries the title is reserved only for the most orthodox leaders.

Muhajirun—emigrants from Mecca to Medina at the time of the Prophet.

Muharram—first month of the Muslim calendar; the first ten days are sacred for the Shi'a festival in memory of the death of Husain.

Mujtahid—a Shi'a religious leader who is competent to pronounce an ijtihad, that is, a religious opinion based on the right use of reason, without contradicting Revelation.

Mullah—a religious leader; usually considered in Pakistan and India to be conservative in his interpretations, and often used there in a depreciatory sense.

Mulud (Mawlid)—the festival of the birth of Muhammad.

Murjites—those who postpone all judgment until the Day of Judgment.

mut'a—temporary marriage; a marriage based on an initial agreement that it will be ended after a fixed time. The Sunnis believe that the Prophet originally sanctioned and later forbade such marriages; Shi'as believe he did not forbid them.

Mu'tazilite—the school of rational theologians in Islam.

Naqshbandi—Sufi order founded some six centuries ago; exists today in India, Central Asia, Turkey, and Indonesia.

nawafil—extra prayers, said in addition to the required ritual worship.

Pir—a Sufi sage or founder of a Sufi order; it means "old man."

Qadarites—those who uphold free will.

Qadi—a Muslim judge who bases his decisions on Islamic law.

Qadiani—follower of Mirza Ghulam Ahmad; Qadianis are generally considered to have placed themselves outside Islam by having recognized him as a prophet after Muhammad; called Qadianis to distinguish them from the Lahoris. (*See* Ahmadiyyah.)

Qadiri—Sufi order in Pakistan, India, Turkey, and North Africa, founded by Abdul Qadir Jilani (died 562; A.D. 1166).

Qarmatian—a radical Shi'a sect which believed in a cyclical process of creation, and that nothing exists outside God; no longer existing.

qiyas—reasoning; deduction by analogy from the Qur'an and Sunnah.

Quraish—the inhabitants of Mecca at the time of the Prophet, a tribal group subdivided into clans.

al-Qurban—*see* Id al-Adha.

Ramadan—ninth month of the Muslim year, the month set aside for the annual fast.

Rifa'i—Sufi order founded in 571 (A.D. 1175).

riya—Arabic word for hypocrisy, or ostentation.

Sab'iya—the "Seveners"; Shi'a sects which limit the number of Imams to seven, looking upon Isma'il as the last Imam.

Salafiya—traditionalists, from *salaf* which means ancestors; those who hold to the traditions of their predecessors; also, those who insist on a literal interpretation of all passages in the Qur'an.

salat—literally, the bowing or kneeling; the daily ritual service of worship; commonly used to refer to the five daily prayers required of Muslims; the second of the five pillars of Islam.

Samanid—dynasty in Transoxiana which at one time extended from the borders of India almost to Baghdad, 261–389 (A.D. 874–999).

Sayyid (Sayed)—a title of honor given to a descendant of the Prophet through Fatimah and the family of Ali; in some countries it may be given to a descendant of the Quraish. Literally it means master, as in the relation of a master to a slave.

Seljuq—Turkish tribe from vicinity of Samarkand which established an empire extending from Afghanistan to the Mediterranean, 429–700 (A.D. 1037–1300).

Senussi—Sufi order, founded in 1253 (A.D. 1837) in North Africa, combining Sufism with Wahhabi ideas.

Shafi'i—school of Islamic law founded by al-Shafi'i (died 205; A.D. 820); followed today chiefly in Indonesia and western India.

Shaikh—title given in some Muslim countries to a man recognized as a qualified religious teacher; also, the head of a Sufi order or tekke, or the spiritual enlightener of a person.

Sham—Syria.

shari'a—Islamic law, the Islamic code. Literally, the clearly defined path to be followed.

Sharif—honorary title given to descendants of Ali's two sons, Husain and Hasan; sometimes given to anyone who can trace his descent from Muhammad. A Sharif is entitled to wear a green band on his turban. Literally, it means "noble, exalted."

Shattari—Sufi order in India and Indonesia, founded by Abdulla Shattar in 818 (A.D. 1415).

Shazili—Sufi order, established in North Africa in 594 (A.D. 1197); found today in North Africa, the Balkans, Turkey, and Indonesia.

Shi'a—literally, "followers"; the followers of Ali, looking upon him as the true successor of Muhammad. The largest group of the Shi'a, the Ithna Ashariya, are found chiefly in Iran and Iraq; other sects, commonly called Isma'ilis, are found in India, Pakistan, the Levant, Oman, Yemen, and East Africa. There are approximately twenty-five million Shi'as today.

slametan—a feast of well-being in Indonesia, customarily held at the end of a religious ceremony or in commemoration of the death of a relative.

Sufi—a Muslim mystic; a member of a religious order which follows mystical interpretations of Islamic doctrines and practices.

Sunnah—the prophetic teachings of Muhammad given either by word or example or by tacit approval.

Sunni—a follower of the Sunnah; by usage it has come to refer to the orthodox position in Islam, those Muslims who are not Shi'as.

Surah—a chapter in the Qur'an.

tafsir—a commentary, usually on the Qur'an.

ta'limis—searchers for truth who require an infallible living teacher.

taqiya—literally, "caution, fear, disguise"; among Shi'as the permission to disguise one's religious beliefs in a time of persecution.

tariqa—order; refers to any Sufi order.

tekke (tekkiye)—a Sufi center or community, made up of residences, a school, and a mosque or a place for performing the ceremonies of the order; sometimes called a lodge or monastery; *ribat* in Arabic.

Tijani—Sufi order founded in Morocco by Abul Abbas Ahmad (died 1231; A.D. 1815); it has spread primarily in the Sudan within the last two centuries.

Tsang—the Tibetan people of China.

Tulunid—dynasty of Egypt, founded by Ahmad Ibn Tulun, a Turkish slave, in 254 (A.D. 868); it lasted only thirty-seven years, but was noted for its wealth and public works.

ulama—scholars well-versed in Islam, regarded by the orthodox as authoritative interpreters of Islamic beliefs and practices.

Umayyad—the first hereditary Caliphate of Islam, ruling from Damascus from 41 to 132 (A.D. 661–750).

Vizier—a minister or high executive officer in the government.

Wahhabi—Muslim reformist sect in Arabia in the last century opposing innovations in Islam, sometimes with violence.

waqf—religious endowment or foundation established to support public works and religious institutions.

Zaidi—Shi'a sect named after Zaid, the son of the fourth Imam; they believe that it is often necessary to fight for their faith; they have Mu'tazilite tendencies, follow the Shafi'i school of law, and are thus close to the Sunnis.

zakat—almsgiving as required by Islamic law; the third of the five pillars of Islam.

zimmi—protected persons; those followers of other religions who, under a Muslim ruler, prefer to keep their own religion and are protected in their choice; literally, those for whom the Muslim state considers itself responsible.

Index